Understanding Aikidō

合気道のりかい:
ひつようなじょうほうやにんしき
(ひつようなじょうほうやアイデア)

Understanding Aikidō:
Essential Information & Perceptions

By Jån J. Sunderlin

Shidosha,
斬突破 合気道会
Zantoppa Aikidō Kai

Nidan,
富木流 合気道
Tomiki-ryū Aikidō
(Japan Aikidō Association & Fugakukai International)

Shihan,
斬突流 合気柔
Zantotsu-ryū Aikijūjutsu

A. A., General Science
Solano College

Text and continuity editing by **Hunter F. Morrigan**

M. Ed., M. Div., M. T. S.,
&
Shodan,
斬突破会 合気道
Zantoppa-kai Aikidō

Published by:

The Zantosu Ryu

(via the *IngramSpark Publishing Platform*)

ISBN-10: 0-692-39675-6
ISBN-13: 978-0-692-39675-9

Hardcover First Edition

First Printing: February 26, 2015
Second Printing: March 15, 2016
(Minor grammar and punctuation corrections.)

Acknowledgements

I wish to thank the following organizations and people for their kindnesses or efforts that have helped to make possible this book.

Kodansha International for permission to reprint certain sections of the book *The Spirit of Aikidō* by Kisshomaru Ueshiba, without which this written effort would not have been possible.

Mr. Stanley Pranin, contributor and editor of the both the *Aiki News* magazine and the *Aikidō Journal*, whose pursuit of accurate historical information pertaining to Aikidō has been helpful in the creation of this written effort.

The following aikidoka were invaluable in their initial support toward establishing the Zantotsu-ryū Aikijujutsu (Z.T.R.A.) and the Zantoppa-kai Aikido (Z.T.K.A.) organizations during the time period 1989 through 1996, in order of initial association:

Mr. Patrick K. Jones (Nidan; Shihanke, Tenjin Shin'yō-ryū)
Mr. William E. Gregory (Shodan; Shodan, Karatedō)
Ms. Jolene S. Cantrell (Shodan)
Mr. John White (Nidan, Tomiki-ryu; Yondan, Zantotsu-ryū)
Mr. Charles R. Davis (Sandan)
Mr. Jason Stacy (Sandan)
Mr. Alan Griswald (Nidan)
Mr. Fred B. McMullin (Shodan)
Mr. Chris Mills (Shodan; Sandan, Aikikai)
Mr. John G. Copeland (Shodan)
Mr. Terry Harder (Shodan)
Mr. Sijer Harder (Nidan)
Mr. Mark Niebuhr (Nidan)
Ms. Hunter F. Morrigan (Shodan)

Special thanks to Shihan Tsunako Miyake of Tomiki-ryū Aikido for her teachings, and later, her kindness when she presented to me her obi following my Nidan advancement test on August 18, 1985.

All photographic images of Japanese persons and places within this book were published before December 31, 1956 or photographed before 1946 under the jurisdiction of the Government of Japan. Therefore, these images are considered to be public domain according to article 23 of Japan's old copyright law and article 2 of the supplemental provision of the copyright law of Japan. A thank you, posthumously, to all the persons who made their historical contribution by taking these photographs, without which this written effort would have been somewhat less interesting.

The book cover design and all illustrations were conceived and drawn by Jån J. Sunderlin. Most of the book cover's elements herald from ancient India, China, and Japan; e.g., the lotus blossom floating on the ethereal *Kū* (空, Japanese) -- *Akasha* in Sanskrit but *Aether* in English. The large eroteme (interrogative mark) or question mark element is derived from Western Culture, which can be shown to have been conceived by the medieval English scholar Alcuin of York. The sideways question-mark-like images at the corners of the front cover and the X-like images of the back cover are from India's Sanskrit language, meaning, respectively, *beginning* and *end*.

This book, **Understanding Aikido: Essential Information & Perceptions**, is typeset in Linux Libertine G, HanaMin A, Chandas, and Uttara fonts.

Understanding Aikido

Historical Accuracy Statement

I have gone to much effort to ensure the accuracy of the historical and technical information provided herein. However, a perfect creation is rarely, if ever, achievable; this is especially the case in large efforts. Errors concerning historical or technical content can be addressed by errata or corrected in future printings. If the reader finds an error of fact, you may consider submitting your concern, with supporting information, to *www.understandingaikido.info.*

Table of Contents

Section VIII – *Special Editorial Comment*

Section IX – *Autobiographical Sketches*

Section X – *Glossary*

Section XI – *Bibliography*

Section XII – *Index*

This effort is dedicated to my teachers in order of appearance:

S.S.H.S. Wrestling Coach (1968 - 1969)

G.R.C.C. Boxing Coach (1970)

Douglas Morris – 2nd Dan Aikido

Carl Geis – 10th Dan Aikido

Tsunako Miyake – 8th Dan Aikido

Takeshi Inoue – 6th Dan Aikido

Patrick K. Jones – Shihanke, Tenjin Shin'yō-ryū

John White – 2nd Dan Aikido, 4th Dan Zantotsu-ryu

Yufu Wu – Sifu, Hung Ga Kung Fu

Foreword

*"... Joyn Sense unto Reason,
and Experiment unto Speculation,
and so give life unto Embryon Truths,
and Verities yet in their Chaos."*

Sir Thomas Browne -- 1646 C.E.

It is hoped that this effort of writing will provide the reader with a better understanding of the discipline of Aikidō.

Jån Sunderlin – Shidosha, the Zantoppa Kai

Preface

Throughout this book the first letter of the word "**aikidō**" has been capitalized in order to state that there does exist for it foundational criterion that yields a definition by application of which a person can understand that it is unique and therefore merits a proper noun status, i.e., **Aikidō**. Concerning the content and organization of this book, frequent attention has been given toward avoiding errors of history, transliteration, grammar, etc. All quoted phrases in this book are placed within double quotation marks and may also be italicized in order to provide a visual separation from the surrounding text, the latter only for that reason; and, sources are referenced in the endnotes of the corresponding chapter. Certain words, phrases, and descriptions herein are italicized or placed in single quotation marks in order to 1) indicate a particular word's unique existence, 2) facilitate either comparison or differentiation, or 3) to imply a special use of the word or phrase in an idiomatic, syntactical, or grammatical sense; when the latter is intended and where an explanation of the special meaning is necessary, an endnote is provided. Some hyphenated words or ideomatic phrases are placed in double quotation marks to indicate that such are not unique to this author. The names of Japanese people given herein are transliterated to romaji, and as such the Japanese tradition of giving a person's family name first (their patronym) is not used; instead, the American English tradition -- first name first, family name last -- is used. Japanese romaji terms -- i.e., the representation of the traditional Japanese logographic writing system with the grammar elements of the English language, which are constructed with the *Hepburn Romanization System* -- is explained throughout the book, especially in Chapters II, XI, and Section VII. 合気道 is romanized as *Aikidō* and, except in certain areas of the book's cover, title page, chapter headings, and glossary, the diacritic (called a macron) above the letter *o* has been omitted throughout the entire text of this book. Furthermore, all other romanized Japanese words, names of people and places, and technical jargon where a diacritic above the *o* or *u* would normally be used, except upon the first occurrence, will be treated the simarlarly. A satisfactory pronunciation of the Japanese word 合気道 can be heard by voicing consecutively in the following order the English words *eye, key,* and *doe.* Numerous Japanese kanji and kana sinograms (logographs) are used in this book, and where such occurs, most are *Shinjitai* (new forms) but some are *Kyujitai* (old forms). Pinyin is used for the Chinese names. B.C.E. (Before Common Era) and C.E. (Common Era) are used for dates prior to the end of World War II, except in the tables of the "Aikido Event Timelines" section. Finally, regarding a matter of linguistics in the English language, singular *they, their, theirselves* is sometimes used in this book to show possession referring back to an antecedent that is of an indeterminate gender or number as well as to avoid the modern culture-dependent use of the problematic masculine generic *he* to represent an unspecified or indeterminate gender; and this is not without a claim of precedence.[1]

Concerning objectivity

An effort of writing presents most authors with the problem of semantics. Words are used to describe words, and this is often a source of misunderstanding when the exact meaning of a word or group of words is not known or commonly agreed upon; which words to use and in which order to arrange them so as to accurately represent the information or idea is an aspect of writing that is often contemplated. The consequence of this type of linguistic difficulty is that it can cause a listener or reader to ponder errantly because of an initial misunderstanding. An objective viewpoint, essential to lessen occurrences of misunderstanding, is greatly helpful when responding to or contemplating the intent or actual meaning of that which people may have spoken or written. I have therefore written a short and pertinent explanation of *the concept of objectivity*[2] in order to make clear the meaning of the words *objective* or *objectively* as well as to initiate a process of <u>objective thinking</u> in the reader; this latter aspect <u>being essential to contemplate reasonably the information, perceptions, and ideas that are presented in this book</u>. The words *impartial* or *unbiased* may be usefully substituted in some cases to assist a reader's understanding. Also, and not only for the preface, *the chapter endnotes are sometimes explantory in quality and therefore important* because they provide additional clarifying information to the reader concerning the meaning of certain assertions, ideas, or concepts or provide other useful details about some historical events. Lastly, the preface should not be considered either as a critical philosophical or psychological analysis of the concept of objectivity because it is simply a guiding discourse for the purpose of moving the attention of the reader toward the importance of objectivity in life.

As used in this book, *objective assessment* or *objectively assessed* derive their useful meaning by contrasting the conceptual idea of these two linguistic constructs to the undeniable fact that any person's thought, verbal or written statement, or action originating therefrom must be considered to be affected by their own perception and or evaluation, this latter having emerged from their innate sensate condition in response to their social environment; and, also, by defining for the purposes of this book the characteristics of the *two most important types of objectivity. Objectivity is the proposition that there is a preeminent or unique reality that is entirely independent of and indifferent to human judgment;*[3] and, upon personal achievement, such is one of several immutable truths of our human realm. Most people know from their experience in life, to some extent or another, that this idea, objectivity, is a valid as well as useful concept. (Narrowing for a moment the area of discussion, there are circumstances that are specific to human societies to which *a certain type of quasi-objectivity* may be applied, but these will only be mentioned and not elaborated upon because their identifiers are known well enough.)

Let's examine briefly the *two preeminent types of objectivity: 1) the human natural core-mentality that is devoid of perversity,*[4] *and 2), the indifferent acts of Nature.* First, a beginning point is necessary: *Conception; and I am formed as being human. In life, I am a human being. As I live and sense in the ways of a human being, I perceive that other people do, too -- i.e., their being is commensurate with mine. In sensing a person who is near to me I can empathize, for in their humanity are found the conditions of existence which permit me to recognize mine -- i.e., he or she is a foundational reflection of me. Reasoning, then, by conscious processes that arise from an unavoidable awareness of my natural membership in humanity, I clearly understand that my existence with others presupposes that I accept and support their innate right to exist; in so doing, I perceive clearly my innate connection with the human creed as well as my own human significance and responsibility in the scheme of life and accept this as my innate and preeminent reality. I am one with being in the human condition.* Such an unequivocal comprehension and full acceptance of this shared human condition is the seminal point from which the highest form of objectivity can arise. *Highest objectivity* emanates from the natural, innate core-mentality that is entirely devoid of perversity within a human being; but, this does not mean that any one person is devoid of perversity. When a growing youth is subjected to any of the various personality-shaping forces of a social environment that incidentally or purposefully obfuscates the recognition of their intrinsic humanity that is the sole attribute or entirety of their natural core-mentality -- the *innate pure-self* [5] -- the result is that they lose rather quickly the cognitive state that is necessary to produce its recognition and or proper expression. This particular social phenomenon hinders a person's ability to practice Aikido with a balance between humanism and the development of self-defense skill; i.e., it hinders the knowing of a higher consciousness that is one prerequisite toward acheiving a valid Budō reality.

Objectivity (type 1) derived from a natural core-mentality

Innate pure-self is the naturally present core-mentality disposition of a human being as conferred by Nature (i.e., genetic code) or, possibly, by a supernatural entity (e.g., a god). Meaning, it is the inherent trait that predetermines an infant's gradual and typically invariable development toward a basic mentality that demonstrates through acts (sensory input preferences, thought, speech, and other physical actions) *1)* a predisposition to comprehend and embrace their genetically (or perhaps supernaturally) bestowed potentiality to be of beneficial significance in humanity and *2)* their membership responsibility to the humane betterment of the shared human condition. However, the pure-self does not stand alone as the essential psychological foundation of the human being. The natural and essential foundation of a person, the *innate-core-essence*, certainly in existence at the moment of their birth, is *constituted of two interactive parts*. What is known commonly as the *survival instinct* trait is one inseparable part, the other is the *pure-self* trait; these two innate, preeminent aspects of a human presently make up the innate psychological foundation of its being, that is, its psychological norm or psychological core-essence. The pure-self can be technically described as a hypothetical *psychic repository* that consists of inherently prearranged neuron groups which function to confer and express, through certain unique and constant bioelectric interactions, its innate essence. Neuron communication interfaces positioned between the pure-self and the survival instinct act as a *psychic filtration adaptation portal* by means of which the pure-self modifies, to a greater or lesser degree, the expression of the survival instinct (hunger, fear, flee or fight, reproduction, shelter, etc.) in society. A visual aid that may assist the reader to understand such a neuro-psychic construct is given in *Figure 1*. The existence as well as significance of the innate-core-essence is not easily apprehended by an individual because the possibility of such discovery is governed by the extent to which a society has obscured the survival instinct, and subsequently, the pure-self. When considering any particular social environment within which a person lives, the interaction of a person's innate-core-essence with that environment is *the primary factor* in determining the evident characteristics that represent their state of being. *Another significant factor* is the extent to which they can bring to bear the 'right' kind of self-generated mental effort (willpower) to perceive and understand cause-and-effect, and then make the necessary adjustments to their behavior toward achieving a productive personal reality. Examples that support this conceptualization of any person's innate psychological norm -- that is, the innate-core-essence, itself comprised of the survival instinct and the pure-self which interact complexly as influenced by family and society -- are abundant; e.g., hundreds of years of Buddhist experiential knowledge and ontological treatment.[5] The typical effect of socializing forces upon the innate pure-self is that of its obfuscation by encasing and limiting the positive effects of its natural qualities with successive layers of erroneous interpretations (e.g., a society's government always acts in the best interest of its people) and harmful imaginings (e.g., mentally entertaining the degenerative fantasy of seeking control for merely the sake of exercising the power of control) whereby these aberrant thinking processes establish a baseline from which further errant thought, unproductive or degenerative behavioral patterns, and egregious acts -- all indications of defilement -- can and frequently do, emerge. Unfotunately, the condition just described is infrequently noticed by the affected individual unless they experience an event that reestablishes their connection to pure-self. A person may continue living in some state of unrecognized delusion because the effect of their society is consistently providing an ever-present and all-encompassing *societal template* (social matrix) to which their mentality attempts to conform. Many people exist, unwittingly, as a clone or mimic of their society's template because socializing forces (e.g., preexisting cultural, political, or religious ideas) tend to obfuscate a person's pure-self trait. Certain benefits that a person or a society could experience from the awareness of pure-self are infrequently realized (e.g., less crime, less warfare, more production). It is from this idea and observations that the following three examples are provided in order to elaborate what may result when pure-self is obscured by adventitious degenerative effects that can emerge from incidental, ill-conceived, and pernicious familial or societal acts. Also, and equally important, in the paragraph immediately following there is a presentation of several other examples that describe a natural, unsullied expression of pure-self. Putting aside the unfortunate situations of genetically induced brain abnormalities, brain diseases that cause genuine cognitive bioelectric dysfunction, physical brain injury resulting from internal or external trauma, or the possibility of *soul*,[6] *one example* is when a child begins to express an ornery intolerance toward other children, such a condition having possibly resulted as a response to parental overindulgence, unnerving psychological events, a beginning awareness of others, or a confounding, perhaps even harsh, survive-or-die social reality. The extent to which a real, not consciously perceived, pure-self state of being is actually experienced by any person is largely a result of the characteristics of their familial and societal circumstances, such as those from apparent or unapparent teachings or propaganda, which have been directed toward shaping their mentality (either accidentally or purposefully); the effect of these being such that they inject, often deeply, a 'socializing' force (e.g., enculturation or indoctrination) that modifies the interaction between the survival instinct and pure-self, the outcome of which can either be for the better or for the worse. It is important to note that there does exist a situation where one or many acts or characteristics of a person can be mistaken as having emerged from pure-self; such are merely the misinterpretations that result from delusions foisted upon an individual by their society. Parents and societies bear the sole responsibility for providing a minimally biased but true socializing reality for children and adults, respectively, in a way that actually improves the human experience. *An example* of the suppression of pure-self in enough members of a society that can relatively quickly result in a society's devolution is when there emerges a preference for a specific type of sociopolitical affiliation or identity-disposition where, for a given country's society that supposedly abides by its governing documents, a thorough-going application of and adherence to that guiding body of documents (which at inception had been so constructed as to improve its member's social condition) often comes to be unsupported by a majority of its members. Such a devolution results because the majority of its members, one by one and little by little, become unable to perceive the egregious cognitive effects upon their thinking that has emerged from the influence of errant information or subversive and pernicious propaganda; and, from this inability, they proceed unknowingly by the means of their own misdirected acts (e.g., uninformed or careless voting, or living in the moment rather than living for the future) and socially erosive attitudes (e.g., education is in its 'best' formulation when designed and administered by governmental entities) toward a degenerated social reality where there exists, in effect, fewer civil rights and less freedom. *Another complex example* of an onset of the loss of the personally-known pure-self that results from a collectively-accrued societal 'ethos' can be seen when the members of a society collude to propose the *troublesome*, often unspoken, and *socially erosive false attitude* that *might* equals *right* while giving only 'lip service' to the ideal virtue that *might must be subordinated to that which is Right*. In this situation, for whatever reason, one person, another, then yet another person has gradually emerged a peculiar but similar brand (type) of *quasi-right*, all having come together via social activities (e.g., coffee shop meetings, sports events, political dinners or rallies, criminal activities, pop-culture conventions, or other types of gatherings designed to attract like-minded as well as unsuspecting people) that indulge certain socio-memetic influenced inclinations whereby each of them experience a subtle or moderate, perhaps even blatant, psychosocial reinforcement of personal attitudinal tendencies. So it comes to pass, little by little, that as this especially important attribute -- the pure-self -- is buried deeply in the unconscious, there begins a concomitant emergence of a layered and interconnected basic cognitive operating structure, somewhat onion-like in essence, which comes eventually to constitute the various aspects of a person's mentality. (E.g., biases, anxieties and or fears, behavioral tendencies and patterns, spiritual leanings or religious membership, and political affiliation are interactive and often hinder an accurate or a complete knowing of their actual, true pure-self.) To offer some support for

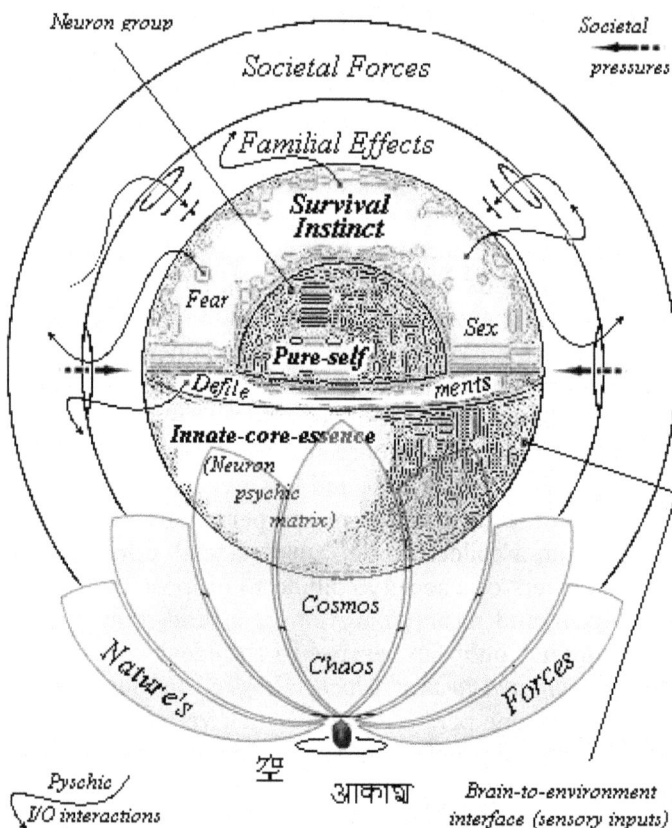

Figure 1

Illustration of the hypothetical **Innate-core-essence Concept** -- existing as a genetically encoded, interactive neuron complex within the human brain -- as conceived and shaped by the forces of Nature or a supreme deity (e.g., God); the latter symbolized by the stylized white lotus blossom (pink on the book's cover) at the bottom, i.e., an event like that related in the **Nasadiya Sukta** of the **Rig Veda** or some other 'creation' event. (Original drawing in color.)

this assertion, consider the Indian guru Sri Swami Satchidananda, who, in his book **The Yoga Sutras of Patanjali**, relates to us that *"Every thought, feeling, perception, or memory you may have causes a modification, or ripple, in the mind. It distorts and colors the mental mirror. If you can restrain the mind from forming into modifications,* *there will be no distortion, and you will experience your true Self*";[7] and, of further support, **Takuan Soho**, a Japanese Buddhist abbot, in an essay to the prominent samurai Yagyū Munenori, relates that "*It is the mind itself that leads the mind astray; of the mind, do not be mindless.*"[8] Beginning at birth, such a condition of being emerges slowly as an intricately constructed psychological response to the subtle or overt, gentle or harsh, and 'good' or 'bad' effects of a person's societal environment. This unavoidable condition of existence is partly a result of being youthful and lacking a consciously functioning linguistic structure by use of which they could begin to produce right-thought[5] sense of their experiences, and, partly a result of the complexly evolved outcome resulting from the interaction of a person's genetically determined brain structure[9] and or possible soul with that of their familial upbringing and their society's ethos. In support of this second assertion, Carl Jung, a renowned psychologist and cognitive researcher of the 20th Century, in his book entitled the **Modern Man In Search of a Soul**, proposes that "*Man's unconsciousness likewise contains all the patterns of life and behaviour inherited from his ancestors, and every child, prior to consciousness, is possessed of a potential system of adapted psychic functioning.*"[10] The modern sciences of today have revealed, by-and-large, that the ideas of these men as well as others were not far from the mark, even hundreds of years ago. When challenged by external information or inquiry, but where their social environment's obscuring effect is thoroughgoing, a person will unknowingly experience over time a suppression of the pure-self and begin to live, to some extent or another, a life of delusion.[11] This problematic personal phenomenon -- the suppression of pure-self -- emerges typically as a complex multifaceted psychological cause-and-effect interaction that can result in, and frequently does, distracting or harmful misperceptions and misunderstandings about the workings of life; this, in turn, can inevitably lead to the formation of anxiety, reality-contrariness, depravity, fear, neurosis, possibly some conditions of psychosis, and social strife. Many people live unknowingly with a certain mentality and personality that has emerged from the ill affects of their enculturation; the pure-self of each, as it were, is *hidden amongst the leaves*. *Highest objectivity* is difficult if not impossible to experience when pure-self is obfuscated.

Though some learned people may argue against this singular and unique source from which the highest form of objectivity can emanate -- the innate-core-essence -- the simplest of observations of human psychosocial development quickly produces information that validates this concept; e.g., a psychologically stable person (i.e., unburdened by any of the disorders previously mentioned) will always attempt to ensure their continued being (excepting a situational condition that may necessitate otherwise). Continuance in life -- being comprised of the innate urge to live and to reproduce -- is invariably expressed by most individuals in a way that is a result of the dynamic interaction of the survival instinct and pure-self traits as influenced by socializing forces. *Exemplifying a pure expression of the survival instinct* is a newborn's urge to seek its mother's breast for nourishment; and, a little further along in an individual's psychological evolution, a child's spontaneous, unsullied act of compassion or protection that comes from a place that is not motivated by avarice, a desire to manipulate, or by a desire for recognition or reward -- a true expression of the pure-self attribute. A person's act of spontaneous and unconditional kindness or protection is an example of pure-self expression if their mentality has been completely devoid of any forethoughts, premeditation, or desire of reciprocation. A satisfactorily functioning (not cognitively impaired) person's continued being is comprised of a reasoning, truth-seeking,[12] and steady mentality integrated with their physical body (without the corpus the mentality dissipates, without mentality the corpus expires) -- perhaps uniquely enlivened by soul; it is from here that the latter example of the previous sentence is associated with pure-self, for an act of kindness or protection does not necessarily or unduly threaten a person's continued being (i.e., survival). From this viewpoint, such action expresses clearly a person's recognition of the innate human qualities present in the other person while exhibiting the meaning of what it is to be human. Put differently, *the recognition of the innate human qualities in the other person is not only the preeminent meaning of what it is to be human but, in fact, it is an authentic revelation of pure-self unto self.* Recognition of pure-self is the basis from which a person can firmly hold in their consciousness the identifying markers of actual objectivity. Even ancient peoples knew of pure-self. *Chuangtse*, an ancient Chinese philosopher, informed us of this concept when he wrote that *"A man feels a pleasurable sensation before he smiles and smiles before he thinks how he ought to smile."*[13]

Connecting these topics -- objectivity, innate-core-essence, and pure-self -- with Aikido, an act of attentiveness or self-restraint while executing a technique (either as a performer or a receiver) so that injury does not occur to your partner is an example of your conscious connection to your pure-self. In effect, this means that *one should treat others as one would like others to treat oneself*, which is a golden ethic of social reciprocity that arises from the *objectivity that exists uniquely in pure-self*. This is, therefore, innate; meaning, a characteristic imbued by and inseparable from its inherent primal genetic and or soul nature. Rising upward and out of this inherent characteristic (the *natural objectivity in pure-self*) -- pushing out of unconsciousness toward a person's memetic portal into, possibly, consciousness -- and, often expressed in various ways in the overall societal consciousness of many of the world's societies, is the expression "*Live and let live.*" It (acting out of, or in accordance with this expression) is representative of objectivity in human societies, for it (the single valid meaning of this expression) emerges from that seminal point -- the pure-self -- unaffected by human activities, teachings, or machinations. Barring those cognitive disorders that were mentioned previously, no matter to what extent a person has been conditioned by family, clan, tribe, work group, culture, society, or Nature, they always have present somewhere in their mentality, even when suppressed by the behavioral effects that have emerged from the cultural forces of their social environment, either a vague or clear awareness of this single basis of objectivity, the pure-self. *Live and let live* should not, however, be errantly utilized toward proposing a behavior or doctrine of idealism, unconditional noninterference, contrived self-initiated ignorance, unbridled living-in-the-moment, or of willful self-harm because when considering the benefits of a human society governed by a valid formulation of liberty and justice (shaped by truth) -- contrary to the effects of 'popular culture' social forces that make possible the emergence of thinking whereby it seems 'good' to allow all that might be suggested by this expression -- such is actually a misguided interpretation. In order to initiate a seminal change whereby a person might begin to peel away their obstructing layers of misperception, confusion, and misdirection, some type of different cognitive processing must arise (from a stimulus) within their mentality through which they could come to know the extent of their ill-shaped mentality. This is often brought about as a result of personal tumult and subsequent contemplation, which might include a method of meditation. When a person experiences an occurrence of enlightenment (satori; in the Japanese language) they have an opportunity to approach nearer to their innate pure-self. *Reconnecting with the pure-self, knowing the pure-self, and acting humanely out of pure-self is the best possible or highest condition of objectivity.*

One type of self-analysis (psychological introspection) begins to arise when a person contemplates information from outside their realm of influence (e.g., facts and opinions from other people); however, the ever present influence of their 'societal template,' which includes a 'familial template,' as it interacts with their preexisting 'comfort-zone-mentality' that itself has been emerged by familiarity with previously held psychosocial constructs, urges them to reject the truth of much valid, extrinsic information. This type of analysis can only be termed as *quasi-objective assessment* because it is *subject to* the possible influence of factors that can interfere with establishing a reconnection with the pure-self; the extent to which it could have any affect at all toward achieving a mentality shift within a person would depend upon the extent to which they would willfully probe their condition of being. Slightly better quasi-objective assessment occurs when the individual is constructively critiqued by their peers; this is however not always to be considered true or valid objectivity because it is subject to the group intentions or agenda and is sometimes utilized *without even the semblance of objectivity.* Interestingly, the essential quality of objectivity within a human society is that it is largely subjective, meaning, subject to the actions of other people. The only *objective viewpoint* that a person can firmly hold in their mind is a clear assessment that their existence is the subject or target of two somewhat differing but interconnected forces. Specifically, *the first* is an act that affects or impinges upon you which has been initiated by yourself, by another person, or by a group of people -- this is the human realm, a subdomain of Nature; e.g., a situation of self-defense gives you information about your ability to protect yourself from injury.

Objectivity (type 2) imposed by Nature's indifferent acts

The other force arrives when Nature itself produces the feedback information as an objective force-entity that imposes, sometimes bluntly, upon one's condition of existence -- this is Nature's dominion, which includes events beyond the control of humankind and all other living things; e.g., an earthquake gives objective information about the construction characteristics of a house or other building, poison ivy gives information about one's human fragility, or, while hiking, a wild animal attack gives information about your ability to protect oneself from bodily injury.

How to reconnect to pure-self: 'objective' self-assessment

A clear, frequently reevaluated, validly achieved (unbiased) assessment as to how one exists or something manifests within the scheme of life is that which constitutes or defines actual, true objectivity. True objectivity, upon obtaining such, is useful in reestablishing full awareness of pure-self. *Attaining true objectivity by unraveling the layers of psychological encumbrances which obfuscate the pure-self is essential toward achieving a personal evolution that reflects a higher consciousness.*

Though there are many methods by which a person can come to know their pure-self, those such as Buddhist derived meditation and or the Shinto ritual process of *misogi*[14] are practiced by some students and teachers of Aikido. Interestingly, the founder of the main style (Aikikai) of Aikido, Morhei Ueshiba, considered the very practice of Aikido to be a form of misogi, for through such a practitioner comes to realize that the other person is a reflection of themself -- in recognizing one's own innate human qualities in the other person an aspect of pure-self is brought into consciousness, thereby revealing the necessity of full respect for the other.

An event during the battle of Ichi-no-Tani in 1184 C.E. between two warring Japanese clans, the Minamoto and the Taira, provides an illustration of the concept of pure-self. Heike prince Atsumori (1169–1184 C.E.) of the Taira clan, and Kumagai no Jiro Naozane (1141–1208 C.E.) of the Minamoto clan met on the shore near Suma as the Taira warriors were fleeing their burning fortress. Atsumori and his warriors were attempting to escape defeat by hurriedly departing in their ships to flee to another Taira fortress in Yashima. As Atsumori, on horseback, entered the water, Naozane, in forward pursuit, alone, rode up. Naozane saw clearly that the opposing warrior was a Commander-in-Chief and called out to him exclaiming that 'it is dishonorable to show your back to an enemy.' Naozane com-manded him to return. Atsumori, honor bound, turned around, re-turned to the beach and engaged Naozane face-to-face, both with swords unsheathed. A youth of perhaps sixteen years, Atsumori was no match for Naozane who was battle tough at forty-three years of age. Their swords crossed. During the short engagement, Atsumori's helmet is knocked from his head and Naozane sees that the warrior is quite young, a youth like any one of his own sons. He hesitated to sever Atsumori's head, but the youth commands that Naozane kill him, as this is the way of the Japanese warrior. Naozane again hesitated, probably quickly contemplating the impending tragedy of this boy's death, the son of another man, or even of permitting Atsumori to escape. But, alas, Naozane's thundering troop arrived, and tearfully promising to offer prayers for him -- being spurred to act in knowing that others of his troop would demand Atsumori's death -- severed his head.

The hesitation of samurai Naozane during his brief encounter with Prince Atsumori is thought by many historians to show that some samurai, perhaps many, were remorseful about their death-dealing acts. In fact, Naozane, after the Genpei War (1180–1185 C.E.), disavowed Bushido and resigned his samurai status to become a Pure Land Buddhist (Mahāyāna) monk. Naozone's hesitation and momentary contemplation had arisen from his pure-self, that part of his essence that knew what was perverse and what was not. In that brief encounter with Atsumori, he had experienced an *objective* glimpse that pierced momentarily through the obscuring layers of his society, which, naturally, resulted in an awakening of his consciousness to the absurdity of his existence.

This event, from the annals of Japanese history, resulted in a life-changing projection of pure-self into Naozone's consciousness, manifesting suddenly as personal awareness about the condition of his being in relation to his society. Though not easy to assess, it is likely that thousands of such *pure-self* moments occurred during Japan's progress from feudalism to a modern constitutional republic. Toward a further understanding of Aikido, it is supportive to mention here that each of these individual pure-self moments, when combined over time, were equivalent to a *social seeding* that helped to stimulate Japan's social progress from feudalism toward its present society, and accompanying this change was the evolution of Budo from Bushido and Aikido from Daito-ryū Jūjutsu.[15]

The fight between Atsumori and Naozane, which is immortalized in a stage drama of the Japanese art of *Noh*, serves as a poignant warning to all people who may come to experience what can happen as life unfolds when pure-self is smothered by any number of noxious cultural or societal structures and their attendant behavioral expectations -- i.e., tragedy. Today, too, many societies -- each composed of people who emerge various, often different cultural and political forces -- emanate a general affect that can obscure an individual's knowing of pure-self; some of these forces or some aspects of those forces have the effect of leading a person's consciousness away from the mental processes by which they could achieve a valid objective viewpoint.[16]

Assisting us to further grasp the meaning of *objective assessment*, consider Takuan Soho's statement of right-mindedness when he tells the reader that "*Right-mindedness is considered to be the substance devoid of perversity that is the core of the human mind; and in using the straightness in that core of the mind as a plumbline, everything produced will exhibit right-mindedness.*"[17] Continuing to elucidate this, James Allen's foreword in his book *As a Man Thinketh* cautions us that "*They themselves are the maker of themselves by the virtue of their thoughts, which they choose and encourage; that mind is the master weaver...*"[18] Then, consider Jean-Paul Sartre's statements concerning the problem of *choice* in his book *Existentialism and Human Emotions*, "*Objective because they are to be found everywhere and are recognizable everywhere ...*"[19] and "*... in discovering my inner being I discover the other person at the same time ...*"[19] Furthermore, in a revisiting of ancient Chinese history, the military officer and philosopher Kuan Yin helps to elucidate what is meant by *objective* or *objectively* when he reminds us that "*If you get away from your point of view, things and forms will appear in their true light by themselves.*"[20] Lastly, as a testament to humankind's effort to discern and clarify the objective viewpoint, Arthur Waley, an early 20th Century Asian studies scholar, in his book *The Nō Plays of Japan*, relates the following: "*Once when Shākyamuni* [Siddartha Guatama] *was preaching before a great multitude, he picked up a flower and twisted it in his fingers. The rest of the hearers saw no significance in the act and made no response; but the disciple Kāshyapa smiled. In this brief moment a perception of transcendental truth had flashed from Buddha's mind to the mind of his disciple. Thus Kāshyapa became the patriarch of Zen Buddhists, who believe that Truth cannot be communicated by speech or writing, but that it lies hidden in the heart of each one of us and can be discovered by 'Zen' or contemplative introspection.*"[21] Herein, "transcendental truth" refers to a preeminent objective truth while "hidden in the heart" (i.e., at the core) is a reference to pure-self.

Finally, regarding *self-defense*, though a specific *how to* is not e-lucidated herein, when the term is used in this book it is done so in association with the relevant concepts, tactics, and techniques that a person who utilizes Aikido may bring to bear in defense of self or others when there emerges a possible life-threatening situation, such being divided into person-to-Nature situations or person-to-person situations against an opponent who is not armed with a bal-listic or explosive weapon; the latter circumstance being a special situation of self-defense that is best taught by a competent teacher in a school setting. In this book I have purposefully omitted the in-depth discussion or illustration of any specific technique or tactic for two reasons. *First*, there exists already a large number of writ-ten and video media that are comprised of such technical inform-ation, many of which are competent and useful. *Second*, when your opponent is equally knowledgeable and adept you'll find that your successful defense will rest upon a fleeting moment of perception that you must instantly act upon, thus assuring your justifiable vic-tory -- if you fail to make use of that moment you are more likely to be defeated than not. There are people in our world who would do you harm for no reason other than that of you happening to make eye contact with them. Those of this type, as well as others who are afflicted with wrong-mindedness and psychoses, have studied to some extent or another the various styles of martial arts and are completely willing to use their knowledge in a destructive way to harm you. It is a disservice to humanity to unwittingly or for gain to provide useful knowledge of martial techniques, tactics, and strategy to members of the public outside of the context of a class-room wherein a teacher might properly shape and control the dis-semination of such. Morihei Ueshiba rarely gave public demonstra-tions, and when he did, if he saw gangsters or hoodlums in the au-dience, he ended his presentation.[22] Media (books, magazines, and video) about Aikido or martial arts in which there is contained photo illustration -- especially where little attention is paid to shap-ing the proper civil attitudes of a reader or viewer from the per-spective of lawful behavior -- frequently contributes to the emer-gence of unfriendly, scurrilous, truculent, and or sometimes vicious disposition where an individual thusly aligned is willing to 'jump bad' at the slightest of slights.

[1] Generic *he* has been a preference in usage, not a binding grammatical rule, as Thackeray's use of both forms demonstrates. "The alternative to the masculine generic with the longest and most distinguished history in English is the third-person plural pronoun. Recognized writers have used *they, them, themselves,* and *their* to refer to singular nouns such as *one, a person, an individual,* and *each* since the 1300s." The 2011 translation of the New International Version Bible utilizes singular *they* instead of *he* or *he or she,* reflecting changes in English usage. The translators commissioned a study of modern English usage and determined that singular *they,* and subsequently *them/their,* is by far the most common way that English-language speakers and writers today refer back to singular antecedents such as *whoever, anyone, somebody, a person, no one,* and the like. See the topic entitled **Singular they** at Wikipedia.org; 2011. See also the article entitled **Theirself or Themself** at http://cliffhays.weebly.com/blog/theirself-or-themself; 2015.

[2] Mortimer J. Adler defines objectivity as "*The objective is absolute; the subjective is relative to individual human beings.*" See, **Adler's Philosophical Dictionary** by Mortimer J. Adler; Touchstone Edition, paperback, 1996, page 14.

[3] While there is no universally accepted articulation of the concept of objectivity, "*a proposition is typically considered to be objectively true when its truth conditions are met and are 'mind-independent'*", i.e., they stand wholly apart from (independent of) those cognitive processes of a conscious being (sentient subject) that emerge feelings, imaginings, dreams, judgment, etc., which latter tends to modify or distort an object's absolute truth in reality. This is in contrast to, and largely opposite of, the concept of *Perspectivism.* See the topic entitled *"Objectivity"* from Wikipedia.org; 2011. For another good discussion of the concept of *objectivity,* see **Adler's Philosophical Dictionary** by Mortimer J. Adler; Touchstone Edition, paperback, 1996, page 14.

[4] Perversity -- turned away from what is right or good; contrary to the evidence; marked by perversion.

[5] Buddhism, particularly Mahāyāna, and other eastern religions such as Hinduism and Jainism, have teachings that similarly propose an *essential self,* that is, *a pure immaterial basis of being* situated at the center of a person's mentality that is in accordance with the Eight Fold Path (right thought, right views, right speech, right action, right livelihood, right effort, right mindfulness, and right meditation). The Mahayana Buddhist

teaching of Tathāgatagarbha expresses clearly its nature. The Lankavatara Sutra describes the Tathāgatagarbha as "by nature brightly shining and pure," and "originally pure," though "enveloped in the garments of the skandhas, dhatus and ayatanas and soiled with the dirt of attachment, hatred, delusion and false imagining." It is said to be "naturally pure," but it manifests impurity as it is stained by adventitious defilements. Also, from the perspective of modern cognitive science, read the article entitled *The Science of Morality* by Abigail Tucker; the Smithsonian magazine, January issue, 2013.

[6] Mortimer J. Adler describes *soul* by invoking the viewpoints of the Greek philosophers Aristotle and Plato, because the concept of *soul* is very difficult if not impossible to quantify or prove. Adler relates that for Aristotle, *"the word 'soul' names the form to be found in the substance of all living matter"* and that *"the intellect, which is one of the soul's specific powers, is immortal because it is immaterial."* For Plato, Adler says, *"the soul was a spiritual substance co[n]joined with a material or physical body."* See *Adler's Philosophical Dictionary* by Mortimer J. Adler; Touchstone Edition, paperback, 1996, pages 180, 181, 182.

[7] See the second sutra in the book *The Sutras of Patanjali* by Sri Swami Satchidanana. Integral Yoga Publications; reprint edition, first printing, 1990.

[8] See *The Unfettered Mind: Writings of the Zen Master to the Sword Master*, by Takuan Soho, translated by William Scott Wilson. Kodansha International, Ltd.; first paperback edition, fourth printing, 1987, page 44.

[9] Today, a developing branch of human psychology called *Memetics* postulates that there exists within the human mentality, along with its cognitive processes and other functions, a mental unit of imitation and replication and of cultural values transmission. This mental unit, called a *meme*, consists of an attitude, behavior, idea, or style that is disseminated or passed person-to-person, one mind to another, through writing, speech, gestures, rituals, symbols, or other imitation-oriented phenomena and results in the transfer of cultural ideas or practices. One theory suggests that a meme (consisting of two or more neurons) or *meme-complex* (consisting of two or more memes) is predisposed toward processing all incoming information in a specific-to-the-person way, and that this predisposition is genetically inherent in the person at the inception of its being but changeable overtime, and that such neuron groups may self-reinforce certain attitudinal, behavioral, ideological, or stylistic tendencies resulting from the action of various affects of various biochemical neuro-transmitter molecules,

e.g., dopamine. A meme or memecomplex that replicates most effectively results in a more thorough or successful inculcation and transmission of its meaning, significance, or portent, but some may replicate successfully and imbed thoroughly <u>even though found to be harmful to the host's overall well-being</u>; this latter aspect provides an explanation for Buddhism's ancient teachings regarding the "*dirt of attachment, hatred, delusion and false imagining*" referred to in endnote 5 above.

[10] See the book **Modern Man in Search of a Soul** by Carl Jung; chapter entitled *The Basic Postulates of Analytic Psychology.* Kegan Paul, Trench, Trubner & Co; hardback edition, first printing, 1941.

[11] Delusion -- a false belief or opinion held, often exhibiting resistance to reasoning or confrontation with actual fact.

[12] Truth-seeking -- a state of cognition where a person, after realizing the effect of their society upon shaping the characteristics of their present state of cognition, has removed bias or predisposition concerning any activity, event, movement, occurrence, phenomenon, or perception, no matter how disconcerting, and, unwilling any longer to dogmatically hold onto a certain perception, idea, or ideology, has mostly if not entirely moved their cognitive processing outside of their personal enculturation shell in order to seek either unvarnished (candid, straightforward, unembellished) or immutable truth.

[13] See the book entitled **The Wisdom of Laotse** by Lin Yutang. Random House, Inc.; hardcover, first edition, 1976, page 203.

[14] Misogi -- this is Shintōism's ritual purification method.

[15] And, Kendō from Kenjūtsū, Jūdō from Jūjūtsū.

[16] One viewpoint of *Objectivism* holds that "*reality exists independent of consciousness, that human beings have direct contact with reality through sense perception, [and] that one can attain objective knowledge from perception through the process of concept formation and inductive and deductive logic.*" See the topic entitled *Objectivism* at Wikipedia.org; 2011.

[17] See **The Unfettered Mind: Writings of the Zen Master to the Sword Master** by Takuan Soho, translated by William Scott Wilson. Kodansha International, Ltd.; first paperback edition, fourth printing, 1987, page 44.

[18] See the *Forward* in the book entitled **As A Man Thinketh** by James Allen. Fleming H. Revell Company Edition, first printing, 1957.

[19] See the book entitled **Existentialism and Human Emotions** by Jean-Paul Sartre. The Wisdom Library, a division of The Philosophical Library, Inc.; hardcover, 1957, page 38.

[20] See the book entitled **The Wisdom of Laotse** by Lin Yutang. Random House, Inc.; hardcover, first edition, 1976, page 32.

[21] See the book entitled **The Nō Plays of Japan** by Arthur Waley. Alfred A. Knopf; hardcover, first edition, 1922.

[22] See the article entitled the **Founder of Aikido: The Principle of Great Harmony and Love** by Kisshomaru Ueshiba; Aiki News magazine, article #70, 1986.

Introduction - Aikidō's Distress

"What is aikido? Even advanced students have difficulty in providing a straightforward answer."

"Similarly, we have difficulty in trying to explain the ultimate essence of aikido when asked by a novice or an outsider."

Kisshomaru Ueshiba -- 2nd Doshu Aikikai Aikido
The Spirit of Aikido (Aikido no Kokoro)[1]

A person who seeks a clear understanding of that which they undertake or seek to achieve, no matter what it may be, challenges oneself with the task of acquiring knowledge, skill, and determining truth. Self-defense, policing, or martial action (warfare) does not permit either quasi-truth or truth masking. There is no room at all for any kind of self-deception because the outcome of physical self-defense action, physical police interdiction, or military combat is either defeat or victory, this being proof of whether a person's spiritual fortitude is lame, murky, and weak rather than skilled, resilient, and tough -- the proof of little skill or ultimate skill. Interestingly, in the physical disciplines that appear useful as a means to ward off aggression (such as martial arts) and where any of these may attempt to inculcate in the practitioner a humanitarian-like behavioral ethos, such as that often present in Aikido training, there is a certain possibility that the necessary mental toughness as well as the essential technique and skill required for successful self-defense can be destructively subverted by that very ethos. The developmental outcome of training for a practitioner of Aikido will vary depending upon how the program of study is designed and emphasized. For example, when a program of Aikido training favors the inculcation of esoteric spirituality over practical self-defense skills, there follows inevitably a certain and evident weakening of its focus upon the essential matters of self-defense. Put simply, the desired outcome or goal of a particular style or program of training affects whether a spiritual or self-defense focus will predominate as its primary identifying characteristic. Importantly, an ideal program of Aikido training will establish within a practitioner's consciousness a functional balance between these two elemental concerns while also ensuring that the spiritual element is actually useful toward developing a reasonable (i.e., protective) and humane (i.e., minimal harm) approach to the variable and difficult situations of self-defense.

Many of the technical aspects of Aikido, perhaps all, are shaped to some extent by its philosophical tenets; yet, this relationship should not produce the circumstances that brands Aikido as an ineffectual means of self-defense, either by some members of the overall Aikido community or by casual observers or analysts. Unfortunately, such a *branding*, that is, as an ineffectual self-defense, comes to pass little by little when one or more practitioners of one Aikido style or another indulges a greater focus on theoretical or esoteric spirituality because they find repugnant and disconcerting the actual behavior necessary to accomplish the reality of successful self-defense. It is certainly less disconcerting, perhaps even enjoyable, to attempt a reworking of one's so-called spirituality without engaging the occasionally uncomfortable mental and physical effort that is required to attain true aiki-aligned self-defense capability. In support of these assertions, consider the comment of Gōzō Shioda (the founder of Yōshinkan Aikido) that "*Current aikido has no core. It is empty in substance. People try to reach the summit without going along the substantial part. So aikido deteriorates into dance or something.*"[2]

Seemingly, for many who practice Aikido, there are two prominent murky aspects concerning that which defines its philosophical basis. *First,* What are the essential characteristics of Aikido's philosophical foundation? *Second,* Is the term *martial art* an accurate descriptive term for Aikido? These questions beckon for answers from all who practice Aikido, but especially from those organizations that claim association with the word *aikido.*

Why is it important to inquire about the essence of Aikido's philosophy? To answer, Aikido's philosophy informs a practitioner about what kind of outcome is expected at the end of a conflict, whether such is verbal or physical, in order to be affirmed as truly adhering to the ethos of Aikido. Thus, in being informed about what is expected as an outcome, a practitioner is made aware of what must come first as mental alignment, then behavior, and finally, further learning toward the development of skill; all this arising out of acceptance and, later, the effort of training. Unfortunately, such has become a difficult task for students of Aikido because it has suffered a differentiation or factionalization process that has resulted in a 'slicing' from its wholeness a number of generalized categorical emphases, those being *1)* self-defense, *2)* spirituality and health (yoga-like in character), *3)* combative sport, and *4)* civilian policing. A fifth category -- military or paramilitary combat -- exists in the thinking of some who call themselves Aikido practitioners, but the type of emphasis necessary to align thusly is more akin to Aikijūjutsu than to Aikido.

The aforementioned matters as well as other important aspects pertinent to the study of Aikido -- such as the ever-present political discord between the differing Aikido styles that has arisen from conflicting attitudes about competition, or the weakening of its teacher's ability to inculcate in a student the proper attitude and skill necessary to accomplish successful aiki self-defense -- comprise its general distress. A significant part of this book is directed toward discussion and resolution of this distress, hopefully to help reestablish Aikido's efficacy, reinvigorate its teachers, and elucidate its role in the improvement of human societies.

The study of how Aikido's philosophy should or should not shape the learning and application of its techniques, whether for the reason of general well-being or functional self-defense, is a matter not to be ignored when one seeks truth from this discipline. True Aikido is done in a manner so as to attain not only a balance between the spiritual need and the physical reality but also to interweave these two in a way where they manifest a humane and productive result that exhibits respect for life. That said, when discussing the emphasis category of self-defense, the functionality of Aikido as a means of self-defense in one society is not necessarily what is required of it in another where societal mores have evolved differently (e.g., compare the nature of violence in Japan with that of the United States of America). In fact, ignorance of this matter can result in not only a breech of a particular country's mores but can also instill in a person a self-defense skill set that is misconceived at best, invalid at worst, and very dangerous when a need to defend against an aggressor arises. A practitioner of Aikido must apply their effort toward gaining an unbiased understanding of this discipline's actual foundational essence because in achieving such they will be better prepared to do that which is necessary to engage the learning of functional, aiki aligned self-defense ability. Having achieved this, one is encouraged to further develop their written and verbal powers of speech so that they may provide clear and valid answers to any questions that a curious outsider or new student may pose.

[1] See, **The Spirit of Aikido** (Aikido no Kokoro) by Kisshomaru Ueshiba, translated by Taitetsu Unno; Kodansha International, Ltd., paperback edition, first printing, 1987.

[2] See the essay entitled **The Process of Forming Aikido and Japanese Imperial Navy Admiral Isamu Takeshita: Through the analysis of Takeshita's diary from 1925 to 1931** by Fumiaki Shishida, 8th Dan, Shōdōkan Aikido, Waseda University, Tōkyō, Japan, 2008.

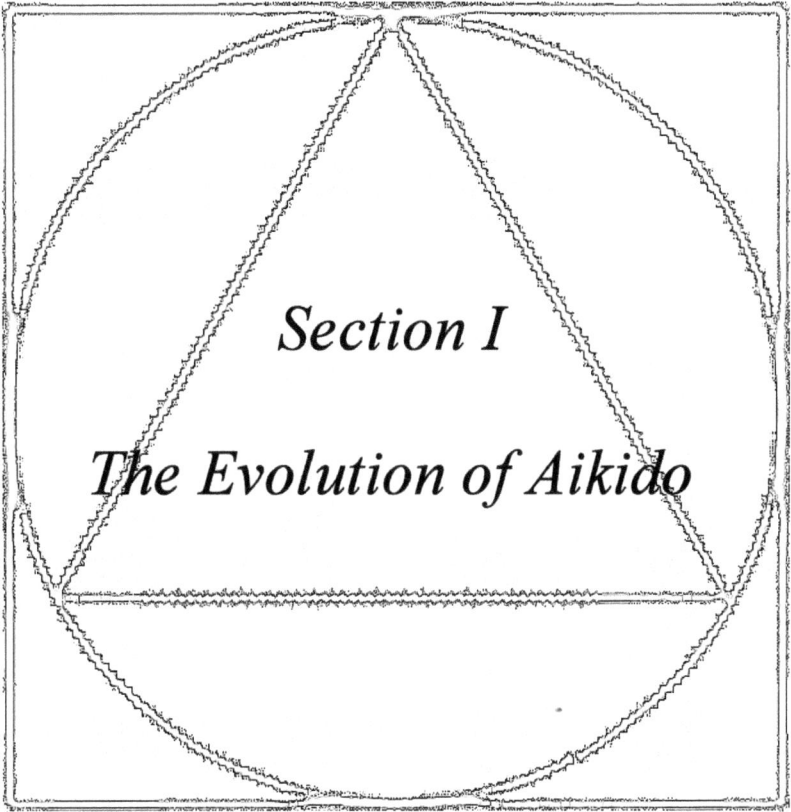

Section I

The Evolution of Aikido

Chapter I

Understanding Aikidō. What is it?

Aikidō (合気道) -- *the way of meeting spirit, the way of uniting spirit,* or *the way of harmonious spirit* -- is a unique physio-spiritual[1] discipline that offers a person a path of study through which they can attain a personal refinement of consciousness[2] while inculcating simultaneously a protective yet appropriate set of self-defense skills, which, when applied out of need during a situation of self-defense, can be minimally injurious to an aggressor. When acting thusly, a practitioner of Aikido shows a certain useful as well as necessary respect for a wrongdoer and thereby diminishes the possibility of an escalated confrontation that might result in a tragic social outcome. Through the development of a certain ability that is conferred by a study of that which comprises the merging or unification of life's energies, the practitioner of Aikido can actually and realistically render harmless many of the disruptive forces experienced in life, including those that can emerge from self-defense situations, thereby establishing a larger, more resilient, and stronger sphere of harmony as the predominating condition in their life. Practitioners of Aikido, called *aikidōka*, point their individual efforts toward understanding that which comprises the concept of harmony as well as how to achieve behavior that manifests it; e.g., in self-defense situations.

Contemplating the kinds of disorder that can erupt during a situation of defense against an aggressor, an aikidoka studies how to resolve such conflict with action that produces the least destructive outcome, yet always protecting their life. Such study results in the development of certain personal abilities that are always realized to be useful beyond the realm of self-defense or pugilism. A core precept of Aikido is that of *non-contention.*[3] (See Chapters IV and IX for discussions about 'non-contention.') If embraced fully by a practitioner, a certain different personal spirituality, the extent of which can only be known by them, may be awakened and evidenced as they take in and internalize Aikido's technical and philosophical teachings. In fact, at a very high level of spiritual and technical development, a few aikidoka may develop an attitude where they consider an opponent as a partner in the search for truth (the truths of life), though such should neither be the goal of study nor, when in a self-defense circumstance, held in thought as an inviolable attitude or approach toward an attacker whose actions express an intent to hurt or kill.

Aikido manifests its philosophy through the practice of specific physical movements and techniques that have a functional basis evolved from certain older and traditional Japanese jūjutsu ('gentle art') and kenjutsu (blade art) schools as informed or moderated by the concept of *aiki,* which is based upon the ideas of *ai* (harmony) and *ki* (energy). Depending on the style of Aikido, the concept of ki may be imbued with mystical or supernatural qualities; however, this is not so for all styles of Aikido. In the personal realm, *positive ki* manifests when a person's thought-intention results in behavior that produces a situation-dependent dynamic where a desired harmonious outcome might occur; the possibility of a successful outcome is enhanced when breath and action are coordinated. To describe it differently, positive ki manifests when the coordination between breath and action is encapsulated by intention that embraces harmony or, in other terms, positive ki manifests when intention produces behavior that engenders harmony while coordinating breath and action. This is especially so for those actions in life which affect other people.[4] For the practitioner of Aikido, two primary conditions must exist in order to produce ki that is positive where such may enable harmonious interaction with others. *First,* one's intention must embrace harmony -- that is, getting along, accord, working together, agreement, moving in unison, etc. *Second,* all action -- mental, speech, body language, other necessary body movement, and particularly breath -- must be coordinated and unified, ideally, with the inherent movements of life, or with the forces of the universe. However, one must realize this: it takes two people in relation to each other or one in relation to Nature to create either harmony or disorder.

Aikido is practiced by tens of thousands of people around the world, and for many it is the single most important physio-spiritual endeavor that they have undertaken. Each person who chooses to embrace a path of aiki through the practice of Aikido will likely experience an awakening self-realization. Inherent in training is an opportunity to make change for the betterment of self and community. For example, a person will likely come to know that a sane existence is most certainly dependent on harmonious interactions with other people, whether it be in acquaintanceship, friendship, marriage, community, nation or the world; and, that a pleasant existence is based upon kindness toward and respect of life. The practitioner of Aikido, empirically and intuitively, recognizes these matters which concern their existence.

The essence of Aikido's philosophy has evolved from both the older Japanese martial disciplines as well as from the influence of Buddhism and Japan's native Shintō religion, but especially by the effect of the Japanese religion called Ōmoto-kyō (大本教). This is important to mentally apprehend because it causes a shaping of the technical characteristics of Aikido, which vary somewhat from one style of Aikido to another.

During the twelfth century, Japan's cultural emphasis shifted gradually away from an aesthetic and scholarly ethos to one represented largely by both devout filial piety and firm loyalty given to a daimyo (territorial lord) or shogun (supreme military commander) by warriors who glorified personal and family honor associated with, imbued in, or attributed to martial skill and weaponry. For the warrior, this thoroughgoing cultural martial attitude was known as *Kyuba-no-michi* (the way of the horse and the bow), and later in the fourteenth century as *Bushidō* (武士道), i.e., the way of the *warrior statesman.*[5] Generally, Bushido's ethical code dictated frugality, loyalty, reverence, mastery of martial arts, and an adherence to the honoring of these attributes even unto death. The ethical teachings of Bushido and *Budō* (武道, *the way of stopping weapons of destruction*) are still pertinent to the study of Japanese martial arts. Bushido is the old code of warrior action and behavioral ethics with attributes that evolved from Japan's ancient times; where Budo, a relatively modern formation with a somewhat different ethical basis -- having been first suggested in 1914 C.E. by a police official named Nishikubo Hiromichi and embraced officially by Japan's Ministry of Education in the year 1926 C.E. -- is an ethos that evolved to guide both *soldier* and statesman to act according to its preeminent philosophical tenet, that is, *to stop weapons of destruction.* This process of transformation was largely influenced by Jigorō Kanō's efforts to establish a new behavioral ethos and worldwide social comaraderie (jita kyōei -- mutual welfare and benefit) as heralded by his creation Jūdō. The term *Bujutsu* (武術) refers to the actual martial techniques, tactics, and strategies used in fighting and warfare, i.e., the technical science of the Japanese martial arts and war, the execution of which is guided by one ethos or another.

Ai Uchi No Kyoukun (合い打ちの教訓), precept of mutual striking, is part of the philosophy of the older martial disciplines of Japan's feudal period which predate Aikido and other martial or martial-derived disciplines of today -- its meaning is the willingness to put one's life near to death, accepting without fear that you may at any moment die, in order to achieve victory over one's opponent. In so acting a person exhibits an attitude of indifference toward their possible death and thereby will have gained a greater chance of living -- though never is one's mind grasping for or desirous of a long life. If one willingly accepts the inevitability of one's death, one is relieved of this fear (not having a long life) and can proceed in life (or, at least, in battle) free of all doubt, full of determination. During those older feudal times, such an attitude was embraced and held by the strongest warriors because the grotesque reality of battlefield close combat was a frequent occurrence. Survival meant that one must develop a mental ability that, on a personal level, would give an advantage of control over the opponent. Any inkling of fear could create, in its instance of occurrence, a mental confusion that might lead to panic. A mind reacting thusly can beget gross uncertainty that could result in an outcome of injury, defeat, capture, humiliation, or death. Obviously then, a stout and skilled warrior could not be uncertain as to what action must occur, must not fear. Ai Uchi No Kyoukun, that older traditional precept, required a certain necessary macabre proximity to death in order to accomplish the feat of vanquishing an opponent. This way of behaving was accepted as practical for a warrior of feudal Japan and his entire mental composure from the time of birth until his death was developed under its affect. Without doubt, to live by the sword as outlined by Ai Uchi No Kyoukun meant that a warrior might also find it severing him from his life.

Today, when practicing a martial art or a martial art derived discipline, Ai Uchi No Kyoukun is still a useful technical concept, especially for many military, police, and security persons. Yet, for the majority of people who currently practice a modern martial-art-derived self-defense discipline, the embracement of such a principle is mostly unnecessary. Today, people, especially those in properly functioning constitutional republics, who live in a condition where police enforce their society's civil laws to thereby protect them from unusual and excessive civil violence have evolved a somewhat gentler and kinder non-feudal social order and societal peace. That is not to say, though, that there are no cultures or subcultures in our present world that do not align with this older martial precept, for there are.[6]

Fortunately, in a society founded on the principles of life and liberty, a sane person has an alternative precept with which he or she may identify and by which they may act when faced with an opponent. The alternate and humanitarian-like precept is that of *Ai Nuke No Kyoukun* (合い抜けの教訓), precept of mutual escape; it's meaning is *the willingness to take action that is either minimally destructive or nondestructive while yet protecting one's own life.* This precept is a most significant one for Aikido, as it transcends those aspects of the older martial attitude that seek closeness to death, thereby evolving a new attitude that is one of two precepts upon which the philosophy of Aikido is founded. The other precept is that of *aiki*, i.e., *harmonizing spirit or harmonized energy.*

It is important to contemplate that some practitioners of Aikido, both novice and professional, have a vague or perhaps muddled mental grasp of the actual or most valid meaning of certain important descriptive words or phrases which are often employed to e-lucidate Aikido's essence. Misunderstanding begets confusion, and confusion in turn usually, unless otherwise artfully devised, produces an undesirable outcome. The word *martial* -- both its English language meaning as well as that conferred by the Japanese term *bu* (武) and the words *ai* (合), *ki* (気), and *aiki* (合気) -- must be thoroughly examined. The latter three will be discussed in subsequent chapters. Turning attention now to the word *martial*, it is often assigned either a creative or destructive meaning in both Western and Japanese societies depending on the circumstance under consideration; and without qualification during its use, as is often the case, misunderstanding the speaker's or writer's intent may easily occur.

Such flexibility, though a useful tool when artfully employed for the purpose of misdirection,[7] is usually unproductive in elucidating actual and important meaning. Contrary to the definition of that which comprises "True martial art"[8] as related in the book *The Spirit of Aikido* by Kisshomaru Ueshiba, who was the second doshu (inheritor of the tradition) of Aikikai Aikido (the Ueshiba family line of Aikido), a martial art is not at all concerned with peace, love and harmony but rather it is concerned either with the immediate elimination of an assault perpetrated by an opponent, or at best, the minimization of violence and destruction in order to resolve the disorder toward a possible peace within which harmony and love may again blossom. This distinction is necessary because peace and love, residing in the dominion of harmony, manifest clearly as pleasant and productive human behavioral aspects only after harmful physical interaction has been stopped or, ideally, prevented (e.g., through societal appropriate, preemptive educational nurturing). Continuing, "True martial art" is better represented as *ideal martial art* because the complete attainment of that type of truth -- i.e., love and peace -- is an idealistic goal that, when considering an event of personal or societal violence, can only be realized through humane self-defense action that neutralizes the violence and restores harmony to the house of peace; having said that, it seems quite incongruous to associate this kind of well-meant idealism with the word *martial.* Surely, examination of this word *martial* in order to ascertain its best meaning and proper place of use can benefit anyone who pursues an understanding of Aikido. Morihei Ueshiba, the founder of Aikido, was a very adept and sagacious practitioner of that which Western Civilization calls the Martial Arts. Yet beyond that, and more significantly, he was a practitioner of Budo, *"The Way of Stopping Weapons of Destruction."*[9] The importance of this latter for Aikido practitioners is that it provides them with an opportunity to fully understand what Aikido is or is not.

To begin developing a feeling of the essence of Aikido, one must experience it. To begin a discussion of whether or not it is a martial art, one must have that experience and must also discern clearly the best meaning of the word *martial.* A dictionary defines it as meaning "of, or suitable for war," or "showing a readiness or eagerness to fight."[10] With the right emphasis, interestingly, and perhaps disturbing to some *aikidoka* (practitioners of Aikido), *the techniques of Aikido are suitable for use in war, for destruction, and can obviously be used to fight.*

To define Aikido employing a word other than *martial* seems to be a difficult task, even for those who are its highest proponents. Is it possible that Aikido is not a martial art? To answer this question one must begin by asking (and answering) yet another question begotten by that aforementioned disturbing statement, that being: *How could it possibly be that the techniques of Aikido are suitable for use in war, can be used to fight, and can destroy when employed toward that end?* Thoughtful inquiry considers well that Morihei Ueshiba achieved, through much effort and tribulation, a high sense of compassion towards humanity. He then developed the foundational aspects of his discipline, which was originally named Aikibudo, and presented Aikido to the world for the purpose of upholding kindness, respectfulness, and sincerity as those human behaviors which are among the best for the development of the human personality; yet, he knew well that one must be prepared for and be able to defend against the violence emerging from inequity that exists in life. Morihei Ueshiba, as well as his son Kisshomaru, understood the necessity for the physical and psychological techniques that would be useful in the defense of self from the attacks of an aggressor.

"Aikido decides life and death in a single strike, so students must carefully follow the instructor's teaching and not compete to see who is the strongest."

Morihei Ueshiba -- Aikikai Founder
1st Reminder in Aikido practice
The Spirit of Aikido
p. 85

"Contrary to what one might assume, Aikido contains several devastating techniques, especially those meant to disarm and subdue the enemy."

Kisshomaru Ueshiba -- Second Aikikai Doshu
The Spirit of Aikido
p. 18

Delving further into what Aikido is, one needs to mentally apprehend that it is a *discipline*. But, what is a *discipline*? A dictionary defines it as being "training that develops character."[10] Think clearly now and understand this, that which defines any discipline is created by the proponents of a discipline, and through sheer power of *will* they adhere to that which defines it. That which defines a discipline is known as its philosophy, and its philosophy is carried forth by its proponents. Men and women, the proponents, choose by their very actions the definition of their discipline (and their actions may, on occasion, go contrary to the previous philosophy of their discipline, thus changing, at the moment of deviance, temporarily or permanently, the very essence upon which their discipline had been based). The proponents of Aikido choose not to war, not to wantonly destroy, not to create ill relations, and not to be eager to fight. Therefore, they do not practice with a martial attitude. Reasonably then, it follows that Aikido is not a martial art! If any aikidoka does choose to fight (though self-defense is permissible) or to war then they revert to Aikido's martial progenitors and they are no longer practicing Aikido. Indeed, when the techniques of Aikido are practiced with a martial emphasis, and when this is the sole manner of practice, then this kind of practice is antithetical to that body of technique and philosophy that Morihei Ueshiba intended as the discipline and art of Aikido -- it would not be true aikido. Conversely, when Aikido is practiced with a concern-for-life emphasis, but not divorced from the real need for personal self-defense, then this kind of practice is clearly recognized to be Aikido.

"The first character for martial art, bu, means 'to stop weapons of destruction'. If its true meaning is understood by people all over the world, nothing would make me happier."

> **Morihei Ueshiba** -- Aikikai Founder
> *The Spirit of Aikido*
> p. 120

Considering further this line of thought, some masters of other martial arts speak similarly. For example, Shi Ming, a Chinese Tai Chi master, informs us in his book entitled **Mind Over Matter: Higher Martial Arts** that *"True martial virtue is the highest morality; on reaching the highest level of virtue, furthermore, it is possible to eliminate this frightening word martial."*[11] Should not this be the case for Aikido, too?

Aikido is a clear and straight path of study toward realizing an ideal, ethically complete discipline that is organized to diminish the need to embrace the martial attitude as the aikidoka comes to understand the true meaning of Budo, i.e., the way of stopping the weapons of destruction.[12] It demands from all aikidoka a way of behavior that exhibits the ultimate ethic, one where the aikidoka is directed to behave in a manner that protects, sustains, and enhances life. Usually, an Aikido teacher (sensei) presents this code of behavior through the concept of *aiki,* meaning the *harmonizing of energy or spirit.* To protect life means to defend it against premature death and, therefore, an aikidoka must always be capable of functional (protective) self-defense action. To enhance life means to reject fighting and war and, instead, replace those behaviors with others that engender health and contentment as well as good relations with other people. Herein is found the best and truly inspiring quality of Aikido.

The *activation force* that gives rise to true Aikido is not resident in its body of physical techniques, but rather, one finds this in its philosophy and is dependent upon the practitioner's intent. In fact, it is not necessary for an aikidoka to disavow a study of functional self-defense ability in order to fulfill the tenets of Aikido's philosophy.

Aikido, a unique physio-spiritual discipline with functional elements of self-defense, aligned specifically with the precept of Ai Nuke No Kyoukun, gives any practitioner an opportunity to transcend the martial attitude so that they might evolve their consciousness to *protect, sustain, and enhance life* -- these latter being the *Three Precepts of the Zantoppa Kai* (three important tenets that help to guide an aikidoka upon a true aiki path). Any practitioner of Aikido can benefit from a mindset that embraces these so long as they maintain an objective, realistic attitude.

Having completely embraced and thoroughly internalized *Ai Nuke No Kyoukun,* the *Three Precepts,* and *functional aiki-based self-defense ability,* an aikidoka can truly be described as having evolved to a higher consciousness, for that which they practice is no longer associated with the martial attitude.

[1] Mortimer J. Adler defines *spirituality* as, "*What is spiritual is immaterial. God is spiritual, the angels are spirits, and the human intellect -- the intellect, not the soul -- is a spiritual power, which is to say it is immaterial.*" See, ***Adler's Philosophical Dictionary*** by Mortimer J. Adler; Touchstone Edition, paperback, 1996, pages 182 & 183.

[2] See the book entitled ***Mind over Matter: Higher Martial Arts*** by Shi Ming; Frog, Ltd., paperback, 1995, pages 3, 10, 16, 28.

[3] See, ***The Spirit of Aikido*** (Aikido no Kokoro) by Kisshomaru Ueshiba, translated by Taitetsu Unno; Kodansha International, Ltd., paperback edition, first printing, 1987, page 12.

[4] Ibid, page 25.

[5] The *first* kanji sinogram, bu, 武, is an onyomi reading that means {military}, {martial}, or {warlike}, and itself is a compound of two other parts, those being 止, meaning {halt} or {stop}, and 弋, meaning {shoot with bow}, {shoot}, or {to spear with halberd}. Here you have a choice of two meanings: either to *stop* (the aggression of) *the spear* (or *shooting*), or to *stop* (aggression with) *a spear* (or a halberd, bow & arrow, or gun); both of which contain a suggestion of defense or pacification rather than aggression. The *second* kanji, shi (士), is the ancient Chinese sinogram character for *educated gentleman*, and it should be noted that such a gentleman was expected to be fully educated in the arts of literature as well as in the arts of war. Its onyomi reading of *shi* can mean {scholar}, {gentleman}, or {soldier}. Interestingly, its single kunyomi reading is *samurai*. The *last* character of this word, do (道), is again a compound showing an eye, or fully, a head indicating intelligence, and the radical for *motion*. It can mean *street* or *way*, but is primarily a way living with continual intelligent observation or thought; or, perhaps, intuition. It is never static or totally defined. Bushido, then, might be defined as a thoughtful way of living, using both the literary and the martial arts in keeping the peace. For further information see William Scott Wilson's comments at Wikipedia under entry entitled ***Bushido***. http://en.wikipedia.org/wiki/Bushido; 2012.

[6] Some gang and cult behavior; and, a number of neo-feudal countries.

[7] *Artfully employed* means that there are a number of psychological methods used by people for various reasons to attain a certain goal otherwise unreachable by direct, i.e., overt means. For example, neurolinguistic pro-

gramming.

[8] See, **The Spirit of Aikido** by Kisshomaru Ueshiba, translated by Taitetsu Unno; Kodansha International, Ltd., paperback, first printing, 1987, page 121.

[9] Ibid, page 120.

[10] See, **The American Heritage Dictionary**; Dell Publishing Company, paperback, second printing, November, 1981. Or, see any other dictionary that has been competently compiled.

[11] See the book entitled **Mind over Matter: Higher Martial Arts** by Shi Ming; Frog, Ltd., paperback, 1995, page 99.

[12] Meaning, primarily, personal attitude not aligned with or inclined toward warfare.

Chapter II

Self-Defense: Sen, Maai, and Aiki

In the previous chapter the task of attempting to discern the difference between the martial attitude and the self-defense attitude began. Subsequently, a little discussion about the practical meaning of the term *self-defense* is helpful for a person who contemplates the study of Aikido or any other physio-spiritual, self-defense, or martial oriented discipline. The etiology of modern violence and a discussion of the specific methods (mock scenarios, strategies, tactics, and techniques) that could be useful in a self-defense situation is not the purpose of this chapter or the book; such has been already authored by many competent martial artists as well as military and police personnel. The discussion herein has been evolved from the normal concept of awareness and the technical concept of combat distance as derived from Aikido.

There is both *restive* and *active* self-defense behavior. Whether one or the other of these modes is initiated is governed by the circumstances of a person's environment as well as by the mental attitude necessarily held in consciousness as response to that environment. Both of these behaviors arise from one's conscious decision to awaken their senses as well as from considerable thought about how a person, a living being, should exist within their surrounding environment. Keep in mind that each state of the United States of America has a general body of legal rules that affect how a citizen, when living within a given state, must shape their personal attitude toward self-defense. Presently, *the two legal attitudes* that have emerged from the state government perspective for the reason of guiding a citizen's self-defense behavior are either *1)* you can *stand your ground*, or *2)*, you must *first make an attempt to retreat*. Refer to your state's code of laws to determine which applies to you. If you live in an area other than the U.S.A., refer to the laws of your country.

Restive self-defense is a mental state of calm awareness that provides a person with information concerning risk within their surroundings -- a condition of aware existence where certain protective behaviors are learned and become a set of useful specific nonconscious[1] responses toward daily life. This condition of being is not present in consciousness but emerges from a person's pre-conscious[1] mentality; it occasionally gives rise to both intuition[2] and sudden enlightenment (satori). This aspect of mentality causes no feeling of nervous apprehension or foreboding. A few simple examples of this kind of self-defense are

1) Walking on the sidewalk facing traffic;
2) Walking toward your car at night, you've already visually scanned the area around it, your key or remote keyless System (RKS) in your hand;
3) When driving your automobile, you maintain the proper following distance from the car in front of you; and,
4) While walking a forest path, you glance upward from time to time to see if there might be a detached tree branch hanging in the tree canopy that could possibly fall. This type of awareness can also be used when driving your automobile upon a road where there is a tree canopy overhanging the road.

After learned and mentally internalized, the above are not predominately active in conscious thought.

Active self-defense is a condition of awareness that exhibits a high alertness as one or more possible threatening events are imminent and you are preparing a response to defend yourself against possible injury. Examples of this are

1) Walking toward your car at night, as you're visually scanning the area around it, with key in hand, you notice one or more individuals suddenly appear from behind a van. They seem to be approaching you with ill intent. You retreat toward a gathering of people and consider whether or not it will be necessary to telephone the police (recommended);
2) You exit a restaurant and suddenly become aware of an automobile careening down the sidewalk, seconds from colliding with you, a pedestrian. You jump into a forward roll

in a direction of safety, narrowly averting injury or death;

3) While walking upon a sidewalk on a breezy day, a branch dangling from an overhanging tree, which you observed at perhaps 15 seconds distant, suddenly drops. As it speeds downward like a spear and strikes the sidewalk, you've a-voided it because you slightly redirected your travel;

4) You, a man, are at a gathering of family members or friends. Someone has consumed too much alcohol. He (or she) is obviously drunk, unruly, and unreasoning. He approaches you, you cannot avoid him, and a very short conversation between you and he occurs in a manner that quickly es-calates to a situation where he attacks you with a punch to your face. You parry lightly while stepping back at an angle to successfully avoid his punch. Again he attacks, swinging a haymaker punch at you. Then, as you merge your defensive movement with his attempted second punch, perhaps you feign a strike or actually hit in order to elicit a response from your attacker which you use to facilitate the neutralization of the attacker's intent; you secure momen-tarily his arm as you throw the attacker to an area of the room that is clear of dangerous obstacles (such as furniture that might impart unnecessary injury). Others who have attended the gathering come and grab the attacker, usher-ing him to an area where both you and he are no longer in the presence of each other. You decide if it is wise to re-main at the gathering (perhaps leave) and whether or not to make a report to the police (recommended). A similar sce-nario can occur to a woman; and,

5) The following situation is described in detail in order to clearly represent the scene; it is less likely to occur to the extent described for a woman. You, a man, are in a retail store. As you approach one of numerous purchase stations you notice that only two are attended by checkout cashiers. You decide upon one and as you approach closer you see that there is a cart full of items, unattended, perhaps aban-doned by a shopper, positioned in a manner that is not in the queue. There is one customer in front of you as you wait for your turn. The purchase in front of you is delayed and a full five minutes passes; you look to the right at the other open purchase station and notice that it would likely

take as long in that queue, so you remain where you are. *Of importance is your attitude regarding that which you perceive to constitute social manners and how you act when your personal set of values (ethics/mores) is disrespected by another person, for many conflicts between people emerge from this area of social interaction.* Just as the person in front of you completes their transaction and begins to depart the purchase station, you begin to move forward to begin yours, and suddenly you notice a man appear to your left to reassume control of 'his' shopping cart, which he had obviously left unattended for at least five minutes now. He looks at you and vocally insists that he was in the queue and that he now wants to get in front of you; but, in fact, he had temporarily abandoned his cart, placed it to the left out of the queue in order to go back into the store and continue shopping, then returned at a moment opportune for him to reassert his 'right' to his position in queue. You have a couple of items held in your hands. He has a cart full that will obviously take at least another five minutes of you waiting in line. The number of people in queue at the other purchase station has increased, and the several other purchase stations show no sign of being opened to attend to the increasing number of customers queuing up behind you and at the other open purchase station. At this point, several seconds have passed since the wayward customer has reasserted his claim to go next, in front of you. You have a decision to make. Will you let him go in front of you, or will you not? So, *your decision,* being made within a second or two, *emerges from your basic set of social manners.* You consider that the wayward shopper has no reasonable right to reassert his position in the queue. You speak, in a calm voice, "No sir, you may not go in front of me. Please consider going to the end of the line"; he is offended and immediately verbally counters you saying that he will resume his position in line; he begins to point his cart toward you. There is yet another delay in front of you -- the previous customer has forgot to obtain the receipt for their purchase and turns around just after having departed the purchase station. You wait, but also attend to the heightened discord between you and the wayward shopper; you ready your cellular phone to telephone 911 in the event that he attacks you, considering that if he does you'll be able to keep relatively calm and keep him away by quickly moving around the many obstacles present in the store. You continue to watch him; thirty seconds more have passed, his vocalizations are getting louder and he continues to exhibit the twitching around his eyes and mouth. Is it anger or fear that you see in his reponse? Soon you'll have to take your position at the sales counter, you consider quickly that if you do not let him go first that the wayward and now irate shopper, who is showing signs of unreasonable behavior, will be at your back while you are attempting to make your purchase. Instantly you consider that this is not a wise idea, and you take action to deescalate this problematic situation. Now that you have made your point about what you consider to be the social manner that dictates how a shopper should behave when they leave their cart behind (rightly or wrongly) you decide quickly to treat the situation differently, you *retreat*, by moving over to another purchase station. Just as you begin to do this, several other cashiers arrive at the other purchase stations, and those people in queue at the two previously open purchase stations move over to the other stations. This, fortuitously, provides you that opening to shift to another line. You take that opportunity, keeping attentive to your observation of the wayward shopper who is not further than six feet distant. Unperceived by you, and yet to be discovered, is another shopper in one of the other queues who has belatedly come upon the scene and begun to become generally aware of a situation between you and the wayward shopper (you'll discover the portent of that shortly). You are now being assisted by the cashier at another purchase station, the wayward shopper is glaring at you; you are relatively calm and remain aware, but attentive to your purchase. You purposefully lengthen your interaction with the clerk so as to cause the wayward customer to finish his transaction first, who has inserted himself in the queue in front of the shopper who was previously behind you, hoping not that he'll depart the retail store before you. The cashier attending you asks you what the problem has been, as most have noticed the conflict; you relate concisely yet quickly the situation that has transpired between you and the wayward shopper to the cashier, as this affords you a little more time to delay your transaction. She says she'll call the manager of the store, but you suggest that such would only serve to heighten the conflict; besides, you sense that the wayward customer will only continue to grumble and very soon depart. Then, within seconds of this thought that is exactly what occurs, the wayward customer leaves the store; but now the thought comes to you that there is the possibility that he'll be waiting for you in the parking lot. You finish your purchase and thank the cashier and walk toward the wide hallway that proceeds to the automatic sliding door exit. You pause, waiting on one side, looking out at the parking lot to assess whether or not the wayward one lies in wait for you. As you do this, another customer who has just finished his purchase, with his woman, walks past you and purposefully turns his head to give you an unfriendly and intimidating look that indicates his displeasure. He begins to pause, as you, calmly, look at him. Instantly, you know what is up; this fellow has likely come in late on the scene, observing only the latter part of your discord with the wayward shopper. This newcomer to the disorder likely thinks, from one ill reasoning thought-strand or another, that you are the culprit, the instigator, and he is considering, probably, just how he might go about kicking your butt and teaching you a lesson. Ah, but you are an aikidoka, right? You did not consider that such a later developing event might occur -- that a third party might consider you as the culprit. The unreasonable newcomer, a second wayward one, is quickly ushered through the door as his woman knows what is going on too and wishes to avert a physical encounter. Wow, what a world, yes? So, now you wait for this third party to enter his automobile, while yet ascertaining if the first wayward shopper has driven away. Fifteen minutes has passed since the beginning of your discord. Finally, you determine that the first wayward shopper has departed the parking lot. You walk outside and begin walking to your automobile, but are keeping your eye to the right as the second wayward fellow and his woman have entered their pickup truck. You decide to wait on the sidewalk close to the retail store. The second wayward one drives right past in front of you slowly eyeing you with that meant-to-intimidate look. Carefully observing him, you are now attentive to what this fellow might do, he slows a little, you wonder if he'll attempt a drive-by-shooting, then he speeds up and departs. You, relieved, walk to your car and depart, considering well all that has occurred. Of course, you could have let the first wayward shopper take his 'rightful' position in the queue, saying nothing more than, "Go right ahead." From this kind of situational discord, a person can understand much about their mental constitution and preparedness to navigate life's difficult trials. Does the strategy of the first wayward shopper, which was comprised of leaving a cart full of merchandise and then later returning to assert preeminence, constitute *the might that makes right*? Would have a different approach -- like conversation with the wayward shopper or perhaps having permitted him to move ahead of you -- produced a different outcome? If you had engaged in conversation, would the wayward shopper have understood you? Of course, all this latter is speculation. Perhaps you, yourself, could be considered as the "wayward shopper."

Consider well what may arise as an outcome of your decisions and actions. In each society there is a general cultural attitude. However, there are also subcultures and all these have codes of behavior with their many inevitable variations; any individual thereof has their own perception of what they might adhere to as that which comprises their own set of values, and these latter may change upon any whimsical thought or threatening event to suit an individual's desire or need. Many people shift erratically or conveniently their mentality around the fringes of that which constitutes a moral, ethical, or manners code, i.e., a set of personally held values.

Whether it be for the reason of safely moving about in the usual day-to-day arena of life or for the sudden arrival of a situation of person-to-person self-defense, either verbal or physical, an understanding of the meaning of *taking the initiative, or when and how to time your action to achieve the best possible result*, is of great importance toward this end. In the Japanese martial and self-defense realms the term *Sen* (先, meaning {before}, {lead}, {ahead}, {preceding}, {previous}, {future}) describes initiative and timing. Sen is derived from the word *sente* (先手, meaning {beforehand}).

In the midst of a situation of self-defense where you have momentarily been caught off guard, *Ato-no-sen* (後の先, where 後 has the meaning of {late}, {behind}, {delayed}) means to retake the initiative just after the opponent's attack. If you've not already been defeated, sometimes it is possible to act with this kind of initiative to regain control and accomplish a successful defense.

Go-no-sen (禦の先), of which the far left kanji sinogram is sometimes confusingly represented by 後 (meaning of {late}, {behind}, {delayed}; with a kunyomi[3] reading of *ato*), is better described with 禦, *gyo* or *go* (onyomi reading[3]), meaning to {ward off}, {defend}, or {resist}, which through an analysis of all the parts that comprise it (often referred to as *bushu*) implies the implementation of *ai*, 合, linguistic root *au*, {fit}, {merge}, {come together}, or {unite} in order to accomplish a successful defense. (See Chapter XI for more information.) In understanding that hand-to-hand fighting is a situation where the opponent is attempting their own offensive, this type of Sen is a dynamic responsive initiative where the defender's action rebounds off of, merges with, or redirects the energy of the opponent's attack in order to thereby initiate a superior offensive toward suppressing any further attack, often utilizing the opponent's mental and or physical off-balance; examples from Aikido include any of its pertinent immobilization or projection techniques. The implementation of this kind of Sen points to skill in perception, timing, counterattack, and suppression or neutralization. The ki (energy/spirit) of aiki (harmonized energy/spirit) is primarily Go-no-sen in character because, in the majority of circumstances where one is pitted against a competent opponent who is equally capable (both equally unarmed or armed with the same weapon), the usual outcome for the person who makes the first move, i.e., the first strike, is defeat.

Sen-no-sen (先の先) means to make your defensive action at the very instant that the opponent begins his movement of attack -- strike as the opponent mentally commits to an attack but before he moves -- in other words, the defender attacks between the opponent's decision to attack and his actual movement to attack.

Clearly then, Sen-no-sen means to take the initiative with a preemptive action, and under certain limited circumstances such a way of acting can be successful; it is during this brief moment that the defender may make an action to elicit a counteraction from the opponent that may in turn be utilized by the defender and taken to a successful self-defense conclusion.

Through astute perception, intuition, speech, or perceived body language one may be able to achieve *Sen-sen-no-sen* (先々の先) -- anticipate the attack. When the aforementioned tree branch falls, you've avoided it because you previously discerned that it could fall at any moment and have taken appropriate evasive action. You've deescalated an argument with another person because you managed to sincerely present an equitable proposition; this assumes there exists flexible reasoning ability from the behavior of the other person, or that you have somehow been able to connect to some part of the other's mentality that itself finds agreement or kinship with your proposition. Deescalation results when there is a functional combination of

1) The perceived removal an injustice or threat; and,
2) The establishment of an interpersonal position or relationship of sameness or fellowship.

The study of how the distance between you and an opponent or you and an inanimate threat affects the outcome of a threatening event is an essential positional element in achieving reproducible, successful self-defense outcomes. Ma-ai (間合い; 間, ma {interval} {space}; 合, ai {fit} {merge} {unite}), with a meaning of {fitting into the interval}, {space-fit}, {space-harmony}, {space-condition}, or {combative distance}; hence, a fitting in or harmony is established by the observance of a distance or interval, is an essential tactic for maintaining the space that will make possible a better assessment of how to respond to a possible threat before it actually becomes threatening. Ma-ai refers to the space between two opponents in combat; i.e., the engagement distance, incorporating both the distance between opponents and the time it will take to cross the distance as well as the angle and rhythm of interaction. Typically, the three conditions of ma-ai are

1) *To-ma* (long interval);
2) *Itto-ma* (middle interval); and,
3) *Chika-ma* (short interval).

Itto-ma is the distance where either person may step forward one step and deliver a strike; this varies somewhat depending on the size of each person and whether or not one person other the other is armed with any weapon other than a ballistic one (e.g., a rock, a throwing star, a bow with arrow, a javelin, a pistol, or any other implement that can be launched to deliver an effective blow upon the adversary). *In order for Aikido to work effectively as a body of self-defense technique while also manifesting classical, idealized curvilinear aikido during defense against an aggressor, careful attention must be given to the function of both maai and kuzushi.* When itto-ma is breeched, it is necessary to employ close-quarters grappling theory and techniques such as those available from Judo or Jujitsu (see Chapter XI for further information about ma-ai). Kisshomaru Ueshiba, the son of Aikido's founder, relates to us that "*Unlike Judo, where you grapple with your opponent, in Aikido you almost always maintain some distance.*"[4] A system of self-defense, a martial art, or an art that could be categorized as a Budo is deficient as a means of self-defense if its technical philosophy does not include preparation for close-quarters grappling; Shōdōkan style Aikido and most of the Shodokan derived sub-styles (e.g., the Fugakukai, Jiyushinkai, Kaze Uta Budokai, and Zantoppa-kai sub-styles in the U.S.A) are competent in offering complete self-defense training that address all the conditions of ma-ai.

How to make maximum use of or take advantage of an aggressor's dynamic actions (e.g., their direction of movement, condition of balance, speed, strength, unpredictability) is an important aspect of the study of *aiki*, i.e., harmonized energy and spirit (see Chapter XI for further information about aiki).

Lastly, a study of both tactics and strategy are important elements of mature self-defense ability. Tactics, that is, specific and useful plans of how to act, are necessary to minimize disorder, violence, and injury when engaged in a self-defense situation. A study of Aikido with a self-defense emphasis will typically include practice in tactics. A general strategy in life is that of preparing one-self for all which may come to pass, including hand-to-hand combat; however, it is wise behavior to move cautiously away from danger that does not require immediate attention toward mounting a defense. Pertinent to the aforementioned, Morhei Ueshiba clearly reminds us that *"True Budo means to win over yourself and eliminate the fighting heart of the enemy."*[5] The type and quality of ethics, mores, values, and or virtues that a society has instilled in its people determines whether or not such an idea could gain preeminence and thereby establish different behavior that diminishes rude mannerisms, manipulative and abusive behaviors, intransigent attitudes, and violence; if these are of the type and quality that inclucates such, then they can act as strong social deterent, i.e., as a citizen's best, inherent, first line of defense. This is an important idea to understand.

[1] *Non-conscious* refers to the general processes that are not mediated by conscious awareness but are not a function of nor reside in a person's unconscious. *Preconscious* is considered to be an occurrence of something, a thought-bit, that may manifest itself in consciousness, having emerged from a person's unconscious or non-conscious, perhaps consciously triggered by the momentary circumstance of their environment which their senses have perceived. In this area of cognitive function where nonconscious mental activity occurs, there arises an interaction of conscious thought with the preconscious function of the unconscious that seemingly generates, perhaps through a reflexive process, the human phenomenon of intuition. Satori, a moment of enlightenment, may occasionally be generated from this interaction.

[2] *Intuition* refers to a perceiving or knowing that arrives into consciousness without active sensing or thinking. Some people consider intuition to be a mystical phenomenon; however, a majority understand it as an unconscious mental (cognitive) processing of unconsciously operating cues, which latter are unconsciously fabricated from the influence of previous experiences or learning, in order to provide a possible solution to or useful assessment of an in-the-present situation or circumstance. According to C. G. Jung, a pioneering psychologist, "Intuition [is] perception via the unconscious."

[3] Onyomi refers to ancient Chinese derivation yet used in modern Japanese language, this showing the influence of the Chinese language upon Japan. Kunyomi refers to Japanese indigenous derivations either uniquely created or uniquely employed; this being a situation of the older Chinese kanji with their traditional meaning being commonly used with that meaning by the Japanese people but with a different vocalization sound. See Section VII for more information.

[4,5] See, Japanese text version of the book 合気道 (Aikido) by Kisshomaru Ueshiba; Kowado, Tōkyō, 1957. This particular statement, and others, were part of a newpaper's interview of both Morihei and Kisshomaru Ueshiba. That interview was included in the aforementioned book, pages 198-219; Stanley Pranin and Katsuaki Terasawa translated this portion of the book, and later it was made available to the public by Mr. Pranin.

Chapter III

Spirituality in Aikidō: Ai, Ki, and Aiki

Apparently, many practitioners of the different styles of Aikido are inclined to imbue its practice with a mysterious spirituality that is usually derived from a personal attitudinal inclination, which itself is usually influenced from a subjective interpretation (an inherent interpretive desire or need) of the numerous and often mythically based aspects of the spiritual traditions of Shinto. For example, Omoto-kyo (an eclectic Japanese new religion that is influenced by Shinto and other spiritual traditions) or esoteric Buddhism, such as Shingon (a Japanese form of Buddhism that emphasizes esoteric experiences, though this does not mean that it is entirely devoid of exoteric teachings), often serve this purpose. At the root of this tricky and sometimes detrimental characteristic -- subjective spirituality that can weaken an Aikido's practitioner's *aiki-based* technical self-defense ability -- are several of its philosophical teachings as well as at least one aspect of its practice methodology. These are, respectively, *1)* the metaphysical part of the concept of *ki* coupled to the *idea of noncontention* and *2)* the favoring of the relatively soft or unchallenging *ki-no-nagare* (ki, the flow of) practice method.[1] The term ki refers to either a real or hypothetical energy or flow of energy. Metaphysical (hypothetical) *ki*, which is, by the nature of its vagueness, possessed by ambiguous and amorphous characteristics, lends itself toward the rise of *magico-religiosity* when certain practitioners, teachers, and students alike, who have a psychological predisposition or desire for a certain kind of spiritual experience, act to imbue their Aikido experience with an aire of mystery in order to either avoid certain aspects of Reality (e.g., the harsh aspects of self-defense) or to create for their leader a special condition of psycho-spiritual control over the others in their group (a school, seminar, meeting, etc.); the latter being a condition that is often associated with cultism.[2] In the book entitled **Mind Over Matter: Higher**

Martial Arts, Tai Chi master Shi Ming poignantly reminds us that *"The philosophical foundation of the essence of the martial arts, including refinement of consciousness, does not belong to religious superstitions like those recognized by so many modern philosophers, which are anesthetics to enable people to passively avoid the world."*[3] Shi Ming's insight is important for the practitioner of Aikido (or for those of any martial art) because "religious superstitions" typically interfere with the development of practical (functional) self-defense ability. Therefore, in an effort to reestablish sensible thought concerning the supposed metaphysical aspects of Aikido, which will be helpful in sorting out Aikido's characteristics and revealing its actual physio-spiritual basis, a good understanding of *ki* is helpful.

There are two important forms of ki. *First* to consider is that of an individual being's life force. Each person seems to possess an immaterial force that animates their being in life. Their personal life force manifests as their attitude toward and behavior in life. This is *personal ki.* Judaism and other Hebrew derived theological traditions, such as Christianity and Islam, may refer to personal ki as a person's soul, but soul here includes the additional aspect of that personal life force being specially overseen by a supernatural entity. One's personal ki interacts with that of other people as well as with other energetic aspects of a person's earthly environment, including those extra-earthly cosmic energies and potentialities impinging upon earth. Personal ki, or soul, may have the powers of intellect, regeneration, and transference.[4] The *second* type of ki is that of the energies of physics, known and unknown, quantifiable or intuited; these kinds of forces or energies -- which are typcially aethereal in their characteristics, mystical in their origin, and infrequently perceived by one's senses -- comprise *external ki.* The not-yet-quantified or intuited ki is the part of external ki that is often *superstitionized*, and this, through purposeful artifice, misunderstanding, or personal need is that which may impart an aire of magico-religiosity to Aikido. No matter if you're a beginning student, learned practitioner, or teacher of Aikido, one must take care not to let this kind of misunderstanding degrade training, i.e., to disregard a based-in-reality understanding of the need for and usefulness of self-defense skill. Understand this: your spiritual quest in life is at an end if you're not alive.

Considering personal ki and that which is necessary to create productive personal ki, the two conditions that must exist are

1) Conscious intention that embraces harmonious interaction with other people; and,
2) All personal action -- thought, speech, body movement, breath -- all aspects of personal ki, must be coordinated with the movements of the immutable, natural (not human contrived) forces of the universe (external ki).

Morihei Ueshiba stated that a person's well being is best realized when one acts to "*harmonize the ki of the universe and the ki of the individual, responding to all things from ki, and becoming one with it.*"[4] His statement strongly posits that *the act of aligning with the forces or energies which comprise ki* is that which comprises *aiki,* and that ki itself is one force or another (immutable law), evident or obscure, but that it *is not,* as his son Kisshomaru Ueshiba correctly explained, a superstitious phenomenon. For Kisshomaru Ueshiba, ki seemed to be the result of a dynamic combining of a person's psycho-spiritual expression of *pure-self* and behavioral vitality with the other naturally occurring external forces (e.g., the movement of another person) of life, and it arises from or within a person when they practice Aikido and therefore does not need to be especially cultivated.

To understand better how the practice of Aikido could lead a practitioner towards a path of spirituality, some initial discussion concerning the Japanese people's native religion of Shinto, Morihei Ueshiba's connection to it through Omoto-kyo, and how his practice of these influenced the philosophic underpinnings of Aikido, is essential. (Further discussion of Omoto-kyo religion is provided in Chapter IV). A good source of information that provides a beginning point for such discussion is Kisshomaru Ueshiba's book, ***The Spirit of Aikido*** (*Aikido No Kokoro*). Consider the following excerpts.

"*Ultimately, Master Ueshiba concluded that the true spirit of Budo is not to be found in a competitive atmosphere where brute strength dominates and victory at any cost is the paramount objective. He concluded that it is to be realized in the quest for perfection as a human being, both in mind and body, through cumulative training and practice with kindred spirits in the martial arts.*"[5];
"*His goal, deeply religious in nature, is summarized in a single*

statement: *'the unification of the fundamental creative principle, ki, inseparable from breath-power, of each person.' Through constant training of mind and body, the individual ki harmonizes with the universal ki, and this unity appears in the dynamic, flowing movement of ki-power which is free and fluid, indestructible and invincible. This is the essence of Japanese martial arts as embodied in Aikido.";[5] and*

"Through the genius of Master Ueshiba the first principle of Budo, as formulated by him -- 'the constant training of mind and body as a basic discipline for human beings walking the spiritual path' -- was transformed into a contemporary martial art."[5]

Furthermore, contemplation of Kisshomaru's understanding of his father's statement, *"the constant training of mind and body as a basic discipline for human beings walking the spiritual path,"* provides some useful information, too. It expresses that a person interested in pursuing a spiritual path must constantly train the mind and body. However, it doesn't state that a practitioner may walk a spiritual path by constantly training mind and body. Toward what goal must one direct the training of their mind and body? As indicated above, Morihei's goal is the unification of individual (personal) ki with universal ki, but just prior to that statement is Kisshomaru's general understanding of his father's goal, *"the quest for perfection as a human being"*; this latter can be construed as Kisshomaru's notion of that which comprises a spiritual path for an aikidoka.

Kisshomaru Ueshiba further clarifies his understanding of the principles of Budo by stating his two main points which concern Aikido's foundational hallmarks, which are

1) *"...the essence of Aikido is the unique Japanese philosophy which affirms the spiritual quest as the first principle of Budo and the tradition founded by Master Ueshiba."*; and,
2) *"And as long as we preserve Aikido's rejection of competitive tournaments, we will not lose the integrity of true Budo."[6]*

In the Aikido sense, then, according to Kisshomaru Ueshiba, true budo is comprised of the previously outlined precepts of *1)*, the pursuit of a spiritual quest, and *2)*, the rejection of competition as a means of elucidating that spiritual path. True budo, according to

Kisshomaru, is only such when it meets these two criteria. Therefore, Kisshomaru Ueshiba's formulation of his father's first principle of Budo has, in effect, completely made the definitive statement that true budo must adhere to these two points and that Aikido, as a budo, is primarily a spiritual quest. Such a statement, as can be expected, has given rise to contention not only among aikidoka but also amongst the practitioners of other martial disciplines. Is any Japanese martial art, such as Jujutsu, Karatedo, or Kenjutsu considered "true Budo" only if its participants align their behavior with Kisshomaru Ueshiba's definition of the first principle of Budo ("...*the essence of Aikido is the unique Japanese philosophy which affirms the spiritual quest as the first principle of Budo and the tradition founded by Master Ueshiba.*")?[7] Is such a statement an attempt to inform the participants of other Japanese martial arts about that which should comprise for those arts the philosophical foundation of Budo?[8] Yes. Is the act of stating such somewhat presumptuous? Probably.

Considering further Kisshomaru's formulation of the principles of Budo, when a practitioner finds these values acceptable, it can sometimes follow (typically in styles that emphasize spiritual development) that any serious thought of technique being useful for self-defense is conveniently put aside in order to avoid any dislike that they may have for addressing the reality of personal combat, ostensibly to pursue spiritual development.

Is the study of Aikido a proxy study of Shinto, the ancient Japanese naturism religion? Perhaps; it depends upon the attitude of the practitioner and upon the school or style of Aikido that they attend.

Stanley Pranin observes in his essay entitled **Morihei Ueshiba and the Ōmoto Religion** that: "*Although he* [Morihei Ueshiba] *and Onisaburo* [Deguchi of the Omoto-kyo] *shared a similar spiritual and moral vision, Morihei's implementation of these ideas through aikido have posed no threat to the power structures of the societies in which the art has been introduced.*"[9] In this quote, note "...*implementation of these ideas through aikido...*," for this is a reference to Aikido's metaphysical underpinnings having been partially developed from certain Omoto teachings. Certainly Morihei's objective, after his relationship with Onisaburo had matured, had been to bring into physical manifestation certain aspects of these teachings by implementing them in the physical realm through his Aiki-budo (later known as Aikido). Therefore, it is important to understand fully that certain aspects of both Shinto and Omoto-kyo are present to a lesser or greater degree in most styles of Aikido. Additionally, it is important to know that there are several Shinto sects, as well as several Shinshukyō (new religion doctrine, or new religion sects) descended from Omoto-kyo, which employ Aikido as a method to disseminate their teachings; a somewhat recent and prominent example of this type of association is that of Kannagara Aikido with the Tsubaki Ō Kami Yashiro (Tsubaki Grand Kami Shrine) Shinto sect. Such purposeful connection -- i.e., where religious, religious-like, and or metaphysically oriented activities are closely intermingled with or woven into Aikido -- is likely to shape the perception of what any particular school of Aikido considers to be that which represents the physical practice that might be termed as Aikido, or, more importantly, that which may or may not exist as its purported self-defense techniques. Kisshomaru Ueshiba and the controversial Kenji Tomiki (the founder of Shōdōkan Aikido), as well as other Aikido teachers of Japanese ethnicity, have voiced their disapproval of this type of intermingling. For example, Gaku Homma, kancho (head teacher) of the U.S.A. based Aikido Nippon Kan Association, himself an uchi deshi student of Morihei Ueshiba, in his Internet article entitled ***The Founder Morihei Ueshiba, a God?: Reflections on the Anniversary of Japan's Surrender to the U.S. Coalition***, informs us that *"For those who believe that the Founder* [of Aikido] *is a god, this is inconsequential, since their beliefs are usually a hybrid mix of Buddhism and New Age fantasy. The Founder as a god is just another extension of their spiritual excursions, and also a marketable product."*[10] When "spiritual excursions" are motivated by fanciful or self-serving thoughts there can emerge misconceived or false mental constructs that result in incorrect, sometimes harmful, assumptions or beliefs. To what extent might *New Age* fantasy, magico-religiosity, and unverifiable metaphysical proposition be utilized by those who believe Moriehi Ueshiba is a god in order that they might transform Aikido into a 'Church of Aiki'?

Traditionally and usually, a non-Japanese is not permitted direct access to Shinto's, or for that matter, Omoto-kyo's core teachings, for in order to benefit from these, as their teachings propose, a person must be ethnically of Japanese descent; this is particularly so if the Shinto or Shinshukyo that a person desires to practice is aligned with Koshintō (the ancient type of Shinto) as outlined and revitalized by Atsutane Hirata (1776-1843 C.E.), who was a strong advocate for classical Japanese nativist/naturism learning. Hirata proposed that all Japanese were descended from Japan's indigenous *kami* (the gods or nature spirits in Shinto), and as such, only the Japanese people, in having this as their unique heritage, could benefit from their kami. Such a teaching has been and is today a significant source of Japanese ethnocentrism. This demonstrable requirement has seemingly emerged an inherent point of control point where any non-Japanese can only benefit from certain, though limited, teachings of Shinto or Omoto-kyo via the study of Aikido. Furthermore, there is evidence that a number of Aikido organizations, which are officially recognized by the Zaidan Hojin Aikikai (Aikikai Foundation) today, are expected to align with Japan's unofficial cultural ethos, an ethos indirectly fostered by the Japanese government and naturally, perhaps unavoidably, embraced by its people. At the time of this writing, of the twenty thousand or so Shinto priests worldwide, there are only seven non-Japanese who are ordained by one Shinto organization or another. Though these type of ordainments can suggest that a weakening of Hirata's ideas could be occurring within organizational Shintoism, such a minor shift is probably useful to it in one way or another and serves to increase its chance of survival as a religion in the larger world culture. With these types of ordainments, other non-Japanese may partake of some of the activities, teachings, and other benefits offered by Shinto; however, few people are likely to do so, as, for example, the most recent combined surveys from the United States, Canada, and Australia estimate the number of adherents at approximately four thousand people, and some of these have Japanese heritage. From the metaphysical as well as the cosmological viewpoint (as this is, in its own way, the *raison d'être* of its practice) there is reason to doubt when considering Shinto's central ethnocentric tenets that such involvement by a non-Japanese would result in an instance of intimate rapport with or guidance from a kami because their bloodline (genetic heritage) is not rooted in ancient Japan. There are five primary denominations of Shinto, with at least thirteen secondary sects, and perhaps one hundred tertiary Shinshukyo. Approximately ninety percent of Japan's population practices some aspect of Shinto. Today, a non-Japanese aikidoka would do well to keep this particular knowledge conscious when considering their position in Aikido's peopled hierarchical ethno-order. In support of this precautonary statement, I turn to various other present and past scholars for their perspectives. For example, Peter Goldsbury, a 6th Dan (degree) Aikikai aikidoka and a professor at Hiroshima University in Japan, in a portion of his web-blog writing entitled *Transmission, Inheritance & Emulation: The General Impact of the Pacific War on Aikido*, published online at aikiweb.com, relates to us that "*Since aikido was a Japanese martial art, there was an unspoken corollary that it was best taught by Japanese - and this has always been the case in Japan.*" Another example that is supportive of this assertion comes from the famous as well as controversial Japanese Nativist Studies scholar Atsutane Hirata (1776 C.E. to 1843 C.E.) who stated that "*We who have been brought into existence through the creative spirits of the sacred ancestral Kami are, each and every one, in spontaneous possession of the Way of the Gods. This means that we are equipped by Nature with the virtues of reverence for the Gods...*"[11]

What are the possible deleterious affects of an Aikido spiritual quest upon a practitioner, and, of what is the Aikido spiritual quest comprised? First, there is possibility for harm, mental as well as physical, to a practitioner of this discipline when a significant part of its foundational essence rests upon a concept that is difficult to quantify -- ki. Such a 'force,' i.e., ki, is easily and frequently imbued with an amorphous meaning that comes about by the interaction of the willing but sometimes differing mindsets of Aikido's practitioners. During contemplation, either in a group setting or as an individual, its possible characteristics or attributes and their attending functions, which have been proposed or 'revealed' after gathering together the metaphysical experiences, thoughts, and knowledge of the sympathetic participants, suggests to them ki's essential character and how it (ki) exerts its aetheric and sometimes ought-to-be quality toward conferring a generalized spiritual quality to Aikido. Also, let's not forget that each of these mindsets have been influenced by the dynamic cultural forces of their own society, thusly manifesting a personal bias that has emerged from a particular psychological inclination or perspective as affected therein; the inherent weaknesses in such a process are those of uncertainty and capriciousness. Complicating this psychosocial phenomenon, actual ki, especially during a self-defense situation, can be difficult to harness and direct toward a productive conclusion. Ki can be negative, i.e., giving rise to disorder and destruction. Ki is what it is -- a force of Nature; it can be demystified. *Second,* adding further to that which may cause this harm, which consists primarily of misunderstanding that could eventually lead to confusion, discontentment, possibly physical injury, or eventual disillusionment, is the very fact that Aikido's often sensed spiritual traits emerge from Shinto, Japan's indigenous racial faith. Expanding this statement a little in order to identify partially the type of discontentment or disillusionment that may occur, and leaving further research unto the reader's own later effort, it is sufficient to relate that Shinto, or any of the Shinshukyo (new religion doctrine or sect) that make use of Shinto's core tenets as their basis, is, for the most part, a *naturally closed* religion -- meaning that, a person who is not ethnic Japanese is not considered to be *naturally eligible* to receive the teachings of Shinto or of its branches or derivations (e.g., Omoto-kyo) unless such is done indirectly, such as through the study of an Aikido style. In support of this assertion, consider that Sokyo Ono, in his book entitled **Shinto: the Kami Way**, relates to us that "*..., while Shinto is a racial faith, it possesses a universality which enriches the lives of all people everywhere.*"[12] Contemplate the part "*while Shinto is a racial faith,*" then notice that the later part is used to soften the meaning of the former. Benign ethnocentrism is present in such a religion and is occasionally present in Aikido, too. However, it is important to remember that many present societies from various origins have ethnocentric peculiarities. Carl Jung, pioneering psychologist and author, notes that many different religious ideas have sprung up around the world as they have because of a response to the perceptions and developing needs of people living in differing geographic areas. Returning to the discussion concerning the possible harm that can result from an errant interpretation and implementation of the characteristics of ki, an example that might inadvertently lead to physical injury, *kotodama* {word-spirit}, which is the hypothesis that the vocalization of certain sounds or groupings of these sounds influences, enlivens, or initiates movement and or phenomenon, or, but often commensurately, the belief that ritual word usage has a magical affect upon the human being and its environment.[13] This metaphysical idea is a teaching of Shinto, several Japanese Buddhist sects, and the Shinto-derived Omoto-kyo sect, and it is sometimes taught in Aikido. A common example of this would be that of the use of *kiai*, 気合, an intentional and purposeful shout or other type of utterance created in accordance with certain kotodama teachings. However, when a person finds it necessary to defend against an attacker, they must not rely upon a structured utterance of any kind to secure their safety, for by itself, such an utterance rarely, if ever, secures one's safety. Interestingly, of the hundreds of Shinto kami, the forty-two that ostensibly protect life and manifest procreative power (according to Morihei Ueshiba), i.e., the *Aiki no Ō Kami* to which the Aiki Shrine in Iwama is dedicated, exhibit a striking resemblance in effect to ancient India's Vedic concept of Chaos being reduced to Harmony by the action of the unique *varna shabda* (letter or syllable speech sounds) that resulted in Nature's creation event -- specifically, the arrival of *All That Is*, perceivable or not. The *Varnas* are symbolically represented by the forty-nine Vedic maruts (gods) of the ancient Rigveda hymns, these latter being a representation of the Vedic metaphysical theory that through the proper use of Vedic Sanskrit's fundamental letters (each a sound when uttered) there arises the 'language,' or process, of Creation; and, that each varna exists with a specific potency, which can only be creatively active when several or many in combination are properly voiced or sung, e.g., as in the *Varnamala* (Garland of Letters).[14] In fact, the *Gojūon* linguistic grid of the Japanese language, which serves to organize its vowel and syllable phonology, is directly connected to the ancient Vedic theory of Creation via its arrangement as influenced by the Japanese acknowledgment that uttered sounds have, ostensibly, 'creative power.' The *First* and *Second* outlined above constitute the possible harm that could occur to a person.

Responding to the latter part of the aforementioned question, *"of what is the spiritual quest comprised?,"* and offering balance with a productive effect, the spiritual quest in Aikido consists of, ideally, the pursuit of an ever-increasing awareness of the workings of life, i.e., a higher consciousness about Nature, while consistently exhibiting compassion, equanimity, and honesty when protecting, sustaining, and enhancing life. Therefore, when studying Aikido, a practitioner's behavior must be such as to manifest in oneself some part of or all of these humane qualities. It is expected, when at the beginning of a new study, that there will be some lesser degree of understanding about the extent of one's development in this ethical arena as well as a limited awareness of the importance of the pursuit of such a meaningful philosophical endeavor. Ideally, the spiritual quest is fully realized when a practitioner, given the extent of their knowledge and skill, can always protect, sustain and enhance life through the benevolent use of *ki-to-ki* alignments; for example, by person-to-person or person-to-Nature acts aligned with the immutable laws of life and all that these manifest.

In itself, *Aikido is not a religion*, i.e., not in the sense of the typical characteristics that denote any particular peopled activity as religion. Somewhat opposing his father's insistence that "... aikido is a religion without being a religion," Kisshomaru Ueshiba made it abundantly clear that, though his father's style of Aikido (Aikikai) was greatly influenced by the teachings of Buddhism, Taoism, and Shintoism, its closest association to religion or being religion-like is found in its quest -- i.e., *"walking the spiritual path"* -- to understand the human condition and its relationship to the forces of Nature.[15] Kisshomaru Ueshiba went to great effort to unpack (explain) and make understandable and useable his father's ideas concerning the workings of Nature and their importance for Aikido. Notwithstanding, since Aikido has been evolved by a man who was nurtured by Japanese culture, any practitioner of Aikido, especially if they partake of Aikido's Shinto-derived rituals while embracing the idea of non-contention toward disavowing the competitive attitude,[16] is participating in some aspects of indigenous Japanese religion and should be aware of the fact that their discipline is 'watched over by' numerous Shinto kami. Evidencing this, Yukitaka Yamamoto, 96th High Priest of the Shinto Tsubaki Grand Shrine, informs us that *"Sarutahiko is the kami of bravery and therefore he acts as the guardian kami of the Japanese martial arts, particularly the form of self-defense known as Aikido."*[17] Now, having expressed this, is it not a good occurrence in the history of humankind that the man, Morihei Ueshiba, made possible a transition, i.e., a bridge, between Japan's indigenous racial faith and all the world's non-Japanese people, specifically, Aikido? Only if his act of doing so is continually shown (by the acts of its practitioners) to contribute toward the maintenance good relations (harmony, peace, etc.) amongst all people who are touched or influenced by Aikido. Does this bridging, which could also be viewed as a concession to the other peoples of the world, come from a place of concern for humanity's future? Probably; and this is evidenced by Kisshomaru Ueshiba's many writings that reflect both his as well as his father's concern about establishing a better and safer reality for all people. Nevertheless, our world is not without violence, and though the spiritual quest in Aikido is an important endeavor for an aikidoka, self-defense ability must not be ignored in favor of a desire to attain an idealized harmony or peace. This is the foremost practical reason that the Aikido master Kenji Tomiki introduced both *randori* practice (free practice; literally, *taming disorder*) and *shiai* (contest or match; literally, a *meeting to test*). Consider that if you cannot defend yourself against personal aggression it is quite possible that you'll not be around long enough to realize the spiritual development that could have been of benefit to humanity. The training in control and martial techniques for the police and military in today's Japan is largely either of Judo and or Aikido origin, and it is markedly rougher, tougher, and to-the-point than the general practice found in the typical Aikido dojo, and for good reasons.[18] Continuing a bit further with this train of thought, one would not be amiss in thinking that Morihei Ueshiba, founder of Aikido, knew well how to defend himself from physical attack, but he learned also how and when to injure, or not injure, any attacker. In fact, prior to World War II (W.W. II) much of his teaching was martially oriented for military purposes. However, during his quest for what he considered would be the ideal form of Budo, he progressed to a skill level that gave him the ability to minimize the amount of harm that he may have found necessary to defend himself in any real self-defense situation. Part of this progression in his ability occurred in a step-by-step process, evolving his thinking and actions toward only that which was necessary to protect him, with no action in excess, at any particular moment within a struggle. Similar to this action is a moving body of water flowing around and shaping itself to overcome any impediment -- *resistance is futile!* Gradually, with ability evolved from incessant training, he manifested a more benevolent attitude, but only from the place of knowing how to defend within the realm of what it meant to be a practitioner of Budo. His characteristic attitudes and behavior were a result of an ever-evolving understanding of and skill in Budo as shaped by the religious as well as the mundane experiences of his life, which interaction was informed and guided by his spirit, i.e., by the unique quality of his innate life force or soul. From this way of dynamic being, Morihei Ueshiba evolved a mental inclination that urged him toward the development of his Aiki-budo, then later, with the help of his son (Kisshomaru), modern day Aikikai Aikido. Morihei's conception of aiki as an *ethereal spiritual container* or a *supernatural etheric* is explained and outlined by the Shinto concept of *Musubi* -- i.e., the union of specific metaphysical forces for the purpose of creation; it was understood and presented to his students as the ultimate force that creates life, makes possible harmonious relationships for all beings, and provides for a certain and necessary balance amongst all things.[19] These forces he explained as being composed of *ki-musubi* (vital energy: a force predisposed to the formation of living things or animate beings), *iku-musubi* (creative e-nergy: an occurrence of a force that begins the process of manifesting a living thing or animate being), and *o-musubi* (connecting energy: an actual force manifested and evident but neither easily quantifiable nor made use of).

Yet, certainly, Morihei Ueshiba's religious temperament did not negate either his martial understanding or his self-defense skill; not, at least, until his very advanced years when his physical abilities were compromised and he began to contemplate even more intensely the role of spirituality in Aikido training. As a person ages and begins to experience various bodily ailments there can occur a decline of their brain's ability to reason nominally (see definition in the glossary). This latter difficulty can manifest one type of cognitive dysfunction or another that hinders balanced reasoning or expression of pure-self. In Ueshiba's book entitled **The Heart of Aikido: The Philosophy of Takemusu Aiki**, printed posthumously, he reminds us of the importance of maintaining the body's physical condition by relating that "*Your body is the temple of spirit, it is the medium in which your true nature is housed. Take good care of it.*"[20] Undoubtedly, Morihei Ueshiba realized that much of the disorder that can emerge from inequity and the oddities of personal character comes forth from the psycho-spiritually hindered, psychosocially underdeveloped, or otherwise socially harassed or misguided person, who, for whatever reason, or no reason at all, commits violence. He demonstrated his understanding of the need for real self-defense in a number of ways. This can be easily perceived in his *Reminders in Aikido Practice.*[21] These reminders are, in fact, a part of Aikido's philosophical ethos, and an aikidoka's embodiment of these is an important part of their spiritual quest.

For a practitioner of Aikido, it is important to comprehend that intention and action supportive of any particular goal is that which brings to life a certain ethos, a certain philosophy, or a certain condition of spirituality. Again, two conditions must exist to engender positive creative ki. *First*, conscious thought-intention embracing harmony. *Second*, all action (thought, implementation of thought through body movement -- speech, facial expressions, limbs, etc.)

and breath should be coordinated and unified with the inherent movement of life or with the forces of the Universe -- this being, in effect, true and complete aiki.

As mentioned earlier, Morihei Ueshiba's understanding of the kanji character 武, *martial bu*, though not unique to him, is "*to stop weapons of destruction.*"[22] This strongly suggests an emphasis on defense rather than on aggression.

A proposition can be made that outlines the Japanese cultural definition of Budo, where such has been a result of collective development, over time, by many Japanese budoka, (e.g., recently prominent: Jigoro Kano, Morihei and Kisshomaru Ueshiba, Kenji Tomiki, Gichin Funikoshi, and numerous others). That which can be said to be its ethos is the

1) Acceptance that *stopping the weapons of destruction* is the best collective meaning of *martial bu*; and that to manifest this in life one must show behavior thusly aligned; and,

2) Ceaseless training that, through whatever discipline, harmonizes the life force (internal ki) of the practitioner with the energies and immutable laws of the Universe (external ki) in a way that unequivocally, clearly, and truly supports *stopping the weapons of destruction.*

Furthermore, an analysis of the following two statements reveals a significant difference that can affect how an Aikido practitioner might study it. Contemplate

"... *the constant training of mind and body as a basic discipline for human beings walking the spiritual path.*"

> **Morihei Ueshiba** -- Aikikai Founder
> *The Spirit of Aikido*; page 15

as contrasted to

"... the essence of Aikido is the unique Japanese philosophy which affirms the spiritual quest as the first principle of Budo and the tradition founded by Master Ueshiba.

> **Kisshomaru Ueshiba** -- Second Aikikai Doshu
> *The Spirit of Aikido*; page 117

Morihei's statement indicates that any person who pursues a spiritual path *must constantly train.* In contrast, Kisshomaru's statement, in no uncertain terms, states that the first principle of budo is *the spiritual quest,* and that the foundations of Aikido rest upon unique aspects of traditional Japanese philosophy as outlined by his father, Morihei. Interestingly, Kisshomaru presents two different inferences, *the first* being that the essence and foundation of Aikido is the spiritual quest based upon certain unique Japanese philosophical constructs derived by his father from the religions of Shinto (e.g., reverence of kami), Omoto-kyo (e.g., kotodama effect theory), and Buddhism and Confucianism (e.g., moral teachings). *The second* being that Budo, from the perspective of its actual (absolute) meaning, is also based in such a spiritual quest.[23]

Is the pursuit of spirituality congruous with the martial attitude? To begin to answer, a clear understanding or definition of that which comprises the meaning of *spirituality* and *martial attitude* is essential.

When the meaning of the word *spirituality* is considered to be the state of *a subjective approach or inclination toward characterizing the phenomenal events of life that are processed by the mind as immaterial or ethereal in character, often commensurately assigned a religious-like or religious quality,*[24] and when *martial attitude* is considered to be that defined by the "*true meaning*" of Budo,[25] that is, "*to stop weapons of destruction,*" then a person who engages in the practice of a Japanese martial discipline while aligning thusly their attitude can be said to be spiritually inclined. Therefore, it could be said, that when these parameters are met, *spirituality* begins a correspondence with the *martial attitude* such that it (the martial attitude) may eventually be reshaped into a *non-martial attitude,* perhaps more humane, that *may* function properly for self-defense. However, the latter is only possible if the person has not favored spirituality over self-defense training.

Notwithstanding, among the many martial artists of the different martial disciplines, there are likely numerous opinions which comprise the body of attitude that forms the basis of what may be considered as *martial attitude;* this being a matter for discussion by those other adherents. From the viewpoint of an aikidoka, though, consideration must be given to that which has been promoted as the *ideal martial attitude* as informed by both the meaning of *Budo* and of *aiki.*

Discussed earlier, the highest meaning of the term *budo* is *to stop weapons of destruction*. Therefore, when a person purports to be concerned with the development of a certain personal spirituality while studying a martial art (but not Aikido), and who considers spirituality to be as delineated previously, and who aligns their attitude toward action that *stops weapons of destruction* (either physical or psychological), then this person's behavior manifests a simple condition of correspondence (a 'discussion' as it were) between spirituality and martial attitude (as they conceive these latter two to be). When a person is studying Aikido (as opposed to a martial oriented discipline), such correspondence may manifest a particularly important aspect of Budo, that of *aiki* -- the idea that harmony of energy, where such may be exemplified by either merging with an energy or through non-resistance (or non-contention), is an essential element *to stop weapons of destruction*.

Congruity between spirituality and the martial attitude occurs when these seemingly mutually exclusive concepts correspond or combine in a way which transcends the typical meaning of each to express Aikido's fullest philosophical intent as elucidated by the Three Precepts -- protect, sustain, and enhance life. The identification and acceptance of *the most valid meaning* of Budo, which process should include cognitive methods to stop the type of mindset that emerges an inclination or tendency to make unnecessary use of weapons of destruction, is the first step toward achieving this transcendence.[26]

[1] This *idea of non-contention* and its application to Aikido is discussed in Chapter IX, while the practice method of *ki-no-nogare* is discussed briefly in Chapter XI.

[2] See the latter part of Chapter IV for a discussion of *cultism.*

[3] See the book entitled **Mind over Matter: Higher Martial Arts** by Shi Ming; Frog, Ltd., paperback, 1995, page 30. The discussion in this book is excellent!

[4] Mortimer J. Adler suggests this. See entry under "Soul," **Adler's Philosophical Dictionary** by Mortimer J. Adler; Touchstone paperback edition, 1996.

[5] See the book **The Spirit of Aikido** by Kisshomaru Ueshiba. Translated by Taitetsu Unno; Kodansha International, Ltd., paperback edition, first printing, 1987, page 22 and 29.

[6] Ibid, page 14 and 15.

[7] See the book **The Spirit of Aikido** by Kisshomaru Ueshiba. Translated by Taitetsu Unno; Kodansha International, Ltd., paperback edition, first printing, 1987, page 117.

[8] For a quite different definition of *Budo* from present day *Bushido* grand-master Fumon Tanaka, see **Sword Techniques of Musashi and the Other Samurai Masters**; Kodansha, hardcover, English language edition, 2013, pages 108 and 109.

[9] See the article entitled **Morihei Ueshiba and the Ōmoto Religion** by Stanley Pranin; Aikido Journal Online, February, 2005.

[10] See the article entitled **The Founder Morihei Ueshiba, a God?: Reflections on the Anniversary of Japan's Surrender to the US Coalition** by Gyaku Homma; published online by the Aikido Nippon Kan, August 15, 2005.

[11] See the book entitled **Shinto: At the Fountainhead of Japan** by Jean Herbert; Allen & Unwin, hardcover, first edition, 1967, page 69.

[12] See the book entitled **Shinto, The Kami Way** by Sokyo Ono, in collaboration with William P. Woodard; Charles E. Tuttle Company, hard-

cover, first edition, 1962, thirteenth printing, page 112.

[13] See the article **Takemusu Aiki: Lectures of Morihei Ueshiba** by Morihei Ueshiba; published by the Aikido Journal Online, Article #118, 1999.

[14] See the book **Manifold Unity: The Ancient World's Perception of the Divine Pattern of Harmony and Compassion** by Vera Christina Chute Collum, Charles E. Tuttle Company, Inc.; hardback, 1992, pages 84 through 88.

[15] Regarding the assertion that "... aikido is a religion without being a religion," see **Takemusu Aiki: Lectures of Morihei Ueshiba, Founder of Aikido** by Morihei Ueshiba, edited by Stanley Pranin; Aikido Journal, article #116, 1999. Regarding "... walking a spiritual path," see **The Spirit of Aikido** (Aikido no Kokoro) by Kisshomaru Ueshiba, translated by Taitetsu Unno; Kodansha International, Ltd., paperback edition, first printing, 1987, pages 14, 15, 16.

[16] See the book **The Spirit of Aikido** by Kisshomaru Ueshiba. Translated by Taitetsu Unno; Kodansha International, Ltd., paperback edition, first printing, 1987 pages 12, 15, 102.

[17] See the book entitled **Kami no Michi** by Guji Yukitaka Yamamoto; Tsubaki America Publications, paperback, 1987, chapter 8.

[18] See **Transmission, Inheritance, Emulation**, section **II -- Budo and Bushido, Kami and Kokutai: Aikido, Religion, and Nationalism**, subsection entitled **The role of the military, considered as a distinct caste, in government and daily life**, an online weblog tome that is available at www.aikiweb.com by Peter Goldsbury, professor, Hiroshima University, Japan.

[19] The word *aiki* is a Japanese term that is not unique to Aikido. Morihei Ueshiba identifies with it by describing its definition or essence to be comprised of a unique set of esoteric physio-spiritual qualities, which he states are exactly those qualities residing in, according to Japanese mythology, the sword *Kusanagi-no-Tsurugi*, which was retrieved by the deity *Susanoo-no-Mikoto* from the tail of the dragon Yamata no Orochi after he slew it. To conceptualize such a hypothetical metaphysical idea or realm, mentally envision a two-edged slit in that which is presently described by modern science as the *space-time continuum*, this being similar in form to that of a double-edged sword blade (but double-pointed, too, with no handle). This

'sword' or 'two-edged slit' could be imagined in the form of a long, flat, and narrow ellipsoid which could be considered as a uniquely existing '*vibrating energy field area*' between Heaven (our Universe within which life as we know it exists) and another, different, here-to-for unpercieved reality (perhaps another dimension of our universe or another altogether different universe), i.e., a cosmic area where exotic subatomic particles interact with the known *four forces* of the Universe in a manner that could emanate (or wherein there could reside) the 'deity-created' forces of *Musubi*; and, in order to begin to bring the idea of harmony unto a person's consciousness, possibly even to bring unto Earth an 'idyllic harmony,' a study of Aikido can only achieve access to this force (Musubi) by engaging certain esoteric processes (like kotodama) by which one gains entrance into this ethereal realm, thus transcending the 'normal' state of mentality that is 'anchored in place' or 'held captive' by exoteric experience and knowledge -- in effect, a personal bridging or unification of Heaven and Earth (In Japanese mythology, the *Floating Bridge of Heaven*). Several pertinent thoughts here are: *1)* Nature causes (creates) a dismantling of both micro and macro portions of itself (which should only be considered as a temporary disharmony) through many of its indifferent events (acts) while or toward maintaining its overall balance, i.e., harmony; *2)* for concscious corporeal life, harmony is a relative condition, for that which is balance or harmony by the effect of Nature is not always considered by people to be harmony for people. Nature's processes occur according to Nature; when Its processes destroy or create, the concerns of people are irrelevant. Regarding Nature's processes, a person should accept that when It causes (creates) an event of unconstruction (i.e., a dismantling), It also sets up the circumstances for something new to come into existence. Idyllic harmony for people would be a condition of no discord of any type at any time; so, when considering the innate mental nature of the human being and how it is affected by Nature's processes, I think that such a condition is probably impossible to realize, perhaps even undesirable. Obviously, the aforementioned is an attempt to provide a different but science-like approach toward making sense of Morihei Ueshiba's *Takemusu Aiki* hypothesis. See, ***Takemusu Aiki - Lectures of Morihei Ueshiba, Founder of Aikido*** by Kisshomaru Ueshiba, translated by Sonoko Tanaka, edited by Stanley Pranin; Aikido Journal articles #116, #117, and #118, 1999. Also, for some quick background information about the Japanese mythical god Susanoo-no-Mikoto, see http://en.wikipedia.org/wiki/Susanoo-no-Mikoto; 2011.

[20] See, ***The Heart of Aikido: The Philosophy of Takemusu Aiki*** by Morihei Ueshiba, edited by Hideo Takehashi, compiled and translated by John Stevens; Kodansha International; hardcover, first edition, 2010, p. 91.

[21] See the book ***The Spirit of Aikido*** by Kisshomaru Ueshiba, translated

by Taitetsu Unno; Kodansha International, Ltd., paperback edition, first printing, 1987 page 85.

[22] Ibid, page 120.

[23] See the book *The Spirit of Aikido* by Kisshomaru Ueshiba, translated by Taitetsu Unno; Kodansha International, Ltd., paperback edition, first printing, 1987, pages 12, 15, 16, 17, and 117, 120.

[24] For another competent definition, see *Adler's Philosophical Dictionary* by Mortimer J. Adler; Touchstone paperback edition, 1996.

[25] See the book *The Spirit of Aikido* by Kisshomaru Ueshiba, translated by Taitetsu Unno; Kodansha International, Ltd., paperback edition, first printing, 1987, page 120.

[26] Here, "unnecessary use" means, generally, the type of action that is inappropriate for the given situation to which the 'weapons of destruction' are applied (this implies a mind-to-hand act), or a use of such to purposefully interfere with, in a foolish, selfish, impractical, malicious, senseless way, the course of life of another person, people, or society.

Chapter IV

Morihei Ueshiba: History, Piety, and the Ōmoto-kyō

Human societies have evolved from numerous peopled groups or clans that gathered naturally for the reasons of defense against threats to livelihood and life, food acquisition, procreation, and concern or fear about mortality. For all ancient human groups, these aspects induced the emergence of various methods or styles of shamanism or native spiritual beliefs; e.g., Tibetan shamanism, Siberian shamanism, Native American spirituality, Nordic Sami shamanism, Celtic polytheism, and the Italian Benandanti visionaries, which are usually characterized, past or present, by the activities of a shaman, medicine man, noaidi, druid, or abbess, respectively. With the passage of time, spiritual methods such as these provided certain social avenues toward the eventual establishment of many grander and intricately built organizational bodies, themselves comprised of myth and tales, perception of origin, contemplation of being and meaning of life, moral and ethical statements, belief and faith, energy ebb and flow, and gods or god which are today known and practiced as the world's many spiritual, healing, and knowledge traditions. In support of this assertion, the well-known historian Charles Page Smith told us in his booklet entitled **The Universal Curriculum** that "*I suspect it could be shown (and probably has been) that all systems of education from the tribe to far more complex civilizations have grown out of and rested upon the religious beliefs of the societies of which such systems or principles were a part.*"[1] Meaning, all human social realities have come into existence as an effort to surivive while discovering and validating those social and immutable truths that provided a sustaining functionality for any particular society.

The Japanese people are not different here, their own history and part of their unique national character having originated from ancient indigenous spiritual perceptions, cosmogonic constructions, myth, and other traditions which evolved a pantheistic view of life, *the way of the Kami,* i.e., *the religion of the Deities of Heaven and Earth.* Beginning around the time of the Meiji Restoration (1868-1912 C.E.) till present, initiated largely by the efforts of Norinaga Motoori (1730-1801 C.E.) and Atsutane Hirata (1776-1843 C.E.), it has since been refined and formalized as *Kannagara no Michi,* i.e., *the Way as was done in the age of the Gods.* Kannagara no Michi, also sometimes termed *Kami no Michi,* is the core of all Shinto; derivations thereof -- typically termed Shinshukyo (new religious doctrine or sect) -- have other characteristics that mark each as either slightly or significantly different and often incorporate aspects of Buddhism, Hinduism, and Christianity. Syncretism is a prominent aspect of Japanese society, which phenomenon is abundantly evidenced in the Japanese spiritual tradition of Shugendō.[2]

From as far back as historians can authenticate Japan's history, its people have expressed a unique attachment to and involvement with kami worship through the tradition of Shinto. The early developmental stage of Shinto was hindered by the introduction of Confucianism, this beginning soon after a Japanese envoy visited the Chinese Han court in 57 C.E. Further interference in Shinto's development occurred by the introduction of Buddhism around 552 C.E. The overall affect of Buddhism upon forming the Japanese culture was profound as it initiated a refining effect upon its early nobility and peasants alike, and a civilizing effect upon the rude and sometimes unnecessary violent behavior of Japan's early warriors; Shinto at that time lacked the philosophical development that was present in Buddhism. Today, the vast majority of Japanese people utilize both Shinto and Buddhism in a syncretistic manner when looking after their spiritual needs. For example, Shinto provides ceremonial ablution which is accomplished through ritual purification to rid oneself of that which might be considered a defilement or an evil while Buddhism offers an easing of earthly misery and ceremonial funeral rites. Confucianism traditionally, but Christianity more recently, offers moral teachings.

Morhei Ueshiba, having been born and nurtured in the Japanese culture of his time, and subject to its effects, was seeking as many a person has, to learn as well as define his purpose in life and thereby substantiate his unique being. For each person during any past or present age, the circumstances of existence within one's social and natural environment provides the stage upon which they must act. Little by little there occurs an awakening of conscious awareness that evolves an understanding of their innate inclinations or abilities as well as the constitution of their personality, and holding knowledge of such in their conscious thought they are provided the means by which they can act to change, to develop, to create, to achieve, often a reflexive response to the stimuli of their environment, thus defining, by their acts, a unique path in life. Morihei's livelihood options during his youth were shaped by the economically tough and dynamically turbulent social changes and events of Japanese life during the middle to late Meiji Period (1868-1912 C.E.), Taishō Period (1912-1926 C.E.), and Shōwa Period (1926-1989 C.E.). It is known that the human mentality exists both with strength and fragility -- the exact nature of its condition varying from person to person -- and that through purposeful action a person's weaknesses can be strengthened, or through deleterious acts or circumstances their strengths weakened. The ideal process of development or improvement consists of making use of one's known innate productive abilities to strengthen their weaknesses, thereby enhancing their powers. Depending upon the condition of a person's naturally given mental constitution and how it interacts with their surroundings, there may come to pass an occurrence of change that will be noted as a significant aspect in their personal development and history. This type of socio-environmental psychodynamic occurred, as one might expect, for Morihei Ueshiba. There were a number of significant events which shaped his personality and provided him with not only a succession of maturing experiences but with several important opportunities that resulted in his founding of Aikido. Most aspects and events of a person's life -- mental inclinations, decisions, acts, and external events occurring around the person -- affect moment after moment the nature (meaning) of their succeeding experiences in life. Some of these encroach upon a person with little or no solicitation, some suggest a possible direction toward which a person may apply their efforts, but, overall, most are a result of a person's initiatory, responsive, or reactionary acts. For Morihei, those of notable significance that are important for the purpose of outlining his relationship with piety (see the glossary for definitions) as well as his martial progression are given in the following list.

1) His early interest in and study of classical Asian literary writings and myths;

2) The attempted political coercion of his father by physical violence and its affect upon the shaping of his youthful development;

3) His early uncertainty about what to pursue as a livelihood and frequent trips to the forested mountains in order to find the solitude necessary to contemplate, train, and begin to determine toward what goals he would direct his efforts and commit his life;

4) His military experiences during the Russo-Japanese War;

5) His leadership of a large group of homesteading families into the frontier of the northern island of Hokkaido;

6) His complex relationship with Takeda sensei of Daito-ryu Jujutsu;

7) Upon his return to his hometown, Tanabe, to assist his seriously ill father, his angst-inspired meeting of Omoto-kyo (Omoto) founder Onisaburo Deguchi;

8) His attraction to and participation in the Omoto religion;

9) The First Omoto Suppression by the Japanese government;

10) The death of his first and second sons;

11) Omoto's Mongolian incident;

12) First Vision (1925);

13) His decision to teach Aiki-budo to Japanese military men at both his Kobukan dojo and various military institutions before and during W.W. II (Manchuria included), thereby supporting Japan's statist Emperor System and Kokutai policy (1931);

14) The Second Omoto Suppression (1935);

15) Second Vision and its affect (1940);

16) His retreat to Iwama during the middle of W.W. II (1942), his Third Vision (1942), and the beginning process of redefining his Aiki-budo under the categorical identifier *aikido*;

17) After WWII, his ever-developing esoteric spiritual pursuits until the time of his death (1942 until his death in 1969).

Importantly, two of the above outlined events, the meeting of the Daito-ryu Jujutsu master Sokaku Takeda and his angst-driven meeting of Onisaburo Deguchi (leader of the Omoto-kyo religion) were seminal, as these resulted in an exposure to a technically superior martial reality as well as to a vastly different psycho-spiritual realm, which in turn, led him to the necessary insight and martial skill that he eventually drew upon to develop the defining technical and philosophical foundation of Aikido. A solid review of all these events will be presented here because they are useful toward the development of a basic understanding of Morihei's depth of character and their formational affect upon his martial endeavor.

Youthful study of classical Asian literary works

Perhaps the earliest indication that the young Morihei Ueshiba would manifest his destiny in a somewhat pious manner, and that such a predisposition in combination with other events of his life would eventually lead toward his participation in Omoto-kyo, was evident, according to his sister Kiku[3], from his interest in and studies of various ancient Chinese and Japanese classical literary works, especially those of the Japanese monk Kūkai (known posthumously as Kōbō Daishi) who founded the Shingon (True/truth word) sect of Japanese Buddhism in the 9th century C.E. From his youthful study of Shingon Buddhism, it is probable that Ueshiba began to develop certain formative ideas during fanciful youthful thought or daydreams as to what behaviors and pursuits might be suitable for him as he advanced forward upon his journey in life. Certain aspects of Kukai's behavior Ueshiba might have considered to be useful for his own personality development; for example, Kukai is known to have sought isolation in the forests of Japan in order to contemplate and chant Buddhist mantras. Morihei Ueshiba, when in his late twenties, often went to the forest,[4] probably with a similar purpose, that of contemplation and or meditation. During one mountain sojourn, Kukai, as he was chanting, reportedly experienced a vision where the bodhisattva Ākāśagarbha appeared and directed him to travel to China in order to understand the teaching and meaning of the Mahavairocana Sutra.[5] Similarly, Ueshiba had experienced a number of visions throughout his life. Interestingly, and of significance in understanding Morihei's attraction toward the teachings of the Omoto-kyo, the Mahavairocana Sutra of Shingon Buddhism contains ritualistic instructions pertaining to the 'proper' use of the letters of the Sanskrit alphabet (preserved in the ancient Indic script called Siddham) so that a devotee may vocalize properly the necessary invocative sounds (as derived from the Rigveda) -- i.e., as it pertains to esoteric Buddhism's *vairocana* (illumination) -- in order to enter into a meditative state that is conducive toward achieving 'enlightenment.' Certainly, the maturing Morihei Ueshiba as well as Onisaburo Deguchi were each quite aware of this and other sutras; each likely attempted to make use of these in an effort to understand the more complex phenomenon of life. In Japan today, as it was during Morihei's time, several rituals performed in Shingon Buddhism invoke the two ancient Indian Vedic deities named Agni and Indra; these gods are the two most significant mythical beings presented in the Rigveda. When the possibility of involvement with the Omoto-kyo began to significantly occupy his thoughts, Shingon, native Shinto and its *Norito*,[6] and the *Man'yōshū*[7] (a set of ancient Japanese poems) provided him with an initial knowledge of kotodama (word-spirit) and its relationship to the Rigveda (the Varnas, i.e., Letters of Creation), all of which were useful during his subsequent interaction and friendship with Onisaburo Deguchi. Revealing a little of the seemingly innate inclination of many past and some present Japanese to associate certain magical (unsubstantiated) effects or outcomes with utterance (spoken or sung),[8] two somewhat flowery ancient classical phrases which were used to identify the Japanese archipelago are found in two poems (numbers 894 and 3254) of the Man'yoshu: *kotodama no sakiwau kuni*, i.e., a "land blessed by the spirit of the word," and *kotodama no tasukuru kunu*, i.e., a "land where word-spirit lends its aid."[9] Of further relevance, the kanji ideograms of the Japanese language are largely descended from the logographic Chinese characters know as hanzi, but another part of its written language is represented by *kana*,[10] which is descended through another path via the ancient Japanese writing script called the *man'yōgana*. Japanese kana script is connected with the archaic Sanskrit of the Hindu Rigveda through the *gojuon* linguistic grid that is used to organize its present day phonology, this grid having been borrowed from the Indic Siddham script, the latter, itself, a descendant of the ancient Brahmi script.[11] Hanzi characters of the Chinese language, though largely a uniquely evolved indigenous writing system, were somewhat influenced by the various ancient Indic scripts through the transmission of the Mahayana Buddhist mantras. Upon his return from China, Monk Kukai introduced the Siddham script to Japan in the year 806 C.E. because the Japanese logographic characters used for writing during this time (largely Chinese hanzi) were deficient in their capacity to properly represent the sounds of the Buddhist mantras (written in

Sanskrit). In Japan today, the esoteric Buddhist schools of Shingon and Tendai still use the Siddham script when their monks are writing and copying sutras. Morihei Ueshiba's study and practice of the esoteric aspects of Shingon Buddhism continued throughout his life.

Youthful development and early martial training

Early in his youth, around the age of twelve, Morihei Ueshiba was faced with contemplating the wrongdoings of people and the injustice of such acts. Concerning these types of unsettling events, the first that likely began to affect the formation of his thought occurred when his father Yoroku, a well-to-do agricultural farmer of the late Tokugawa Period's *shi-nou-kou-shou* or *mibunsei system*[12] as well as a councilman in the town of Tanabe, was accosted in his sleep by several thugs who had been hired by a rival political opponent. The ensuing action, which included fisticuffs, likely awakened within him concern for his own safety as well as that of his family's and established a real connection with the stories his father told of the exploits and physical encounters of his samurai great-grandfather, Kichiemon Ueshiba.

His first boyhood encounter with manly tussling likely occurred when his father, after the work activities of the day, would take him to the beach to participate in sumo wrestling with the children of other families. Also during this period, Morihei learned to use efficiently the hand-held harpoon and spent a fair number of his hours on the ocean fishing; some historians suggest that his later interest and skill in bayonet use was initially simulated by these activities. Not only was the young Morihei Ueshiba engaging his thought in the spiritual realm of Shingon Buddhism study, but also beginning to connect his unique being with a useful set of general mental and physical tools, i.e., understanding, perception, intuition; the development of agility, strength, and body maneuvering.

Though having a strong inclination toward mathematics but finding the curriculum in high school generally unsuitable, Ueshiba quit; however, he enrolled at the Yoshida Abacus Research Institute which was focused on mathematics and its application in business. He excelled in this school and after completion, at the age of eighteen (1901 C.E.), he traveled to Tokyo to work in a mercantile store. While working competently as well as diligently, he came to realize that his type of personality was best suited to *musha shugyō*, i.e., a pursuit of ascetic martial training with many teachers of differing disciplines in order to achieve the best possible martial skill. It was during this time in Tokyo that he first began his martial training. After completing his daily work obligation, he studied Tenjin Shin'yō-ryū Jujutsu. Unfortunately, after six months or so of training, he contracted the disease known as Beriberi (a vitamin B deficiency) and, in poor health, he returned to his family's residence in Tanabe after less that one year in Tokyo. This inclination toward musha shugyo was an indication that his attitude in life would be aligned with piety.

From late 1901 C.E. until his enlistment in the Japanese Army in 1903 C.E., Morihei Ueshiba spent his days assisting his family and community in the daily matters of life, courting the young woman who would become his wife, recovering from Beriberi, and attempting to further identify his path in life. Most male youth during the development of their personality and process of identifying where to direct their effort toward establishing a livelihood do not know how to go about doing so, this being a result of minimal self-awareness and a limited understanding of the reality of the environment within which they exist. Life happens around and to a person until they make purposeful and direct engagement with their environment, thereby gaining information that is useful in shaping the direction of their journey. At some point, often between thirteen and nineteen years of age, each person has some vague or sudden realization that they must find their own way in life. As this realization appears, most people begin to contemplate, willingly or not, what they must do. This can be a process of "try this and try that," and sometimes it is attended by travail or tribulation if the constitution of their innate personality does not fit well with the circumstances of their natural and social environment. How often has the reader seen a teen or older youth running on a beach or upon a hiking trail, running and running, perhaps training for a marathon, but certainly 'trying out' their body to understand its limits while probing also, whether they know it or not, their mental constitution? Morihei Ueshiba was no different here. Reportedly, beginning around the age of eighteen or so, he engaged in self-initiated physical and mental training in the mountains, similar to that of the stalwart *yamabushi*,[13] and as a result there developed a rumor that he was akin to tengu (a long-nosed goblin of Japanese mythology). Richard N. McKinnon relates to us in his book the **Selected Plays of Kyōgen** that for the Japanese, *"The image of the yamabushi was one of invincibility." "Some regarded him as a demigod, others, a demon incarnate."* It seems like Morihei Ueshiba was 'trying on for size' this Japanese archetype. Furthermore, Kanemoto Sunadomari, an Omoto-kyo devotee as well as Ueshiba's first biographer, relates to us that *"It was not surprising to think that he was a Tengu or an insane man."*[14] At twenty years of age Morihei Ueshiba intensified this type of training as he prepared to meet the Japanese Army's requirements for enlistment. Later, after completion of his tour of duty, he continued to evolve and apply this kind of ascetic practice toward the acquirement of esoteric knowledge as well as the further expression of his character and shaping of his personality.

Japanese Imperial Army service

As the struggle and ugliness of war will do, the Russo-Japanese War, February of 1904 C.E. through September of 1905 C.E., was another experience that shaped Morihei's personality. At the age of twenty-one, the year 1903 C.E., Morihei enlisted in the Japanese Army, contrary to his father's wishes. Morihei was an 'only' son, and later, upon suspecting his son could be sent into battle, his father wrote the commanding officer of Morihei's army unit requesting that his son not be sent into battle. The request was not granted. During his time of service, Morihei Ueshiba was promoted to sergeant in the field for his outstanding bravery while in combat and his dutiful, "can do" attitude. His demonstrated skill in bayonet use, likely a result of harpoon and early martial training, was noticed by his command and put to use in training other enlistees. During his enlistment, Ueshiba began study of Yagyu-ryu kenjutsu. In 1906 C.E., he was honorably discharged. It's informative to note that one of Morihei Ueshiba's primary biographers, Kanemoto Sunadomari, states that, regarding Ueshiba's actual combat tour of duty, *"Space limitations do not permit me to describe Morihei's life during the war..."*[15] Sunadomari's biography of Morihei Ueshiba was completed in the year 1969 -- the year of Morihei's death. Why would a biographer defer a discussion of Morihei's actual combat involvement? In pondering over possible answers for this question, it is useful to call attention to one effect of the after-math of the Second World War (The Pacific Arena of World War II, W.W. II) upon the collective social attitude of the Japanese people. Generally, the majority of Japanese people who survived W.W. II, remembering its awfulness, achieved a profound spiritual solace during the making of a new Japanese identity that aligned itself with harmony and peace.[16] It is likely that Morihei Ueshiba and his son, Kisshomaru Ueshiba (the third son of Morihei Ueshiba who took over his father's role as the leader of Aikikai Aikido in 1969), as well as Sunadomari considered that any discussion and publication of matters concerning Morihei's personal involvement with or sup-port of the ugly aspects of war, even twenty-four years after W.W. II, would only tend to slow or weaken both personal and group ef-fort toward shaping of Japan's new peaceful and productive social reality. Therefore, the telling of Morihei's military combat experi-ences during the Russo-Japanese War as well as his involvement in the training of members of the Japanese military before and during W.W. II was not useful toward achieving and ensuring this mean-ingful new reality. Kisshomaru Ueshiba's post W.W. II attitude a-bout Japan's national angst can be clearly discerned when one con-templates the following statement from his book entitled **Aikido Ichiro**: *"Look! There is something good here, even from Japan. It is a budo without fighting and with a positive philosophy towards the op-ponent." "Especially now, in the present circumstances, aikido has a role to play in Japan's reconstruction."*[17] At one point Kisshomaru Ueshiba even went so far as to state that his father had not been in-volved at anytime in any military combat; his reason for making such a statement can only have been to move the attention of the curious away from his father's military experiences in order to fo-cus on Aikido's post W.W. II development.[18] Notwithstanding this attempt at diversion, Kanemoto Sunadomari, Morihei Ueshiba's first biographer, tells us that Ueshiba had indeed experienced military engagements during the Russo-Japanese War. After the war, his disinterest in applying to the Toyama Military Academy in order to pursue a military career, which numerous officers of the Japanese Imperial Army had urged him to do, was more likely to have been a result of the sobering reality of combat brutality (a recognition of his own mortality and perhaps a beginning repugnance about kill-ing) rather than any other reason. Arising therefrom, any fanciful or unrealistic thoughts (i.e., the daydreams of his youth) that he may have earlier had about following in the footsteps of his great-grandfather Kichiemon Ueshiba, who had been a respected samurai, were likely somewhat modified.

Years afterward, when teaching, on an occasion where Ueshiba found it necessary to illustrate a technical principle or philosophical tenet of Aiki-budo or Aikido, he would draw out from his experiences in fighting a pertinent event or occurrence to clarify or substantiate that which he was attempting to express or teach; for example, "*I became able to see the enemy's bullets as they came flying in. So it was easy for me to escape them.*" Also, in a later combat episode of Ueshiba's life, he states that "*...when the bullets flew at us we could only avoid them by twisting our necks and bodies.*" "*A pebble-like white flash would come flying at us one second before the bullet. I got away from the white flash in an instant and afterwards the bullet would pass by. Everyday was a repeat of this and in time I naturally came to understand the secrets of Budo.*"[19] Many, if not the majority, of military combat veterans are frequently unwilling to discuss the details of fighting experiences. Such is frequently the behavioral response of war veterans -- that of silence for one personal reason or another -- particularly those who experienced killing and the death of others. Similar responses from numerous other Japanese army veterans concerning a reluctance to talk about military combat, like Aikido master Rinjiro Shirata, occurred post W.W. II. And, on the other side, in the European war theater, Capt. Lee A. Sunderlin, the author's father, a U.S. Army Air Corps Martin Marauder B-26 bomber pilot during W.W. II, rarely mentioned any aspect of his military Air Corps combat experiences; when it did occur such was an innocuous abstraction of the reality of those experiences for the reason of his sons' guidance.

Shirataki settlement on the Island of Hokkaido

During his 'spearheading' of a settlement near the frontier area known as Shirataki in the Abashiri prefecture, island of Hokkaido, in the year 1912 C.E., Morihei Ueshiba led a small group of approximately eighty-four pioneers (consisting mostly of families) to establish, with much effort and difficulty, a small village located in the forested area of Futamata. Much of Hokkaido at this time was unsettled and people were encouraged by the Japanese government to inhabit and colonize certain areas -- among several reasons, the Japanese main island of Honshu during the late nineteenth century was becoming overpopulated. In the autumn of 1917 C.E., the village was about eighty percent destroyed by a forest fire that had been ignited by floating embers from the farming practice of burning crop and land clearing debris. After the fire, a number of the original settlers returned to the island of Honshu, but in spite of these setbacks Ueshiba redoubled his own efforts to rebuild the village and its economic viability. In June of 1918 C.E., Ueshiba was elected to a twelve-member governing council of the greater Kami-Yubetsu community (consisting of several villages) of which the Shirataki village was part. His commitment to fulfill his responsibilities in the role of head leader of this frontier group, an indication of piety, is well documented by several historical writers, including his first biographer, Kanemoto Sunadomari. In December of 1919 C.E., he received a telegram from Tanabe that his father was seriously ill. Concerned about his father and still somewhat distraught from the fire tragedy and its lingering problems, but also having previously entertained thoughts of returning to Tanabe to visit his family and teach Jujutsu, he decided to make the journey to be at his father's side. He resigned his councilman position. His wife, Hatsu, having just given birth to their third child, had already returned to Tanabe before him while he began disposing of their property in Shirataki. Certainly his role as a leader and devotion to the people of the newly established village of Shirataki counts as fidelity toward his social obligation, i.e., piety. (Shirataki village merged with the larger town Engaru in the year 2005; and, in 2010 the Abashiri prefecture was renamed to Okhotsk.) Somewhat pertinent, also, is a little bit of historical information suggesting that Ueshiba had earlier heard rumors of the relatively new, spiritually dynamic Omoto-kyo religious sect in the town of Ayabe, island of Honshu.[20]

Initial meeting of Sokaku Takeda and Daito-ryu Jujutsu

Aikido's connection to the martial art of Daito-ryu Jujutsu is a result of Morihei Ueshiba's complicated and sometimes difficult relationship with Sokaku Takeda, the inheritor or *chuko-no-so*[21] of the Daito-ryu tradition. Takeda's knowledge and skill in his profession, that of a traveling martial arts teacher, was highly respected among many Japanese police and military men of that time. For example, Sanehide Takarabe, the Police Chief of Akita prefecture, island of Honshu, upon being reassigned to the Abashiri prefecture asked Takeda to accompany him on his latest assignment to the new and rough-and-tumble frontier of Hokkaido.[22] Takeda had been residing at a local inn in the town of Engaru while he assisted Takarabe, and it was during this time that he was also giving Daito-ryu lessons to other people in the greater Engaru area. Public awareness of the acts of people travels fast, even back then, particularly where any act was noteworthy, so it was no surprise that Takeda and others became aware of Ueshiba's efforts to establish a thriving community in the Shirataki area of Hokkaido (see paragraph following). Vice versa, Ueshiba had likely heard of Takeda (Kanemoto Sunadomari, Morihei Ueshiba's first biographer, reports that Ueshiba had first heard of Takeda from a Sumo wrestler whom he met while hiking the path over Kitami Ridge between Shirataki and an area know as Asahikawa, near the small mountain settlement of Shirushibe). One of Takeda's students was Kotaro Yoshida, an ex-samurai who had become a journalist and was working in Engaru. Yoshida likely had knowledge of Ueshiba, perhaps having applied his journalistic endeavors to the reporting of what were the most recent activities and events that had come to pass in the new Hokkaido frontier. Yoshida offered to arrange Ueshiba's introduction to Takeda. Soon after, sometime in February, 1915 C.E., it happened that Ueshiba, who was visiting Engaru on business for his Shirataki community, met Takeda in the hallway of the inn where they were both staying. Whether this was entirely by chance or orchestrated by Yoshida is unknown. During the brief conversation, Takeda invited Ueshiba to stay on at the inn in order that he might partake of some already ongoing Daito-ryu instruction. Ueshiba accepted, and during this initial training over the period of about one month he began to understand Daito-ryu's unique effectiveness. Though by this time Morihei Ueshiba was learned in at least one martial art, most notably Yagyū Shingan-ryū Taijutsu (see Section VI -- Aikido Event Timelines) in which he was certified. His initial training in Daito-ryu was seminal for the eventual development of Aikido; it seemingly began to motivate his thoughts toward evolving an enlightened understanding of certain technical aspects of movement and energy applicable to the martial realm. So thoroughly inspiring was this training that Ueshiba invited Takeda to stay in his home, which

Takeda accepted, and subsequently urged about a dozen or so of the younger boys and men from the Shirataki village to study as well. Among these students was Ueshiba's nephew, the young and sometimes irreverent Noriaki Inoue, who later, after W.W. II, would teach his martial discipline using the name *Aiki-budo* (resolutely abandoned by the Ueshibas after WWII , but later renamed Shin'ei Taido by Inoue). In fact, Morihei's father, Yoroku Ueshiba, and his uncle-in-law, Zenzo Inoue, together consented to provide funding for the building of a dojo in Shirataki. From 1915 C.E. until late in 1919 C.E., Morihei Ueshiba, as often as his responsibilities to the Shirataki community would permit and often in a regularly scheduled manner, trained under Sokaku Takeda. For Ueshiba, this interaction with Takeda signaled the beginning of a lifelong relationship during which he devoted to his teacher significant personal attention, effort and resources -- such was the bargain struck as recompense for Takeda's knowledge and tutoring. According to Daito-ryū Aikijūjutsu's records, Morihei Ueshiba partook of Takeda's instruction, sometimes intensively, over a period of approximately twenty years.[23] Was Ueshiba's expression of a dutiful personality of, or related to, piety? Perhaps, as it is very difficult to show that piety can exist without motivation from self-interest. However, when Ueshiba had firmly decided to depart Hokkaido in order to return to Tanabe, he transferred his home and acreage to Takeda, which act was more than that necessary to fulfill the contractual arrangement for his lessons. Throughout their relationship, despite the fact that Ueshiba sometimes found it necessary to be conveniently unavailable when Takeda visited him (which was a result of Ueshiba's awareness of Takeda's cantankerous and sometimes pugnacious personality), Ueshiba treated his teacher with the respect due a master of Budo.

Later, Kisshomaru Ueshiba, in his biography about his father, Morihei, would describe his father's recollection that "*During one of the town council meetings in Shirataki a farm owner had spoken of a certain old woman, Nao Deguchi, of Ayabe, who was famous for being an oracle, or 'tip of the writing brush' (fudesaki), of God's redemption of the world. I myself had felt the great need of reforming this world and upon hearing this story, something clicked.*"[24] This indicates that Morihei Ueshiba had had some prior knowledge of the Omoto-kyo and its activities, which probably stirred within him thoughts about visiting its headquarters. Some historians report that he had probably gained knowledge of Omoto-kyo's teachings via his nephew, Noriaki Inoue, who had previously become an Omoto devotee.

Initial meeting of Onisaburo Deguchi and the Omoto-kyo

Having sent his wife and their three young children ahead of him to Tanabe, island of Honshu, Morihei Ueshiba departed the island of Hokkaido to be at his father's bedside. After arriving in Aomori town, the northern most part of Honshu, he traveled via rail (locomotive) to Kyoto. While on this trip he reportedly engaged in conversation with a fellow traveler who spoke to him of the spiritual teachings and miracles of the new Omoto-kyo religion located near to Ayabe town. Kyoto was for him a personal crossroads; which path to take. With every clickety-clack of the train's wheels passing over the rails, time was counting down. Upon arrival in Kyoto in late December, 1919 C.E., rather than taking the train to Osaka from where he would have taken a ferryboat to Tanabe, Ueshiba's burgeoning spiritual quest combined with his existential angst (having arisen from the effect of the Shirataki fire and his father's grave illness) caused him to make the decision to reroute to Ayabe. After arriving in Ayabe he walked promptly to the Omoto headquarters, and while doing so reportedly sensed an interestingly upbeat spiritual vibrancy that seemed to expansively emanate from the purpose driven, dynamic activities of the town's people; as Kisshomaru Ueshiba later stated in his biography of his father, "*A sacred and pure atmosphere pervaded all.*"[25] Upon entering the magnificent main hall of the Omoto headquarters, Ueshiba was led to the temple area and directed to quiet his spirit, contemplate his circumstances, and pray, which he obliging did. A goodly number of minutes passed when he heard faint footsteps and, as if out of a mist, there appeared a human figure gently walking toward him. As this person approached closer, Ueshiba reportedly experienced an intriguing and thoroughgoing sensation of willful surrender. Such a response is often considered to be an indication of a personality that is especially pious. This seemingly ephemeral figure was, as history informs us, Onisaburo Deguchi, the keenly intelligent and charismatic head priest of the Omoto-kyo religion. Reportedly, Onisaburo spoke prayers for Ueshiba's father, which had the effect of consoling the distraught Ueshiba. Thusly, Morihei

Ueshiba met Onisaburo, a meeting that was seminal toward quickly attracting him as a devotee of Omoto-kyo; but, also a meeting that propelled him toward involvement in several tumultuous events that would affect both his family and his newly adopted religion. When considering the nature of his earlier self-studies -- an indication of his basic predisposition or character -- such an attraction, particularly when under the mental stress of his father's impending demise, is easily understood. After spending several days in Ayabe listening to and contemplating the teachings of the Omoto-kyo, Ueshiba departed for Tanabe to be at his father's side. These teachings likely affirmed his earlier decision of quickly and completely leaving behind his efforts in Shirataki and probably cemented in his thought the necessity of taking a different, more spiritual path of endeavor. To establish even further that Ueshiba was at a personal crossroads, Kanemoto Sunadomari in his telling of Ueshiba's life informs us that "*As a child he had seen spiritual places when taken to Shinto shrines and Buddhist temples for worship by his parents and grandparents and so he had already acquired religious faith. But this faith was nothing but a vague, ideological belief.*" "*Morihei learned the true nature of the spiritual world at Omoto for the first time and what he had vaguely understood now became clear.*"[26]

Death of a father: harbinger of change

Upon arriving in Tanabe in early January of 1920 C.E., Morihei Ueshiba became profoundly chagrined when he learned that his father, Yoroku Ueshiba, had already passed. After tending to family matters, Ueshiba, his wife, their two children, and his mother, Yuki, moved to Ayabe -- a move likely for the reason of seeking answers that might sooth his existential angst -- but not without substantial protest from both his wife and his mother.[27] Hatsu, who was pregnant, had just recently moved from Shirataki back to Tanabe with her children Matsuko and Takemori; then, shortly afterward, her husband's father passed away. It was a tumultuous time for the family. About seven months after settling near the base of Mount Hongu where the town of Ayabe is situated, Hatsu gave birth in August to their second son, Kuniharu. Reportedly, both young sons of Morihei and Hatsu Ueshiba rapidly fell ill; in August their first son (Takemori, age 3) died, and in September the same befell their second son (Kuniharu, age 30 days), possibly from influenza or tuberculosis.[28] In the face of these tragic events, Ueshiba's resolve to remain in Ayabe as a devotee of Omoto-kyo only strengthened,[29] which was likely a result of a further deepening of his psychological angst regarding human mortality and death. Considering the expressions of his character up to this point, these actions, *1)* giving his property to Sokaku Takeda and leaving behind his Shirataki efforts in Hokkaido, *2)* visiting the Omoto-kyo temple in Ayabe despite the fact that his father was seriously ill, and *3)* moving from Tanabe to Ayabe to pursue the teachings of Omoto-kyo in spite of his family's protestations (which decision may have been even more difficult to justify after the death of his sons), describes a type of person who seems to have been from the onset a seeker of things metaphysical with a strong inclination toward piety of one kind or another, but also with a tendency to make decisions that were occasionally disliked by his wife and extended family. So captivated was Morihei Ueshiba by the teachings of the Omoto-kyo and its charismatic leader that he and his family remained as residents in Ayabe until the beginning of 1927 C.E.

Interlude 1

To provide a little background for all of the following episodes in Morihei Ueshiba's life, it is important to know that during the time period from approximately 1890 C.E. through the end of W.W. II in late 1945 C.E., Japan's government, consisting of its parliamentary Diet and the Emperor, did not have thoroughgoing control over the actions of its military abroad; this was especially the case in that part of today's Northeast China, known during this time period as Manchuria. The Japanese government in Japan proper had good, solid control over its various police forces; however, this was not the case with its military forces. During the Meiji Period (1868-1912 C.E.), as Japan began forming a modern military and intelligence service, many men from the disenfranchised samurai class, some of whom were disgruntled, had necessarily as well as expectedly developed influence over the attitudes and ethics that comprised the Japanese military's training policies for its military forces. As a result, at pivotal times, numerous administrative officers, commanders of operational military units, and enlisted soldiers found themselves at odds with certain decisions of the Diet and initiated military actions contrary to the latter's decisions and orders. Morihei Ueshiba's existence was inextricably intertwined with the Japanese experience of his time, and, as he had chosen Budo as his primary profession, it was only a matter of time before he was drawn into an ever deeper association with the Japanese military by the effect of Japan's prevailing social *zeitgeist* (aire-of-the-age), i.e., the *Yamato Damashii* ideology and the statist *Kokutai* policy, which emerged a fascist social reality.[30] Most Japanese experienced a thoroughgoing indoctrination due to the deleterious effect of these social policies. Prior to W.W. II, one person amongst a small minority of Japanese who held back and rejected such a woeful social philosophy was Jigoro Kano, the founder of Judo who died in 1938 C.E. In comparison, Morihei Ueshiba did not begin to step away from his nation's top-to-bottom fascist reality until mid 1942 C.E., when he ceased his teaching of military personnel and withdrew to his residence in Iwama prefecture. In Manchuria, Kenji Tomiki continued to teach military personnel and toward the very end of the war he was required to fight when the Soviet Army overran Northeastern Asia. After W.W. II, Kisshomaru Ueshiba, Aikikai Aikido's second Doshu, a young man who had been in the fortunate position of not being required to fight, reshaped his father's discipline (i.e., Aikibudo) into the modern Aikikai Aikido of today. Kisshomaru largely rejected such an errant philosophy, that of Yamato Damashii, by taking an attitudinal stance against violence. His stance was founded upon the idea that when a person embraces "*non-contention*," the very act of doing so usually lessens conflict and often results in the evolution of better relations among disputing people.[31] Yamato Damashii was a societal philosophy that emerged a Japanese future shaped by two somewhat differing proponents of mythology and spirituality, the Emperor's line of Shinto (traditional) and, in this case, Omoto-kyo's version (non-traditional), whose frequently opposing efforts to aid in their collective Japanese experience were improperly handled by not only these two but also by a relatively new and therefore somewhat immature governing institution, Japan's parliamentary Diet. The Diet, which was replete with many self-serving politicians who were fond of romanticizing some aspects of late feudal Japan rather than getting down to the difficult work of creating a thoughtfully envisioned civil society, suffered pervasive manipulations by numerous Japanese ultranational factions that influenced its decisions and 'sowed' within Japan's military the disruptive idea that allegiance to civilian authority was errant behavior when considered 'in the light of the Japanese people's unique ascension from heaven' and, subsequently, their 'inherent right to reshape the world according to a divine plan that had been bequeathed' by their ancient Japanese deities.[32]

During the 1920 C.E. to 1927 C.E. time period, much occurred in Morihei Ueshiba's life. *First*, the death of his father. *Second*, the suppression of the Omoto-kyo's activities by the Japanese government in early February of 1920 C.E., and certainly the Ueshibas' discussions about their upcoming move to Ayabe where Omoto-kyo was headquartered were affected by this event. *Third*, after their move to Ayabe in June of 1920 C.E., Morihei Ueshiba established upon the urging of Onisaburo Deguchi what comes to be known as the *Ueshiba Juku* (the Ueshiba Coaching School). *Fourth*, Morihei and Hatsu Ueshiba's sons die. *Fifth*, Hatsu Ueshiba gives birth to her third son Kisshomaru Ueshiba in September of 1921 C.E. *Sixth*, Ueshiba's mother, Yuki, dies in 1922 C.E. *Seventh*, Sokaku Takeda and his family arrive in Ayabe in the month of April 1922 C.E. to certify Ueshiba as a *"teacher in absence of the headmaster,"* five months later awarding Ueshiba a *Kyoju Dairi* certification. *Eighth*, Morihei Ueshiba journeys to Mongolia from February through July of 1924 C.E. with Onisaburo Deguchi on what turns out to be an ill-fated venture, which had the intent to found a utopian community based upon the teachings of the Omoto-kyo; and, lastly, his first vision in 1925 C.E., which he considered to be a momentous occurrence of enlightenment originating from a divine source. Mulling over only the tumultuous events, it's a wonder, isn't it, that Ueshiba continued his relationship with the Omoto-kyo? But, this hints further about the nature of his character, its relationship with piety, and his need for spiritual direction. Morihei Ueshiba must have found in Omoto exactly that for which he was seeking.

Regarding the significance of the Ueshiba Juku to the development of modern Aikido, this where the basis of Aikido really begins to be developed and established. It is here that Onisaburo introduced Ueshiba to Seikyo Asano, a retired admiral in the Japanese Imperial Navy, who had moved to Ayabe to be closer to his younger brother, the prominent Omoto-kyo devotee Wasaburo Asano. From then onward, with a short interruption in 1925 C.E. resulting from his adventure in Mongolia with Onisaburo, Ueshiba had a steady enrollment of personnel from the nearby naval base at Maizuru, Japan. During this time, i.e., from 1920 C.E. until he moved from Ayabe to Tokyo in 1927 C.E., he began to gain a reputation amongst the officer corps of the Japanese Imperial Navy as a very capable and unique budoka. This certainly helped Onisaburo to insulate or strengthen Omoto-kyo's various activities against harassment by the Japanese government. For Ueshiba, this type of social path, i.e., association with the military, seemed to be his destiny. As noted earlier in this chapter, before his honorable discharge from the Japanese Imperial Army following the Russo-Japanese War, he had been encouraged by his divisional and regimental commanders to continue with a military career.[33]

Move to Ayabe and the First Omoto-kyo Suppression

By the time the Ueshibas had made their decision to move to Ayabe, the Omoto-kyo had acquired a large following, popularity as well as notoriety, a newspaper, and real estate. Onisaburo's inspiring leadership, which emanated from his exciting oratory, good organizational and promotional skills, 'revealing' spiritual insights, teaching, and literary efforts had helped to create a dynamic socio-spiritual movement whose message had begun to reshape Japanese society. Unfortunately, various controlling entities of the Japanese government had been watching Omoto's activities. (Even today this is the situational reality for any attention-getting social movement or organization that exhibits a full-of-possibility and or opposed-to-the-established aire. The preexisting, powerful organizations are watching and making an account of who's who and what they're up to; such movements are often openly suppressed while others are quietly or covertly repurposed or suffer dissolution.) A powerful devotee of the Omoto-kyo, Wasaburo Asano, who, in the years before 1920 C.E. had been a prominent professor of English at Japan's Naval Academy and therefrom had retained significant influence among the navy's officer corps, had become so thoroughly fixated by one of Omoto's earlier predictions of apocalyptic societal upheaval in Japan that he found it necessary to openly speak out to the public that such a fate would become an inescapable reality in 1921 C.E. Onisaburo, who had replaced Nao Deguchi (1836 C.E.-1918 C.E.) as head of Omoto-kyo, found it difficult to moderate Asano's viewpoint and subsequent public oration, which resulted in unwanted and counterproductive attention from the Japanese government. Wasaburo Asano headed a strong faction within Omoto that believed in and attempted to make sociopolitical use of its foundress' (Nao's) predictions for the future. (See endnote 24 in this chapter for information about Nao Deguchi.) Being a new devotee, it is likely that Ueshiba was not fully aware of the extent of the government's concern about and surveillance of Omoto-kyo's activities and it is quite probable that both he and his family were surprised and concerned when it was raided on February 11, 1920 C.E. Onisaburo and other top members of Omoto were arrested and charged with newspaper-publishing violations and Lèse-majesté by the effect of the Public Security Preservation Laws of Japan.[34] Awaiting trial, Onisaburo was jailed for one hundred and twenty-six days before making bail, then was tried, convicted, and sentenced to five years in prison by the lower Osaka judicial court. However, after his case was submitted to Japan's highest court for review, it was found by the court that there was "a serious defect in the previous ruling" and his conviction was overturned. Undaunted, the government's prosecutorial team reevaluated and reorganized their charges against Onisaburo and presented their case again. Once again the lower court found in favor of the government. Onisaburo -- who was absent because he had 'jumped' bail, departed Japan and traveled to Northeast Asia to scout for a new geographic location to which he could possibly relocate the Omoto-kyo's headquarters -- was convicted in abstentia of lesser crimes. After Onisaburo was returned from Mongolia to Japan by the Japanese police to serve his sentence, he appealed once again to the higher court. During these proceedings, the reigning Japanese Emperor Taisho died (December 25, 1926 C.E.), which resulted in his pardon.[35] In spite of the government's harassment and suppression of Omoto-kyo's activities, the Ueshiba family moved to Ayabe around the time that Onisaburo was first released on bail; by itself, this 'speaks loudly' about the quality of Morihei Ueshiba's conviction to pursue Omoto's teachings and is an indication of his spiritual zeal and 'blossoming' piety. Following Onisaburo's bail release -- but before the lower court had issued a decision on the government's reorganized case, and before he had 'jumped' bail in order to travel to Mongolia -- Onisaburo had assigned Ueshiba as the *Head of Agricultural Affairs* for the Omoto-kyo. Onisburo had assigned this role to Ueshiba because he knew of the latter's relatively successful Shirataki endeavor on Hokkaido. In addition to Ueshiba's agricultural duties, he also gave lessions regularly in Daito-ryu at his *Ueshiba Juku* dojo.

Omoto's Mongolian Incident

This episode of Morihei Ueshiba's life is quite important because it reveals the extent to which a strong condition of piety naturally infused his character. Without doubt, his rearing within Japanese society shaped his 'personality blue-print' with a certain urge or obligation to 'live up to' its unique set of expectations, one of which was loyalty to your teacher -- in this case, his spiritual teacher, Onisaburo Deguchi. In Japan, then, once such a teacher-pupil relationship had been established, especially one in the realm of spiritual matters, many a person so situated would find it dishonorable, therefore repugnant, to act otherwise. Ueshiba's relationship with filial and religious piety, in fact, his particular conceptualization of all the varieties of loyalty and obligation, which are often attended by perseverance or stoicism, drew him toward making certain decisions that resulted in some of the more 'colorful' events that tested his character.

Several years had passed since Morihei Ueshiba's spiritual guide had suffered arrest and court proceedings by the Japanese government, though the passage of time did not assuage the government's desire to have Onisaburo removed from Japan's socio-political stage. Ueshiba, by this time, was certainly cognizant of the problem that the Japanese government had with Omoto-kyo's social message for Japan's people as well as its ever-growing membership. Nevertheless, in the face of possible persecution if not outright danger to himself and his family, he continued to associate with the Omoto-kyo because he had become fascinated with its teachings and enamored by Onisaburo Deguchi's charisma.

In early February, 1924 C.E., Ueshiba (leaving behind his wife and children in Ayabe) and Onisaburo (who was still on bail with pending prosecutorial and court actions) departed from Japan on a mission to lay the foundation for an Omoto-kyo utopian community in Mongolia. Yutaro Yano (an Omoto significant and retired naval captain who operated a successful business in Manchuria) and two other Omoto followers accompanied them. Numerous members of

Omoto-kyo were connected with Japan's government in one capacity or another. However, these connections were neither of sufficient political level nor loyal enough to keep Onisaburo informed as to the real intentions or plans of the Japanese monarch and his government's sociopolitical maneuvers; from the point of view of the government, these governmentally positioned Omoto members added to the concern it had about Omoto's ever-increasing social force.

The reasoning that led Onisaburo to push forward with his Mongolian adventure was faulty, no matter how it is characterized or described. *First,* he had long had a personal desire to expand the teachings of the Omoto-kyo into the Asian continent; but, without a well thought out plan, one with proven points of strength, his mission was one where only *"fools rush in where angels fear to tread."*[36] *Second,* Ueshiba, after he'd received his *Kyoju Dairi* certification from Sokaku Takeda, had begun to experience frequent episodes of disagreement with his teacher about his methods of teaching and the teaching fees owed him. The emergence of this difficulty in Ueshiba's relationship with Takeda was partially Onisaburo's responsibility because he had encouraged Ueshiba to attain recognition as the most prominent budo teacher in Japan. Following along with his spiritual master's advice, Ueshiba made some decisions that irritated Takeda. As a result, Ueshiba accepted Onisaburo's decision to go to Mongolia when the latter suggested that he could escape his predicament with Takeda. *Third,* Onisaburo was approached by a member of his Omoto organization, Yano, who managed a commercial business in the city of Fengtian, Manchuria to assist with the Japanese government's effort to open *"a 'new frontier' which would in fact be a new colony."*[37] (Later, Fengtian was renamed to Shenyang, but it was called Hoten by the Japanese then.) This particular 'commerce business' was actually one of numerous facades for various Japanese covert operations on the Asian continent, and it is possible that this member was 'helpful' to Onisaburo only because he, Yano, was carrying out orders from a government that had just several years earlier raided the Omoto-kyo. It is probable that the Omoto-kyo had been infiltrated by various operatives of the Japanese government or ultranational groups and that the 'assistance' provided by this particular Omoto member was a complex attempt by one or several of these factions to use Onisaburo as a means of changing the balance of power in northeast Asia, something with which he was willing to cooperate because of Omoto's persecution in Japan and his driven desire to promulgate Omoto's teachings.[38] Its not at all far-fetched to consider the possibility that some men of various Japanese agriculture and materiel firms that were strengthening their operations in Manchuria would not at all have found it unsettling if imprisonment in a Chinese prison or death awaited Onisaburo, for at least this scheme would provide some information about the strength and tactical abilities of the Chinese, Manchurian, and Mongolian forces; meaning, those elements of the Japanese government that found him to be a nuisance would be rid of him.

It is interesting to contemplate Onisaburo's mindset leading up to his decision to organize and carryout such an undertaking. Just several years earlier the Japanese police forces, authorized by their government, had raided all of Omoto-kyo's establishments throughout Japan, destroyed and seized some of its property, and imprisoned as well as subjected both Onisaburo and others to interrogation and court proceedings. Did he ever consider that some of his 'dedicated' Omoto followers might have had deeper loyalty elsewhere? Perhaps Onisaburo considered his trip to Mongolia useful for the following reasons.

1) To escape the circumstances of Omoto-kyo's persecution in Japan, which could permit the situation there to calm down;

2) To facilitate Omoto-kyo's mission of world salvation by positioning its headquarters more centrally in Asia;

3) To show to the Japanese emperor and his government that he and Omoto were supportive of Japan's time-honored imperial philosophy of Yamato Damashii, thereby establishing Omoto's social stature -- although this particular 'face' of Onisaburo's agenda was somewhat genuine, he knew well that Omoto's teachings regarding the hierarchical order of Japan's kami weakened the Yamato Emperor's right to rule;

4) To investigate further the mythical tales of India's ancient Rigveda, particularly those relating to both the creative and destructive powers of utterance as proposed in its mythical Varnamala and the latter's relationship to the Omoto-kyo's kotodama theory; and,

5) To help Ueshiba escape his predicament with Takeda.

Some Aikido historians suggest that Onisaburo had learned prior to their departure that there was the possibility of a second wave of police raids for the reason of arresting even more members of the Omoto-kyo, and, combined with his already known desire to spread its teachings, decided that it might be a good tactical move to make a journey to Mongolia in order to relocate the Omoto-kyo headquarters there.[39] Whatever else might be considered as his reasoning or motivation, Onisaburo, along with Ueshiba and the others, shrouded in secrecy, departed for Mongolia on February 13, 1924 C.E. in an undertaking that turned into a dangerous misadventure.

After traveling by ferryboat from Japan to Korea (Chōsen to the Japanese),[40] then by train through Korea to arrive at their destination in Manchuria on February 15, 1924 C.E., Onisaburo, Ueshiba, Yano and the others of their group proceeded to the location of the Sanya Company office in the city of Fengtian.[41] While at the office of the Sanya Company they met with other important Japanese of the area in order to discuss the details of the Omoto group's mission as they pertained to the goals of the *Manchukuo Chokokukai*, which was a Japanese organization in Manchuria that had been dedicated to the establishment of an official Japanese province there. Later that day they met with Zhankui Lu (Senkai Ro to the Japanese), who was a Mongolian chieftain commissioned as a lieutenant general in Manchuria's Fengtian Army and served under the Manchurian military governor, Zuòlín Zhāng (Sakurin Cho to the Japanese). Lu was sympathetic with Onisaburo's mission. Generalissmo Zuolin Zhang was the ultimate authority from whom law and order issued in the northeastern Asian provinces of Heilongjiang, Jilin, and Liaoning, i.e., Manchuria;[42] as a military commander, Zhang held Lu directly accountable to him. The meeting with Lu, who was a superstitious man,[43] went well, and a strong though somewhat psycho-spiritually unbalanced brother-in-spirit connection quickly developed between them. Onisaburo's reputation as a spiritual master was previously known to Lu, and this permitted Onisaburo's charisma to easily convince him that a joint endeavor would likely produce a beneficial social and spiritual reality for not only the Mongolian people but, eventually, for all peoples of Asia.

After Lieutenant General Lu had presented Onisaburo's *omotemuki*[44] (apparent) reasoning and plan to Generalissmo Zhang, who cautiously approved and ordered him to use the name Xibei Zizhi Jun (Northwest Autonomous Army) to identify their army, Lu whole-heartedly committed his efforts and resources to the journey into Mongolia. However, Lu had also been ordered by Zhang to inform the Omoto group to wait before departing Fengtian until he produced for their use a legitimate military pass that would authorize their travel and help ensure their safe passage during their mission. Obviously, this could have also served as a tracking method so that Zhang might be frequently updated as to the group's location and activities.

Zuolin Zhang was an adept military man as well as a crafty, self-made statesman. Zhang tenuously controlled Manchuria, held sway over some of the chieftains of Inner Mongolia,[45] had complex and uneasy relations with other Chinese warring factions, and was also subjected to influence by various Japanese interests; he could ill afford to have one more problem in or around his Manchurian dominion.[46] Zhang cared little for Onisaburo's spiritual endeavors or aspirations but saw an opportunity to mobilize some of the Mongol groups through a unified leadership of Lu and Onisaburo to later attack certain elements of a rival Chinese Clique, the Zhili. As a group, the Mongol peoples were spiritual but quite superstitiously inclined, and their leaders were apt to make decisions based upon magical divinations. Though Zhang was 'helping' with Onisaburo's scouting mission, neither Lu nor Onisaburo were entirely aware of his motivation to do so. Regarding the history of Manchuria from 1905 C.E. until the end of W.W. II in 1945 C.E., this was certainly a time of intrigue and duplicitous behavior in which there were competing Chinese and Japanese factions that viewed Northeast Asia similar to the westward expansion of the United States of America on the North American Continent in the Nineteenth Century, while the Mongol peoples were largely attempting to retain autonomy over their traditional lands upon which they had roamed and lived for hundreds of generations. For an improved understanding, review Japan's *Amau Doctrine*, which can be considered as having similarities to the U.S.A.'s *Monroe Doctrine*.

Upon the urging of Tesshu Okazaki, who was a land cultivator in Manchuria and a member of the Manchukuo Chokokukai, and with whom Onisaburo and his group had met to discuss Japanese interests in Manchuria and organize the details of their mission,[47] Onisaburo, Ueshiba, Okazaki, and one other, before they had received the required military pass, departed Shenyang on March 3, 1924 C.E. Their destination was the Manchurian military outpost at Taonan. Rather than take the train from Shenyang northward to

Sipin (New Shiheigai to the Japanese), the group decided to travel by automobile over rough dirt roads and paths in order to avoid unwanted attention. Just a little south of Changtu, a small town on the way, one of the automobiles had a mechanical failure. While awaiting parts to effect its repair, the group was approached at a local inn by several Chinese policeman and an official from the Japanese Embassy who questioned them.[48] This event was probably the incident that alerted both Japan's police forces as well as Zhāng of Onisaburo's whereabouts. (Remember, Onisaburo had fled Japan while on bail during the higher Court's reconsideration of a lower court's findings about Omoto-kyo's supposed Lèse-majesté activities and other charges, and had ignored Zhang's order to wait for a military pass.) In fact, the Japanese police had issued a 'wanted alert' and monetary reward for information regarding Onisaburo's whereabouts;[49] Morihei Ueshiba continued to participate unreservedly as Onisaburo's bodyguard, yet another indication of the extent of his devotion to Onisaburo and spiritual embrace of Omoto's teachings. After arriving in Sipin, they boarded the train for Chengchiatun (Teikaton), a westerly but necessary intermediate destination before traveling further northward by train to Taonan, which was a military outpost area under the control of Zhang where Onisaburo and his group would meet up with Zhankui Lu to gather troops and supplies. On the train from Chengchiatun to Taonan, they were unavoidably seated in the same coach with several Chinese officials who were curious about Onisaburo's reason for traveling to Taonan where there was always much trouble arising from banditry. (Remember, the group had departed Shenyang before receiving the required military pass.) Each time these officials directed questions to Onisaburo, Okazaki would interject conversation that seemed to satisfy their curiosity; but, it is reasonable to think that these officials could have reported this encounter to both Zuolin Zhang and the Japanese Embassy. After a trying five days of travel via both automobile and train they arrived in Taonan on March 8, 1924 C.E. Taonan was an temporary destination before they proceeded onward to Guanjiatun, which is an area just to the northwest of Taonan that was the designated as the gathering place for troops and provisions, but due to distressing bandit activity in the area, they waited two weeks before the group could safely depart for Guanjiatun. During this interlude, Onisaburo, probably 'playing his cards close to the vest,' meets with Generalissmo Zhang and they discuss Onisaburo's desire to possibly relocate Omoto-kyo to somewhere in Mongolia. From Guanjiatun they would ride, either on horseback or wagon, into the Suolun District of Inner Mongolia in order to setup a base of operations around the base of Mt. Suolun, where there was a large administrative building that had earlier been vacated by the Russians after several military engagements between the Mongolians and Russians.[50] As the Omoto group entered the Guanjiatun area on March 26, 1924 C.E., which was a fairly well-known and populated center of Lamaism (Tibetan Buddhism), they changed their clothing to reflect its look so as not to arouse unnecessary suspicions while attempting to convey to the curious onlookers the importance of Onisaburo and his group; this was an idea that both Onisaburo and Lu had conceived earlier during their discussions in Fengtian, and for which they had later obtained the appropriate clothing.[51] Lu and Onisaburo thought it would be beneficial to their cause to exhibit a religious aire with which the area's indigenous people could easily identify. Interestingly, and somewhat counter to their concern about arousing suspicion, the name 'Dalai Lama' was usefully but illegitimately assumed by Onisaburo; his manner of dress was such that it gave support to this largely fraudulent but expedient claim, thus completing the ruse. Ueshiba was supportive of this deception and, in fact, it is reported that he was hurriedly 'ordained' in *Omoto Lamaism* by Onisaburo for this purpose when their group was approached by hundreds of people in the area who sought healing and spiritual guidance.[52] Can this bestowment be considered as a legitimate ordainment? Well, it is known that Ueshiba had thoroughly immersed himself and his family in the Omoto experience, that roughly three years had passed since doing so, and that Onisaburo was Ueshiba's spiritual teacher. Today, every April 29, the Omoto-kyo holds a ceremony to honor Morihei Ueshiba's efforts to help establish the Omoto-kyo as a respectable spiritual tradition, but they do not consider him as an ordained Omoto priest. It is important to note that the spiritual teachings of the Omoto tradition of today are somewhat different than those of its past.

Weeks passed as alliances and other preparations were made just to the northwest of Taonan, in the Guanjiatun (Gongyefu) area, which was the location previously arranged by General Lu for the gathering of troops and provisions for the Northwest Autonomous Army. Though Zuolin Zhang by this time had begun to become uneasy as to whether Onisaburo's mission statement (to scout for a suitable location in both Inner and Outer Mongolia to relocate Omoto-kyo) was entirely truthful, Zhang was both obligated by his previous agreements with Lu (who was a Mongol ally and officer in Zhang's Fengtian Army) and urged by his own motive (which was the use of the Northwest Autonomous Army to attack and defeat elements of the rival Zhili Clique) to continue to provide supplies, guide its operations, and help organize its manpower. However, Zhang was learned in deception, intelligence gathering, and control of his forces; and though he provided much that was necessary to establish the basis for this new army, he also assigned a loyal officer (a relative) who was conversant in the Japanese language to participate with Lu and Onisaburo when the army began its operations.[53] Though numerous Mongolian militia and Fengtian Army elements had been promised by various Mongol chieftains and Zhang, when Lu and Onisaburo departed the Guanjiatun area on their northwesterly march to Mt. Suolun, the soldier count of the Northwest Autonomous Army was only about two hundred. These were a troop that Lu had brought on horseback on April 14, 1924 C.E., after Onisaburo and his group had relocated from Taonan to the Guanjiatun area. This author does not have information concerning how or when Lu learned of Zhang's complete scheme, but it is plausible, though speculative, that some knowledge of what Zhang was planning was gained when Lu arrived in the Taonan area, where he learned that Zhang had already visited Onisaburo there, had had pertinent conversation with him, and had assigned a translator as well as guide of his choosing to assist Onisaburo and his group. It is likely that Zhang was still in Taonan when Lu arrived, and they must have subsequently had some tense conversation about Zhang's reason for visiting and overseeing operations in Taonan; earlier, in January of 1924 C.E., Lu had been ordered by Zhang to assemble as well as command a new army. Sometime after Lu had initially met with Onisaburo but before he departed to setup a base outpost in the Suolun District, he had discovered, either in his discussions with Zuolin Zhang or from other independent sources, that Zhang's opinion of Onisaburo expressed a general disregard of life's spiritual nature. Zuolin Zhang, reportedly, thought Onisaburo to be a charlaton, but would sometimes make use of Onisaburo's abilities when necessary to smooth out relations with people as his military campaign against the Zhili Clique progressed; Onisaburo's mission, whatever it might eventually turn out to be, was a minor concern for Zhang. Upon fully realizing Zhang's intended use of the new army, Lu was disconcerted; he convened further discussions with Onisaburo, Ueshiba, and the others of the Omoto group at Guanjiatun and, urged forth by his spiritual beliefs (indigenous shamanism combined with elements of Lamaism) and mystical analyses (fortune-telling and physiognomy) of Onisaburo's personality (which he related later to Onisaburo after the latter had arrived at Mt. Suolun), decided to covertly and entirely disassociate from Zhang's plans.[54] (Onisaburo himself was one who heeded o-mens or signs.) On April 24, the commander of the Taonan Division of Zhang's Fengtian Army (another relative of Zhang) had brought weapons and other essential provisions to the Guanjiatun area where the new army was forming up, but the full assembling of sol-diers had not yet occurred. If the army had come together accord-ing to Zhang's plans, its soldier count could have quickly rose to 30,000 or more, but it seems that Lu and Onisaburo departed pre-maturely.

On April 25, 1924 C.E., General Lu rode northwesterly into the Suolun District with several dozen of his two hundred loyal soldiers that he had earlier brought with him in order to make preparations at what was soon to become their army's headquarters near the foot of Mt. Suolun; Onisaburo, his Japanese group, and the larger part of Lu's troop with supply wagons would depart a day later. At this historical juncture, Lu had already finalized in his mind a dramatic decision to irreversibly split from Zhang's authority and move to-ward a loyal partnership with Onisaburo in support of establishing a new social reality in both Inner and Outer Mongolia; this was made easier because Onisaburo had brought with him approximate-ly 250,000 Japanese yen, money that was necessary to fund any pos-sible operations toward this end.[55] When Zhang learned of Lu's ini-tial insubordination, which was their unauthorized marches into the Suolun District, it confirmed Zhang's earlier precautions (e.g., his earlier ordering of a military pass for Onisaburo's group and, after-ward, the assignment of a trusted translator as well as a trusted guide to Onisaburo's group). Zhang was gravely concerned because the Northwest Autonomous Army was supposed to act in concert with his Fengtian Army to attack, overwhelm, and subdue the rival Zhili Clique of Northern China. But, he did not take immediate ac-tion against Lu and Onisaburo; probably because some of Zhang's supplies had just gone with them into the Suolun District,[56] and since he had given command of the Northwest Autonomous Army to Lu, he waited to gather information about Lu's seemingly mutinous act and its portent before making a decision about what to do. When Lu arrived in the southern area of the Suolun District he established an initial lower outpost around and in the ex-Russian administrative building that was located there, then rode out to rejoin with Onisaburo's troop, which had departed a day later than he from Guanjiatun. As General Lu and Onisaburo marched northwest toward their lower outpost, two other changes were initiated, without the approval of military governor Zhang. *First*, Onisaburo would act as an adjutant 'military general' to their small army but Zhankui Lu, a respected Mongol chieftain with military experience, would act as its commanding general; both would cooperate to lead their army.[57] *Second*, as Lu and Onisaburo were approaching their lower outpost, they likely discussed further Lu's recent discussions with Zhang, and as they entered Inner Mongolia they changed the name of the Northwest Autonomous Army (Xibei Zizhi Jun) to Neiwai Menggu Duli Jun (Inner and Outer Mongolia Independence Army).

Slowly, hundreds of Mongolian freedom fighters and mounted bandits began to arrive at Lu's lower outpost; these were assessed for their fitness for service and sent to Onisaburo's 'upper' camp where the troops were barracked in tents at sixteen-mile intervals, with Onisaburo's headquarters in the middle. It is not known what happened to the translator or the guide that Zhang had assigned to Onisaburo, but it is not unreasonable to think that they were either left behind at Guanjiatun or they were disposed of on the way to the Suolun District.

The Inner and Outer Mongolia Independence Army, which would actually have included numerous Mongol chieftains and their men as well as lesser-known Asian spiritual leaders, quickly metamorphosed into a 'spiritual' force dedicated to securing and maintaining independence from Chinese, Manchurian, and Russian governance while also establishing an Omoto-kyo utopian-like society; when Zhang fully realized what was occurring, he began to take action to stop this revolt. Lu and Onisaburo's plan and revolt fit in well with the ever-growing ultranational sentiment within Japan's military to devise a conflict in Manchuria so that Japan could justify a military invasion, but something that Zhang, though at times cooperating with Japanese interests for his own benefit, did not at all want to see come to fruition. It is uncertain as to whether or not Onisaburo and Ueshiba were acting solely upon a desire to escape Omoto-kyo's persecution in Japan because in Shenyang they had met with other Japanese nationals to discuss the desired goals of the Manchukuo Chokokukai and the difficulties that would have to be overcome in order to realize further colonization of Northeast Asia by Japanese. Instead, it seems reasonable that they were working to ameliorate and eventually resolve Omoto's persecution problem by accomplishing something to help along Japan's goal of colonizing Northeastern Asia. Onisaburo thought that if he could achieve this goal it might provide him an inroad to smoothing out Omoto's difficulties at home by establishing in the thoughts of the emperor and members of Japan's government that he was a well-meaning and patriotic man who was supportive of Japan's international goals, which should, in turn, generate within these entities the necessary respect for the Omoto-kyo religion such that it would not suffer further persecution. However, all this was wrong thinking for two important reasons. *First*, at that time and until after W.W. II, the Japanese emperor did not at all need a new and powerful religious organization competing with his inherited royal privilege to guide Japan's Shinto and Buddhist traditions; as a result, no matter what Onisaburo did to build Omoto's popularity or to support Japan's international goals and policies, he would always fall short of the acceptance he desired from the emperor and his government, or as it actually was, from the government and its emperor figurehead.[58] *Second*, the possibility of success in achieving this goal was small because of the extent of military governor Zuolin Zhang's control over Manchuria, part of which consisted of his liaisons with certain other Mongolian chieftains who, besides Lu, were either serving in Zhang's Fengtian Army or sometimes aligned with Zhang when it served their interests; as a result, the goal that Onisaburo and Lu had in mind would have to be achieved quickly, forcefully, and with a series of successful deceptions. Yes, if they had succeeded in their attempt to secure Inner Mongolia from the control of Zhang or any of the other competing Chinese factions, this could have provided Onisaburo with the geography that would have made it possible for him to establish Omoto there; but, he must have also realized that such an achievement would not necessarily garner him the respect in Japan that would alleviate Omoto's persecution there or elsewhere, for he and Lu would have been a force to be reckoned with, something that neither Japan's government and its emperor nor the Manchurian military governor Zuolin Zhang wanted. A fallback position that would consist of geography in Inner Mongolia protected by the Neiwai Menggu Dulijun (Inner and Outer Mongolia Independence Army) could provide Onisaburo with the option of moving his religion there in the event that he never gained the type of respect in Japan that would alleviate Omoto-kyo's persecution. Morihei Ueshiba must have understood these ramifications, too, and at this point, he continued to act as Onisaburo's personal bodyguard. It seems that Onisaburo knew little of the behind-the-scenes potential for internecine sociopolitical maneuvers of the various minor and major actors of the Chinese and Mongol power factions, or perhaps, at best, thought he could somehow avoid or make use of such struggles by employing his social prowess and spiritual charisma.[59]

At their encampment around the base of Mt. Suolun, General Zhankui Lu, who three times each day would toss 6 copper coins to divine 'information' that could help him make daily decisions,[60] and adjutant General Onisaburo, having by now thoroughly embraced the grandiose idea that his undertaking was heavenly ordained,[61] awaited the arrival of more freedom fighters that a 'trusted' chieftain had previously said would be available to assist in their Army's move to unify inner and outer Mongolia. Had these fighters joined up with their small army, it could have swelled quickly to a number over 20,000 men. Morihei Ueshiba continued dutifully in his role as Onisaburo's bodyguard, but also took to teaching Aikijujutsu to numerous Mongol freedom fighters. It is probable that Zhang had been informed that Lu was awaiting reinforcements, and if so, fully realized that Lu, Onisaburo and their army were a threat to his governance and control of Manchuria. For Zhang, the final piece of evidence which convinced him that he would soon be dealing with insurrection became clear when he was notified that the Northwest Autonomous Army had changed its name and flying banner to *Neiwai Menggu Dulijun* (Inner and Outer Mongolia Independence Army) at the moment it crossed the border between Manchuria and Inner Mongolia on its march into the Suolun District. Though well provisioned, commanding General Lu and 'General' Onisaburo had not yet seen the arrival of additional fighters in response to their call-to-arms. Then, sometime in May, 1924 C.E., their army, yet encamped around the base of Mt. Suolun, suffered numerous small attacks from unidentified bandit groups.[62] Rather than remain in the Suolun District while awaiting the arrival of fighters promised by other Mongol chieftains, with the strong probability of suffering more bandit attacks, they made a decision to march southward following the eastern edge of Inner Mongolia to set up a second base of operations near Tongliao; once there, they could reassess their situation, so they thought. It is very likely that military governor Zhang intercepted Lu's call-to-arms requests and threatened reprisal against any group of fighters that had been thinking about joining up with the Inner and Outer Mongolia Independence Army. As Lu, Onisaburo, Ueshiba, and their army hastily departed their encampment at Mt. Suolun, the army had only grown to some number between one thousand and two thousand men. A short time later, Governor Zhang's scouts notified him of the renegade army's southward movement, and he quickly ordered elements of his Fengtian (Hoten) Army to intercept and suppress what he considered to be a rebellion.[63]

In July, as the Inner and Outer Mongolia Independence Army marched south from the Suolun District in order to set up a second base in Tongliao, Inner Mongolia, it came under attack by elements of military governor Zhang's Fengtian Army, just northwest of the town of Chengchiatun (Teikaton), in the area of Bayantala village, province of Jilin, Manchuria (today part of northeast China). On the run and under constant attack, General Lu, unable to reason under pressure, and having no time to consult the possible futures by a 'revealing' coin toss, was unable to think clearly and made decisions that frequently placed their army in more serious circumstances. Upon Lu's orders, apparently contrary to Onisaburo and Ueshiba's advice, their army continued a frantic march toward the town of Tongliao while experiencing numerous randomly occurring flanking attacks until, as it approached Tongliao, after many hours of on-the-run violent conflict, it was overwhelmed and captured. At some point during these attacks, Ueshiba, Onisaburo, and the other members of their spiritual entourage had been forced to take up arms to defend themselves (which means that one, some, or all of them may have wounded or killed Fengtian Army soldiers). Shortly after the army's capture, Zhang ordered the immediate execution of Lu and many of the subordinates that served under him. Up to this point,

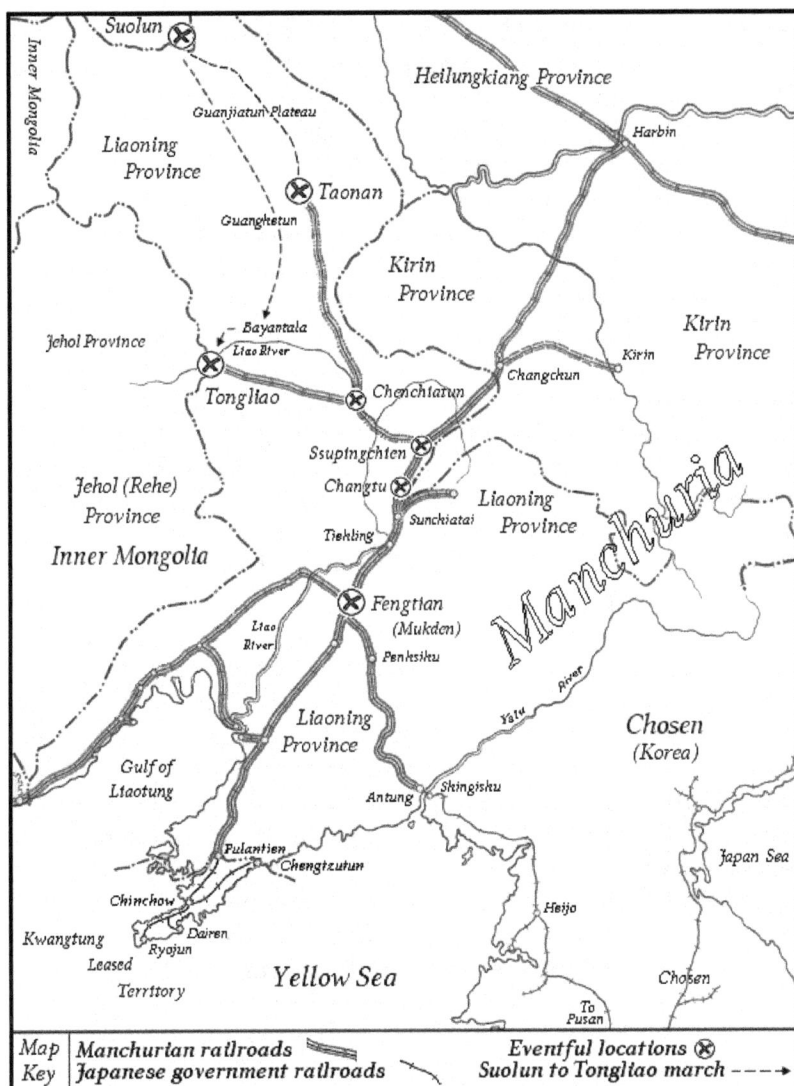

Figure 2

A map of the Omoto group's adventure in Northeast Asia, 1924 C.E.

Morihei Ueshiba's decision to accompany Onisaburo was probably the strongest indicator of the level of his loyalty and obedience. Apprehended and shackled, Onisaburo, Ueshiba, and the others of their group were quietly removed from their temporary place of incarceration (an inn) by a squad of Fengtian Army soldiers and roughly marched to an execution site where there lay strewn about many corpses of the freedom fighters of the Inner and Outer Mongolia Independence Army. (Numerous historical pictures of Onisaburo, Ueshiba, and the others as prisoners are available from sources on the Internet.) During this short march, Ueshiba exhibited protective loyalty to his spiritual master, Onisaburo, when he made several interventional attempts to stop the rough treatment that Onisaburo suffered at the hands of Zhāng's soldiers; this was dangerous for Ueshiba, for he risked immediate death, which, in this case, is associated with his piety.[64] Returning briefly to the Omoto group's short incarceration at a local inn, a Japanese guest staying at the same inn recognized the seriousness of its predicament and quickly acted to inform the Japanese Consulate in the nearby town of Chengchiatun (probably by telegraph). Fortuitously, just minutes before the group's scheduled execution, a representative of Japan's consulate arrived and intervened, thus saving them from death.[65] Seemingly, the Japanese government, or at least some Japanese colonists in Manchuria (perhaps those of the Manchukuo Chokokukai) had been monitoring their activity and whereabouts and did not want them dead. Onisaburo, Ueshiba, and the other members of the Omoto-kyo group were promptly returned to Japan by police escort, where, in the press, they received unexpectedly something like a hero's welcome. (I wonder what Hatsu, after her husband had been returned, thought of this excursion?) Prior to Onisaburo's misadventure in Manchuria, Japan's press corps, which was largely under the control of the Japanese government, had consistently disparaged the Omoto-kyo's religious foundations as largely contrary to the established, traditional view of Shinto mythology, the latter being the sovereign dominion of the Japanese Emperor.[66] This unexpected but very temporary reversal of the press's attitude toward Omoto was probably a result of the Japanese government's desire to make good use of the Omoto group's adventure as a propaganda device to highlight the hardships, efforts, and loyalty of Japanese citizens in Manchuria, which Japan was actively and slyly attempting to colonize. The Japanese government probably believed it could make

good use of this small international episode to help support its reasoning about its colonization efforts in Northeast Asia, all the while
continuing its deceptive support of Zuòlín Zhang. However, the
hero-like newspaper reports of the group's adventure were not an
indication of change in the Emperor's attitude about the popularity
of the Omoto religion, for Onisaburo went straight to jail. At what
point might loyalty or piety give rise to unreasonable behavior?

Onisaburo Deguchi and Morihei Ueshiba's ill-fated adventure in
Manchuria and Inner Mongolia occurred just before the start of
Northeast Asia's second Zhili-Fengtian War, which began in the
month of October, 1924 C.E.[67]

Interlude 2

All the members of Onisaburo's wayward group were returned
to Japan under Japanese police escort. Upon setting foot in Japan,
Onisaburo Deguchi was interred, having been earlier sentenced to
jail by a lower court after a second trial that had been held during
his absence.[68] In spite of some fanfare and popular approval, largely
a result of Japanese newspaper publicity, Onisaburo's failed plan for
a new Omoto empire in Asia only heightened the Emperor and his
government's concern about Omoto's ability to acquire power and
threaten the ruling status quo. With Onisaburo once again in jail,
Omoto-kyo's ability to further interfere with Japanese government
policies, maneuverings, and goals was curtailed for the time being.
Morihei Ueshiba returned to Ayabe and continued to carry out his
role as Omoto's Head of Agricultural Affairs as well as teach what
he now called *Ueshiba-ryu Aiki-budo*; no apparent prosecutorial action seems to have been taken by the government for his role as an
accomplice in Onisaburo's plan to create an Omoto empire, but it
could only be reasonable to think that he and other Omoto devotees
were under close observation.[69] Whatever the Japanese government
may have considered as its options for legal action against Morihei
Ueshiba, he did not likely return to an entirely pleasant familial situation with his wife. Hatsu, who had remained behind in Ayabe
with her three children, was annoyed with his participation in the
Omoto-kyo's recent escapade in Northeast Asia; as were numerous
other members of their extended family. They thought that he had
been unduly influenced by Onisaburo's charm and was inattentive

to the needs of his family.

Spiritual Traditions, Mythology, and Visioning

Up to this point I've mostly organized the events pertaining to Morihei Ueshiba's connection with piety in a timeline order, usually placing any nonconsecutive or to-be-discussed-in-the-future events within the "Interlude" subsections. Now, however, it is necessary to diverge briefly from that format (in this one subsection only) so that I can outline and discuss a collection of especially important and unique psycho-spiritual events that Ueshiba reportedly experienced. These events, his spiritual visions -- both at the time when they occurred and later when gathered together after his passing -- have had an undeniable psychosocial affect upon the shaping of Aikido's general characteristics as understood by its practitioners and considered by the public. At one far end of the spectrum, they have either imbued it with an alluring aire of mysteriosity and a promise of esoteric supernatural power or, on the opposite end, branded it as a quirky and ineffectual pseudo-martial art; the latter ignominious labeling being a special problem for Aikido's image around the world.

Shamanism has long existed amongst the peoples of Asia, with Siberian and Chinese shamanism being the prominent types that undoubtedly influenced the shaman traditions of Japan, especially those of Shinto. The activities of a shaman sometimes rely upon a psychologically altered state known as *ecstasy* to access a supposed hidden reality in order to, ostensibly, divine future events, gain esoteric knowledge, or affect a change in normal reality for the reason of assisting other people to overcome personal difficulties. This process typically includes contact with 'spirits' or 'transcendental beings.' A shaman's mastery over the condition of ecstasy includes, at the least, the psycho-spiritual techniques of trance, rapture, and separation of the soul from the body.[70] Such an altered psychological condition is self-induced by shamans through various methods of autosuggestion or rituals, which can include drumming or chanting, in order to attain a temporary psycho-spiritual condition that is said to transcend normal reality; this being the usual process. However, in addition to the aforementioned, it is sometimes facilitated by the use of a psychoactive plant extract, smoke, or vapor,[71] which, when used in spiritual, shamanic, or perhaps religious context, are known as *entheogens.*[72] Older traditional Shinto as well as the several sects of Japanese Buddhism, particularly before 1945 C.E., made use of the well-known biology of several Cannabis plant species to shape some of their spiritual characteristics -- such as rituals and trappings -- that conveyed a unique culture-dependent imagery to their devotees and other members of the public. Over the course of centuries, but prior to the end of W.W. II, the Japanese people had evolved an intricate, multifaceted relationship with the Cannabis plant. Many aspects of daily existence, comfort, and pleasure, e.g., hempen rope, garments, and intoxication, were derived therefrom.[73] Prior to Japan's Showa Period (1926-1989 C.E.), the consumption of alcohol as an intoxicant was restricted to certain privileged groups (e.g., the Emperor and his family, governing officials, the samurai). Being distilled primarily from rice, which was an important food staple, alcohol production and consumption was necessarily limited. After WWII, the cultivation and use of all Cannabis species was restricted throughout Japan by the Supreme Commander of the Allied Powers (S.C.A.P.) as part of the process of dismantling State Shinto. S.C.A.P. had identified Cannabis as one facet of the Japanese government's social control methodology that had been used to mislead its people toward supporting a national policy of unrelenting geographic expansionism.[74] In Japan today, Cannibis cultivation for the production of industrial hemp fiber or medicine is permitted by special license, but its illegality for personal use as an intoxicant is still strongly enforced. Both Shinto and Japanese Buddhism still utilize the plant's fibrous element for many of their trappings and garments. However, in spite of Japan's restrictions and strict guidelines about how the various characteristic elements of Cannabis can be used, there is anecdotal evidence to suggest that some devotees who seek to fully carry out a culturally imbued role as a highly evolved shaman may yet make use of its psychoactive effect. Before the end of W.W. II, most of the ritual ropes (*shimenawa*) used in the Shinto purification rite were woven from hemp fibers. Today, in some Aikido dojos that are aligned strongly with Aikido's Shinto heritage, there is a "high place" or altar situated on one side of the mat area that consists of a rope and many lightning-bolt-like strips of white cloth (*shide*), this being indicative of the area's sacredness. Depending on the shrine, temple, or dojo, these ropes may be woven from legally obtainable industrial hemp fiber, but some have also been woven from the fiber of rice straw. A large part of the agriculture of Japan was devoted to the growing of hemp for use in rope, cloth, paper, and spiritual uses for hundreds of years. Various Cannabis species are (and were then) naturally occurring in India and Asia, and a certain weedy (hardy) variant growing on Hokkaido Island has (and had then) an especially strong psychoactive effect upon the human brain. Though speculative, it is possible that part of Ueshiba's agricultural leadership in Shirataki (on Hokkaido) as well as in Ayabe (on Honshu) included the cultivation of Cannabis. When S.C.A.P. imposed the Cannabis Control Act in the year 1948, approximately 4000 hectares (9884 acres) of farmland in Japan had been dedicated to Cannabis growing; today, that amount has been greatly reduced to approximately 15 hectares (37 acres). Comparatively, the country of France today has dedicated approximately 8,000 hectares to the legal production of industrial hemp, medicines, and food product from Cannabis, while the United States has less than 5 legal hectares under cultivation. (However, this may change soon due to attempts by several states to legalize it.) Yet another entheogen is derived from the mushroom plant *Amanita muscaria*,[75] which is commonly used by Siberian, Korean, and Japanese shamans, past and present. Sometimes, Cannabis and Amanita are mixed, too, and either inhaled as a smoke or ingested in order to effect a state of ecstasy.

Shamanism is, generally, a personal behavioral conceptualization that gathers together a uniquely enlivened person's experience and knowledge into a form of a self-conceived spiritual vocation -- ostensibly for the reason of helping other people to quiet anxiety or allay fear, guide curiosity, cure ill health, foretell the future, reveal life's workings, or solve the mysteries of life. Such a person, known as a shaman

1) Offers theirself as a knowledge source to their community with a set of typically esoteric practices or skills (e.g., rituals, healing methods, sometimes ceremony, etc.) that can seem magical or mystical;

2) Performs services for people in accordance with the general social characteristics of a given community;

3) Acts as a 'spiritual connector' to an alternate but hypothetical realm through the practice of ecstasy, which is typified by rapture, trance, separation of the soul from the body, or visioning;

4) Has structured rituals that are used to carryout the services,

affect a change, or achieve ecstasy; and,

5) When mentally 'visiting' their alternate realm (via ecstasy), is dependent upon a 'transcended spirit' or 'transcended being' to attain the insight, understanding, or information that they seek.

Japanese Shamanism is often, but not always, the spiritual vocation of a 'lone wolf,' one where the shaman sets the initial parameters of their spiritual investigations but must largely abide by the dictates of a guardian spirit, i.e., the spiritual outcomes of a shaman's altered state of consciousness are informed or shaped by the characteristics of their guardian spirit. Though a shaman usually exists within the context of community and provide certain types of service to it -- typically divining or foretelling in quality -- they are often solitary individuals; though not so much so that they might be considered reclusive. In contrast, Shintoism, which developed gradually from Shamanism over the centuries as the idea of family (or clan) gods and family succession took hold upon Japan's collective social conscience, had been refined to such complexity that it involved a religious-like relationship with the concept of possession by gods or spirits, which was facilitated by experiencing ecstasy.[76] Before the end of W.W. II, so thoroughly had this idea been woven into the Japan's cultural identity that a majority of the Japanese people were simply 'with it,' i.e., identifying with it as something indigenous and natural.[77] It is helpful to mention that, according to the Japanese author Ichiro Hori, "*Shamanism is by no means a phenomenon peculiar to primitive societies. Among the founders of new religious movements in Japan are several with shamanistic characteristics. Even in the higher religions with their metaphysical and theological embellishments, 'enlightenment' or 'conversion' at bottom appear, despite the erudition of their philosophical elaborations, to possess a structure remarkably similar to that of shamanism.*"[78] In particular, Siberian Tungustic Shamanism has had a significant influence on the spiritual traditions in Japan. To show how any indigenous spiritual tradition can be affected by other external spiritual influences or social movements, and how these external influences can also be reshaped by any set of prevailing indigenous spiritual traditions, let's consider briefly the case of Tibetan Buddhism (Lamaism). Though popularized in the United States of America and parts of Europe as a 'true' form of Buddhism that contains and transmits many of the teachings of Shakyamuni (Siddartha Guatama) Buddha, these, in Lamaism, at the ecclesiastical level, have been undoubtedly influenced by *Tibetan Animistic Bön Shamanism* (which itself is connected to the traditions of *Siberian Shamanism* around Lake Baikal in Siberia) as well as by the native Tibetan folk spirituality called *Mi Chos*. This helps a reader to establish a better understanding of the socio-spiritual characteristics of the Japanese culture within which Morihei Ueshiba grew and matured, especially Omoto's influence upon it because Lamaism was an important subject of study for Onisaburo Deguchi during his time. (Remember, Onisaburo had hurriedly ordained Ueshiba and one other in Omoto Lamaism when their Omoto group had ventured into Northeast Asia.)

Onisaburo Deguchi seemed to exhibit often somewhat of a "lone wolf" characteristic in that he was constantly in conflict with the status quo of Japan's established Emperor System and its government, but not in the sense that he was a solitary loner, for in fact he was Omoto-kyo's spiritual dynamo, its consummate leader. Morihei Ueshiba, though having briefly experimented earlier in his life with the Japanese mountain-ascetic archetype and at this time somewhat influenced by Onisaburo's teachings, was beginning to shape an approach to life that was different than that of his spiritual teacher; he cannot be thoroughly associated, as can Onisaburo, with the characteristics that identify a shaman. An example of this difference can be found is his move from Ayabe to Tokyo where he begins to use his martial knowledge and skill to increase his involvement in the training the men of Japan's military, thereby showing an unwillingness to oppose the prevailing Japanese zeitgeist. (In one sense, the latter is a form of piety, i.e., dedication to support of the existing form of society and its governance by those who control.) Morihei Ueshiba, who was certainly a uniquely enlivened person, never presented himself to his community as a man who was frequently 'voyaging' to an alternate spiritual realm in order to obtain answers to the problems that were, and are today, typically brought before a shaman; e.g., foretelling of future events (which was Onisaburo's behavior). Instead, Ueshiba experienced visions and therefrom received (divined, i.e., spiritually discovered) answers to certain perplexing martial problems.

Mysticism is, basically, the idea that a person can, through the implementation of certain esoteric processes that are comprised of specialized cognitive or other behavioral techniques

1) Experience and understand the meaning of heretofore unknown phenomenon that are inaccessible in normal cognitive reality (objective reality); and,

2) Achieve a 'oneness' with the Absolute, the Infinite, or the Divine, and where such a metaphysical argument has acquired a degree of 'validity' over the course of time by the presence of a vast collection of distinctive practices (e.g., rituals, methods of attaining ecstasy, etc.), oral transmissions, and written records that attest to its relative 'truth' within the context of an individual-dependent subjective reality or *metareality* rather than objective reality.[79]

Aspects of mysticism are clearly evident in Japan's spiritual traditions of Shamanism, Shintoism, Buddhism, and Shugendo. Though each of these are syncretic to some degree or another, the Shugendo tradition of past and present is probably the best example of the social phenomenon of Syncretism in Japan today; and those people who practice it are typically referred to as either *shugenja*, meaning "a person of training and testing" or as *yamabushi*, meaning literally "mountain concealment," but figuratively as "one who lies hidden in the mountains." During Ueshiba's stint as a mountain ascetic, it seems that his behavior was more characteristic of shugenja rather than yamabushi.

The basic features of Shamanism, Shintoism, and Mysticism as well as those characteristic of the altered mental state of ecstasy have now been sufficiently outlined to enable reasonable considerations about Morihei Ueshiba's visions from a cultural perspective; but, this is probably not sufficient to produce either an explanation of the reason for their occurrence or a thorough understanding of the general quality of his several visions. What could modern scientific methodology and its analyses of the many facets of the human condition have to offer toward explaining his visions, especially from the viewpoint of the interconnected sciences of Neurology and Psychology? For example, is there anything good to be said of a calmed, focused, or meditative state of mind, where during such a mental state, a person's cognitive processing may produce an envisioning of a solution to a problem? These are questions that I'll attend to later.

Two primary considerations that can help to develop a better understanding of Morihei Ueshiba's visioning and its relationship to piety are those of *1)* his psychological relationship with Syncretism and *2)* whether he could be considered as a warrior personality (i.e., a man primarily oriented to martial attitude and action) with the characteristics of a shaman or, more generally, a warrior personality with the characteristics of a mystic. Obviously, he was born into a culture where not only did native folk spiritual traditions exist (e.g., Shinto) but also one in which there existed both esoteric Buddhism (Shingon, Tendai, Zen) and Syncretism (e.g., Omoto-kyo, Shugendo). From earlier in this chapter we know that

1) Ueshiba was formally schooled as well as self-taught in Japanese esoteric Buddhism (including knowledge of ancient Buddhist warrior-monk sects) and seemed to archetypically identify with the visioning that had reportedly been experienced by the Japanese Buddhist monk Kukai;

2) Being born Japanese, he was naturally exposed to every facet of Shinto during the course of his life;

3) For a while he pursued mountain asceticism combined with martial training, with a few people thinking him to be similar to tengu;

4) Prior to enlisting in the military, he had been certified by a Shingon Buddhist priest as having obtained a certain stage of Buddhist spiritual enlightenment;

5) He joined the Japanese Imperial Army in the early 1900s and probably saw combat;

7) He pursued consistently martial training and esoteric knowledge during the entire course of his life;

8) When not teaching budo he was actively, thoughtfully, and spiritually involved with agriculture;

9) He thoroughly immersed himself in the teachings and mission of the Omoto-kyo, itself a syncretic Shinshukyo, while also, it appears, observing many of the rituals and rites of Shinto as well as those of Esoteric Buddhism;

10) He had been ordained, though hurriedly and perhaps out of necessity, by Onisaburo Deguchi in *Omoto Lamaism*, remember, when they entered Guanjiatun in northwestern Manchuria;

11) While accompanying Onisaburo on their ill-fated Omoto-kyo adventure in Northeastern Asia, he engaged in combat; and,

12) Occurring shortly after he and Onisaburo returned from Mongolia, he had reportedly experienced an ecstasy-like vision that emerged for him a personal, though subjective, enlightenment.

Can these behaviors, acts, and experiences be considered as characteristic of a *sōhei*, i.e., a Buddhist warrior monk, or perhaps, those of a something a little different, such as a *warrior mystic*? The 13th Century C.E. Buddhist warrior-monk named Eizon, who paved the way for the development of several Japanese yoga disciplines, was of this archetype -- a historical personage amongst many, but one of whom Ueshiba was probably knowledgeable. However, most sohei were typically Buddhist and banded together to act from the position of group power. During Ueshiba's time, priests of the Japanese syncretic spiritual tradition of Shugendo still emphasized the use of warrior-like equipment, garments, and trappings; with little doubt we can think that he must have been aware of this, too. Ueshiba's mountain sojourns, which reportedly had, in addition to their physicality, both an introspective and ascetic quality, were, when the behavior of introspection is considered, more characteristic of a *shugenja* than of a *yamabushi* because he did not tend to be reclusive or eremetic. Unlike a shaman, he did not make himself thoroughly and solely available to his community for shamanistic reasons only, such as for divination, as would the typical shaman; but it is probable that his advice in matters that would typically be brought before a shaman -- or for that matter before a Buddhist monk or Shinto priest -- was sought by some people on some occasions. Instead, he made himself available as a 'guru' of agricultural matters and all things martial; yet he also had a strong reverence for all things spiritual as well as a strong relationship with piety. Generally, he seems to align better with the definition of Mysticism rather than with that of Shamanism. Certainly, some of Ueshiba's unique sense of spirituality was at this time forming, but it was not until later, especially after 1942 C.E., that he began to thoroughly mix his syncretic and subjective spirituality with his martial teachings to eventually form a quasi-theologically oriented philosophy, called *Takemusu Aiki*,[80] which could later be associated with his Aiki-budo. However, Kisshomaru Ueshiba during his post W.W. II reconfiguration of the Zaidan Hojin Aikikai (the Aikikai Foundation) never fully implemented his father's proposed philosophy, probably because he found it to be too subjectively derived for it to be useful in the development of what would eventually become known as Aikikai Aikido (from Ueshiba-ryu Aiki-budo) in a world where Japan was sorely in need of divorcing itself from its myth-driven governance and militarism.[81] So, the evidence points to an Ueshiba who -- after having *1)* conditioned his youthful vitality and attributes during ascetic mountain training; *2)* fought in the Russo-Japanese War; *3)* led a group of settlers in an agricultural effort on Hokkaido; 4) engaged the learning of Omoto-kyo spirituality; *5)* achieved a large degree of autonomy in his ability to teach Daito-ryu Jujutsu; *6)* accompanied Onisaburo into Mongolia on an ill-fated Omoto adventure; *7)* learned the foundational teachings of Omoto spirituality; and, upon his return from Mongolia, *8)* returned to his teaching of budo and work in agriculture -- was well on a path of self-development that began to reveal his personality as a type of a warrior mystic rather than that of a shaman or warrior monk. However, he was yet missing one essential experience that would thoroughly, in retrospect, qualify him as a mystic -- that of ecstasy. Sometime after he had returned from Mongolia in mid 1925 C.E., Morihei Ueshiba, shortly after a vigorous, competitive bout (shiai) with a navy officer who was highly skilled in kendo, experienced his first spiritual vision. According to an account of this event that was given by his son (Kisshomaru Ueshiba), the ground trembled as golden vapors of ki welled up from underneath his feet and, as the 'golden ki' gently enveloped him, he was transformed into a 'golden body' that was marvelously etheric in quality, whereupon he 'expanded' outward into the Universe and, as he became unified with It, he realized that a warrior must thoroughly manifest the 'Divine Love' which has been bequeathed to people by the gods (kami).[82] It is at this point, immediately following his vision, that Morihei Ueshiba could be considered as a self-styled warrior mystic, in my opinion, whose most revered, perhaps guardian, deity was *Sarutahiko no Mikoto*, with the diety Susanoo-no Mikoto positioned in second place.[83]

If Ueshiba's vision had occurred differently he would have related it differently, don't you think? For example, he could have said something like: *After participating in shiai with a highly skilled kendoka, I realized that even a warrior should manifest 'Divine Love' when engaged in a contest for his life.* Or, he could have said it a little different, like this: *After pondering from several different men-*

tal angles a difficult martial problem and its relationship to the expectations of society, I engaged a highly skilled kendoka in shiai. Shortly after it ended, I suddenly realized the importance of 'Divine Love' as it relates to the opponent when engaged in a contest for one's life. (Of course, all this talk about 'Divine Love' is interesting, especially as we consider Ueshiba's later role in the training of military men in bayonet use and other fine points of fighting.) To be fair, we must assume that the story about his vision is accurate, and what happened was that which was described first. However, this brings us to an important question. Why did Ueshiba experience this enlightenment, and any of his later ones, as he did? Not unexpectedly, that question returns us to those two questions mentioned above which concern what modern science might have to offer toward explaining his visioning.

Undoubtedly, there can be no analysis that will satisfy all the questions that any person might formulate and ask of any other person about anyone or about any particular thing or phenomenon because the innate condition of human existence is such that a certain part of it is entirely subjective, i.e., subject to the mental processing of the individual, and this may include imaginings or mental pictures that are influenced by the circumstances of their familial and societal upbringing. Sometimes when I'm in a favorite coffeehouse writing, I attempt to mentally grasp the essence of Morihei Ueshiba's life. With my eyes closed, I mull over the stories of his experiences, then think of mine, compare and contemplate, and await for the moment when there will enter my thoughts what I believe is something useful to relate to the reader. It is not easy to arrive at a reasoned positioned on many of the matters that I have presented herein because I'm neither Japanese nor from his era. I can relate well to personal challenge, trials and tribulations, for I, as well as all other people both past and present have had these. I have not experienced visions, neither voluntary nor involuntary. However, I have benefited from the experience of enlightenment, so to speak, i.e., a suddenly occurring understanding or realization about some problem or phenomenon; but I have not interpreted these occurrences as a spiritual or religious experience. Today, the modern sciences of Neurology and Psychology have enabled investigation into the workings of the human mind that have never before been possible. Some of those investigations have revealed the following information.

1) **Psychoactive plant components or extracts** have an undeniable and specific mind altering effect on the cognition of any human brain, and these produce an altered mental state that frequently include imaginings or hallucinations;

2) **Pareidolia**, a benign mental condition or state where a person can experience awake imaginings or hallucinations while cognitively functioning nominally (i.e., without any brain anomaly or disorder), can be either externally induced by the circumstances of their environment or self-induced, and is a psychological phenomenon well know to affect those people with an inclination or desire for a certain type of religious experience;

3) **Transcranial Magnetic Stimulation** (TMS), where a person's brain is stimulated with certain electromagnetic waveforms, typically produces the temporary effect of hyperreligiosity in the subject;

4) **Temporal Lobe Epilepsy**, a human brain disorder, almost always causes hyperreligiosity;

5) **Schizophrenia**, another human brain disorder, causes the person thus affected to imagine voices, experience paranoid delusions, and have, generally, disorganized thinking;

6) **Hypnosis**, a psychological method that calms the mind by greatly reducing the extent to which extra-body sensory stimulation enters the sensory cortices of the brain, can increase consciousness in the 'here-and-now' as well as help in remembering obscure memories.

7) **Apophenia** is the mental condition or state of a person that enables them to experience or identify 'meaningful' patterns in seemingly meaningless randomness (often subjective in character);

8) **Hierophany** is the name given to describe an experience that is claimed by a person to be a manifestation of the sacred, which includes claims of an appearance of a deity (largely if not entirely subjective in character); and,

9) **Left-brain Confabulation**, a nominal (normal) brain function, predisposes the left hemisphere of the human brain to suggest or come up with the best possible answer to explain inconvenient facts or events when its given state of consciousness does not include the necessary information to generate an answer that correlates the new sensory input

with its known experiences (In other words, when confronted with data that "does not compute," the left-brain makes an 'on-the-fly' hypothesis, which may or may not result in an approximate, let alone accurate, evaluation of the actual fact or event. This seemingly peculiar way in which the brain operates is probably involved to a certain extent in the psychological phenomena of pareidolia, apophenia, and hierophany).

It has been proposed by some researchers that *pareidolia*, when combined with *apophenia* and *hierophany*, may have helped early humans and their societies organize chaotic events and make sense out of their world as the mental faculty of consciousness of each member gradually changed or evolved.[84] Mircea Eliade, a very well-known religious historian and author informs us that spirituality and religion manifest with their peculiar characteristics because of a sharp distinction between that which is considered as sacred in contrast to that which is adjudged to be profane. According to Eliade, for traditional man -- as contrasted to a modern man who questions the value of spirituality and religion with his secular mindset -- myths describe as well as announce "*breakthroughs of the sacred (or the 'supernatural') into the World*" and serve to draw attention to the "*mysterium tremendum et fascinans*" of inexplicable phenomenon, typically in the form of hierophanies.[85] In mythical hierophany, the sacred appears in the form of an idealized sociologic model whose characteristics are pertinent or significant to the place and era into which it has entered (e.g., the visual characteristics and acts of a deity). By manifesting itself in this way, the sacred self-generates its credentials (its 'truth') while at the same time inspiring in its subject the feelings of awe and alluring fascination, thereby imparting to the world (the subject's desired view of it) a certain value (quality of experience) that has, upon its very occurrence, reflected back into the mentality of the subject where it lodges itself permanently as awesome and transfixing, and from which experience the subject is bequeathed or derives a certain direction and purpose. For the subject to be able to affirm the truth of such an experience and accept it as valid in reality (i.e., his or her reality), it is necessary that all the characteristics of such an experience replicate or conform to the models of sacred that have been previously established within their culture. Mircea Eliade informs us that, for a traditional man or woman, all aspects of life -- the existence of things, the events or work-ings of Nature, and the acts of people -- *"acquire their reality, their identity, only to the extent of their participation in a transcendent reality."*[86] What aspects of Morihei Ueshiba's behavior might con-form to Eliade's "traditional man," in the Japanese sense? Well, such has already been answered, hasn't it?

Though Morihei Ueshiba was very spiritual, he never ardently pursued a thoroughgoing identification with 'full on' religious devo-tion, as is the case with people who have actually become ordained as a priest. Instead, his spiritual piety manifested as it did as a re-sult of a personality that had conformed to a "traditional man" mod-el, albeit, a Japanese version, as influenced by Onisaburo's teach-ings. When this assertion is combined with the facts and determin-ations previously mentioned, identifying Morihei Ueshiba as the quintessential embodiment of a *Japanese warrior mystic* is not at all difficult.[87] In realizing this, is it not reasonable to consider him as the originator or giver of the truth of aiki, or, in his conceptuali-zation and terminology, "Takemusu Aiki"? In this sense, one could consider his form of Aikido -- known today as Aikikai Aikido -- as a unique Japanese *physio-spiritual discipline*, which he began to form when he retreated to Iwama in 1942 C.E., but later, following W.W. II, more thoroughly developed by his son, Kisshomaru Ueshiba. No Aikido style, not even the Aikikai style, is wholly a spiritual tradi-tion, because any style's purported philosophical theory is unified with both physical theory and physical techniques that have been derived from Budo, which latter reside in objective, physical reality. But, in its idealized conceptualization, that of the Aikikai organiza-tion, Aikido is a physio-spiritual discipline wherein its technical theory is guided as well as shaped by a spiritual philosophy called Takemusu Aiki. (Compare this to the general definition of Aikido in Chapter I.) However, the theory of Takemusu Aiki is not the ba-sis for all Aikido styles. It is additionally important to understand that the body of ideas that constitute the metaphysical theory of Takemusu Aiki are derived and intricately woven from Buddhism, Shinto, Shugendo, and several precursor Japanese martial arts, and that Ueshiba's particular fusion of the physical reality of martial movements with his esoteric, subjective, myth based, and syncretic spiritual claims, i.e., his esoteric metaphysical theory, was not ad-vanced as such until after W.W. II. Following W.W. II, Morihei Ueshiba remained in seclusion until the year 1956, and when he emerged he began to present his reformed, martial-derived discipline, with the help of Kisshomaru Ueshiba and other sensei, to the public. Sometime after this, but before the publication of Aikikai Aikido's book entitled **Takemusu Aiki** in 1976, the elder Ueshiba expressed that "... ai*kido is a religion without being a religion.*"[88] So, is Aikido a religion, or is it a martial art? It must be one or the other, because the two concepts -- a spiritual path to God and martial activity -- are probably quite mutually exclusive, especially when contemplating what could be considered to be the best spiritual methodology by which one may commune with a transcended being or God, which, incidentally, should probably be without a weapon in hand. Aikido, no matter the style, is not a discipline in the sense of that which typically characterizes religion. Notwithstanding, today, many aikidoka, some Shintoists, and some New Age followers seem to want to use it as a ritualized vehicle to advance a religious or social movement agenda. It would have been much better for solidarity amongst the aikidoka of all styles if something like *Aikido is a spiritual path without being a religion* could have been said, which would have probably precluded Aikido's present distress.

If the reader would contemplate the spiritual characteristics of the numerous religious movements of past and present, *particularly those where weapons have been or are involved*, it is not too difficult to mentally apprehend how the activities and rituals of some Aikido groups could be considered as characteristic of *cultism*. The general characteristics of a spiritual or religious *cult* are

1) A reliance upon an intricately constructed hypothetical body of ritual, typically offered up by a dynamic and convincing leader who has produced his or her answer(s) to various social and spiritual problems as -- though hypothetical, subjective, and often egocentrically arranged in its conceptualization and methodology -- a rallying call and micro-social 'insemination' so that there can 'sprout' a growing new reality for the group's members or overall society toward what is suggested as a 'proper' or 'better' relationship to Nature, the spirits, God, or the gods;

2) An offer of esoteric spiritual methods by the implementation of which the devotee can acquire special but subjectively arrived at knowledge that may be useful toward self-

empowerment;

3) An organizational basis, which is comprised of its philo-sophic teachings, administrative functions, and public mes-sages, that is constructed in a manner where it attracts a re-latively small number of devotees when contrasted to other larger spiritual traditions;

4) A tendency toward factionalization or dissolution due to inconsistent, incoherent, or controversial teachings and a weak sociological, i.e., organizational, structure;

5) A tendency to discourage contact of its devotees with mem-bers of the general public, especially those who have pre-viously been friends or are family; and,

6) If associated with purposefully obscured or secret aspects, can be considered an *occult*, i.e., a cult with hidden esoteric rituals and teachings that are performed or taught only in secret because such secrecy is deemed necessary in order to obscure any non-benevolent characteristics, and where the meaning of these may not even be known to all of its de-votees.

To illustrate my concern when weapons are involved, I'll dis-cuss the reverence given to a katana, which is a particular type of Japanese sword. Among the numerous foundational characteristics of Shinto, there is one that concerns the profanity of the shedding of blood, which it considers to be impure. Interestingly, several of its rituals make use of the katana, whose design is specifically e-volved to be decisively effective in killing a living being -- the out-come of which, besides death, is the letting of much blood. So, on one hand Shinto abhors the shedding of blood, but on the other, it includes in many of its rituals a weapon that, when used for its in-tended purpose, typically results in bloodletting. Even if the intent of Shinto's sword related rituals are simply for the reason of imag-ing certain philosophical ideas or mirroring certain indigenous so-cial constructs or values, this type of relationship with the sword is untenably incongruous. Though the intricacies of this problematic relationship are neither easily discerned nor culturally unwound, here is a large dish of the human spiritual tendency served up with a dash of absurdity. Though numerous accomplished martial artists who make use of edged weapons will express again and again that the primary reason to practice with such is to clarify the mind so that it may focus keenly on the here-and-now, which they consider to be a method useful toward bettering themselves, they are obviously using a weapon known for its killing effectiveness. Similarly, though the devotees of Shinto will tell you that the weapon is used only as an implement to accentuate the meaning of a certain part of a ritual and that such an event is 'traditional,' what is meant is that they make use of the innate characteristics of the katana to bring into an observer's mind a clear mental image of purposeful design in order to briefly draw it away from a multitude of fleeting or chaotic thoughts so that it is sharply focused on the ritual, which process serves as a small and preparatory neurological 'slatecleaning,' thereby making the necessary and useful 'psychological cut' into which a graft of traditional Japanese culture, according to the Shinto viewpoint, may be permanently embedded into their mind. In every instance and place where it happens, a well-crafted ritual can be considered as a strong and useful psychological tool.[89] When a spiritual tradition incorporates the use of imagery of weapons within their rituals or when a martial art associates its technical foundation with a spirituality derived from the mythical acts of mythical deities, e.g., offering up a weapon in an honorific manner to thereby evidence a weapon's divine quality -- irregardless of any reasoning offered to justify such, and even if the ritual act is a salute to humility -- there emerges slowly and surely an unavoidable psychological reshaping of a person's mentality wherein they construct and imprint into their mind some type of belief that the weapon connects them to the energy that animates a transcended being in an otherworldly realm. However, the observance of such ritual does not guarantee that the weapon will not be used to commit an accidental, unthinking, unjust, or outright brutal act of violence. Despite the cautionary statements from many sword masters to inform us that the ethical calling of the study of sword fighting is to challenge one's own mind to recognize the seriousness of life so that one might attain a state of higher consciousness, which, when attained, ideally expresses a *magnanimity of the heart*, there have been innumerable acts of brutality with sword in hand.[90] (This is not to say that such has not occurred in other countries, too, for it has.) What happens when one who 'plays with swords' (or with any weapon) cannot find the necessary magnanimity of the heart to prevent an unreasonable, unjustified act of violence? (See Chapter VII for further discussion.) Assuming the reader has read the preface of this book, let us recall the outcome of the sword engagement between Heike prince Atsumori and samurai Naozane.[91] Such a sociological problem has existed in some cultures of past societies and exists today, too; e.g., respectively, the ancient Norse peoples and some Cargo Cults of today. The Japanese katana, or any other configuration of the sword, was especially designed as a warfare implement for the purpose of slashing, cleaving, or piercing flesh and bone; it was not first conceived of as a religious ritual implement, though it was and is sometimes used as such.[92] In my opinion, ritual implements that are used to evidence or connect with a supposed benevolent life-giving deity or metaphysical force, or chase away evil spirits, etc., should neither be a weapon nor an idealized image of a weapon, and all religious icons, rituals, writings, and teachings should not reflect an association with weaponry. Today, Morihei Ueshiba's Takemusu Aiki metaphysical theory is not embraced by all aikidoka.

The sword of the Imperial Regalia of Japan, the *Kusanagi-no-Tsurugi*, possibly shaped like a leaf of the calamus plant, and which is bestowed with the concept of valor by virtue of its time-honored associations with the deities of Japanese mythology, is a sacred and highly revered quasi-mythical object from which all traditionally crafted Japanese edged weapons -- which sometimes receive blessings of variable meaning by a Shinto priest at the onset of their forging -- derive their reverential quality.[93] As related by Japanese mythology, the Kusanagi-no-Tsurugi sword was supposedly discovered and retrieved by the mythical deity Susanoo-no-Mikoto, and later given by him to *Amaterasu-no-Mikoto* (goddess of the Sun and Universe) who then passed it on to her son *Ninigi-no-Mikoto*, who himself was later sent to Earth in order to 'pacify' Japan, bringing with him the *Three Sacred Treasures* -- those being the sword known as *Kusanagi-no-Tsurugi*, the *Yata-no-Kagami* mirror, and the jewel know as *Yasatani-no-Magatama*. These treasures, according to legend, remained on the islands of Japan and became identified and revered as the Imperial Regalia of Japan; they are ostensibly kept hidden and secure somewhere in the Atsuta Shinto Shrine, but it is uncertain as to whether they exist because no verifiable showing of them has occurred since 688 C.E. Today, the Kusanagi-no-Tsurugi sword is believed by some people to be imbued with the spirit of *Amaterasu-no-Mikoto.* The reverence bestowed upon edged weapons by some people of Japanese society, or by non-Japanese thusly inclined, is primarily a result of the attendant psychological and sociological influences whenever the mythical tales of Susanoo-no-Mikoto, Amaterasu-no-Mikoto, and Sarutahiko-no-Mikoto -- that is, Shinto's myths -- are taught, but in combination with its obvious use as a weapon. The complexity of the various forms of Japan's spiritual traditions are sometimes difficult to fathom because much of the information that comes unto any thinker's cognition from which they might begin an analysis (e.g., historical regression analysis) has largely emerged out of an ancient peoples' needs and responses within their indigenous environment. Over a long course of time, both superstitions and literary creativity shaped the recounting of some of their experiences into the unverifiable stories that are today recorded and told as myth. This process of myth-making is apparent in other cultures, too. For example, the Briton legend of King Arthur and the mysterious qualities of his sword Excalibur and its scabbard, which, interestingly, is considered by most enthusiasts of Arthurian Legend to be a sign of rightful sovereignty when gripped and wielded by a person whom the sword has magically identified as a blood-related heir to Arthur. The association of a weapon or other items with a divine right to sovereignty is a recurring archetypical theme throughout the world in many societies. Returning to Japanese mythology, some scholarly researchers and learned aikidoka in the recent past have tried to make sense of these myths in order to determine what portions of them, if any at all, are intrinsically valid so that they might obtain some evidence that supports Morihei Ueshiba's metaphysical theory of Takemusu Aiki. In my opinion, when a theory or philosophy is constructed from or around a body of myth, especially where that mythology is seemingly fantastical in its presentation, and where little effort is given to exposing its weaknesses and thereby revealing what truth it holds (other than its quality as myth), there can only result a new myth based upon the previous mythology. In his book entitled *The Spirit of Aikido*, Kisshomaru Ueshiba, sensing this problem, made a request of all aikidoka for *"a scientific explanation..."* while *"listening to what foreign students of aikido have to say..."* about Aikido; this was wise of him.[94]

After his first vision, Morihei Ueshiba had two more that were publicly revealed. The second happened in December of the year 1940 C.E. Then, after moving to Iwama in 1942 C.E., Ueshiba experienced his third vision, one which is described as happening during the worst fighting of W.W. II and refers probably to the Battles of Coral Sea and Midway in May and June respectively of the same year.

Interlude 3

After Morihei Ueshiba had been returned under police escort from Mongolia to Japan in 1924 C.E., life begins to unfold a little differently for him. The newspaper accounts of the Omoto group's venture in Northeastern Asia is described by and large as beneficial to Japan's prestige; notwithstanding, Onisaburo is returned to jail. Having resumed his teaching Aiki-budo and agricultural duties in Ayabe, Ueshiba is encouraged by Onisaburo to dissociate from the Omoto-kyo and move to the Tokyo area to teach, as he, Onisaburo, is uncertain as to how long he might be jailed. It has been stated by some historians that Onisaburo had suggested this to Ueshiba because such would move him and his family away from Ayabe, thus insulating them from further personal distress if the Japanese government acted to again harass and suppress the Omoto-kyo religion. Ueshiba, as mentioned earlier, is not prosecuted but instead, due to his connection with Admiral Seikyo Asano who had become a student of Ueshiba's, is spoken of as a highly skilled budoka and capable teacher to Admiral Isamu Takeshita, who was another prominent and influential military man with a strong personal interest in Budo. Asano had likely heard from Onisaburo (either indirectly via an intermediary or directly if he visited him in jail) or directly from Ueshiba about the Omoto group's difficulties and fighting in Mongolia, which further impressed him with Ueshiba's bujutsu ability. At this point, it is probable that Asano expressed to Takeshita the idea that it might be worthwhile to consider Ueshiba as a candidate to help the Japanese military strengthen its preparedness and fighting capability. Prior to Omoto-kyo's escapade in the northeast of Asia, Ueshiba had already been teaching naval personnel at the navy base in Maizuru, which was near to Ayabe. This can be considered as having been a fortuitous opportunity for the military to analyze his character and overall martial skill. At some point in the year 1925 C.E., Admiral Takeshita visited Ayabe for the reason of meeting Ueshiba and to view a demonstration of his Aiki-budo. In 1925 C.E., yet another Japanese 'peace preservation' law called the

Chian-iji-ho (Public Security Preservation Law) was passed, which further strengthened the government's ability to restrict freedom of speech and assembly. Having sought out and met Morihei Ueshiba earlier in 1926 C.E., Kenji Tomiki began to study from Ueshiba in Ayabe during the summer of 1927 C.E. Sometime between the latter part of December of 1926 C.E. and May of 1927 C.E., Onisaburo, who was then languishing in jail and had been awaiting week after week for the Japanese high court's decision on his second appeal, is informed that the Emperor Taisho has died; Japanese law during that time provided for the pardon and release of people who had been incarcerated for political reasons. Onisaburo is pardoned and released from jail in the month of May, 1927 C.E.[95] Soon thereafter, Onisaburo began to reevaluate Japan's political climate and formulates a different and somewhat perplexing approach to injecting his idea's of social reform or support into its society, which includes, once again, Ueshiba's involvement. (Review Onisaburo's incarceration during this time; see endnote 68 in this chapter). Meanwhile, Admiral Takeshita organized a demonstration of Ueshiba's Aiki-budo, and later in the year of 1927 C.E., Ueshiba visited Tokyo to demonstrate his Aiki-budo to various important political and military personages. During the month of September in the same year, Ueshiba and family moved to Tokyo, and a temporary dojo in Shiba (part of the greater Tokyo metropolis) was set up not too far from their residence. In 1930 C.E., Ueshiba and family moved to Mejiro, which is another part of the greater Tokyo metropolis, and set up another temporary dojo. During the autumn of this year, Jigoro Kano (the founder of modern Judo), who was dedicated to the goal of recording the old Jujutsu styles that had begun to vanish in Japan as a result of the modernization of its military, visited and observed Ueshiba's Aiki-budo. (See Chapter V for more information about Jigoro Kano's visit to Morihei Ueshiba.) Between late 1927 C.E. and 1937 C.E., Ueshiba taught top military men and civilian government persons; thusly, there gradually developed a ruling class awareness of Ueshiba's budo skill and his important potential as a loyal participant in strengthening the fighting capability of the Japanese military. This, once again, can be considered as an occurrence of piety, i.e., his dedicated participatory role in the prevailing military agenda, which by this time had been moving toward facilitating Japan's expansion into Northeast Asia. Much later, Kisshomaru Ueshiba disclosed that his father had regularly taught Aiki-budo classes at the Japanese Naval Staff College (the *Kaigun Daigakkō*, i.e., the Naval War College) from late 1927 C.E. until early 1937 C.E.[96] During this time period, Sokaku Takeda would find it necessary to visit Morihei Ueshiba in order to demand the teaching fees due to him according to their teacher/student financial agreement; Ueshiba was frequently amiss in his duty to pay the fees due to Takeda. In 1931 C.E., after thoroughly embracing his country's military establishment, Morihei Ueshiba moved to Ushigome (a part of the greater Tokyo metropolis) and, with the help of Admiral Takeshita and the beneficent Ogasawara family, established the *Kobukan dojo*, meaning *Imperial warrior hall* dojo; due to the type of training that occurred there (i.e., combat oriented), its student's dubbed it the "Hell Dojo of Ushigome."[97]

On June 4, 1928 C.E., the Manchurian military governor Zuòlín Zhāng was assassinated by an operative of the Japanese Kantōgun (Kwantung) Army, which at that time was garrisoned at Ryōjun (Port Arthur) on the Liaodong Peninsula of Manchuria; though he was succeeded by a somewhat competent interim ruler, his son Xuelian Zhāng, Manchuria's economy and civil order subsequently collapsed. Three years later the Kantogun Army, on September 18, 1931 C.E., in an attempt to craft a 'legitimate' way to 'justify' an invasion of Manchuria in order to 'restore' civil order, purposefully initiated another explosive false-flag operation in the proximity of the city of Fengtian (Shenyang), which incident the Army used as its 'reasoning' to invade Manchuria. (This incident is known to the Chinese as the *Liutiaohu Incident*, but to the Japanese it is known as the *Manchurian Incident*.) Onisaburo, earlier freed from jail, returned to Ayabe to take care of Omoto's mundane matters. While doing so, he realized that Ueshiba's unique potential was becoming recognized by influential officers in the Japanese military, e.g., Admiral Takeshita's interest in Ueshiba. During this time, Ueshiba's Aikibudo had also become recognized by other higher government officials (due the efforts of Admirals Asano and Takeshita) as an advanced style of budo that was worthy of evaluation alongside of Judo and Kendo for military purposes. Onisaburo's ever-present desire to inject his ideas into Japanese society still motivated him, even under the pall of the government's continuing hostility to both him and the Omoto-kyo. As a result, Onisaburo conceived the idea that he could reestablish Omoto's vigorous role in Japanese society with Ueshiba's help by forming within the Omoto-kyo a different and legitimate department whose activities consisted of and were shaped by Aiki-budo, but this was only an *omote-muki* 'face'; from the *ura-muki* perspective, Onisaburo began to consider a different but hidden plan. While Ueshiba was continuing to strengthen his relationship with the established Japanese ruling elite, Onisaburo decided to get cozy with several ultranational organizations, i.e., the *Gen'yōsha* (Dark Ocean Society) and the *Kokuryūkai* (Black Dragon Society), for assistance in advancing Omoto's vision of Japan's future. In 1932 C.E., Onisaburo formed the *Dai Nippon Budo Sen'yokai* (Society to Promote Japanese Martial Arts). Out of loyalty to his spiritual master, Ueshiba agreed to participate in Onisaburo's new endeavor; though considering Omoto's past problems with Japan's government, he probably should not have done so. The Dai Nippon Budo Sen'yokai was a covert attempt to develop a security force (or possibly a paramilitary force) whose purpose would have been to protect the Omoto-kyo from government harassment. Its openly stated (omote-muki) or supposed mission -- to assist the goals of Japan's government through the furtherance of an 'imperial budo' (*Kobukan* means *imperial warrior hall* or, better, *imperial warrior training hall*) -- was, in part, meant to be a distractive facade while serving as a covert methodology by which Onisaburo could purposefully and discretely probe Ueshiba's military connections for intelligence about the Japanese government's agenda or plans (this being his ura-muki purpose). The ultranational factions with which Onisaburo had aligned the Omoto-kyo had a different agenda for Northeast Asia (or at least a different timetable) than that of Japan's then prevailing government. The former had minimal regard for the international politics with which the relatively inexperienced, uncoordinated, sometimes corrupt, and frequently politically ambiguous Japanese Diet were necessarily concerned. Whether or not Ueshiba had been fully aware of Onisaburo's omote-muki/ura-muki scheme is unclear. However, it is known that during the early 1930s the right-wing militaristic faction called the Sakurakai (the Cherry Blossom Society) met frequently at his Kobukan dojo to train and converse. Ueshiba was conveniently absent when these meetings were held, but they were held with his knowledge.[98] Though often cooperative as a result of their common ties, the Omoto religion, Onisaburo, and Ueshiba were each motivated by their own unique personal 'calling' and individual agendas. Onisaburo had a different view of the hierarchical order of importance of his culture's pertinent top-level kami that conflicted with those promulgated by the Emperor and wanted a future for Japan where he and his Omoto following could be free of government restrictions and oppression; but, by this time, he had garnered the sympathy of and become acquainted with those ultranational factions whose covert efforts were directed toward obtaining complete control of Northeast Asia, which frequently found themselves opposed to the plans of the Japan's homeland government. Ueshiba, on the other hand, wanted to pursue a budo career, and having come from a family that had traditionally supported and honored the Japanese Emperor as the head of state, embraced the military (which was a time-honored instrument of the Emperor) as his primary means of achieving his personal goal. As a result, Onisaburo and Ueshiba, though some-what yet bonded in friendship by their shared experiences in and with the Omoto religion, were headed in opposite sociopolitical directions.

Upon consideration of some of the more obvious facts that per-tain to Morihei Ueshiba's personality, he shows us a reoccurring behavioral inability to say 'No,' which prevented him from choosing a different personal direction when certain types of difficult inter-personal social dynamics existed. The significant occasions when he had been unable to refuse participation, but when he probably should have, were

1) Onisaburo's request that he participate in Omoto's venture into Mongolia in 1924 C.E.;
2) Onisaburo's request of him to act as the Aiki-budo teacher for the Dai Nippon Budo Sen'yokai and to assist in the car-rying out its administrative duties in 1932 C.E.;
3) The occurrence of numerous and sundry meetings of the far right-wing Sakurakai society at his Kobukan dojo; and,
4) The psychological lure that consisted of attention from the Japanese ruling classes and a once-in-a-lifetime opportunity to make his reputation as a master budoka, affect the direc-tion of development of the Japanese military's hand-to-hand combat training methods and policy, and contribute to the time-honored imperial ideology of Yamato Damashii.

History has recorded his choices. The *first three* of these occasions he probably embraced out of a culturally imbued *sense of loyalty or duty* to those individuals who had made them even though they heaped upon him significant personal concerns and distress; but, during this period of his life, his support of Yamato Damashii reflected a type of piety. Occasion *4)*, which was probably more one of choice (that resulted from personal interest) rather than one resulting from a sense of devotion to an imperial ideology, produced for him a certain amount of fame, provided some protection from any unjust governmental scrutiny (which was rampant during this time), and made possible his desired career as a professional budo teacher. A *second behavior* (perhaps related to loyalty) was one where Ueshiba occasionally found it useful to 'tip-toe' around difficult social relationships; when such arose, he would avoid them by using the circumstance of his absence as a type of surrogate, which was, in effect, a decision, but not necessarily one that would permanently resolve any interpersonal difficulty. The manifestation of these two behaviors, the inability to say "No" and avoidance (both likely a result of the effects of culture interacting with his innate character), seems to have comprised a behavioral methodology that helped him to function within the context of his society. However, these behaviors, especially the inability to say "No," came to a sudden halt sometime around the middle 1942 C.E., when he refused to continue teaching the military, resigned from his military teaching positions, and retreated into seclusion at his residence in Iwama. This important decision, likely a result of his recognition that Japan's aggression (which began with its invasion of Manchuria in 1931 C.E.) could no longer in his mind be justified; the Battle of Midway in early June of 1942 C.E. served to 'underscore' that Japan's might in the Pacific theater had been challenged as well as partially 'checked.' Ueshiba's decision marked a new beginning for him, one where his Aiki-budo would evolve over about a ten year period, while he was in seclusion, into the discipline that today is known as Aikikai Aikido.

Morihei Ueshiba's occasional avoidance behavior seems to have been somewhat transmitted to his son, Kisshomaru Ueshiba, who later, if this proposition is supportable, further shaped it as one aspect of Aikikai Aikido's overall philosophy -- that being, the theory of *non-contention.* (See Chapter IX for more discussion concerning "non-contention.") Furthermore, from the viewpoint of an observer of history, a pattern can be seen in Ueshiba's psychological makeup regarding the manner in which he took action to distance himself

from or avoid some difficult, 'tired,' or 'worn-out' personal relationships -- he moves and relocates elsewhere (thereby putting physical
distance between himself and the difficult circumstances), is conveniently absent, or is so busy at different locations that it is difficult to know where he is. An example of this type of behavior can
be found in Ueshiba's distress with his Daito-ryu Jujutsu teacher,
Sokaku Takeda; the former being remiss in his responsibility to pay
monetary fees that were due to Takeda for the latter's instruction of
him. However, when contemplating Ueshiba's relationship with his
spiritual master, Onisaburo Deguchi, this type of behavior manifested a bit differently. Though he respected Onisaburo as a guru of all
things spiritual, when Onisaburo began cozying up to Japanese ultranational factions, Ueshiba began moving in the opposite political
direction toward further support of the time-honored and traditional idea of the Emperor's right to rule as he increased his teaching at
numerous other military training facilities (i.e., the Imperial Yamato
viewpoint, which was opposed by that of Omoto's).[99] The primary
functionaries of Omoto's Dai Nippon Budo Sen'yokai, Onisaburo
and Ueshiba, were not entirely operating from the same 'instruction
manual.' An important aspect of the interpersonal dynamic between them seems to have been that Onisaburo was making use of
Ueshiba's martial skill to train his Omoto-kyo security force while
also cautiously gathering intelligence from him. On the other hand,
Ueshiba was making use of Onisaburo's charisma and social adept-
ness to contact and make social inroads with certain members of the
Japanese high-level military class and numerous aristocrats. The
actual intent of the activities of the Dai Nippon Budo Sen'yokai,
combined with the ongoing popularity of the Omoto-kyo (its parent
organization) contributed significantly to the government's discomfort about Omoto-kyo's social role in Japanese society. As a result,
in 1935 C.E. the Omoto-kyo suffered a Second Suppression that was
carried out by Japanese police forces.[100] Fortunate for his family
and Aikido today, Morihei Ueshiba escaped most of the harsh consequences that could have been imposed by Japan's then existing
court system, which probably was a result of his importance as a
master budoka who was training Japan's military. Nevertheless, he
did suffer official curtailment of his ability to openly express Omoto
teachings as well as significant interfamily discord.

The 'stage' is now set for Morihei Ueshiba's next major appearance with piety, that being his enthusiastic support of Japan's pre-

vailing Yamato Damashii and Kokutai social policies through his participation in strengthening the Japanese military's fighting capability. The Kobukan was one of numerous efforts that had been organized to support Japan's expansion into the Asian continent and the Pacific Islands (whether or not Ueshiba was fully aware of it) by training many members of the military in combat oriented hand-to-hand, bayonet, and sword techniques, but it also served as an initial proving ground for those technical principles and techniques that would later be drawn upon to form the various styles of Aikido. In 1933 C.E., with the help of the young Kenji Tomiki as an editor, he published the book entitled **Budo Renshu**, which was, for all intents and purposes, a military training manual that contained many descriptions and photos of hand-to-hand, bayonet, and sword techniques. From the beginning of 1931 C.E. until he withdrew from his numerous teaching responsibilities in 1942 C.E., Morihei Ueshiba unreservedly applied his thought and efforts toward the performance of his role in Japan's expansion of its imperial empire.[101] A psychosocial effect that occurs to every person who grows and matures within any given society is that it (the society) shapes their behavior and view of life. A difficult endeavor it is to mentally position oneself temporarily outside the effects of one's birth society in order to ascertain its affect upon oneself; often a person goes-with-the-flow not realizing that they are participating in a social movement or society that later will be understood to be unproductive, errant, or destructive.

The Second Omoto Suppression

With the advent of Onisaburo's release from jail, he attempted to reinvent the public face of Omoto-kyo's message over the next several years, though keeping its spiritual teachings true to Omoto's original interpretation of hierarchical order of importance of Japan's kami, which was in conflict with that of the long established line of Japanese Yamato emperors. However, he and the Omoto religion had been stigmatized by the earlier 1921 C. E. suppression, and finding it legally difficult (Japan's "Peace Preservation Laws" were very restrictive of speech) to convey his message to the public without incurring the wrath of the prevailing Japanese government, he began to align his efforts with the Gen'yosha and Kokuryukai ultranational factions, which had dedicated right-wing followers in the Japanese military, while forming with the help of Morihei Ueshiba the Dai Nippon Budo Sen'yokai in August of 1932 C.E. Omoto's Dai Nippon Budo Sen'yokai was located in a new dojo, separate from Ueshiba's Kobukan dojo, in Hyogo Prefecture.

The secret military faction Sakurakai (abovementioned), which was comprised of many right-wing militarists who opposed the often faltering and somewhat corrupted quasi-representative form of government (where some deference was given to the ideas and requests of the Japanese Emperor), had been 'secretly' founded in 1930 C.E. Its singular purpose was the overthrow of the then existing Japanese national parliamentary body known as the Diet in order to replace it with a kokutai framed, Emperor-centric, military-controlled socialism, wherein 'full' deference (the supposed ideal) would be given to the ideas and goals of the Emperor. The Sakurakai had held numerous meetings at Ueshiba's Kobukan Dojo up until the time of its coup attempts during the year 1931 C.E. These coups, one in March (the March Incident) and the other in October (the Imperial Colors Incident), were unsuccessful. Numerous members of the Sakurakai who were not arrested shifted to another faction within the Japanese Army called the Tōseiha (Control Faction). The Toseiha was headed by Generals Tetzusan Nagata and Hideki Tōjō. Morihei Ueshiba's involvement with the Sakurakai is a little murky; though some of his attitudes were in alignment with its goal. It is probable that he disagreed with the idea of change via the method of coup. Notwithstanding, *first* and foremost, he was a thorough supporter of Yamato Damashii, the core of any version of ethnocentric Japanese kokutai policy. *Second*, he was loyal to Onisaburo and earnestly devoted to the Omoto-kyo; during this era, Onisaburo was in league with both the Gen'yosha and the Kokuryukai, which supported the coup. *Third*, Ueshiba permitted many meetings of the Sakurakai in his Kobukan dojo. *Fourth*, he actively taught numerous members of the Sakurakai, such as his life-long friend Shumei Okawa, who was sentenced to five years in prison for his involvement in the March Incident.[102] *Fifth*, nine months after Sakurakai's failed coups, Onisaburo, with Ueshiba's willing participation, founded Omoto-kyo's Dai Nippon Budo Sen'yokai, whereupon numerous members of its other newly established organizations, such as the *Showa Shinseikai* (Showa Sacred Association) and *Showa Seinenkai* (Showa Youth Association), began training in Aiki-budo and other

studies.[103]   Beside these activities, leading members of the Showa
Sacred Association were active in promoting a sociopolitical movement referred to as the *Showa Restoration*, part of which included a
means of 'unifying' the various prominent Japanese religions with
government in an attempt to create a new governing cabinet -- an
Imperial House Cabinet -- while another part had been a proposal to
eliminate party-line (political party) governance in order to eradicate extensive corruption in Japanese politics, business, and social
thought. Such a cabinet could have helped to moderate the censor-
ship and oppression that the Omoto-kyo had been experiencing because a representative therefrom would have resided within it. The
petition to establish this type of political cabinet was gaining support in the Imperial Court because the Emperor's brother, Prince
Chichibu, was openly supportive of various right-wing causes. Had
such a cabinet been established, it would have interfered with the
Emperor's customary influence over the government. As a result,
the Emperor's political advisors notified the Prime Minister, who
then notified the Home Ministry, that it should take all actions necessary to accomplish the official dismantlement of the Omoto religion (by police action) because it threatened the Emperor's traditional role as head of state.[104]

Concerned about the numerous and well-organized attempts to
topple Japan's government, the Home Ministry acted promptly upon
the go-ahead and directives of the Emperor's advisors and ordered
its Police Bureau (the Keihōkyoku), which oversaw all civilian police entities throughout Japan, to 'ferret-out' and render harmless
any indigenous organization that threatened the Japanese government's then extant status quo condition. Subsequently, the Police
Bureau took on the task of gathering further intelligence about the
character, influence, and potential to stir up trouble of numerous
'troublesome' political organizations, religious sects, and 'secret' societies. Prominent among these was Omoto, whose spiritual leader,
it was 'discovered,' had to some degree or another allied himself
with certain ultranational or right-wing factions (the Gen'yosha,
Kokuryukai, and the army's Sakurakai faction) that had lent support
of one type or another to the Sakurakai's coup attempts. From the
Bureau's perspective, Morihei Ueshiba was also suspected of com-
plicity because he was a prominent member of the Omoto-kyo, co-
led and taught at the newly formed Dai Nippon Budo Sen'yokai, and
had permitted the Sakurakai (quite probably at Onisaburo's request)

to hold meetings in his Kobukan dojo.[105] The director of the Police Bureau, Toshiki Karasawa, was given specific directions as to what was necessary to begin the dismantling of the Omoto-kyo organization in order to achieve its removal from prominent social existence in Japan. That which Onisaburo had wanted to avoid by his earlier attempt to relocate the Omoto religion in Mongolia -- i.e., the total suppression of Omoto in Japan -- was about to begin.

As December 8, 1935 C.E. dawned, several prefect-level police headquarters launched a suppression action against the Omoto-kyo that included arrests of its leading members, property seizures, and building structure demolition throughout Japan. Onisaburo and his wife were arrested as were all of the other top members of Omoto. Morihei Ueshiba, though on the arrest list, initially escaped arrest because the Osaka Police Chief, K. Tomita, who was a student of Ueshiba's, notified him just before the police arrived and hid him for about a month in a subordinate police officer's home (G. Morita's). Of course, this particular intrigue was kept mostly secret until after the end of W.W. II. Many of the arrestees were harshly interrogated, jailed to await trial, convicted of Lèse-majesté and numerous other offenses, and sentenced to lengthy as well as personally challenging jail terms. Onisaburo Deguchi was not released from prison until 1942 C.E., and six years later, in January of 1948, he passed away. The government's suppression was thorough, as it was meant to eliminate the Omoto's organization structure and its ideas from Japanese society. After W.W. II, the Omoto religion was reestablished, but it has never regained the prominence, either in Japan or elsewhere, that it had enjoyed before its second suppression.[106] Several new Japanese religions have since evolved from the Omoto-kyo; the most notable among them is Aizen-en, which was founded by Yasuaki Deguchi, Onisaburo's eldest grandson.

At the moment when Morihei Ueshiba was notified that the police were about to launch a nationwide effort to squash and eradicate the Omoto-kyo, he had a decision to make. He could await the arrival of the police and endure what would come soon thereafter, or he could accept G. Morita's offer to be hidden away for a while in the latter's home until the initial police fever had abated. Loyalty and piety up to a point, Ueshiba chose the latter, though probably not without some challenging and disruptive mental tumult. After all, he could not afford a stymying or loss of his efforts in the development of Aiki-budo to be lost with his imprisonment, possible torture, and stigma arising from association with the Omoto-kyo as it crumbled under the government's final assault.[107] Ueshiba's act of temporary escape seems to have been one of tactical avoidance, but this decision caused him much personal grief because many top members of the Omoto religion as well as some of those of his family considered him something akin to a Christian "Judas." Police officers who were sympathetic with Ueshiba due to his personality and skill as a budoka had shielded him. After coming out of about one month of hiding, Ueshiba surrendered to the local police and was interviewed and released by those who had earlier forewarned and hid him, but pending a later police hearing and decision about whether he should be taken into custody and subjected to court proceedings. Those police officers who had previously sympathized with Ueshiba crafted a report for their superiors at the Police Bureau that suggested only minimal action, if any at all, be taken against him. In those days, some of the numerous policing agencies in Japan had the powers to impose certain restrictions upon a person's behavior without a court hearing.[108] Later, the official punishment that was levied upon Ueshiba consisted of the curtailment of his ability to associate with Omoto-kyo's leaders and prominent followers, which consisted of a 'no contact' order for an indefinite period of time and forbade him from using or displaying any of its symbology or writings.[109] The significant and disruptive inter-family discord that was visited upon Morihei Ueshiba consciousness consisted largely of his nephew Noriaki Inoue's ire, who considered Ueshiba to have been unfaithful to the Omoto cause as it was progressively subjected to further persecution and harassment by the Japanese government. Inoue, who was also a devoted Omoto follower, had studied Sokaku Takeda's Daito-ryu Jujutsu in Shirataki commensurately with Ueshiba. Some researchers believe that Inoue was the first member of the Ueshiba/Inoue family to embrace the teachings of the Omoto-kyo, and that he was the one who pointed his uncle's attention to its early history and teachings. It's during this time that Ueshiba's loyalty to Onisaburo began to wane as he fully apprehended the futility and danger of Omoto's attempts to oppose the prevailing government. The suppression of the Omoto religion as an active and vital sociopolitical organization, though disturbing and life changing, released Ueshiba from involvement in its political affairs, thus 'freeing' him to lend his unique Aiki-budo expertise in thorough, unencumbered support of Japan's military establishment. Nevertheless, his piety toward the teachings of the Omoto religion remained strong even though during the years between the Omoto's second suppression and the end of W.W. II it was necessary for him to hold these privately.

Interlude 4

Between the years 1935 C.E. and 1943 C.E., Morihei Ueshiba continued to train members of Japan's Imperial Army and Navy. Numerous first generation Aikido teachers were trained in Aiki-budo during this period, a time when many different and often conflicting indigenous social forces were steadily moving Japanese society toward a top-down, Emperor led, military controlled, national social fascism rather than continuing its progress toward a sociopolitical course characterized by a constitutional republic-like structure. The members of the Japanese Army's Toseiha (Control Faction), who had been opposed to most of the Sakurakai's ideas as well as to those of the Kōdōha (Imperial Way Faction), which was yet another influential Imperial Army faction, were successful in gaining full control of the Army after the latter's attempted coup of February 26, 1936 C.E. failed. There were two important characteristics that set the Toseiha apart from the Sakurakai and the Kodoha. *First,* the Toseiha did not subscribe to the body of ideas that characterized the Showa Restoration movement, which, primarily, called for a return to an idealized, pre-westernized Japan that was free of the polluting influences of both liberal democratic and Marxist ideas, whereby the nation would be purged of bureaucratic, economic, political, and thought corruption; e.g., graft, greed, opportunism, and the erosion of traditional family and societal customs and values. The Showa Restoration movement was supposed to supplant these social problems through a return of the nation's control to Japan's 'divinely imbued' Emperor (the Imperial Way), but advised by a new cabinet (the proposed Imperial House Cabinet) and assisted by a military that would have been revitalized with a new spiritual élan in order to create a 'divinely mandated' nationalist state that would act like a light in the dark to reveal to all Asian peoples their importance in the scheme of life as given by a supposedly well-meaning Japanese suzerainty (e.g., Japan's Co-Prosperity Sphere). The Japanese military's new spiritual character would have been crafted by the proposed Imperial House Cabinet, an idea that was agreeable to the Omoto-kyo religion. Onisaburo Deguchi and Morihei Ueshiba were vigorously active in promoting the Showa Restoration movement. *Second*, the members of Toseiha believed strongly that Japan needed to focus on the modernization of its military forces in the light of European and American industrial, technological, and war science advances. In contrast, the Sakurakai and Kodoha believed strongly that the focus should first be on shaping a new spiritual élan in the military. Both Onisaburo Deguchi and Morihei Ueshiba, who were spiritually animated men caught up in a changing world, were like two puzzle pieces that could no longer be fit into the image of a puzzle (Japan's pre-westernized way of life) that was steadily and unavoidably disassembling -- their efforts to reposition themselves into the then newly developing Japanese social reality (i.e., Japan's newly developing puzzle image) were frequently hampered by certain sociopolitical changes that were increasingly indifferent to traditional Japanese spirituality. Omoto-kyo's support of the proposed establishment of a new Imperial House Cabinet and Onisaburo's founding of the Dai Nippon Budo Sen'yokai and Showa Shinseikai associations, along with Ueshiba's devout relationship with Omoto's religious teachings and support of the Sakurakai (not forgetting the meaning of the word *kobukan*, which was used by Ueshiba to identify his Kobukan dojo's connection with the idea of the Imperial Way) can be understood as alignment with the Showa Restoration movement. After the Kodoha's coup failure, some members who had not been imprisoned or otherwise removed from the Japanese Imperial Army merged with the Toseiha. As a result, the Toseiha's control of the Army benefited, which thereby destined Japan for a different course of military action that eventually came to a conclusion with its W.W. II defeat. Interestingly, the strengthened cadre of proponents for a modernization of Japan's military forces then named its faction the *Imperial Way Ethnic Customs Doctrine System* (Kōdō Minzoku Shugi Seitō), which was a nationalist party (fascist-like in character) that thoroughly embraced the *Imperial Way* societal ideal. The name *Toseiha*, where *tōsei* has the meaning of 'control,' was a derogatory and misleading labeling that had been given purposefully by the members of the Kodoha in order to belittle those military men who had been opposed to its ideas and purpose and to the Showa Restoration movement, with an intent of diminishing any truth or usefulness that may have been present in opposing ideas.[110] The subsequent decline in the popularity of the Showa Restoration movement was largely a result of the downfall of the Sakurakai in 1931 C.E., the suppression of the Omoto-kyo in 1935 C.E., and the purge of the Kodoha in 1936 C.E. Hideki Tojo's rise to notorious prominence in the Japanese government was furthered by the Kodoha's failed coup. Late in the year 1941 C.E., under Tojo's orders, the Dai Nippon Butoku Kai (the Greater Japan Martial Virtue Association) forced Ueshiba into accepting a generic category identifier for his Aiki-budo, which was the name "aikido." (See Chapter VIII for more about Hideki Tojo). Ueshiba had been a supporter of the Showa Restoration movement, while Tojo had been opposed to it. The Japanese Imperial Navy did not suffer from disgruntled members who were inclined to form factions for the purpose of overthrowing its government; it obeyed the orders that had issued from the Japanese Emperor. However, it did have two factions during this time period, the Kantaiha (Fleet Faction) and the Jōyakuha (Treaty Faction), that arose as a result of Japan's concern over the *Washington Naval Treaty* of 1922 C.E. The Joyakuha wanted to operate Japan's Navy within the bounds of this treaty, whereas the Kantaiha did not. The Japanese government did not renew this treaty with the other four signatory nations. As a result, its provisions, which limited the Japanese Imperial Navy to a certain size and function, became ineffectual by the end of 1936 C.E. At this juncture, Japan's commitment toward a policy of military facilitated expansionism was unavoidable. Soon thereafter, a reshaped and 'revitalized' Japanese government moved strongly toward a fully militarized approach to bring all of Asia and the South Pacific islands under Japan's control. Six months later, on July 7, 1937 C.E., war between China proper and Japan broke out with the military engagement at the Marco Polo Bridge, near Peking.

During the 1930s, Jigoro Kano, the founder of Judo, was a vocal advocate for peace and spoke out against Japanese military aggression. On May 4, 1938 C.E., Kano died (age 78) on board a passenger ship while returning from Egypt where he had secured Japan's entrance into the 1940 C.E. Olympic Games. The 'official' cause of his death is described as either pneumonia or food poisoning. Kenji Tomiki, who much earlier had been training with Ueshiba, beginning in 1927 C.E., relocated to Manchuria in 1936 C.E. in order to teach Kano's Judo and Ueshiba's Aiki-budo to Japan's Kantogun Army and Kempeitai (Military Police) as well as to some members of Japan's Imperial Household Ministry who had been stationed there. Toward the end of W.W. II, Tomiki was captured by the Russians and held in a Siberian prison for a number of years. Gōzō Shioda, the founder of Yoshinkan Aikido, who had previously attained a 3rd Dan in Judo, began his Aiki-budo training at Ueshiba's Kobukan dojo in 1932 C.E. After his graduation from Takushoku University in 1941 C.E., Shioda was posted as a civilian secretary to General Hata in China. Late in 1942 C.E., he was reassigned to Borneo and acted as the Director of General Affairs for the *Taiwan Colonization Co.*, which was a collaborative effort between the occupying Japanese government and various zaibatsu with the assistance of sympathetic Taiwanese. The somewhat reluctant Aikikai teacher Rinjiro Shirata, who had obtained a 2nd Dan in Judo by age 17, began training at the Kobukan dojo in 1933 C.E., was inducted into the Japanese Imperial Army in 1937 C.E., fought in Manchuria and Burma, and was repatriated to Japan in 1946 C.E. The controversial Kōichi Tōhei, the founder of Shin-shin Tōitsu Aikido, who had begun training in Aiki-budo in 1940 C.E., was inducted into the Japanese Imperial Army in 1942 C.E., fought in China until the end of W.W. II, and was repatriated to Japan in 1946 C.E. Minoru Mochizuki, the founder of Yoseikan Aikido, one of Jigoro Kano's first generation Judo teachers, began study of Ueshiba's Aiki-budo in 1930 C.E. From 1933 C.E. until 1938 C.E. Mochizuki taught his own evolving style of budo at numerous locations in Northeast Asia and participated in improving its rudimentary communication systems and irrigation projects. Following the outbreak of the Sino-Japanese War in 1938 C.E., Mochizuki and his family moved into Inner Mongolia where he, in cooperation with its governmental entities, served as the Director of the High School for the Mongols in Pao-t'ou (today renamed *Baotau*, China) in addition to teaching Judo, Kendo, and Aiki-jutsu. Later, in 1940 C.E. he was appointed as the under-prefect of the department of Chinese Sei Ga (*Shih Ching* in Chinese, i.e., the Book of Odes, a book of the *Chinese Five Classics* group of ancient literary works). After W.W. II, the irrigation projects that Mochizuki had designed were completed by the Chinese government. Minoru Hirai, the founder of the Korindō style of Aikido, had studied numerous Japanese martial arts before he began his Aiki-budo training with Ueshiba at the Kobukan Dojo in 1938 C.E.; among these was Kito-ryu Jujutsu, which Jigoro Kano had much earlier mastered. During W.W. II, Hirai was the head bujutsu teacher of the Japanese Imperial Army's Kempeitai (military police). In January of 1942 C.E., Hirai was appointed by Ueshiba to act as the Director of General Affairs of the Kobukan Dojo. In late 1945 C.E., after Japan's surrender of W.W. II, he established Korindō Aikido's first dojo. Kenshiro Abbe, who also had studied numerous Japanese martial arts before he began his Aiki-budo training, began training with Morihei Ueshiba sometime in 1941 C.E. after his tour of duty in the Japanese Imperial Army. Abbe introduced Judo and Aikido to Great Britain in 1955. Noriaki Inoue (Yoichiro, Ueshiba's nephew) was active in Tokyo as Ueshiba's senior instructor from the mid-1920s until 1935 C.E. Later, from 1932 C.E. to 1935 C.E., he was a senior instructor for Omoto's Dai Nippon Budo Sen'yokai. In 1933 C.E. Inoue traveled to Manchuria in order to teach Aiki-budo for a short period of time at the Japanese Daido Gakuin Academy in Changchun (then known as Shinkyo to the Japanese). Up until the time of the Omoto-kyo's suppression in 1935 C.E., Inoue had acted as Ueshiba's right-hand man. In the aftermath of Omoto's suppression, Inoue suffered the same restrictions that had been put in place by the police regarding active expression of the Omoto-kyo's religious teachings and its symbols, and his personal relationship with his uncle deteriorated. After W.W. II, he continued to teach using the name Aiki-budo to identify his discipline for about ten years, while Morihei and Kisshomaru Ueshiba took up the categorical identifier term *aikido*. In 1956 C.E., he changed the name from Aiki-budo to Shinwa Taidō, but later modified it to its present name of Shin'ei Taidō. Since W.W. II, Inoue had contended that the functional basis of Ueshiba's Aikido of today was co-developed by him. He died on April 13, 1994. In 1937 C.E., Kisshomaru Ueshiba began to take seriously his training in Aiki-budo. In 1938 C.E., Kisshomaru Ueshiba acted as uke for his father for a series of pictures used to illustrate Aiki-budo's techniques in his father's book entitled **Budō**. In 1940 C.E., Morihei Ueshiba established the Zaidan Hojin Kobukai organization, whose first administrative director was the retired Admiral Isamu Takeshita, and in 1942 C.E., at age 21, Kisshomaru Ueshiba was assigned to act as this organization's director, which probably spared him from conscription into military service. Initially mentioned above, late in 1941 C.E., Prime Minister Tojo directed the Dai Nippon Butokukai to bring all martial disciplines under its control; Aiki-budo is categorized as a form of "aikido," which term was designed as a generic category identifier, a term negotiated between the Butokukai and Ueshiba by the latter's represent-ative, Minoru Hirai, but a term with which Ueshiba felt entirely uncomfortable. So uncomfortable with this term was he that he did not acquiese to it being used as the identifier for his Aiki-budo until sometime in 1957, a year after Kenji Tomiki had begun to employ it to describe his new combative sport and self-defense discipline -- Tomiki-ryu Aikido.

After the Manchurian Incident of 1931 C.E., and certainly after the outbreak of war with China (July 7, 1937 C.E.), up to the time when Morihei Ueshiba retreated into seclusion at his residence lo-cated in Iwama Prefecture (sometime not later than the end of June, 1942 C.E.), his teaching of Aiki-budo was structured specifically for Japanese military and police uses, i.e., for killing, arrest, and riot control techniques and strategies.

Ueshiba's Second Vision, retreat to Iwama, and Third Vision

Sometime in December, 1940 C.E., Morihei Ueshiba experienced what he described as another visioning, his second vision. Report-edly, he suddenly could not recall anything about any of the tech-niques or characteristics of his Aiki-budo; but soon afterward, as his visioning continued, everything that he had learned from his teach-ers and had been applying toward military personnel training reap-peared in his mind as *"vehicles for the cultivation of life, knowledge, virtue, and good sense, not devices to throw and pin people."*[111] Also, Kisshomaru Ueshiba tells us that his father Morihei *"... was also wor-ried about the crisis confronting his homeland."*[112] About one and a half years later, before the end of June, 1942 C.E., Ueshiba resigned from his military teaching posts and retreated to his other residence in Iwama prefecture. His resignation can be considered as

1) An expression of his objection to Prime Minister Tojo's re-structuring of certain aspects of civilian support functions for Japan's war efforts, where one directive therefrom had forced the category identifier of *aikido* upon his Aiki-budo;
2) His beginning concern for his position in Japan's endgame maneuverings as he gained insider knowledge about the Japanese Imperial Navy's losses at the battles of the Coral Sea and Midway in May and June of 1942 C.E., which, as

Japan was proceeding toward its ignominious fate of losing the war, would have been an unsettling but necessary consideration for most Japanese people; and,

3)   A steadily increasing concern about his role in helping to train members of Japan's military to kill other people, the enemy, which situation he may have reasoned (that of aggression and war) had been domestically evolved by the effect of a collective unconscious psychosocial load, generationally accrued, that had conferred upon Japanese society, no matter what status individuals therein had held, certain social characteristics that had emerged Japan's path of aggression.

Shortly after his resignation in 1942 C.E., Ueshiba retreated to his primary residence in Iwama Prefecture. There, Ueshiba reportedly experienced a third vision, one which is described as happening during the worst fighting of W.W. II, which most likely refers to the Battles of Coral Sea and Midway, mentioned previously. Ueshiba's third vision suggested to him that Budo had been misunderstood by many people as well as misinterpreted by others in order to purposefully facilitate Japan's aggression, that competition is a harmful attitude, and that such a societal condition (that of aggression and war) is the worst offense against humanity that people can commit. The ideal objective of Budo, he says, is the attainment of peace attained through the power of love.[113] I wonder what role the metaphysical teachings and spiritual message of Aikikai Aikido, or later, Shin-shin Toitsu Aikido, played in the Anti-War Movement of the 1960s in the United States of America?

The affect of these visions, perhaps better described as envisionings, was to begin the process of reinventing Aiki-budo by attempting to either remove or defocus its distinctive martial character and supplant it with an Omoto-derived, humanitarian-like ethos and character. Eventually, after S.C.A.P. gradually lifted the ban on the practice of various disciplines of Budo,[114] and after Morihei Ueshiba had spent years in seclusion contemplating a new conceptualization of his Aiki-budo, the eclectic metaphysical and technical foundation of his evolving physio-spiritual discipline began to take shape. (He didn't entirely terminate his self-imposed seclusion until 1956, when he gave a public demonstration in Tokyo.) Today, many decades after W.W. II, its reconceived character is all that which is apparent in

Aikikai Aikido; and Omoto's influence upon it is set before us in Ueshiba's collected discussions about his experiences, perceptions, and ideas that, when collected together, constitute his general metaphysical theory of Takemusu Aiki. Morihei Ueshiba's visions, which may have been discussed amongst certain close members of his family but were not made accessible for the public's consideration until sometime after he reengaged the public, have been necessarily woven into the story of Aikido. These visions came slowly unto the realm of public knowledge via Kisshomaru Ueshiba, his son, who determined it was useful to explain a few of his father's cognitive experiences as they cooperated to reshape Aiki-budo's martial imagery into the techni-spiritual shape of modern Aikikai Aikido. Essentially, after W.W. II, Morihei Ueshiba's visions served as a seminal impetus to change the martial focus of his Aiki-budo, while certain Omoto-kyo teachings served as his metaphysical basis of understanding from which Aikido's own philosophy and mythology was crafted, the outcome of which was an idealized style of 'Budo' that today is characterized by its practitioners' efforts to experience and manifest a generalized condition of harmony in life. No doubt, Ueshiba's reclusive contemplations and practice resulted in his esoteric Takemusu Aiki hypothesis (Aikikai Aikido's metaphysical underpinning), which was his unique expression of a continued commitment toward understanding the matters of life within the context of the older Japanese societal reality. Can this be considered as a further indication of his pious character? If not, certainly it was a commitment to ensure that his efforts in Aiki-budo would never again be hijacked by a misguided sociopolitical condition for the purpose of aggression and war (such as occurred in the Empire of Japan in which he had been complicit). After his father had emerged from seclusion, Kisshomaru Ueshiba, particularly after his father's death in 1969, greatly influenced the modern look and feel of Aikikai Aikido, doing much to moderate his father's esoteric and sometimes unfathomable spiritual teachings. Akwardly, for a short while at the beginning of this new chapter in world history, Morihei Ueshiba was reluctant to offer practice in Aikido to non-Japanese, and only did so upon the insistent urging of his son. The Frenchman Andre' Nocquet, who had been earlier encouraged by Aikikai Aikido's Tadashi Abe (who had moved to France in 1952)[115] to visit and study with Ueshiba, was Aikikai Aikido's first non-Japanese uchi-deshi, from 1955 through 1957. An American, Walter

Norton Dobson III (also known as Terry Dobson), was the second, from 1964 up until Morihei Ueshiba's death in 1969.

Morihei Ueshiba's ever-developing esoteric spirituality

The final consideration pertaining to Morihei Ueshiba's relationship with piety concerns his ever-developing esoteric spirituality, which had the effect of rather quickly shifting Aikikai Aikido from a martial focus toward a spiritual focus. This shift caused dissent among many of his top teachers during the period of time from 1956 through 1975. For example, Gozo Shioda, Kenji Tomiki, and later Koichi Tohei all branched off from Aikikai Aikido and developed their own styles of Aikido. However, interestingly, the latter's split was a result of Kisshomaru Ueshiba's insistence upon a core philosophy for Aikikai Aikido that was less dependent upon metaphysical teachings that were difficult if not impossible to substantiate. Noriaki Inoue, Ueshiba's nephew and quite probably the person who had first exposed Ueshiba to the Omoto religion, had earlier split off from his uncle as a result of the Second Omoto-kyo suppression. As Morihei Ueshiba aged, his esoteric spirituality became increasingly more evident.[116] Ueshiba traveled to the U.S.A. state of Hawaii in the year 1961 to participate in a ceremonial opening of Aikikai Aikido's Honolulu dojo. On April 26, 1969, Morihei Ueshiba, age 86, passed away of what was reported to be liver cancer. Then, Kisshomaru Ueshiba assumed control of his father's Aikikai organization. Today, he is considered to have been an advocate of quasi-secular[117] and non-competitive Aikido, which purports to be founded on teachings that have been objectively validated. Kisshomaru Ueshiba passed away on January 4, 1999. His son, Moriteru Ueshiba, now directs the Aikikai Aikido organization. Kenji Tomiki said of his teacher Morihei Ueshiba that *"He was also a very pious man and is believed to have received enlightenment, often referred to as 'shinjin aiki.'"*[118]

Morihei Ueshiba
~1939 C.E.

Born: December 14, 1883 C.E.
Died: April 26, 1969

Photo courtesy of the Aikido Journal.

Sokaku Takeda
~1939 C.E.

Born: October 10, 1859 C.E.
Died: April 25, 1943 C.E.

Photo courtesy of the Aikido Journal.

Onisaburō Deguchi
(Recorded birth name: Ueda Kisaburō)
~1939 C.E.

Born: August 22, 1871 C.E.
Died: January 19, 1948 C.E.

Photo courtesy of Wikimedia Commons repository.

Manchurian warlord Zhāng Zuòlín
~1924 C.E.

Born: March 19, 1875 C.E.
Died: June 4, 1928 C.E.

Photo courtesy of the Wikimedia Commons repository.

Japanese schoolgirls with influenza filtration masks
~1919 C.E.

Influenza advisory poster
Japanese text reads: "If treated quickly it gets better right away."
~1919 C.E.

Photos courtesy of the Wikimedia Commons repository.

A maiden emanating her etheric body
in Castle Corbin while presenting the Holy Grail

(Her aura in the original picture is a golden hue. Note the etheric vapors
rising up from beneath her feet. "Corbin" is the name of the castle of the Holy
Grail in the Lancelot-Grail cycle. *From the book: **The Romance of King Arthur**
and His Knights of the Round Table by* Alfred W. Pollard, 1917 C.E.)

Photo courtesy of the Wikimedia Commons repository.

Understanding Aikido

Onisaburo Deguchi, co-founder of Omoto-kyo (left)
Mitsuru Tōyama, head of Gen'yosha (center)
Ryohei Uchida, founder of Kokuryukai (right)
Mid to Late 1920s C.E.

Photo courtesy of Wikimedia Commons repository.

[1] See, *The Universal Curriculum* by Charles Page Smith; published by the William James Press, Santa Cruz, California, saddle-stitched paperback, 1975.

[2] Syncretism is the combination of different forms of belief, faith, spirituality, or practice. Shugendō brings together elements of Buddhism, Shintoism, and Taoism.

[3] See, *Founder of Aikido: From Weakness to Strength* by Kisshomaru Ueshiba, translated by Stanley A. Pranin and Midori Yamamoto; published by the Aiki News magazine, article #35, January, 1980.

[4] See, Goldsbury, Peter, *The General Impact of the Pacific War (WW II) on Aikido*, the section entitled *Essential Background: The Legacy of Meiji and Taisho* and, the section entitled *The Answer Lies in the Soil: Agricultural Budo and the Japanese Essence*, published online at Aikiweb.com, 2008. Also, see the *Founder of Aikido: Opening a Dojo* by Kisshomaru Ueshiba, edited by Stanley Pranin; published by the Aiki News Journal, article #38, July, 1981.

[5] Thematically as well as spiritually central to Japanese Shingon Buddhism are two sutras (tantras in Chinese), these being the *Mahāvairocana Sutra* and the *Vajrasekhara Sutra*. The Mahāvairocana Sutra was probably composed at the great ancient Buddhist university of Nalanda situated in the far-east Indian state of Bahir sometime during the middle of the 7th century C.E. This sutra is the earliest known thorough presentation of Vajrayāna Buddhism (sometimes loosely referred to as tantric Buddhism). Vajrayana Buddhism is a late stage development of Mahayana Buddhism combined with other, later esoteric Buddhist thought. Kukai, the founder of Japanese Shingon Buddhism, became aware of this sutra in 796 C.E. and traveled to China in 804 C.E. to receive instruction in it.

[6] *Norito* - the ancient Japanese Shinto ritual prayers. See, Philippi, Donald L., *NORITO: A Translation of the Ancient Japanese Ritual Prayers*.

[7] The *Man'yoshu* (with a possible meaning of *Collection of Ten Thousand Leaves*) is the oldest anthology collection existing in Japan. It contains approximately 4,500 poems of different forms, mostly of Japanese origin, as well as some Chinese poems and letters. The literary works thereof range across about 350 years from 347 C.E.., (poems #85-89), through 759 C.E., (poem #4516).

[8] Donald Philippi relates of Shinto ritual prayer that "*there is evidence that*

there was a special musical technique for reciting these rituals" and that *"Japanese scholars love to dwell on the role of the kotodama, the mystical power believed to dwell in words, or in words arranged in certain magical formulas."* See, **NORITO: *A Translation of the Ancient Japanese Ritual Prayers*** by Donald L. Philippi, with a new preface by Joseph M. Kitagawa; Princeton University Press, paperback, 1990, pages 1, 2, and 3 of the introduction.

[9] See, ***Japanese Journal of Religious Studies***, 1992, Issue 19/4. Book review -- Donald L. Philippi, *Norito: A Translation of the Ancient Japanese Ritual Prayers* -- an article by Norman Havens, Kokugakuin University, pages 398 through 401.

[10] ***Kana*** are the written scripts of the Japanese syllabary. There are three syllabic scripts used in the Japanese written language: the present-day *katakana* and *hiragana*, and the ancient *man'yogana*. Man'yogana developed as the Japanese made use of Chinese hanzi during the early development of their written language. Katakana and hiragana are derived from the man'yogana script, with the former a development of a highly stylized cursive implementation of the man'yogana, the latter a result of the efforts of Japanese Buddhist monks' development of a shorthand style. The gojuon (fifty sounds) linguistic grid is a system of organizing the present day sounds of the Japanese language, represented by *kana* script.

[11] The ***Rigveda*** is believed by many scholars to have not been placed in written form until the advent of the Brahmi script, which script is thought to have been created sometime between the 6th and the 3rd century B.C.E. Until that time, this Veda was committed to memory and transmitted verbally; archeology and linguistic evidence points to a time somewhere between the 17th and the 11th century B.C.E. for its composition -- the early Vedic Period.

[12] ***Shi-nou-kou-shou*** or ***mibunsei***: the four primary peopled classes of the late Tokugawa Period carried forward into use during the Meiji Period, those being the samurai, farmers, artisans, and merchants. The samurai class suffered dissolution during the early Meiji Period, and men of this class entered military service in the Japanese Army, took positions as civilian police, or applied entrepreneurial effort toward the development the so-called *zaibatsu* firms (resource identification, extraction, and materiel companies).

[13] ***Yamabushi*** -- a reclusive person residing in the forested mountains of Japan who places emphasis on asceticism, training in feats of endurance,

and experiential understanding of the profound relationship of man and his natural environment, typically guided by a synthesis of Shinto and esoteric Buddhist concepts and teachings, today identified by the doctrine of Shengudō. Gichin Funakoshi, founder of Shotokan Karatedo, had a similar attraction to this archetype; see his book **Karatedo: My Way of Life**; Kodansha International, paperback, 1981, page 86.

[14] See, **Founder of Aikido: Idol Among the Soldiers** by Kisshomaru Ueshiba, translated by Stanley A. Pranin and Midori Yamamoto; Aiki News magazine, article #37, June, 1981. See also, **Morihei Ueshiba, Founder of Aikido (Part 2)** by Kanemoto Sunadomari, edited by Stanley Pranin; Aiki News magazine, article #73, December, 1986.

[15] See, **Morihei Ueshiba, Founder of Aikido (Part 2)** by Kanemoto Sunadomari, edited by Stanley Pranin; Aiki News magazine, article #73, December, 1986.

[16] Today, there is concern among some social analysts that as the members of the generation of Japanese people who experienced W.W. II pass from this earthly realm, Japan's national identity could redevelop a somewhat different type of ultranationalism; such an ignominious trend would have to overcome the strength of its present societal ethos, an ethos that has been thoroughly shaped by its post W.W. II governing constitutional documents and its subsequently evolved humanitarian oriented institutions, like Aikido, that are seemingly dedicated to the maintenance of peace.

[17] See, **Aikido Ichiro** (My Life in Aikido) by Kisshomaru Ueshiba; published in October 1995 by Shuppan Geijutsusha, Tokyo. See also, Peter, **The General Impact of the Pacific War (WWII) on Aikido** by Peter Goldsbury, the section entitled **Beginnings of a New Beginning**; published online at www.aikiweb.com, 2008.

[18] Kisshomaru Ueshiba denied that his father had participated as an active combatant in the Russo-Japanese war in spite of strong evidence to suggest otherwise. See, Pranin, Stanley, **Did Morihei ever injure or kill anyone? Here is what we know...**, published online at the Aikido Journal, July 2011.

[19] See, **Founder of Aikido: Idol Among the Soldiers** by Kisshomaru Ueshiba, translated by Stanley A. Pranin and Midori Yamamoto; Aiki News magazine, article #37, June, 1981. Also, the popular television investigative program **Myth Busters** verified that the unaided viewing of a speeding bullet is, in fact, under certain conditions, possible. When certain common atmospheric conditions exist, slower speed bullets, less than 1300 fps, or at

least their outlined path through the air created by the pressure dynamics around the bullet, can be seen by the unaided human eye. The primary rifle used by the Russian Army during the Russo-Japanese war was the bolt action 1891 Mosin Nagant with a muzzle velocity of approximately 2018 fps. However, if some of the small arms were of older vintage, some of the bullets fired during any engagement in which Morihei Ueshiba may have been involved might have been moving at a speed slow enough to be seen. Later, Morihei Ueshiba also stated when he described his accompaniment of Onisaburo Deguchi on an ill-fated venture to Mongolia to establish there an Omoto-kyo utopia, that, right before their group's apprehension during an ongoing exchange of gunfire, he could see an indication of a bullet's departure from the gun barrels of their many attackers. See the article entitled *Founder of Aikido: Enlightenment at the Edge of Death (Part 2)* by Kisshomaru Ueshiba, translated by Stanley A. Pranin and Midori Yamamoto; Aiki News magazine, article #50, 1982.

[20] See the article entitled *Founder of Aikido: Your Father Is Just Fine as He Is* by Kisshomaru Ueshiba, translated by Stanley A. Pranin and Midori Yamamoto; Aiki News magazine, article #43, 1981. Also see, *Yoichiro [Noriaki] Inoue: Aikido's Forgotten Pioneer* by Stanley Pranin; Aikido Journal article #121, 2011.

[21] A title emphasizing that a person is functioning as an agent to revive, impart, and disseminate specific technique, attitude, and skill.

[22] See, *Sokaku Takeda and Daito Ryu Aikijujutsu* by Stanley Pranin; Aikido Journal, article #104, 1995.

[23] See http://www.daito-ryu.org/en/daito-ryu-and-aikido.html.

[24] *Nao Deguchi* (1836-1918 C.E.) is considered to be the foundress of the Omoto-kyo. She was a Japanese housewife and mother who came from a poverty-stricken family; at the lowest point of her misery she reportedly experienced a spiritual connection with or possession by the kami (deity) *Ushitora no Konjin* (Deity of Metals), which is associated with the traditional Japanese cosmological and divination system called *Onmyōdō*. Regarding these actual oral statements by Morihei Ueshiba, review *Founder of Aikido: Your Father Is Just Fine as He Is* by Kisshomaru Ueshiba, translated by Stanley A. Pranin and Midori Yamamoto; Aiki News magazine, article # 43, 1981.

[25] Ibid.

[26] See, **Morihei Ueshiba, Founder Of Aikido (Part 5)** by Kanemoto Sunadomari; Aiki News magazine, article #76, 1987.

[27] For further information about Hatsu's response to her husbands behavior during this time, see, **Founder of Aikido: Move to Ayabe** by Kisshomaru Ueshiba, translated by Stanley A. Pranin and Midori Yamamoto; however, there is an inaccuracy herein, which concerns the birth date of Kisshomaru's older brother, Kuniharu. See, **Documented Events in the Life of Morihei Ueshiba** by Stanley Pranin for an accurate accounting of what happened when.

[28] There seems to be little or no information concerning the circumstances of the deaths of Takemori and Kuniharu Ueshiba. However, the January 1918 C.E. through December 1920 C.E. Spanish Influenza Pandemic seriously affected Japan during this time period. For information about the 1918 C.E. Influenza Pandemic see, **Spanish Influenza in Japanese Forces, 1919-1920** at http://wwwnc.cdc.gov/eid/article/13/4/06-0615_article.htm; a research paper from **Emerging Infectious Diseases**, Vol. 13, No. 4, April 2007. Yoroku Ueshiba, though elderly, may have also succumbed to the flu. For further information about tuberculosis in Japan during this time period see, Fukuka, Mahito, **A Cultural History of Tuberculosis in Modern Japan** at http://www.lang.nagoya-u.ac.jp/~mfukuda/english.html.

[29] See, the **Founder of Aikido: Move to Ayabe** by Kisshomaru Ueshiba, translated by Stanley A. Pranin and Midori Yamamoto; Aiki News magazine, article #44, 1984.

[30] **Yamato Damashii** - the philosophy that the Japanese people's spirit, qualities, and traditions, given to the world by the Yamato line of emperors, were unique to the world and, being such, should be aggressively disseminated around the world. Onisaburo Deguchi was entirely supportive of this ethnocentric idea, but his viewpoint concerning certain Japanese mythological facts from the **Kojiki** (Record of Ancient Matters) was contrary to that of Japan's reigning sovereign; this was the other significant reason that the Japanese government was 'out to get' Onisaburo and dismantle Omoto's societal influence and power. **Kokutai** -- prior to World War II, a specific national social policy presented, taught, and enforced by the Japanese government that included Yamato Damashii.

[31] The idea of "non-contention" is a valid proposition as part of a hypothetical psychological concept that can be applied toward obtaining accord or peace. In the case of humankind vs. Nature, non-contention has the potential to be fully realized; but, in the case of human vs. human it does

not always hold true because certain human mental conditions (e.g., un-resolvable anger-in-the-moment, self-indoctrination, and various mental disorders or diseases) and societal forces (e.g., societal indoctrination as it manifests in Statism, Fascism, or Ultranationalism) often result in a tumultuous outcome no matter what is done to avoid it. In Aikido, "non-contention" is supposedly accomplished by 'channeling' into a person the power of "creative love," which had been claimed by Morihei Ueshiba to be the primary force of Budo; unfortunately, full embracement by an aikidoka of such a theory tends to impair the inculcation of the technical skill that is necessary for self-defense when they begin to favor a psycho-spiritual approach as their preferred method of resolving potentially unsettling or destructive human vs. human encounters. See, *The Spirit of Aikido* (Aikido no Kokoro) by Kisshomaru Ueshiba, with Taitetsu Unno as translator; Kodansha International, Ltd., paperback edition, first printing, 1987, page 12. Also, see Chapter IX of this book for a detailed discussion of "non-contention."

[32] That which had been bequeathed was *1)* the *Kojiki* (Record of Ancient Matters, ~ 721 C.E.), which is a collection of ancient Japanese literary works that consists mostly of myths and poems but with some accounts of historical events and primarily relates 'the creation' of Japan's four main islands; and *2)* the *Nihon Shoki* (Chronicles of Japan, ~ 720 C.E.*)*, which, regarding historical events, is less inaccurate, more elaborate, and more detailed than the Kojiki. Over a three hundred year period, beginning in the Edo Period, both of these ancient literary works were interpreted from an ethnocentric viewpoint and subsequently drawn upon by a number of significant Japanese scholars, emperors, and statesmen to errantly craft the pre W.W. II ideology called *Yamato Damashii*, i.e., the 'divine plan,' known to the Japanese as the societal idea of *kami-kaze* (divine wind).

[33] See, *Morihei's Ueshiba Juku, Launchpad of a Martial Arts Career* by Stanley Pranin; published online by the Aikido Journal, October 31, 2011. See also the article entitled *Founder of Aikido: Idol Among the Soldiers* by Kisshomaru Ueshiba, translated by Stanley A. Pranin and Midori Yamamoto; Aiki News magazine, article #37, June, 1981.

[34] *Lèse-majesté* is an offense against the authority or dignity of a reigning sovereign, i.e., a crime against a monarch's authority or dignity. Omoto's newspaper violations stemmed from the effect of the *Safety Preservation Law* of 1894 C.E. and the *Public Order and Police Law* of 1900 C.E.

[35] Onisaburo Deguchi had left Japan, with Morihei Ueshiba in tow, against his bail conditions to lead a scouting mission to Northeast Asia to deter-

mine if he could relocate the Omoto-kyo there. Onisaburo was pardoned in May, 1927 C.E. See, the article entitled *Founder of Aikido: Omoto Affair, Prelude and Repercussions* by Kisshomaru Ueshiba, translated by Stanley A. Pranin and Midori Yamamoto; Aiki News magazine, article #53, 1983. See also, *Yasuaki Deguchi The Omoto Religion and Aikido (07)* by Stanley Pranin, published by the Aikido Journal, article #103, 1995.

[36] See, An *Essay on Criticism* by Alexander Pope, 1711 C.E.

[37] *Ultranationalism* is socio-political stance of people or groups of people within a nation that are opposed to excessive or unnecessary international interference with their nation's internal affairs.

[38] See the article entitled *Founder of Aikido: Death-Defying Trip to Mongolia* by Kisshomaru Ueshiba, translated by Stanley A. Pranin and Midori Yamamoto; Aiki News magazine, article #48, 1982.

[39] See, *Escape to Mongolia* by Stanley Pranin; Aiki News magazine, article #14, 1975.

[40] *Manchuria* is a name derived from the translation of the Japanese word *Manshū*, which refers to the historical Manchu Dynasty that at one time existed in certain northeastern provinces of the Asian continent; today it is part of the nation of China. "A Japanese, Takahashi Kageyasu, invented the name Manchuria in 1809 in the *Nippon Henkai Ryakuzu*, from where Westerners adopted the name." -- see webpage at http://en.wikipedia.org/wiki/Manchuria; 2011. Travel to Fengtian (often romanized as Mukden and know today as Shenyang, but know as Hoten to the Japanese) during that time was by ferryboat from Japan proper to Chōsen (Korea, but today divided into the separate countries of North and South Korea), then by locomotive through Chōsen into southern Manchuria (today part of China). Prior to 1910 C.E. and until the end of W.W. II, the two Korea's of today (i.e., the north and south states) were a single territory known as Joseon, but when Japan annexed Joseon in 1910 C.E., it was called Chōsen by the Japanese; today, when considered as a single territory, the two states are known as Hanguk by the south Koreans but as Chosŏn by the north Korean's.

[41] The Sanya Company was operated by the Japanese agricultural and land entrepreneur Yutaro Yano, a retired Japanese Imperial Navy captain and Omoto-kyo devotee. See, *Morihei Ueshiba: Founder of Aikido (Part 13)* by Kanemoto Sunadomari; Aiki News magazine, article #84, 1990.

[42] These became unified as Manchukuo (the state of Manchuria) after the Japanese invaded this area in 1931 C.E.; this invasion was later termed the *Mukden Incident.* Since the rise of the Peoples Republic of China after W.W. II, these provinces have been subdivided.

[43] Lu's superstitious inclination frequently interfered with reasonable decision-making. For further information, see, **Morihei Ueshiba: Founder of Aikido (Part 14)** by Kanemoto Sunadomari; Aiki News magazine, article #85, 1990.

[44] *"Omote-muki refers to that which is public, open, official; ura-muki suggests something private, closed, personal." "Omote o tateru is 'to put up a front.'" "Omote o tsukurou is 'to keep up appearances.'" "Omote o haru means 'to keep up a facade.'"* From Takeo Doi's **The Anatomy of Self: The Individual versus Society**.

[45] During this time in history, the term **Mongolia** referred to two separate geographic areas north of traditional dynastic China (China proper), west of Manchuria, south of Russia's Siberia, and east of East Turkestan, but comprised of two geographic areas. The southern of these two areas was called *Inner Mongolia* and the northern was called *Outer Mongolia*, both areas where Mongol peoples had for many centuries lived and roamed throughout. **Inner Mongolia**, in general, was that geographic area consisting of several frontier provinces that had been somewhat annexed by both China proper and Manchuria, 'sandwiched' between these on the south and east respectively, Russia and **Outer Mongolia** (which today is the officially recognized country of Mongolia) to the north, and East Turkestan (or, disputedly, Chinese Turkestan) to the west, and somewhat 'arc shaped' in its geographic outline. Inner Mongolia was partially controlled by 1) China proper, 2) Manchurian interests via military governor Zuòlín Zhāng, 3) Japan's interests there and its desire to control both Inner and Outer Mongolia, and 4) indigenous Mongolian chieftains, the latter who were frequently at odds with the former but sometimes joined their forces with the Chinese or Japanese when it served their own purposes. Manchuria itself was partially under the sociopolitical (i.e., cultural) influence of Japanese interests due to concessions that Japan had won there after its military engagement with Russia at the end of the Russo-Japanese War in 1905 C.E.; during this war, the Peking government of China proper was unable to muster the political and military might to intercede and took the position of neutrality, hoping that future efforts by powerful foreign leaders could produce a return of Manchuria to its control. The social nature of Mongol peoples of Inner and Outer Mongolia during this time was yet largely tribal and nomadic; Inner Mongolia was beset with much

banditry and violence. The history of the Asia continent between 1905 C.E. and the year 1949 is quite complex.

[46] Review the history of the First and Second Zhili-Fengtian Wars, which occurred between Zuòlín Zhāng's Fengtian army and the Chinese Zhili army. Though Zhāng had been partially defeated at the end of the First Zhili-Fengtian War during his attempt to gain control of Peking and northern China proper, he retained control over Manchuria. Onisaburo's Mongolian misadventure can be considered as either a side event that is simply a chapter in the history of both Omoto-kyo and Aikido or, in addition, as an event that helped Zhāng to further understand the tenacity of his rule over Manchuria and subsequently helped him to realize the urgency of attempting to consolidate Manchuria and northern China under his rule in order to resist the 'rising tide' of undesired Japanese expansion into northeast Asia. Since the end of the Russo-Japanese War in 1905 C.E., Japan had gained geographic and other concessions from Russia as well as China proper; one of the geographic concessions was the southern tip of the Liaodong Peninsula of Manchuria, which concession was called the Kwantung Leased Territory (1,350 square miles). This territory provided Japan with a 'legitimate' geographic area from which it could begin an open as well as covert colonization attempt of Manchuria; if Japan could control Manchuria then there was a possibility it could eventually move to take China proper and Mongolia. From 1905 C.E. until the end of World War II, the overt part of this far-reaching plan was presented to Asia and the world as the Greater East Asia Co-prosperity Sphere, while the behind-the-scenes part was comprised of the efforts of covert operatives of the Japanese *Kempeitai* (*Military Police Corps*) and those of Japan's unauthorized secret ultranational societies, such as *Gen'yosha* (*Dark Ocean Society*) and later, the *Kokuryukai* (*Black Dragon Society*). Zuòlín Zhāng had his 'hands full' with other difficult socio-political and military problems, and though frequently influenced by the Japanese interests, was wholly unwilling to let Onisaburo's activities interfere with his governance of Manchuria and his plans for North East Asia.

[47] See, *Morihei Ueshiba: Founder of Aikido (Part 15)* by Kanemoto Sunadomari; Aiki News magazine, article #86, 1990, page 1.

[48] See, *Morihei Ueshiba: Founder of Aikido (Part 15)* by Kanemoto Sunadomari; Aiki News magazine, article #86, 1990.

[49] Ibid.

[50] See, *Morihei Ueshiba: Founder of Aikido (Part 16)* by Kanemoto Sunadomari; Aiki News magazine, article #87, 1991. The *Suolun District* was a geographic area between Inner Mongolia and Manchuria that had been wrested from Russian control by rebellious, indigenous Mongols. At that time, it was separate from any official Manchurian or Chinese governance and was controlled by the Mongolian leader Man Tuohan. Today it is partially located in a small, western protrusion of Jilin Province in China to the northwest of the city of Baicheng, and part in the eastern Hinggan and Horqin areas of historical Inner Mongolia; its name is derived from the geologic prominence known as the Soulun Massif, geographically situated in the lower Khingan Mountain Range on its southeasterly slope.

[51] For more information regarding Onisaburo's brief association with the title of 'dalai lama,' see the *Founder of Aikido: Enlightenment at the Edge of Death (Part 1)* by Kisshomaru Ueshiba, translated by Stanley A. Pranin and Midori Yamamoto; Aiki News magazine, article #49, 1982 and the article entitled *Morihei Ueshiba: Founder of Aikido (Part 14)* by Kanemoto Sunadomari; Aiki News magazine, article #85, 1990. For another reference concerning the group's use of Tibetan Buddhist titles, see the article *Morihei Ueshiba: Founder of Aikido (Part 16)* by Kanemoto Sunadomari; Aiki News magazine, article #87, 1991. For a slightly different perspective of Onisaburo's adventure in Northeast Asia, see the book *Pan-Asianism in Modern Japanese History: Colonialsim, Regionalism and Borders* by Sven Saller and J. Victor Koschmann.

[52] It was illegal at that time in China proper as well as in Manchuria to preach any Japanese religion. Had Onisaburo succeeded in his mission, he would have permanently changed Omoto-kyo's name to Omoto Lamaism and taken on the name of Dalai Lama. See *Morihei Ueshiba: Founder of Aikido (Part 14)* by Kanemoto Sunadomari; Aiki News magazine, article #85, 1990. For Ueshiba's ordainment see, *Morihei Ueshiba: Founder of Aikido (Part 15)* by Kanemoto Sunadomari; Aiki News magazine, article #86, 1990. Such a bestowment was seemingly more a matter of necessity for Onisaburo rather than something that Ueshiba was actually prepared to receive at the time. Was it legitimate?

[53] See, *Morihei Ueshiba: Founder of Aikido (Part 16)* by Kanemoto Sunadomari; Aiki News magazine, article #87, 1991.

[54] See the web-log article *Transmission, Inheritance, & Emulation* [of Aikido] by Peter Goldsbury, section entitled *Mongolia*, published online at www.aikiweb.com, 2008 & 2009.

[55] Ibid.

[56] It is unknown if Onisaburo paid for some or all of these supplies. Zuòlín Zhāng had previously authorized the creation of this army in January of 1924 C.E.; the monies necessary to properly fund it probably came from Manchurian coffers, via Zhāng's finance director, Yongjiang Wang.

[57] When Onisaburo met with General Lu in Shenyang, it was agreed, among other considerations and decisions, that Onisaburo would act as an advising general to their army; this tends to support the alternative idea that both Lu and Onisaburo may have actually had the intent, from the beginning, to make use of military governor Zuòlín Zhāng's support until the point where Lu, with Onisaburo's assistance, mutinied. Onisaburo's participation as an advising general must have been kept a secret, as there does not seem to be mentioned anywhere that Zhāng was aware of this. See, *Morihei Ueshiba: Founder of Aikido (Part 15)* by Kanemoto Sunadomari; Aiki News magazine, article #86, 1990. The army's name, Xibei Zizhi Jun, had been previously approved by Zuòlín Zhāng, military governor and general of Manchuria. See, *Morihei Ueshiba: Founder of Aikido (Part 14)* by Kanemoto Sunadomari; Aiki News magazine, article #85, 1990 and the book entitled *Pan-Asianism in Modern Japanese History: Colonialsim, Regionalism and Borders* by Sven Saller and J. Victor Koschmann.

[58] This is clearly seen when Onisaburo returns to Japan after his misadventure in Inner Mongolia. Though he is praised by many of his fellow Japanese, he and the Omoto-kyo's activities and wealth are later the object of a second, thoroughgoing suppression in 1935 C.E. Since Omoto's persecution in Japan had originated at the royal level, he should have expected that Omoto's continued popularity and reestablishment of its power could only be viewed as a threat to the Emperor's sovereignty.

[59] It is also possible that during his conversations with his Omoto member Yano, and later with the Japanese *Manchukuo Chokokukai* in Manchuria, that he had been given either overt or covert surveillance or protection by one or more secret operatives of any of the Japan based governmental police organizations or Japanese secret societies; for example, the Japanese *Kempeitai* (*Military Police Corps*) or *Gen'yosha* (*Dark Ocean Society*) respectively.

[60] See, *Morihei Ueshiba: Founder of Aikido (Part 14)* by Kanemoto Sunadomari; Aiki News magazine, article #85, 1990.

[61] See the book entitled *Pan-Asianism in Modern Japanese History: Colonialsim, Regionalism and Borders* by Sven Saller and J. Victor Koschmann.

[62] See the article entitled *Founder of Aikido: Enlightenment at the Edge of Death (Part 1)* by Kisshomaru Ueshiba, translated by Stanley A. Pranin and Midori Yamamoto ; Aiki News magazine, article #49, 1982.

[63] Lu's intent seems to have been to free all of Mongolia from Chinese influence and control, but whether or not he openly and completely revealed this and its ramifications to Onisaburo is unknown; e.g., 'I intend to do this (or that), but if we fail it is likely that we'll be faced with execution. Do you understand what I mean?' For more information concerning this event, see *Pan-Asianism in Modern Japanese History: Colonialsim, Regionalism and Borders* by Sven Saller and J. Victor Koschmann.

[64] See the article entitled *Founder of Aikido: Death-Defying Trip to Mongolia* by Kisshomaru Ueshiba, translated by Stanley A. Pranin and Midori Yamamoto; Aiki News magazine, article #48, 1982.

[65] See, *Founder of Aikido: Enlightenment at the Edge of Death (Part 2)* by Kisshomaru Ueshiba, translated by Stanley A. Pranin and Midori Yamamoto; Aiki News magazine, article #50, 1982. It is reported that Onisaburo's group was lined up for execution, and that the executioner raised his rifle and pulled the trigger but its mechanism malfunctioned without firing; literally moments later the representative of from the Japanese Consulate in Chengchiatun arrived -- a Japanese Embassy clerk -- who 'negotiated' for their release. It is probable that their release was gained after the officer-in-charge secured a monetary sum for the Fengtian Army as well as a mutual understanding that Onisaburo and his group would be immediately returned to Japan.

[66] Omoto's persecution is more complex than I present, though this statement is sufficient to describe its general aire. Another factor that emerged for Onisaburo more problems that usual, but also, interestingly, may have saved him from even harsher treatment, was the fact that he was the illegitimate son of the Japanese Imperial Prince Taruhito Arisugawa [1835-1895 C.E.], who had been the governor general of the Eastern Japan Expedition during part of the Meiji Restoration. For an in-depth understanding of all the socio-political dynamics between the Omoto-kyo and the Japanese Emperor and his government, see 1) *Pan-Asianism in Modern Japanese History: Colonialsim, Regionalism and Borders* by Sven Saller and J. Victor Koschmann; 2) blog article *Transmission,*

Morihei Ueshiba: History, Piety, and the Ōmoto-kyō

Inheritance, & Emulation [of Aikido] by Peter Goldsbury, the section entitled **Mongolia**, published online at www.aikiweb.com, 2008 & 2009; and 3) **Yasuaki Deguchi The Omoto Religion and Aikido (07)** by Stanley Pranin, published by the Aikido Journal, article #103, 1995.

[67] A little pertinent history is useful: Military governor Zuòlín Zhāng suffered irrecoverable losses over the course of this war as he attempted to expand his control into northern China. Weakened by the loss of soldiers and equipment as well as from the financial chaos in Manchuria brought about by the military's demands upon its economy, his reputation as a competent commander and governor waned. The Japanese Kantogun (Kwantung) Army (based in Japan's leased area of the Liaodong Peninsula) urged him to decouple from his military conflicts with the Zhili Clique because he had over-extended his forces and weakened Manchuria's e-conomy. Finally relenting under continued Japanese pressure, Zhāng departed Peking (Beijing) on June 3, 1928 C.E. by train. On June 4, 1928 C.E., as this train passed under a viaduct on the southern outskirts of Shenyang, a bomb was dropped onto the roof of the coach in which he was riding by an operative of the Kantogun Army; the resulting explosion killed Zhāng quickly. With Zuòlín Zhāng dead and Manchuria's economy in shambles, Zhāng's son, Xueliang, assumed command as the military governor of Manchuria, but only for a short period of three years. Uncomfortable with the enticements and not-so-veiled threats applied by Manchuria's Japanese ultranationalists, Xueliang Zhāng was not as pliable as his father had been. When he assumed control of Manchuria, Xueliang Zhāng immediately formed an allegiance with the Chinese KMT faction, thus strengthening his control in Manchuria but infuriating the various Japanese pro-colonial, military, and ultranational factions. The KMT was a Chinese faction organized by Sun Yat Sen along the lines of the Soviet Union's Communist Party and often received funding from the Soviet Union, with whom the Japanese were at odds. The Manchurian (Mukden) Incident of 1931 C.E. was staged by the Kantogun Army as a 'false-flag' military action to justify, though erringly, a full military invasion of Manchuria; this was partially a response to Xueliang Zhāng's alignment with the KMT, partially out of Japanese ultranationlistic desire to colonize Manchuria, and partly out of Japanese outrage emerging from Zhāng's previous execution of two prominent Manchuria-based Japanese officials at a dinner party in January, 1929 C.E. Mao Zedong and other early re-volutionary Chinese who eventually formed the Chinese Communist Party joined the KMT in 1923 C.E. Later, in 1927 C.E., due to internal left and right wing strife, the KMT emerged two differing factions that found it difficult to cooperate in their desire to unify China toward putting an end to its Warlord Era. Eventually, in 1946, after Japan's defeat in W.W. II,

148   *Understanding Aikido*

these two factions -- the Chinese Nationalist Party headed by Chiang Kai Shek, and the Chinese Communist Party headed by Wang Jing Wei -- experienced a complete dissolution of cooperation and full-scale civil war broke out, the result of which was victory for the Chinese Communist Party and the creation of the People's Republic of China. Chiang Kai Shek and the remnants of his KMT party retreated to Taiwan in 1949, where he ruled until his death in 1975. At the end of the Chinese Civil War, Xueliang Zhāng departed mainland China with Chiang Kai Shek. In the year 1994, Zhāng immigrated to the United States of America, state of Hawaii, where he lived until his death in 2001.

[68] Having returned to Japan under Japanese police escort in July (perhaps August), 1925 C.E., Onisaburo Deguchi, was again brought before the Japanese court system. Remember, he had already been convicted in a lower court of *Lèse-majesté* and newspaper-publishing violations under the Public Security Preservation Laws of Japan for which he had been sentenced to five years in jail, but while on bail, awaiting the result of an appeal to Japan's high court, he departed Japan for Northeast Asia. Meanwhile, the higher court found problems with how the government had charged and handled its prosecution of Onisaburo and as a result overturned the lower court's decision. The government then reorganized its case and pursued a conviction on the newspaper violations only. Once again the lower court found in favor of the government and, *in absentia*, Onisaburo was convicted. Sentenced a second time to jail, he began serving that sentence as soon as he was returned to Japan from Northeast Asia. While in jail, yet another appeal was brought before the Japanese high court, but, on December 25, 1926 C.E., before his case was decided by the higher court, Japan's Emperor Taisho died; as a result, in accordance with Japanese law at that time, in May, 1927 C.E., he was pardoned. Onisaburo's problems had begun in early 1921 C.E. and came to a close, for this chapter of his life, in mid 1927 C.E.

[69] As a result of Omoto's Mongolian misadventure, several ultranationalist leaders had become aware of Onisaburo's conflict with the Japanese government and began to 'sympathize' with his struggles against it. It is likely that Ueshiba's connections with the Japanese Imperial Navy, which had been cultivated earlier as a result of his teaching at the Maizuru Naval Base, helped him to avoid prosecution; early on, the Japanese Imperial Navy considered Ueshiba to be a valuable teaching asset.

[70] See, **Shamanism in Japan** by Ichirō Hori; Japanese Journal of Religious Studies, 56 pages, December 1975. See also the different research with the same title, **Shamanism in Japan** by William P. Fairchild, Nanzan Institute

for Religion and Culture, Nanzan University, Nogoya, Japan, 122 pages, 1962.

[71] See, *Shamanism in Japan* by William P. Fairchild, Nanzan Institute for Religion and Culture, Nanzan University, Nogoya, Japan, 122 pages, 1962; *The Way of the Shaman: A Guide to Power and Healing* by Michael Harner, Bantam Books, paperback, second printing, 1982; *Hemp in Religion* at http://www.japanhemp.org/en/shinto.htm#moore; *An Overview of Shinto* at http://www.japanhemp.org/en/shintoinfo.htm; *Psychoactive Cannabis in Japan* at ://www.japanhemp.org/en/thc.htm; 2012.

[72] From Greek, meaning literally a 'becoming divine within'; originally used by an informal research group that studied the numerous inebriants of shamans in the 1970s. For a good, quick overview of entheogens, see the article entitled "Entheogen" at http://en.wikipedia.org/wiki/Entheogen; 2012. Siberian shamans have typically made use of the entheogen muscimol that is derived from the mushroom *Amanita muscaria*, which is an indigenous species in most of the Northern Hemisphere, including Japan.

[73] A similar relationship existed (exists) with the rice plant, too.

[74] Some historians and social observers suggest that Japan's Cannabis agricultural industry was also halted in order to create a situation where Japan was dependent upon Western cotton and synthetic fibers.

[75] Interestingly, it has been reported by people who have eaten the mushroom *Amanita muscaria*, without first subjecting it to parboiling in order to render ineffective its psychoactive component, that objects in view changed size rapidly and their visual perspective moved somehow to a position around or outside their body, all while breathing and perspiring heavily.

[76] See, *Shamanism in Japan* by Ichirō Hori; Japanese Journal of Religious Studies, 56 pages, December 1975.

[77] See, *Shamanism in Japan* by William P. Fairchild; Nanzan Institute for Religion and Culture, Nanzan University, Nogoya, Japan, 122 pages, 1962.

[78] See, *Shamanism in Japan* by Ichirō Hori; Japanese Journal of Religious Studies, 56 pages, December 1975.

[79] See the Glossary for a definition of "*metareality*" as well as other terms.

[80] *Takemusu Aiki* is Morihei Ueshiba's metaphysical thesis that he pro-

posed as a guiding philosophy for Aikikai Aikido. See, *Takemusu Aiki - Lectures of Morihei Ueshiba, Founder of Aikido (1)* by Morihei Ueshiba, edited by Stanley Pranin; Aikido Journal, article #116, 1999; *Takemusu Aiki - Lectures of Morihei Ueshiba, Founder of Aikido (2)* by Morihei Ueshiba, edited by Stanley Pranin; Aikido Journal, article #117, 1999; *Takemusu Aiki - Lectures of Morihei Ueshiba, Founder of Aikido (3)* by Morihei Ueshiba, edited by Stanley Pranin; Aikido Journal, article #118, 1999.

[81] Kisshomaru never fully implemented those aspects of his father's theological philosophy that he thought were too subjectively derived and could not prove useful toward shaping a reasonably, i.e., objectively, arrived at techni-philosophical basis for Aikido. Anyone can see his concern about subjective hypothetical theory when reading his book entitled *The Spirit of Aikido*; e.g., he presents a major concern about whether or not the concept of *ki* can be verified as imagined or experienced by his father, and therein he requests that students around the world make a <u>scientific analysis</u> of it in order to attempt to prove its validity from an objective viewpoint, if possible. The Aikikai Aikido of today still largely reflects Kisshomaru Ueshiba's influence. In spite of his efforts and those of others like Gozo Shioda and Kenji Tomiki to keep Aikido away from excessive or unnecessary, often distracting, and frequently unproductive association with subjective spiritual esotericism, there is today an assault upon Aikido from several modern quirky subjective esoteric spiritual movements as well as from an attempt by at least one shrine Shinto group to thoroughly imbed Aikido into its rituals. I say this in spite of Morihei Ueshiba's statement that "Aikido is a religion without being a religion." *What he meant by this is that when a person practices Aikido, they practice a discipline that endeavors to inculcate in a student the philosophic idea that one should act to protect, sustain, and enhance life; and that Aikido engenders, manifests, or gives support to such as an ideal.* He did not mean that Aikido's essence resides solely in subjective esotericism or that it should reflect the quirky characteristics that are so often found in cult or cult-like spiritual movements.

[82] I've rewritten the account of what was reported but retained the essence of this vision. For Kisshomaru's description of what happened, see the article entitled *Founder of Aikido: The Founder Becomes a Golden Body* by Kisshomaru Ueshiba, translated by Stanley A. Pranin and Midori Yamamoto; Aiki News magazine, article #54, 1988. Interestingly, Morihei Ueshiba's first vision is remarkably similar to many other's that had occurred around the world during the decades, if not centuries, preceding him. As proposed by neo-Theosophy, the etheric body is a name that identifies a vital force or energy that is the first or lowest layer of the human aura.

It is claimed to be in contact with the physical body, where it functions to sustain or animate a person's body as well as to provide a means by which they may 'connect' with 'higher' bodies or beings that exist in different dimensional planes. Additionally, see Morihei Ueshiba's writings that were posthumously entitled *The Art Of Peace*, those having been translated and edited by John Stevens; published by Shambhala Publications, Inc., paperback, first printing, 1992.

[83] *Sarutahiko no Mikoto*, among other mythical roles, is considered to be the guardian deity of Aikido. For some quick background information about this deity, see, https://en.wikipedia.org/wiki/Sarutahiko_Okami; 2012. For some quick background information about the Japanese mythical deity Susanoo-no-Mikoto, see http://en.wikipedia.org/wiki/Susanoo-no-Mikoto. Chapter III, endnote 19 of this book contains a refresher concerning this deity's role in Japanese mythology. See also, *Transmission, Inheritance, Emulation*, section *III -- Deguchi, Ueshiba and Omoto*, subsection entitled *Myths and Doctrines*, an online weblog tome by Peter Goldsbury, professor, Hiroshima University, Japan; available on the internet at www.aikiweb.com.

[84] See the Wikipedia references. http://en.wikipedia.org/wiki/Apophenia, http://en.wikipedia.org/wiki/Hierophany, and http://en.wikipedia.org/wiki /Pareidolia; 2013.

[85] See, *Myth and Reality* by Mircea Eliade; HarperCollins, 1968. See also, *The Idea of the Holy: An Inquiry into the Non-rational Factor in the Idea of the Divine and Its Relation to the Rational* by Rudolf Otto; Oxford University Press, 1936.

[86] See, *Cosmos and History: The Myth of the Eternal Return* by Mircea Eliade; Harper & Row, 1959.

[87] However, such a condition is historically known to be true for some shamans or mystics; e.g., some Shinto priests where shamans, but it is quite unusual to find a shaman who identifies with a fixed set of spiritual traditions, such as those specific to any particular Shinto shrine.

[88] See, *Takemusu Aiki - Lectures of Morihei Ueshiba, Founder of Aikido (1)* by Morihei Ueshiba, edited by Stanley Pranin; Aikido Journal, article #116, 1999.

[89] See, *A Year in the Life of a Shinto Shrine* by John K. Nelson, University of Washington Press, paperback, 1996, page 37.

[90] See, *Japan Times and Mail,* July 25, 1926, p. 4. See, **Nakayama Hakudō** at http://en.wikipedia.org/wiki/Nakayama_Hakudō; 2013. See also, **The Fall of Japan** by Craig William, The Dial Press, New York, NY; hardback, 1967. German *Academic Fencing*, also sometimes called *Mensur* (meaning "dimension," which is an approximate corollary to Japanese combative distance known as *ma-ai*), has a similar goal. During Japan's flight from the old to the new military model during the Meiji Restoration (1868 - 1912 C.E.), it is probable that the Japanese military's early and intense interest in German fighting methods during the 19th and early 20th centuries was partly stimulated by this type of swordplay.

[91] Also, contemplate what had occurred in Japan between 1890 C.E. and the end of W.W. II. In 1890 an imperial edict was issued that had the effect of defining the fundamental principles of Japan's educational system. These principles had been carefully crafted from Confucianism in a way so as to emphasize loyalty to Japan's emperor and filial piety as a national virtue. Upon his birth, Morihei Ueshiba was shaped, i.e., subtly and surely indoctrinated, by this and other Japanese social policies. Expressed a little differently, the way in which Ueshiba grew, evolved, and existed was significantly a result of the effect of the Japanese societal template from the time of his birth until his death. Though Onisaburo Deguchi 'opened' Ueshiba's mind to other possibilities, the effect of Japanese society required Ueshiba to conform, or else -- meaning, else suffer persecution and imprisonment in a manner similar to what happened to Onisaburo. For more information, see **Introduction to Japanese Law** by Yosiyuki Noda, University of Tokyo Press, English translation, hardback, 1976, pages 60, 61, and 62.

[92] Suwa Shinto performs at least one ritual that makes use of a sword. See, **A Year in the Life of a Shinto Shrine** by John K. Nelson, University of Washington Press, paperback, 1996, pages 85 through 90.

[93] There are several known ritualized blessings for swords in European cultures, too, e.g., the ancient Druid blessing ritual that involves a maiden and the presentation of the sword to certain celestial bodies.

[94] See the book **The Spirit of Aikido** by Kisshomaru Ueshiba. Translated by Taitetsu Unno. Kodansha International, Ltd., paperback edition, first printing, 1987, pages 27 and 30.

[95] See, **Morihei Ueshiba and Kenji Tomiki** by Stanley Pranin. Article first published by the Wushu magazine, a Japanese publication, and made available as article #70 at Aikido Journal's Internet site.

[96] See, *Founder of Aikido: The Turmoil of War* by Kisshomaru Ueshiba, translated and summarized by Larry and Seiko Bieri; Aiki News magazine, article #65, 1984.

[97] See the article entitled *Founder of Aikido: The Kobukan Hell-Dojo Period (Part 1)* by Kisshomaru Ueshiba, translated by Stanley A. Pranin and Midori Yamamoto; Aiki News magazine, article #60, 1984.

[98] See the web-blog article *Transmission, Inheritance, & Emulation* [of Aikido] by Peter Goldsbury, section entitled *The Sakurakai Assassins and Morihei Ueshiba*, published online at www.aikiweb.com, 2008 & 2009.

[99] The significant police and military institutions where Morihei Ueshiba taught were the *Naval Staff College (Kaigun Daigakku)*, *Army University (Rikugun Shikan Gakko)*, *Military Police School (Kempei Gakko)*, *Toyama School (Rikugun Toyama Gakko)*, and the *Nakano Spy School (Rikugun Nakano Gakko)*. See the article entitled **Kobukan Dojo Era** by Stanley Pranin, published by the Aikido Journal, 2002.

[100] The *Tokubetsu Kōtō Keisatsu* (Special Higher Police) was a special secret police corps that operated solely in Japan proper. The *Kempeitai* (Military Police Corps) operated in Manchuria.

[101] See the web-log article *Transmission, Inheritance, & Emulation* [of Aikido] by Peter Goldsbury, section entitled *The Emperor System and the Kokutai*, published online at www.aikiweb.com, 2008 & 2009.

[102] See the web-log article *Transmission, Inheritance, & Emulation* [of Aikido] by Peter Goldsbury, section entitled *The Sakurakai Assassins and Morihei Ueshiba*, published online at www.aikiweb.com, 2008 & 2009.

[103] See the article entitled the *Founder of Aikido: The Budo Enhancement Association and Takeda Dojo* by Kisshomaru Ueshiba, translated and summarized by Larry and Seiko Bieri; Aiki News magazine, article #62, 1984.

[104] See the web-log article *Transmission, Inheritance, & Emulation* [of Aikido] by Peter Goldsbury, the section entitled *Government Investigates Omoto*, published online at www.aikiweb.com, 2008 & 2009.

[105] See the web-log article *Transmission, Inheritance, & Emulation* [of Aikido] by Peter Goldsbury, section entitled *Showa Shinseikai*, published online at www.aikiweb.com, 2008 & 2009. See also the article entitled the

Founder of Aikido: The Budo Enhancement Association and Takeda Dojo by Kisshomaru Ueshiba, translated and summarized by Larry and Seiko Bieri; Aiki News magazine, article #62, 1984.

[106] See *Founder of Aikido: An Unforgettable Benefactor* by Kisshomaru Ueshiba; Aiki News magazine #64, 1984. This type of suppression has happened to many religious sects throughout history. For a recent example, review the Branch Dividians' suppression of 1993 in Waco, Texas.

[107] Many arrestees were tortured and afterward became mentally instable. Some committed suicide or died as a result of the imprisonment conditions. See the *Founder of Aikido (34): An Unforgettable Benefactor* by Kisshomaru Ueshiba; Aiki News magazine #63, 1984.

[108] See Wikipedia article entitled *Police Services of the Empire of Japan*. http://en.wikipedia.org/wiki/Police_services_of_the_Empire_of_Japan; 2013.

[109] See *Morihei Ueshiba and the Omoto Religion* by Stanley Pranin, published by the Aikido Journal, 2005.

[110] See the following Wikipedia articles for more information about these Japanese military factions: the *Sakurakai* at http://en.wikipedia.org/wiki/Sakurakai, the *Imperial Way Faction* (Kōdōha) at http://en.wikipedia.org/wiki/Imperial_Way_Faction, the *Tōseiha* at http://en.wikipedia.org/wiki/Tōseiha; 2014. Also, see the article entitled the *Founder of Aikido: The Budo Enhancement Association and Takeda Dojo* by Kisshomaru Ueshiba, translated and summarized by Larry and Seiko Bieri; Aiki News magazine, article #62, 1984 for information about Onisaburo's involvement with the Showa Restoration movement and his belief that Japanese budo was divinely bequeathed.

[111] See Morihei Ueshiba's writings that were posthumously entitled *The Art Of Peace*, those having been translated and edited by John Stevens; Shambhala Publications, Inc., paperback, first printing, 1992.

[112] See *Founder of Aikido: The Turmoil of War* by Kisshomaru Ueshiba; Aiki News magazine #65, 1984.

[113] I've rewritten the account of what was reported but retained the essence of this vision. See Morihei Ueshiba's writings that were posthumously published and entitled *The Art Of Peace*, those having been translated and edited by John Stevens; published by Shambhala Publications,

Inc., paperback, sixth printing, 1992.

[114] After S.C.A.P. had lifted the ban on the practice of Japan's indigenous martial arts, which began to occur around 1952, the military branches of the member nations of the Allied Powers were very interested in the various Japanese martial disciplines, especially Judo and Aiki-budo/Aikido. As a result, numerous expert budoka were permitted entrance into the U.S.A., Australia, Great Britain, and France to teach their knowledge to military personnel. For example, Kenji Tomiki taught Aiki-budo/Aikido to the U.S. Air Force when he participated in a joint Japan/U.S.A. martial art/cultural exchange program, which consisted of numerous budoka and had been organized by the efforts of Professor Sumiyuki Kotani (of Kodokan Judo, Japan) and Emilio Bruno (Director of the U.S. Strategic Air Command's physical enhancement program), beginning in 1953.

[115] See the Wikipedia reference concerning Aikikai Aikido's Tadashi Abe, who was notorious for his objections to the dilution of the martial characteristics of Aiki-budo as it changed into Aikido, which process resulted in an effeminate discipline (Aikikai Aikido) that should not be considered to be a martial art. http://en.wikipedia.org/wiki/Tadashi_Abe; 2013.

[116] For further information about "quasi-secular," see the article entitled *The Founder Morihei Ueshiba, a God? Reflections on the Anniversary of Japan's Surrender to the US Coalition* by Gyaku Homma; published online by the Nippon Kan, August 15, 2005. http://www.nippon-kan.org/senseis_articles/05_uishiba-god/05_ueshiba-god.html.

[117] Ibid.

[118] See Kenji Tomiki's *Greeting at the Opening of Shodokan*, an article transcribed from his speech at the ceremonial opening of the Shodokan Aikido headquarters, March 28, 1976. http://en.shodokanaikido.com/about/greeting.html. *Shinjin* means {faith}, {belief}, {devotion}, or {godliness}; e.g., faith in *aiki*.

Chapter V

Aikikai versus Shōdōkan: Conflicting Views of Budō

There are a number of different styles of true Aikido that exist today, and all have been strongly influenced by its founder, Morihei Ueshiba. A significant number of Japanese Budo professionals were influenced to a lesser or greater degree by his teachings. Notable are Noriaki Inoue, Kenji Tomiki, Minoru Mochizuki, Gozo Shioda, Minoru Harai, Kisshomaru Ueshiba, Kōichi Tōhei, Morihiro Saitō, and Kenshiro Abbe. Differences in the perception of that which comprised the essence of Budo was the primary harbinger of disagreement that set the path for each style's arrival, but so too, though secondarily, was the natural inclination of these people to make their own mark in history while doing what they did best, i.e., combative arts. The reasoning of one or another of these individuals produced certain personally-held attitudes that were influenced by their contemplation of the foundational characteristics of Budo; but, what was truth for one was not necessarily so for the other. Of primary importance were two areas of contention. First, *When compared to Japan's historical martial tradition, how should the kanji for **bu** be interpreted and then applied to the performance of any martial art, policing discipline, self-defense discipline, or combative sport?* Second, *What was the best role of the concept of aiki[1] in relation to the performance of these, i.e., was its primary role that of facilitating technical prowess or was it an ethereal one that was difficult to both quantify and utilize in a way that did not beget unwarranted or useless magico-religiosity?* (See Chapters I and III.) The differing ideas of these men can be clearly discerned and appreciated by comparing the statements of each individual during Aikido's evolution from a form of Jujutsu to Aiki-budo, from Aiki-budo to its present name, Aikido, and from a sole Aikido to the emergence of various styles of Aikido. (See Section VI.) There are four primary participants: Jigoro Kano (Judo's founder), Morihei Ueshiba (Aiki-budo's founder), Kenji

Aikikai versus Shōdōkan: Conflicting Views of Budō

Tomiki (Shodokan Aikido's founder), and Kisshomaru Ueshiba (the co-founder of Aikikai Aikido). However, before examining the personally held attitudes of these important individuals, a little foundational discussion concerning an earlier formative period of Aikido, 1915 C.E. thru 1942 C.E., is worthwhile. During this period there arose an ongoing multifaceted and ever-fluctuating cross-organizational conflict of ideas and social positioning that would shape a small but important part of Japan's history; it was comprised of the differing attitudes promoted by Jigoro Kano's Kōdōkan Judo organization, Morihei Ueshiba's coming-of-age Aiki-budo discipline (this is the name by which his discipline was known before it became named *aikido* in 1942 C.E.), Sokaku Takeda's Daitō-ryū Aiki-jūjūtsū, and the Dai Nippon Butokukai (the Greater Japan Martial Virtue Association). Struggles of this type, where competing ideas result in interpersonal squabbles, usually come about between people or organizations when unique or powerful personages, each holding certain attitudinal positions, take action toward implementing their agendas as shaped by the effect of their cognition intertwined with the culturally imbued traditions present in their society. Such was the situation for each of these historical participants during that period. Morihei Ueshiba's behavior was partially shaped by his religious tendency, and this evolved for him as well as for his devotees *a statement of collective attitudinal difference* that resulted in what amounted to an attempted redefinition of that which had traditionally comprised the ethics and activities of Budo.[2] Of course, the reader may know that during this period of time the traditional martial arts were undergoing a restructuring process. Jigoro Kano, who established the basis for modern Judo (The Gentle Way), having established his Kodokan organization, was the preeminent motivational force in reshaping and revitalizing many of the old Jujutsu forms while also clarifying the modern meaning of the values of Bushido that would later become redefined and renamed as Budo. Any discussion of the development of Aikido must consider the effect of Kano and his Kodokan. Here, to begin your thought, an interesting initial comparison is quickly found in their organizational names -- the Kodokan (Kano's official organizational body) established in 1882 C.E., and, the Kobukan (Morihei Ueshiba's first official organization body for Aiki-budo), established in 1931 C.E. (In fact, somewhat confusingly, there is even an Aikikai affiliated style of Aikido in Okazaki, Japan named Kodokan Aikido, which was initiated by Morihei Ueshiba in the year 1957). Jigoro Kano was on a mission to save the techniques and the unique martial characteristics of these old Japanese martial arts, and in order to do so he found it expedient to send out many of his most accomplished Judo students to study with the old school masters. After observing a demonstration given by Morihei Ueshiba in the autumn of 1930 C.E., Kano sent his student Minoru Mochizuki in late 1930 C.E. to Tokyo (the Shinjuku ward) to study with Ueshiba at the latter's Kobukan Dojo. Kenji Tomiki, on his own initiative, had begun training much earlier with Ueshiba in the summer of 1927 C.E., a result of an introduction in Tokyo by a senior judoka of Waseda University; later, in 1936 C.E., after a lengthy conversation with Jigoro Kano (then age 75), Tomiki was encouraged by him to continue study with Ueshiba so that the latter's knowledge of Daito-ryu Aikijutsu could be assimilated into the Kodokan.[3]

During Japan's late Taisho Period (1912-1926 C.E.) and through the majority of its Showa Period (1926-1989 C.E.), Morihei Ueshiba initiated a reshaping of Daito-ryu Jujutsu in a manner that had some similarity to that which Jigoro Kano had accomplished for Kitō-ryū and Shinyō-ryū Jujutsu, yet there was a significant difference based in Morihei's emerging piety toward the Shinto derived Omoto-kyo religion. Morihei's devout study of Omoto-kyo had helped infuse his being with a certain sincere and unique metaphysical urge, and this spiritual quality in him is that which has shaped the philosophical essence of all Aikido, whether it is the founding style, Aikikai Aikido, or other, such as Shōdōkan Aikido (Japan Aikido Association, founded by Kenji Tomiki) or Shin-shin Tōitsu Aikido (often referred to as Ki Aikido). The loose collection of philosophical tenets and spiritual teachings which were to become Aikido's philosophy gradually coalesced into a unified philosophical and technical statement as Morihei Ueshiba experienced life, responding to it from an attitudinal position that was inherent in his own human nature, thus giving rise to a *wind of change* that would apply its force toward reshaping the meaning of that which today comprises Japan's traditional Budo. (This same effect shaped his son's guidance of Aikido when Kisshomaru Ueshiba assumed control of Aikikai Aikido in 1969.) Up until his untimely death in 1938 C.E., Jigoro Kano had been such a force of change, too, when he extracted from Kitō-ryū and Shinyō-ryū Jujutsu the necessary technical and philosophical elements that were necessary to form

Judo. Morihei Ueshiba was undoubtedly subjected to the affect of this other reform, that is, Kano's perception of that which constituted the meaning of Budo. Kano's reformation of several of the old Jujitsu forms was characterized somewhat differently than that of Ueshiba's synthesis of Aikido from Daito-ryu and other forms of Jujutsu, though each had in mind, at some point, a similar underlying ethic -- that of developing healthy, productive, and benevolent people who would act to protect, sustain and enhance life. Kano's reasoning was two-fold, *first*, the presentation of the important philosophy of the harmonious development within a person of his *Three Culture Principle*, consisting of the improvement of the physical, moral, and intellectual attributes of the human being, and *second*, the introduction of Judo, both competitive and noncompetitive forms, as a method to facilitate inculcation of this principle. In contrast, Ueshiba's reasoning, as it evolved later in his life, was to provide a bridge to peace by encouraging harmonious interaction among all people, and Aikido was the method that he felt was eminently useful toward accomplishing this goal. Morihei Ueshiba applied purposefully the force of his unique personality, vitality, knowledge, and skill toward redefining Bushido's ethics as well as clarifying its spiritual elements: an example of this is his important translation of the character that represents martial art, 武, written in romaji as *bu*. In his later years, he was considered as Japan's most revered Budo expert. Yet, notwithstanding, and in spite of Aikido's many proponents today, this clarification has only affected its meaning for those who have accepted its "true" meaning as translated by him -- that being, the way of "*stopping the weapons of destruction*." It is important, now, to pause for some brief thought about the meaning of "stopping the weapons of destruction." A rhetorical question: Can the activities of randori (meaning *free play*; better translated as *taming disorder)* and shiai (with a general meaning of *competition* but translated better as a *meeting to test each other*) be useful in training aikidoka about how to stop the weapons of destruction? Morihei Ueshiba and some of his successors may have been able to attach to Budo a more peaceful meaning through his particular reading of martial *bu*, but such a meaning is subjective, and interestingly, is today largely unknown. The foundational brush stroke for this kanji sinogram is the halberd or spear, known as the *yari*; with additional strokes, its meaning is best expressed as that of "*suppressing revolt*"[4] with an emphasis on regaining order. A spear, no matter how modified, is a dubious image for harmony. Of course, social changes that occur throughout or over time can manifest as an evolution rather than devolution, and when the former occurs, the old symbolism, the meaning of a symbol or linguistic construct, not the symbol or construct itself, often changes to thereby represent a higher societal consciousness.

For aikidoka and martial artists alike, in fact, for any person who may contemplate the ethics of Aikido or any other martial art, Morihei Ueshiba clarified, through his great effort, keen perceptions, and skill, that which comprised the primary ethical foundation of Budo. To some martial proponents, however, Budo's true meaning was then, and is now, arguably different; e.g., Sokaku Takeda's and Minoru Mochizuki's.[5] Today, its best definition arises probably from meaning given by the attitudes of collective generations of Japanese martial art and physio-spiritual self-defense proponents (both native and foreign), each of whom placed either a defensive or offensive emphasis at the forefront of their personal attitude, with some attempting a balance between these two positions. As an exercise in contemplation, is the first principle of Budo (as elucidated by Morihei Ueshiba) considered to vary or to fluctuate in its ethical composition depending on its interpretation by the proponents of any different Japanese derived martial art or martial society, or for that matter, by any succeeding doshu? Among those who may be able to speak for the other martial arts, it is likely that some disagreement or uncertainty exists.

Is a purported aikido only Aikido if it comports with the teachings of the Aikikai? Let's compare Morihei Ueshiba's elucidation of the first principle of Budo with that of Kenji Tomiki, then, discern the effect that Kisshomaru Ueshiba's interpretations of his father's elucidations have had in shaping the philosophic essence of present day Aikido.

To begin, as stated earlier, Morihei Ueshiba relates that the true meaning of martial bu is "to stop weapons of destruction." Though no such concise statement exists from Tomiki he does state in his book ***Judo and Aikido*** that "*It is against the spirit of the Japanese martial arts to be fond of killing and using violence.*"[6] Furthermore, from his treatise ***On Jujutsu and Its Modernization***, he states "*At its heart, Jujutsu, of whatever kind, is for protecting oneself against the attacks of an opponent.*"[7] It is evident from statements such as these that Kenji Tomiki held in his thoughts a similar conceptualization of that which comprised martial bu. Notwithstanding, he and his teacher Morihei Ueshiba each had evolved divergent opinions about that which defined some of the important foundational aspects of Aikido as given by both the definition of *martial bu,* as in Budo, and by that which past proponents of Budo had embraced as true Budo, such as in its traditional sense; furthermore, Morihei Ueshiba's son, Kisshomaru, was soon to enter the arena of Aikido's history to make clear that which he considered to be Aikido's identifying philosophic tenants.

The divergence between Kenji Tomiki and his teacher became more evident after World War II when, in the year 1948, Tomiki was released from Russian incarceration. Yet, considering that he had had strong connections with Jigoro Kano, founder of modern Judo, and in light of the views promulgated by the Kodokan concerning the modernization of all budo forms (excepting its pre W.W. II anti-governmental control position), there can be little wonder that such divergence would eventually cause the birth of a some-what different style of Aikido; Kano was instrumental in the push to collect all old Jujutsu traditions under one organizational body. The primary point of difference was to what extent the metaphysical and theological emphasis in Aikido would be permitted to diminish the importance of randori and shiai when considering whether or not practical self-defense effectiveness could be maintained in Aikido.

Some who contemplate the spiritual essence of Kenji Tomiki in contrast to Morihei Ueshiba would likely say that he was not an especially pious man; but such judgment comes only from those who have either their own special bias toward obfuscation or are making a judgment based upon their own belief system. Tomiki's spirituality manifested itself differently than that of his Aikido teacher's, and in addition to his physical fitness, self-defense, and sport-oriented endeavors he was also known for his artistic expression through calligraphy, which can be considered an aspect of his spirituality. His personality can be partially understood through his statements:

"What are the distinctive features of Japanese Budo? They are surely matters of spirit and philosophy.";[8]

Aikikai versus Shōdōkan: Conflicting Views of Budō

"A man's worth on the spiritual side consists in being possessed of reason and dealing with things intellectually, while on the physical side it lies in being able to make an extensive use of modern tools.";[9]

"Judo is a way to refine our spirit by using the Way of those principles.";[10] and

"Considering from the spiritual side, the martial arts of Japan were a form of self-discipline for the perfection of personality. In this respect they had something in common with the practice of austerities to attain a spiritual enlightenment in religion."[11]

From these statements, one may begin to develop an understanding of Kenji Tomiki's spiritual as well as practical attitudes. Certainly, he deeply valued matters of philosophic and spiritual nature, but in a somewhat different way than Morihei Ueshiba.

Returning to the interpersonal dynamics that caused the divergence between Tomiki and his teacher, and as well with Morihei Ueshiba's successor, Kisshomaru Ueshiba, there is Tomiki's statement from his book *On Jujutsu and Its Modernization*:

"It has been a special character of Budo down through the ages that it does not tend to abandon either randori or kata, but rather embraces both and sees value in both."[12]

Standing alone, this statement is sufficient to understand the nature of the concern that Tomiki felt with the philosophical direction that Aikido was beginning to take during the late 1950's. During this period of Aikido's development, Kisshomaru Ueshiba, a young man, was formulating the concept that *"true"* Budo could only be realized when a practitioner disavowed the competitive attitude, thus positioning them in a mental stance that was more completely focused on, ostensibly, the spiritual journey. It is interesting to contemplate that this particular collectively evolved and mutually held attitude (as such was embraced by other significant aikidoka as well) was neither solely nor necessarily arrived at by the means of a careful psycho-spiritual evaluation of the human condition, but rather, in part, as a protective response to two societal aspects that occurred for all Japanese people following their defeat in W.W. II. *Firstly*, the Japanese people immediately following the Japanese surrender in

1945 C.E. experienced collectively a great loss of cultural identity around that which had comprised traditional Japanese character and society -- the majority of Japanese seriously questioned what had caused their nation to descend into the miserable state of initiating a war that emerged such destruction. Defeated, they were continuously scrutinized by the occupation forces under the guidance of the Supreme Commander of the Allied Powers, S.C.A.P. During the period from 1945 C.E. until the year 1952, most Japanese people, including Morihei and Kisshomaru Ueshiba, reflected upon all of that which comprised their personal being and identity as well as that which would, in the future, establish the new qualities of the Japanese national character; in fact, Morihei retreated to Iwama, Ibaraki Prefecture in 1942 C.E. to begin his own considerations and did not emerge from seclusion until sometime in the year 1956. *Secondly*, S.C.A.P. had immediately abolished all of the organizations that had supported the Japanese military, including all martial art organizational entities, and forbade the practice of any martial art. During this time, Kisshomaru was with his father at Iwama training in and reshaping his father's Aiki-budo, both preparing for the postwar reality. Shortly after the Japanese Emperor's radio surrender broadcast in 1945 C.E., in his book entitled *Aikido Ichiro* (Aikido One Path), Kisshomaru Ueshiba, disturbed by the events and outcome of the war, relates that "*Certainly there is much of Japanese culture that we can be proud of, but now that the war has ended, the estimation of this has fallen to zero.*" [13] He continues further and writes that "*Even though I have not progressed so far in aikido, I believed that aikido was an excellent part of this culture: not only the waza, but especially the spiritual aspects of this budo. I wanted some day to bring this aikido to America and Europe and say: 'Observe! There is something good here, even from Japan. It is a budo without fighting and with a positive philosophy towards the opponent... .'*" [13] Under the scrutiny of S.C.A.P., Aiki-budo, newly renamed Aikido, the Aiki-budo demonstrated on the pages of Morihei Ueshiba's previous published book entitled *Budo Renshu*, published in 1933 C.E. and edited by Kenji Tomiki, was certainly martial in its characteristics (specifically oriented toward military use), a budo definitely to be proscribed during the occupation. Therefore, in the minds of both Morihei and Kisshomaru Ueshiba (the latter who would soon enough become the inheritor of the Aikikai's tradition of Aikido), no competitive practice or event, particularly shiai, could be a useful training element in or for Aikido. Shiai, they felt, or at least the mental formation of the attitude required to engage in such, had been a harmful part of Japan's Jujutsu systems that had fostered a certain degree of troublesome national pride, which had errantly led Japan upon its ethno-economic march toward modernization and attempted dominance by the means of aggressive, belligerent, ultranationalistic militarism. For both Ueshibas, the role that Aiki-budo had had prior to the end of W.W. II, i.e., training people to destroy other people, must not be revisited in the new era after W.W. II.

Strongly influenced by the ugly events and outcome of the war, Kisshomaru Ueshiba, even forty years later, states adamantly that "*Aikido rejects all forms of violence, justified or unjustified. Otherwise, we would be no different from the forms of martial arts in which fighting and winning are selling points*"[14] and that it is "*... primarily a spiritual path which decries any form of competition or tournament where victors or vanquished are decided and everything hinges on winning.*"[15] At this juncture, according to Tomiki, and likely to hundreds of other preceding Japanese martial art masters, "true martial bu" frequently and typically embraces both randori and shiai in order to validate technical practicality as well as express sociological characteristics that might be considered as having a spiritual aire. In opposition, according to Kisshomaru Ueshiba, "true martial bu" as manifested in Aikido does not include randori or shiai, particularly in the form of modern tournament, as these are forms of violence.[16] Which of these attitudes is correct? Or, is it reasonable to combine the merit in each of these viewpoints to thereby transcend their antithetical nature? Stanley Pranin, in his informative article entitled **Background on Kenji Tomiki Sensei**, clearly presents to us that "*... Tomiki, like O-Sensei, saw the budo of old as being cruel and overwhelmingly concerned with fighting and victory.*"[17] Notwithstanding this shared viewpoint, Pranin goes on to tell us that "*While O-Sensei developed an approach based on harmony of movement and a non-fighting mind, Professor Tomiki felt the answer lay in channeling the aggressive energies stirred by martial training into sport.*"[17] This difference of opinion became the major part of the basis of unresovable contention between Kenji Tomiki and both Ueshibas.

Unwittingly, today, the Aikikai has relinquished its once exclusive heritage right, or ownership, of the term *aikido* when it made the decision to completely divorce itself from shiai, itself a type of dialectic in the form of physical contest. Other than the obvious desire to preserve Morihei Ueshiba's Aiki-budo in a post W.W. II Japan, and other than philosophical ideology which itself had been shaped by various personal attitudes and societal forces, yet another reason the Aikikai made this decision was to minimize the extent to which Kenji Tomiki would influence Aikido's future development from the viewpoint of the Judo perspective, a competing line of thought. Though much can be considered from the position of what might have been, it is not much of a mental stretch to consider that a refusal to embrace some form of shiai has weakened not only certain technical aspects of some styles of Aikido but also the Aikikai's organizational guidance and influence over other Aikido brethren; from this latter has emerged a great problem for Aikido as a whole -- i.e., factional divergence.

Resultant from this stark difference concerning shiai, there are today a number of divergent aikido styles. Aikikai Aikido, founded by both Morihei and Kisshomaru Ueshiba, is the strongly established progenitor style. Shodokan Aikido is a prominent style founded by Kenji Tomiki and includes a voluntary one-on-one competitive event that is safely structured. This event consists of two participants, one unarmed, the other armed with a rubber knife; each participant switches roles during the competitive bout; points are awarded for a successful defense against the permitted knife attacks, and points are awarded for a successful attack with the knife. This type of competition is the primary matter of contention between the Shodokan and Aikikai Aikido styles. Tomiki, who was head of Physical Education Department at Waseda University in Japan, believed that such a competitive event was necessary in order to promote participation in Aikido, which would help to secure its existence in a new post-war era and maintain its self-defense viability, thus continuing to support and honor Budo's tradition of shiai, i.e., *a meeting to test.* Interestingly, any type of randori practice that may occur in any Aikido style which abhors shiai can be considered as a type of competition. In order to verify or improve the techniques, tactics, and strategies of one's discipline while also testing one's condition of mental composure, a person must challenge their own being by placing themself before another person or before the forces of Nature (a struggle to survive in the wilderness is an example of man or woman versus Nature). One can reasonably argue, contemplating from the point of view of this long venerated tradition in Japanese martial arts, that any martial or martial-like (self-defense) discipline that does not include such in its activities is not a discipline of Budo. A discipline whose primary goal is spiritual enlightenment should neither be considered a self-defense discipline nor a martial discipline; rather, the term *spiritual discipline* is more appropriate. A discipline wherein the primary goal is to provide a balance between the martial and spiritual arenas is best described as a *physio-spiritual discipline* and must include functional self-defense elements, thus establishing and evidencing a *physio-spiritual self-defense discipline* where neither the martial nor the spiritual supercede the other, i.e., neither predominate in a manner where one weakens the importance of the other. Instead, each has interwoven with the other in a manner that transcends the typical manifestation of either toward achieving a functional balance.

Having experienced Aikido as both a student and a teacher, having experienced both good and bad behavior from the typical person, particularly in the arena of martial endeavor, this writer's attitude shapes up like this:

1) As a unique physio-spiritual discipline, Aikido, comprised of all of its styles, lends its force to the shaping of the foundational definition of Budo's ethics, though it is only one contributor. There are numerous other physio-spiritual disciplines that are more martially oriented that also lend to that shaping. Realizing this, those that direct the organizational aspects of Aikido should refrain from attempting to define that which is considered to be Aikido's philosophy as the best ethical foundation for Budo;

2) Aikido, if it's to be considered a form of Budo, must have a dynamic physical activity such as randori, perhaps even shiai, that validates its waza (techniques) and kata (forms) as useful for instilling within a person the skills necessary for real-world self-defense scenarios and provides an aerobic workout, with such belonging to a course of study that evolves an ever-increasing understanding of life whereby the student begins to refine and advance their consciousness toward protecting, sustaining, and enhancing life; and

3) Any form of kata, randori, or shiai must be presented such that it is guided by 2) above.

Aikikai versus Shōdōkan: Conflicting Views of Budō

The construction of an all-encompassing competitive event for Aikido must be directed toward a goal that is greater than the individual competitor, yet organized to develop humble and respectful participants who seek a higher state of consciousness about the nature and meaning of life so that they may consciously participate with behavior that protects, sustains, and enhances its grand schema Yes, part of the goal of each participant would be to validate the self-defense functionality of Aikido's techniques for both theirself (themselves) as well as for all other aikidoka. However, an equally important part is to direct that personal knowledge and skill toward the overall improvement of the human condition. Awarding of points, trophies, or other forms of ego-bolstering, laudatory notice is likely to be discovered as contrary to the realization of such personal development or social contribution. The problem in giving recognition or accolade for one person's victory over another is that it sometimes has the effect of inclucating in the recipient a certain self-serving pride, but a type that manifests with some socially self-defeating characteristics, which can begin a mental process that suppresses *right* in favor of *might*. When such occurs, it is considered to be a negative or counter-productive martial prowess.

The primary disruption of unity in Aikido has been this disagreement as to whether a competitive event is an activity that could fit into and strengthen the philosophy of Aikido; it is the largest manifestation of Aikido's reality conflict -- a struggle between the necessity of functional self-defense ability and the unique aspects of its philosophy, i.e., its intent to present and uphold a higher ethos that is designed to protect, sustain, and enhance life.

That which could unify the various Aikido styles would be to structure a new competitive or cooperative event, a new form of shiai, such that the two participants would clearly understand that their effort is a collaboration where the goal would consist of a dual purpose toward 1) an effort to validate aikido technique for the participants and for the greater benefit of all aikidoka and 2), an effort of each individual to determine how to evolve toward a higher level of consciousness such that they understand clearly how to fit into the worldly schema in a way that protects, sustains, and enhances it.

What I propose as a modification to shiai, then, is something similar to the interactive verbal dialectic procedure that was pioneered by the ancient Greek citizen Socrates. A discussion of a new shiai is presented in Chapter IX.

The practice of Aikido in a manner that would allow it to be accurately described as true aiki does not need to be largely concerned with the spiritual quest, for Aikido is not a religion. However, true aiki is not simply physical technique, rather it consists of physical technique joined with the philosophy of aiki, where aiki consists of both harmonized energy (as in one's personal energy harmonized with all the laws of physics) and of harmonized spirit (as in one's life force, e.g., thought, intention, motivation) being in relation to other people in a way that creates harmony rather than disorder. A person is one with aiki, so to speak, when such harmonizing occurs, and during the practice of Aikido, one can truly be said to be an aikidoka if such is evident.

Kisshomaru Ueshiba believed that "*Aikido rejects all forms of violence, justified or unjustified. Otherwise, we would be no different from the forms of martial arts in which fighting and winning are selling points.*"[18] From his experience of life, in his opinion, this is that which comprised the best attitude for achieving harmony. However laudable, this statement is unfortunately one of several that have set some Aikido styles upon the path of becoming more a proxy study of religion rather than a valid study of martial or self-defense art; within it lies the basis for arguing that some styles of Aikido can no longer be considered a martial art, and therefrom arises the reasons for Aikido's factionalization.

When confronted with aggression, the necessary and lawful violence of your self-defense action is justified provided that one acts with no malicious or vindictive intention and attempts to minimize the harm to an aggressor; the latter being an important marker of true aiki alignment, true Aikido performance, and lawful behavior. Rik Ellis, a professional MMA fighter and British aikidoka relates to us that "*Anyone who has used Aikido in a truly hostile situation will tell you that it looked nothing like the training in the dojo, one needs to be able to adapt [oneself] and their technique to the situation they are faced with.*"[19] Remember, if you're not alive you'll not be pursuing any further spiritual development, at least not in this life.

The statement, "*Aikido rejects all forms of violence, justified, or unjustified*" is, when the real and harsh self-defense circumstances of life emerge, philosophically empty and unpractical as well as unsafe; in fact, it is a dangerous statement if taken literally and internalized as a guiding ethic by which one lives. Aikido is presently, without making such an improper and harmful philosophical alignment, uniquely different than martial arts, for it affirms at the least a quest for a higher ethos while seeking to promote harmony with its teachings. Is it necessary to disassociate from the reality of life's inequities in this manner to gain enlightenment? I think not, for in facing those iniquities is found the very behavior that is required to achieve a higher awareness of one's proper role toward protecting, sustaining, and enhancing life. There will always be disorder that one must resolve into relative order, and there will always be violence against which one must defend. Whenever Aikido is separated from its technical self-defense functionality it devolves quickly toward exhibiting its remaining parts -- its spiritual teachings -- as a quirky proxy study of various Asian religions through eccentric attitude and dubious action that is aligned with the various, often wobbly, metaphysical facets of the theory of Takemusu Aiki. When such occurs, is it reasonable and honest to describe Aikido as a physio-spiritual self-defense discipline that belongs to the tradition of Budo? Lastly, is Aikikai Aikido a more valid aikido because of its association with the Takemusu Aiki metaphysical theory than that of, for comparison, Shodokan Aikido, which has only its connection to Aiki-budo (therefore, to Aikikai Aikido and Budo) via its Koryu no Katas?

Kanō Jigorō -- Founder of Judō
~1936 C.E.

Photo courtesy of Wikimedia Commons repository.

Morihei Ueshiba (left), **Kenji Tomiki** (right)
Tokyo ~1935 C.E.

Photo courtesy of the Aikido Journal.

Aikikai versus Shōdōkan: Conflicting Views of Budō

[1] For further information about the origin of the concept of *aiki*, see, *Encyclopedia of World Sports: from ancient times to the present*, entry on *Aikido*, ABC-CLIO, Inc., 1996; see also the article entitled **Aikido** by Fumiaki Shishida, published by Aikido Journal online, 2011.

[2] See the book *The Spirit of Aikido* by Kisshomaru Ueshiba, with Taitetsu Unno as translator; Kodansha International, Ltd., paperback edition, first printing, 1987, pages 9, 14, 15, 16, 117, 120. Regarding religious attitudes and behavior arising therefrom, it is known that religions which have had or do have scriptures or tenets that propose (either purposefully or incidentally) a superiority of a people or a superior philosophy are more likely to be made use of (either openly or subversively) by non-religious organizations (such as government or a rogue military) as a psychosocial tool toward controlling the direction of cultural movements or societal direction. From an early age, Morihei Ueshiba was thoroughly imbued with the Japanese ethnocentricity of the age. Ueshiba did not completely apprehend the necessary direction of change that his discipline should take until sometime in 1942 C.E. when he purposefully entered seclusion by retreating to Iwama; also, the shape of modern Aikikai Aikido is as much a result of Kisshomaru Ueshiba, Morihei's son and successor, as it was of the elder Ueshiba. Aikido did not arrive on the world's stage as a fully formed discipline of aiki; rather, it came into being as a result of personal efforts, cross-organizational struggles, and the trials and tribulations of a people at war. Prior to 1931, Japan's expansionism into Manchuria, Mongolia, and other area's of Asia was a slow but ever-progressing takeover of land and resources. However, the Mukden Incident of 1931 C.E. in Manchuria was the beginning point of Japan's use of military force to secure its goals; and, Morihei Ueshiba and other budoka of the time participated, knowingly or not, in Japan's agenda for the Asian continent.

[3] See the article entitled *The Process of Forming Aikido and Japanese Imperial Navy Admiral Isamu Takeshita: Through the analysis of Takeshita's diary from 1925 to 1931* by Fumiaki Shishida, 8th Dan Shodokan Aikido.

[4] See the article entitled *Bu, Ken, Ju* - article by Dave Lowry: http://www.koryu.com/library/dlowry8.html.

[5] See the articles entitled *Reminiscences of Minoru Mochizuki (Part 1)* and *(Part 2)* by Stanley Pranin. Aiki News magazine, articles #71 and #72, 1986.

[6] See the book entitled *Judo and Aikido* by Kenji Tomiki. Japan Travel

Aikikai versus Shōdōkan: Conflicting Views of Budō

Bureau, Japan; hardcover, sixth edition, 1963, page 157.

[7] See the article entitled *On Jujutsu and Its Modernization* by Kenji Tomiki, chapter 4, 1986. http://www.tomiki.org/files/Article_Jujutsu_and_its_Modernization.pdf.

[8] See the article entitled *On Jujutsu and Its Modernization* by Kenji Tomiki, chapter 1, 1986. http://www.tomiki.org/files/Article_Jujutsu_and_its_Modernization.pdf.

[9] See the book entitled *Judo and Aikido* by Kenji Tomiki. Japan Travel Bureau, Japan; hardcover, sixth edition, 1963, page 130.

[10] See the article entitled *On Jujutsu and Its Modernization* by Kenji Tomiki, chapter 2, 1986. http://www.tomiki.org/files/Article_Jujutsu_and_its_Modernization.pdf.

[11] See the book entitled *Judo and Aikido* by Kenji Tomiki. Japan Travel Bureau, Japan; hardcover, sixth edition, 1963, page 157.

[12] See the article entitled *On Jujutsu and Its Modernization* by Kenji Tomiki, chapter 4, 1986. http://www.tomiki.org/files/Article_Jujutsu_and_its_Modernization.pdf.

[13] See, *The General Impact of the Pacific War* [WW II] *on Aikido*, the section entitled *Interlude Part I* by Peter Goldsbury; published online at www.aikiweb.com, 2008.

[14] See the book *The Spirit of Aikido* by Kisshomaru Ueshiba. Translated by Taitetsu Unno. Kodansha International, Ltd., paperback edition, first printing, 1987, page 54.

[15] Ibid, page 117.

[16] See the book *The Spirit of Aikido* by Kisshomaru Ueshiba. Translated by Taitetsu Unno. Kodansha International, Ltd., paperback edition, first printing, 1987, pages, 14, 15, 16, 117.

[17] See the article entitled *Background on Kenji Tomiki Sensei* by Stanley Pranin; Aiki News article #43, December, 1981.

[18] See the book *The Spirit of Aikido* by Kisshomaru Ueshiba. Translated

Aikikai versus Shōdōkan: Conflicting Views of Budō by Taitetsu Unno. Kodansha International, Ltd., paperback edition, first printing, 1987, page 54.

[19] See Rik Ellis' blog at http://rik-ellis.blogspot.com/.

Chapter VI

The Manchurian Factor

Emperor worship -- having arisen in part from Shinto in a time even further distant than its authenticated Yamoto line -- played a significant role in the events leading up to W.W. II as well as influenced certain events that led toward the evolution of Aikido from Aiki-budo. One example of this type of social phenomenon is the occurrence of the second Omoto-kyo incident (see Chapter IV for details) where the societal dynamics of Japan during the 1930s were such that both Morihei Ueshiba and Onisaburo Deguchi were unavoidably existential participants in the turmoil generated by the various the power struggles of *1)* the Japanese Imperial Army's internal factions -- specifically, the Sakurakai, the Kodoha, and the Toseiha (see Chapter IV for details) -- and *2)* the Showa Restoration Movement in its opposition to the then controlling form of Japanese government. (The latter had derived its legitimacy and authority from Japan's Meiji Constitution of 1890 C.E., which documents had established a constitutional monarchy). All of these factions had engaged in 'unhinged' or asymmetric political and military action to some extent or another in order to attempt to set the course and manner of Japan's expansionism while making use of its royal figurehead as a sometimes unwitting political device to further their own, but often differing, sociopolitical agendas. During this time, the Japanese government had good control over its homeland based army and naval forces, but this was not the case with its army force in Manchuria. The Emperor, who was supposed to be the ideal controlling or balancing figure that inspired loyalty among his military officers, frequently found himself, his cabinet, and his government the object of military connivery, plotting, and numerous coup attempts. This was especially the case within the army, which, as we have earlier learned, was the instigator of numerous plots and coup attempts. Also, occasionally, there was an Imperial Family member who was opposed to the Emperor's policies, which emerged further intriguing complications. The type and extent of control that the Emperor and his civilian governmental departments had over the military (which had been specifically enumerated by Japan's Meiji Period Constitution) was not at all firm or certain, especially over the Army, because no strong tradition of trust in or respect for control by elements of the civilian government over military matters had been previously established within Japan's military and populace.[1] The Kantogun Army (Kwantung Army), which was garrisoned at a communication distance from Japan on the southern tip of Manchuria's Liaodong Peninsula where communications were often unreasonably slow, and into which there had enlisted many sociopolitically disaffected men who desired a return to the former 'glorious days' of the samurai, was frequently subjected to 1) the multiple influences brought forth by the agendas of certain important citizens and military men (of the Sakurakai and Kodoha), secret ultranational societies, religious organizations (such as the Omotokyo), and *zaibatsu* firms (resource identification, extraction, and materiel companies) as well as by 2) the typical needs and concerns of the various farming collectives (organizations of farmers/settlers) that had been involved in Japan's attempt to colonize Manchuria. As a result, the Kantogun Army was significantly more difficult to control than the Japanese homeland army, navy, and police forces.

A better understanding of Aikido's evolution can be gained by considering its development in relation to the events leading up to and during Japan's colonization attempts of the geographic area of Northeast Asia that, prior to the end of W.W. II, was known as Manchuria. The Empire of Japan, during its ambitious colonial era, spread itself far and wide to influence and control most of the South Pacific islands as well as certain parts of what today is modern China. Its overall goal or proposed future was that of some type of economic cooperation with the many different ethnic peoples of these geographic areas, this being its best (though destined to vanish) political formulation. Unfortunately, that which eventually emerged as its final political form was an ethnocentric inspired economic control over these non-Japanese peoples, carried out by both covert and overt methods, most of which were neither beneficial nor benign. This egregious economic policy, whose underlying agenda had been purposefully hidden from the numerous controlling entities of these geographic areas, was termed *The Greater East*

Asia Co-Prosperity Sphere. The northeastern area of the Asian continent called Manchuria (Manchukuo to the Japanese) were very important to Japan's economic viability as a new industrial nation, and the lure of this new frontier, though illegitimately conceived, influenced many individual and group movements of Japanese origin. Included among these were the evolution of Aiki-budo toward the Aikido of today and the religion of Omoto-kyo. Though other important evolution of Aiki-budo occurred in the China and South Pacific arenas during W.W. II with Koichi Tohei, Gozo Shioda, and others, this writing will focus only on the significant importance of the Manchurian factor. Manchuria was a land of new opportunity (as was the western geographic region, south of Canada, north of Mexico, for the development of the United States of America) and as such became an object of desire and need for not only Japan as a nation but for numerous smaller Japanese business interests, too. The Japanese government and its military, Japanese zaibatsu firms, Japanese ultranational societies (such as *Gen'yosha* and *Kokuryukai*), Onisaburo Deguchi (the leader of the Shinto derived, syncretic new religion called Omoto-kyo), Morihei Ueshiba, and Kenji Tomiki all acted significantly in this geographic arena.

During the Japanese historical periods known typically as the Meiji Restoration (1868 C.E.-1912 C.E.) and the Modernization of Japan (1868 C.E.-1931 C.E.), Japan's quick but turbulent progress in the economic and political arenas of its society created unavoidable new demands and pressures that, when combined with its national ethnic pride (which arose from emperor worship and militarism influenced by samurai traditions), produced a national ambition that drove it to subjugate and colonize new territories beyond its traditional territories and legitimate purview. This ambition comprised the dominant aspect that shaped Japanese history from 1868 C.E. until the end of W.W. II in 1945 C.E. In analyzing Japan's imperialistic colonization during this period, it can be understood that such resulted from the combination of a number of different indigenous as well as external forces. I'll enumerate these only as general categories because many historians have already covered this period of Japan's history in many different written works. The *first of these forces* was a result of the dismantlement of Japan's unique feudal structure, which caused disenfranchisement, disillusionment, and anger among the members of the samurai class because little government assistance had been given to them toward establishing a reshaped raison d'être in Japan's modernized society. The *second* of these was Japan's headlong rush to develop itself into a worldly significant modern state because, as a result of its past policies of isolationism that had been instituted in order to protect it's unique ethno-cultural identity, had fallen behind the agricultural, industrial, and technological advancements of several Western nations (e.g., Germany). *Third*, Japan's ever-increasing homeland population could, within a few generations, result in an 'overgrazing' of the nation's indeginous rescources and reduce its standard of living to a condition that might cause grave social difficulties. The *last of these forces*, the form of government known as the Emperor System, previously mentioned, was culturally unable to imbue itself with the sufficient juridical and political ethos, foresight, and wherewithal such that it could definitively control its distant provisional government and military forces; that is, prevent these from acting contrary to the orders of its government.

The Meiji ('enlightened rule') Restoration was a period bequeathed by the nominal rule of Emperor Meiji, a time when the restoration of the prominence of the Japanese Imperial household occurred following the overthrow of the Tokugawa Shogunate. This period can be considered to represent the first half of the Empire of Japan. The demise of the samurai class begins here, as modernization pressures necessitated its gradual absorption into governmental administrative or modernized military roles, or, as occurred with many, forced retirement. Attendant with this demise, there arose a slow decline of hand-to-hand and edged-weapon based martial fighting arts in favor of European martial methods of gun, bayonet, and artillery. With the creation of a modern Japanese military that was patterned on the Prussian/German model of the age (which was adopted in 1878 C.E.), the need for edged weapon fighting and subsequent close quarters hand-to-hand combat diminished. As a result, the traditional martial schools (ryu) began to languish and disappear, and so too did their influence upon the manner by which street-level civil law was administered. The need for a less harsh, gentler method of policing -- which had been previously performed by the samurai during the Tokugawa Era -- became apparent. Subsequently, the politics and methods of policing gradually changed to reflect methods that were a little less harsh for maintaining civil law and order. These policing changes brought with them a different understanding of how, when, and to what extent to use physical force when arresting an individual, handling crowd unrest or insurgents, or responding to societal emergencies. Relatively quickly, across a fifty-year period (1880 C.E. - 1930 C.E.), there evolved newly conceived martial art styles (somewhat more 'civilized'), such as Judo and later Ueshiba's Aiki-budo, as a response to the changing times. Many of these new styles retained older forms of edged weapon techniques in groupings of techniques that were classified as old style or old school (koryu) forms (kata). It was during this time of change that the term *Budo* replaced the older term *Bushido* as the classification name for a modern Japanese martial art (See Chapter I). As Japan's civil society struggled toward something that began to resemble a constitutional republic, police forces for maintaining civil order and military forces for protecting its national identity and advancing its economy evolved. The methods of hand-to-hand control in arrest and civil disobedience situations differed from that needed by the military, and the martial arts of old either changed to meet that need or began to disappear. Aged samurai or samurai resistant to change either retired or became free agents, ronin-like, with many experiencing significant difficulty in earning a living and maintaining relevance and status, which resulted in a large group of Japanese who became quite disgruntled with their lot in life. Social outcasts of this type tended to join and support secret ultranational societies and military factions that leaned toward respect of samurai-like ideals, and, if yet young enough, which was not the typical circumstance, sought employment in the various police, military, or zaibatsu organizations. Life in Japan was replete with factional intrigue, conflict, and social complexity during the Meiji Restoration and Modernization of Japan.

During the Taisho Period (1912-1926 C.E.), defined by the reign of Emperor Taishō, Japanese militarists orchestrated overt as well as covert propaganda campaigns to instill in the people a thoroughgoing worship of the Emperor while craftily positioning themselves and their operatives in key, influential political and military positions -- actually, most of the thoughts and acts of the Emperor pertaining to the governance of the Japan were those of his influential civilian and military advisors. The militarists of these two groups promoted a policy of geographic expansionism and steadily orchestrated certain events in Manchuria to further the goal of territorial and natural resource acquirement by establishing a system of governmental puppetry there. In Japan, despite the militarist's efforts to orchestrate a social order where the people found contentment through the adoration of and obedience to the Emperor, workers with many grievances became disenchanted and began to form labor unions and to support socialism. Many militarists opposed such social movements and attempted by their influence upon government to actively suppress them through the use of various police agencies. The first and second Omoto suppression incidents that occurred in Japan in 1921 and 1935 C.E., respectively, were two such cases. It was during this era of Japanese expansionism and indigenous social unrest that Morihei Ueshiba and Onisaburo Deguchi, in 1924 C.E., carried out their ill-fated excursion to Mongolia in order to attempt the establishment of an Omoto utopian enclave, which included far reaching plans for the formation of a new nation.

During the Shōwa Period (1926 C.E.-1989 C.E.), worship of the Japanese Emperor was embellished and strengthened, which stately role was agreeable to Emperor Hirohito during his reign until the end of W.W. II. Numerous militarists pressured sympathetic politicians to create administrative governing bodies and rules to point ultimate control to the military with the Japanese emperor as a 'puppet.' This portion of the Showa Period was replete with much political intrigue, attempted coups, and military action, and many influential soldiers of the Japanese Imperial Army had the idea they could achieve an expansion of Japan's empire in Manchuria and Mongolia that would be able to provide a stable livelihood to farmers and industrial workers; both Onisaburo Deguchi and Morihei Ueshiba had taken up this position, too. Militarists -- i.e., certain government and secret society operatives, politicians, industrialists, and military men -- organized and carried out carefully contrived intimidations and covert assassinations of political adversaries in order to eliminate any opposition that might interfere with the annexation of territories in Asia and the South Pacific Archepelago. Many Japanese were aware of and contrary to Japan's expansionism. It is well known that the great Jigoro Kano, founder of modern Judo, was clearly opposed to his county's expansionist policies on the Asian Continent. There are some who think that his death in 1938 C.E. might have been an assassination rather than an illness (pnuemonia) that impinged upon the health of an aged man.

Any person who is pressured or motivated by the circumstances of their dynamic societal environment -- being urged by that aspect of the mental self known as ego, being motivated by their unique personality to act in one way or another, being motivated by the survival instinct -- finds that the act of choosing is unavoidable. A person may choose or not choose, but in choosing or refusing to choose, a decision is made. Onisaburo Deguchi, Morihei Ueshiba, Kenji Tomiki, Gozo Shioda, and Koichi Tohei all chose to associate with and lend support to various socio-political currents or undercurrents of Japanese society during this period. For example, Onisaburo cooperated briefly with the Gen'yosha and Kokuryukai ultranational societies while Ueshiba was well known to support the Emperor and his military forces. Morihei Ueshiba's friendship with Admiral Takeshita (the admiral who later would become the first president of the Zaidan Kobukai Foundation, the predecessor to the Zaidan Hojin Aikikai, a.k.a. Aikikai Aikido), his training of military men in Aiki-budo, his authorship of a book pertaining to defense and counterattack against knife, pistol, spear, sword, and bayonet and another concerning the best techniques for combat use of a rifle-attached bayonet, further inform us about the extent of his enculturation and loyalty to the Empire. Also, Kenji Tomiki taught Judo and Aiki-budo to the military in Manchuria, Gozo Shioda supported the Japanese war efforts against China, and Koichi Tohei fought there. To what extent, however, were each of these historical players shaped by their culture as well as coerced by pressures inherent in their society?[2] When a person is born into a particular society, then matures within it, a large part of one's identity and livelihood is nurtured and developed therefrom. A reevaluation of one's overall psychosocial relationship to their society may require years of careful investigation into their psychological conditioning, which may reveal certain unproductive or noxious, personally held attitudes that interfere with manifesting a proper overall attitude, i.e., an objective one that is respectful of life, while determining where they are positioned as a person on their society's stage and in relation to the larger workings of life. Is it probable that such an introspection began for Morihei Ueshiba when he resigned his teaching duties in 1942 C.E.? Yes, I think so.[3]

As it pertains to Aikido's evolution, the Manchurian factor of the historical Japanese experience affected the development of Aiki-budo's basis from which numerous styles of Aikido eventually evolved. Many of Morihei Ueshiba's first generation students gained practical, real-world martial application experience with their involvement in Japan's military operations in Manchuria.

[1] The Kantogun Army had more men sympathetic to the plight of the dispossessed Samurai Class. On August 5, 1876 C.E., all samurai pensions were commuted. For further reading, see *Japan: Its History and Culture* by Scott W. Morton; McGraw-Hill, Inc., second paperback edition, 1994. For detailed information, see the article *Transmission, Inheritance, & Emulation* [of Aikido] written by Peter Goldsbury, published online at www.aikiweb.com in its web-log forum, 2008 & 2009.

[2] See Sartre, Jean-Paul, *Existentialism and Human Emotions*. The Wisdom Library, a division of The Philosophical Library, Inc.; hardcover, 1957, pages 41, 42, 43, and 44.

[3] An enlightening article to read that describes some of Morihei Ueshiba's thoroughgoing support of the Japanese Emperor System is *Kobukan Dojo Era* by Stanley Pranin, published online by the Aikido Journal, 2002.

Chapter VII

The Competition Dilemma

Inability to Diminish Bloodsport Popularity

Aikido, as a peopled multi-faceted physio-spiritual entity, has been unable to make full use of its unique qualities to stop the rising tide of Romanesque bloodsport and, equally unfortunate, to prevent the decline of public interest in pursuing a study of an ontologically oriented martial art or physio-spiritual self-defense discipline for the reason of evolving people toward a higher state of consciousness. Since the people as well as the societal forces of Japan and the United States of America (U.S.A.) have been uniquely intertwined, even before the start of W.W. II, the discussion in this chapter concerns mostly Japan, the country of Aikido's origin, and the U.S.A., the country in which there exists a large presentation of commercialized sport events. Bloodsport (a combative sport) presents to us an unravelling of yet another thread from a gentler yet 'always prepared' type of socializing fabric (e.g, as influenced by the ideas of *semper paratus, allzeit bereit,* or *sonae-yo tsuneni*). An analysis of this type may be undertaken for any country in which Aikido is practiced. Before going further, it is important to know that no Aikido organization, small or large, has ever set forth a public statement or policy regarding a desire to influence any particular society toward attaining the kind of higher being or consciousness that could reduce the extent to which the aforementioned problems have existed or do exist today. Nonetheless, it is clearly obvious that much of the philosophy associated with the performance of Aikido creates, when properly embraced by a practitioner, a certain quasi-spiritual quality that can persistently move them to an evolution of a higher state of being or consciousness, which is typically represented by a desire to protect, sustain, and enhance life. The opening proposition, a criticism that is obviously imbued with the potential for misunderstanding, requires a reasonable explanation of the definition or meaning of the term *bloodsport* as used herein. Bear with me as I 'flesh it out.' ***Bloodsport*** *-- an arranged or specifically contrived, specially designed, and purposefully staged event of a person-to-person, peopled group-to-group, animal-to-animal, or person-to-animal contest, conflict, fight, or battle, for whatever reasons, sometimes presented to a public as a game or sport and usually both customarily and legally sanctioned, but not always; where typically, yet sometimes fraudulently, such events identify with the idea of the socially flexible so-called 'spirit-of-competition,' whereby there occurs the type of physical interaction that results in any type of physical injury to the contestants with or without bloodletting (e.g., brain jiggling); and, finally, where many or the majority of the participants, contestants and observers alike, have either an apparent or a hidden expectation of acrimony or temper flareups, grudge matches, or combat-like clashes, which necessarily and unavoidably involve physically severe or violent struggling where even the victorious do not emerge unscathed.*

When a person contemplates the extent to which any particular country's societal conditions have evolved a large presentation of sporting events -- some which are invigorating and replete with positive qualities, but others, often with a large fandom, which are oriented purposefully toward bloodsport (e.g., professional boxing, professional cage fighting) or have been crafted at their inception in a manner that might allow the participants (contestants and fans) to emerge an attitudinal predisposition toward and, later, expectation of acrimonious encounters, temper flare ups, grudge matches, and combat-like clashes that result in, at the instance of occurrence, characteristics that are indicative of bloodsport (e.g., as sometimes found in Gridiron (Professional) Football, Pro Wrestling, Pro Ice Hockey, and Soccer) -- some discussion of the probable causes that have emerged this particular aspect in many of today's societies is necessary to understand Aikido's distress as well as its own role therein. Notwithstanding, I would like to state that the primary focus of this discussion is to reveal Aikido's inherent qualities that can assist an evolution toward a reality in which there is less violence rather than on the why or how large sport institutions have come into being in some modern societies.

Though a large part of Aikido attempts to position itself on the ethical high ground by aligning its philosophy and activities with a noncompetitive attitude (primarily the Aikikai and Shin-shin Toitsu organizations), such, though an understandable position when considered in the light of its historical events and theology-like teachings, has caused, separate from its positive qualities, the emergence of its own self-limiting efficacy. Self-limiting efficacy, an aikidoka-made outcome, hinders Aikido's influence upon the direction of general public attitude toward the creation of a collective societal awareness that manifests the sporting ethic in a way that truly sustains, protects, and enhances the human experience. Yes, it could be argued that without the existence of the Aikikai's ongoing historical position there might have come about the circumstances for a faster and even more prominent rise of Romanesque bloodsport; however, in spite of some evidence that would likely support the validity of such an argument, such is a foregone conclusion when given its already socially verified ethical corpus of physio-spiritual tenets. Rather, though difficult to quantify, the important matter to ponder now is the extent to which Aikido's post W.W. II efficacy in the world has waned or is lacking, and to what extent this waning or lacking may have affected a rise in bloodsport popularity; such might be accomplished by considering to what extent this particular position (non-competition, a position embraced by a majority of aikidoka) has been effective in creating a better, i.e., more pleasant, condition of life for any country or the world community. Today, establishing the criteria by which such a study might provide useful data would be very difficult. It is unlikely that any of the early Aikido organizations had the foresight to purposefully setup long-term goals and criteria by which they could understand Aikido's affect upon the world's societies. Instead, survival of this discipline in some form or another was of paramount concern immediately after W.W. II, and, necessarily so, they directed their effort toward preserving the philosophical, spiritual, and technical body of their discipline. Any so-called betterment of societies over the course of time, of whatever that might have consisted, was due to happenstance being very slightly predisposed toward a slightly more positive outcome by the geographic presence of an aikidoka here, or an aikidoka there. Then (post W.W. II) and now, the various forms of media (then: newspapers, magazines, books, radio, public gatherings and oratory; now: newspapers, magazines, books, radio, television, some public gatherings and oratory, the digital internet and ebooks) were and are the primary methods of information conveyance, be it benign or propaganda, by use of which change was and will be seeded to effect an evolution or devolution within society. Currently, media companies continue to control (make apparent or obscure) exposure to events and information. How, then, can we arrive at a reasonable understanding of Aikido's effect upon the societies of the world and the role it has played in the decrease or increase of bloodsport? The following are seven useful criteria that can reveal to what extent it has had the effect of bettering the human experience, and to what extent its efficacy here has or has not waned.

1) The extent to which factions or offshoots of Aikido have increased/decreased;

2) The extent to which participation in Aikido has increased /decreased;

3) Reported, verifiable self-defense engagements, recorded by dojo instructors or police, where Aikido was used successfully to defend against an aggressor and where the outcome reflected a conclusion that could only be the result of an attitude aligned with the concept of aiki, not mattering whether the engagement was physical or verbal;

4) The extent to which aikidoka, practicing or not, when conducting their daily life activities, communicate or otherwise interact with people with an attitude aligned to the concept of aiki;

5) The extent to which the general public of any particular society has recognized the word *Aikido*, i.e., understanding what Aikido is, or is not; (Such recognition may arise from a person's exposure to any of the various forms of modern audio-visual media. For example, in the television fiction program **Star Trek: Enterprise**, Episode 11, which is entitled the *"Observer Effect,"* Ensign Hoshi, a linguistics expert, makes reference to her accomplishment of a *black belt* (dan grade) in Aikido. Though sometimes controversial, the film actor **Steven Seagal**, a 7th Dan in Tenshin Aikido, has drawn attention to Aikido as well. *YouTube*, a streaming-media Internet site, hosts hundreds-of-thousands of digital audio-visual recordings, many which concern the martial arts.)

6) The extent to which each member of the general public of any particular society outwardly expresses toward another an attitude in alignment with the concept of aiki; and,

7) The extent to which Aikido is respected as a valid, truly functional *physio-spiritual self-defense art* when its viability as a method of self-defense is analyzed by the proponents of the numerous other contemporary martial arts, e.g., Jujutsu, Kenjutsu, Judo, Karatedo, Kung Fu, Hapkido, and Boxing.

When considered from the perspective of their personal history, it is likely that an aikidoka who embraces the so-called non-competitive position finds that they are entirely content with such, for this is what they have sought out. Unfortunately, this is nothing less than escapism, for even in that so-called noncompetitive atmosphere of physical interaction there is yet to be found competition; e.g., competition for attention from the teacher, or the mental comparison of one's own knowledge and skill with that of another student's. Competition, whether it be innate or a purposeful contrasting in order to obtain a basis from which to evaluate, occurs naturally among people. The challenge for citizens of any society is to discover how to continue to direct this innate condition toward instilling within their society an attitude that protects, sustains, and enhances life, rather than unthinkingly or purposefully emerging a dystopian outcome. *Denial of the innate condition of competition,* which is a conscious thought process decision, activates within it an inherent tendency (a tendency latent in denial) aligned toward the probable emergence of a self-limiting efficacy in the individual, and, furthermore, can emerge an incongruous reflexive opposition that represents or causes a further muddling of the individual's perception of reality (objectivity); this in turn can result in mistaken and or absurd thoughts which can lead to other wrong-headed decisions and misplaced efforts that manifest collectively as their contribution to the devolution of their society. Nonetheless, in contrast to an individual's denial of this condition, there is a scenario where groups of people (such as sport industry or governmental entities) purposefully embrace it in an intentionally misconceived manner (typically in the pursuit of profit and control of a society's populace) which, along with other social weaknesses, can emerge a corrupted, perhaps even depraved societal ethos where bloodsport is customarily sanctioned as well as idolized; e.g., the Games of Ancient Rome. Therefore, when mulling over the challenging nature of defense against an opponent (a form of competition), particularly when the practitioner considers Aikido to be a self-defense or martial discipline, where such points ultimately to the learning of a functional aiki-aligned self-defense ability that can secure their well-being, and, toward achieving this end, to some form of activity that objectively tests that ability -- like *randori* ({free play}{sparring}{taming disorder}) which is one type of competition, or *shiai* ({bout}{contest} {match}), another type of competition that is discussed in detail in Chapter IX -- it is essential that the outcome of this training doesn't inadvertently lend itself, even in the smallest way, to the emergence of a less humane social ethos. Each specially crafted competition whereby the physical prowess of one creature is pitted against that of another through an event of direct, potentially injurious body-to-body contact has an inherent tendency to manifest brutish, blood-sport qualities when not carefully managed by rules and referees. So, the challenge for those who oversee the rules and moderate the competitive interaction is to ensure that such sanctioned events of conflict do not emerge a less humane social ethos. In contrast, there are a different type of people who think that all such events should be banned, as even the exchange of punches, kicks, joint locks, throws, strangleholds, and pins in a controlled manner is indicative, to them, of moral turpitude.

Other than Aikido's previously noted role in the emergence of this phenomenon, another important factor has been the steadily increasing public preoccupation with one kind of entertainment stimuli or another; e.g., the highly evolved organizational sport entities such as the U.F.C. (Ultimate Fight Championship) and the N.F.L. (National Football League), digital social media companies such as Facebook and Twitter, travel via aircraft and oceanliner for the sake of travel promoted by the travel agencies, a multitude of other entertainment options such as those offered by the city of Las Vegas and the Disney Company, and digital streaming home media. Subsequently, the effect has been the diminishment of the extent to which people have engaged in thought concerning the participation in a study of an ontologically oriented martial art or physiospiritual self-defense discipline for the reason of evolving toward a higher state of consciousness. Perhaps the organizations (both corporate and governmental) which stand to gain currency (societal control and money) from such *games* or *entertainment*, where violence is presented as a pastime, should shoulder the primary responsibility for the rise of bloodsport in any society so affected. Aikido's role, albeit minor, is an important issue. Why? Aikido's guiding corpus of highly evolved physio-spiritual tenets, truly admirable in their intent and significance for an individual and any society, has fallen very short of achieving prominence in the minds of the majority of citizens in Japan and the United States of America, and similarly so, in other countries of the world. Instead, for example, the U.F.C., one of the many definite indicators of the rise of bloodsport popularity, is prominent there, this being the quintessential example of the ineffectiveness of passively avoiding the *dilemma of competition.*

During the span of time between 1950 and the year 1970 there arose from the destruction of W. W. II a reshaping of scientific inquiry, achievement, and humanitarian effort. This era was popularly termed *The Space Age*, and its societal thrust was imbued with a unique zeitgeist (aire-of-the-age/characteristic-of-the-age) that consisted of three significant yet different intermingling societal forces. *One* manifested the special characteristics of the *scientific method* as exemplified by a reinvigorated exploration of the workings of the physical laws of science while advancing forward into a new frontier called *outer space.*[1] *Another* of those forces was marked by the advent of a *"cold war"* where two opposing groups of countries -- Western Europe, Japan, Australia, and North America cooperating as a 'protagonist,' and the Union of Soviet Socialist Republics and the Peoples Republic of China as 'antagonists' -- entered into a decades-long ideological struggle consisting of political posturing and militaristic intimidation. *Lastly*, a renewed current of humanitarian efforts directed toward attempting to secure a world where such miseries as those experienced by humankind during W.W. II might never again occur. Out of necessity, Japan initiated (under the direction of S.C.A.P.) a reevaluation of its entire societal ethos in a manner shaped by a need to identify those good and productive aspects of the Japanese people; a time when Japan's people critically assessed their cultural past, took account of their society's good aspects, and began to shape a new future where the errant attitudes of the past would never again, ideally, lead them toward war. An important as well as telling result that had evolved for a majority of the Japanese people was a thoroughgoing distrust of its government and military. Japan's defeat in W.W. II ushered in an era where

Japan adopted governing constitutional documents similar to those of the United States of America; Japan sought to create a new societal foundation. Feeling culpable, many Japanese shunned as well as shed many of the past attitudes and cultural traditions which had previously shaped their society's ethos (see Moriteru Ueshiba's comment from his recent book). Immediately following Japan's surrender, the practice of all Japanese martial arts were forbade by S.C.A.P. (see Chapter V) until a time when its government and societal ethos reflected the type of structure that was desired by the victorious Allied Powers. Few citizens of Japan had escaped the effects of the war. Morihei Ueshiba and his son, Kisshomaru, each having certainly experienced various emotions reflecting grave concern about the future of an autonomous Japan, each having personally experienced the tumultuous effect of war and grief over Japan's social misdirection, were faced with an uncertain future. When martial arts were finally permitted in the early 1950s, most martial proponents, like Morihei and Kisshomaru Ueshiba, had gone through much sincere contemplation and soul-searching regarding how to present their martial skills to the world. Both the Ueshibas considered that part of the blame for Japan's societal misdirection had to be attributed to their society's misinterpretation of the meaning of the concept of *Budo*. Relatively quickly both came to consider that martial art competition of any type, like that in Judo, was attitudinally hinged to a fighting spirit that was essentially warlike in its essence.

Kisshomaru Ueshiba believed that one outcome of what he considered to be the identifying philosophy and teachings of Aikido could be that it might have a limited affect upon helping to instill a more thoroughgoing condition of culturally embraced humanitarianism in societies throughout the world. Specifically, he was concerned that the stereotypical attitudes which people held regarding what constitutes both the need for fighting (arising from the attitudes held, ego, and the reflexive oppositional nature of the human psyche) and the actual fighting forms (the behavior emerging from a particular mentality) *"may present some obstacles to the popularization of this art."*[2] Though sensing these obstacles, he made a decision -- the refusal to embrace any form of competitive event -- that has caused some people, both martial artist and incidental observer alike, to consider the Aikido of today as sometimes ineffectual as a means of self-defense. However, this is not the truth of the matter for some Aikido styles, or for certain dojo of all styles.

Kisshomaru Ueshiba accomplished great work toward strengthening the technical, philosophical and organizational aspects of all that is Aikido today, but his inability to formulate reasoning by which he could validly associate Aikido with a new form of shiai, as informed by the concept of aiki, has been the harbinger of factionalization as well as an unintended yet contributing factor to the emergence of further public interest in bloodsport.

From historical evidence, the Roman Games of Ancient Rome seemingly began as relatively harmless demonstrations of prowess and sportive competition. The early Roman games, which included acrobats, wire walkers, trick riding, trained animals, chariot races and general athletic events such as track and field events, wrestling, and boxing with padded leather straps over the knuckles, evolved over a time period of several hundred years, from approximately 550 B.C.E. to 250 B.C.E.. The intent of the games during this initial period was for the reasons of non-injurious entertainment, sportive comaraderie, and an exhibition of Roman prowess. Bloodshed was either accidental or incidental, not something that the typical participant or spectator was expressly desirous of experiencing or viewing.

However, beginning around 250 B.C.E. -- partially a result of the practice of slavery, but largely emerging from the deleterious tendency of any human being to fall victim to its own self-generated psychophysical condition where nerve ending desire can lead a person to seek successively higher thrills through an ever escalating series of stimulus-response driven activities, and where such psycho-physical phenomenon was gradually and intricately woven into the social structure of Ancient Rome in a way that elicited a wicked societal outcome -- the Roman Games gradually and irreversibly changed to include slave-fighters (gladiators) as well as various other truly depraved and perverse activities, events, and exhibitions. This was especially the case during the historical era known as the Roman Empire.

The extent of this change toward an astonishing condition of cultural turpitude and debauchery, where sadism was often the order of the day, is the quintessential example of what can emerge as a significant part of a society in turmoil. This reprehensible condition was apparent to many of Ancient Rome's citizens, and numerous Roman emperors attempted to institute changes. In spite of such efforts, the depravity of the games did not end until the weaknesses of the Roman Empire's sociopolitical structure had elicited a gradually progressing and thoroughgoing psychosocial malady that insidiously eroded many of its connective threads; leading eventually to instability in numerous areas of its political system. Slowly yet surely the collapse of the Roman Empire would arrive, for its societal attitudes, internal struggles, outwardly directed conquests by force of arms, and attacks launched by external warring peoples who were opposed to Rome were unavoidable consequences that emerged from the devolution of its once dynamic early-period Roman ethos. In 330 C.E., the Roman emperor Constantine I declared Byzantium (Istanbul today, in the country of Turkey) as the capital of the Roman Empire, and, upon this decision, renamed the city Constantinople, which politically and geographically divided the Empire into eastern and western Roman domains. After the sacking of Rome by the Vandals in 455 C.E. -- which was a turning point in the hegemony of the Western Roman Empire -- a series of riots and martial law actions in Constantinople in 532 C.E. killed approximately 30,000 citizens and hastened its death throes (The Eastern Roman Empire, later known as the Byzantine Empire, did not fully collapse until 1453 C.E. when Mehmed the II conquered Constantinople). Only through the demise of the Western Roman Empire came the dissolution of the Roman Games. As mentioned earlier, though there were many citizens and a few emperors over many centuries who spoke out against the brutal and perverse condition of the Roman Games, never did there evolve a popular self-initiated Roman social countermovement that might have ended their depraved condition of 'entertainment' and 'play' involving bloodsport. Minoru Mochizuki, founder of Yoseikan Aikido, relates that "...*despite the fact that the order of sports is based on the morality of European knighthood, the rapid degeneracy of this ethic has recently come under criticism. At the same time, the commercialization and politicization of the Olympics have become more conspicuous and loud cries have been raised in favor of the games being returned to Greece. Furthermore, the crime rate among juvenile delinquents rises in proportion to the popularity of sports. This fact has darkened the world of sports...*"[3]

When considering that which constitutes any particular type of society, destructive trends may occur over centuries, and under certain circumstances, even quickly, over a period of several decades; e.g., review Stalin's Russia, Germany's Third Reich, and the Empire of Japan during the 20th Century C.E. Most conventional, modern sports are institutional constructs that reflect a society's self-created ethos. That which constitutes a society's ethos emerges from the thoughts and behaviors of the people within it, but, invariably, this is always controlled and directed by peopled groups which are often fraudulently termed the '*intelligentsia*.' Though the so-called intelligentsia frequently includes the *lettered* or *literate* people who had or have been carefully, i.e., '*usefully*,' schooled by their past or current '*educational opportunities*' and '*academic*' institutions -- typically a conditioning or training not clearly apprehended by the individual, occurring from birth until each begins to play their adult societal role, and organized and taught by previous initiates who are stalwart *professors* of certain attitudes or viewpoints which manifest one brand of political philosophy or another -- this does not at all mean that it is benign, or especially aware, entirely well meaning, and honest, or, for that matter, incapable of unintentionally or purposefully misleading either their group or society. The part of organized Aikido that could be identified as its intelligentsia -- especially where that part has purposefully and understandably led many aikidoka to wholeheartedly embrace the idea that "*Aikido rejects all forms of violence, justified or unjustified*," thereby enabling denial of the innate competitive condition, and wherefrom there has emerged its own outcome *of self-limiting efficacy* -- has actually had the effect of decreasing many an aikidoka's self-defense skill while also contributing ever-so-lightly to weighting the balance of chance toward a further popularization of bloodsport. Unfortunately, this double-edged phenomenon is exactly the opposite effect desired by the proponents of non-competition.

Today, professional pugilism (Boxing), the recent rise of the popular mixed martial arts as presented through the U.F.C. organization, and the increasing incidents of spectator violence in some modern ball sports are examples of modern society's bloodsport culture that have emerged from the innate condition of the human being as shaped by various societal forces. Many present day *sport* games align similarly with the conditions that produced the depravity of the Roman Games.

The Hollywood film industry, having produced films like *Fight Club*, *Bloodsport*, and many others of this ilk, as well as the effect of Pro Wrestling in all its spectacle, have interacted with the many other deleterious forces of life (e.g., desire, avarice, fear, quest for money and power) that have set the scene for the resurgence of quirky misconceived personal attitudes and misdirected or wholly unproductive behavior that tends to degenerate an individual's ethics and devolve a societal ethos. This type of personal and societal devolution emerges gradually and subtly from one type of fallacious reasoning or another by the accidental or purposeful subversion of healthy values, mores, and ethics, which in turn result in the presentment of a partially or entirely new set of such -- typically less noble or even ignoble -- thus making possible the emergence of that which is erroneously considered to be important (though when objectively assessed, it is not) to the people of any society thus afflicted.

Illegal underworld fights of various types, such as animal fights, bare-knuckle fight clubs, and brutal man-to-man death matches are today largely hidden or masked in our newly *enlightened* Western Age. Note that only 562 years have passed since the Eastern Roman Empire dissolved. Daniel P. Mannix, in his book *The Way of the Gladiator*, presents several pertinent correlations between today's society and that of the ancient Roman Empire.[4]

In the United States of America, consider the types of martial arts that were promulgated by one type of social entity or another (sole proprietorship or corporate) in any given decade after W.W. II. During the 1950s, Jujitsu and Judo were prominent. During the 1960s, Judo continued as a popular martial-like sport and both Karatedo and Kung Fu came into public view. In the 1970s, Kung Fu and Karatedo were prominent, with Judo still present and historically secured as an Olympic Games sport, while awareness of the Korean martial art of Taekwondo was increasing. During the 1980s, with the social presence of those arts just mentioned still strong, further popularity of Taekwondo and awareness of Aikido was rising. During the 1990s, Aikido having securely established itself, though often regarded by the observer as ineffectual and sometimes quirky, was now becoming known worldwide; Brazilian Jujitsu was swiftly becoming a new martial fad. In the year 2000, Taekwondo became an official Olympic Games sport. In the new millennium, post 2000, all these are suffering a decline in participation. Presently, the U.F.C. is the fight promoter's new 'golden egg' -- financial gain to be obtained through the proposition that strength, technical cunning, and brutal skill are to be glorified as mighty, where the *might* herein is typically inferred, though wrongly so, to be *just* and *right.* Interestingly, it is possible to argue that the Aikido community's unwillingness to embrace a competitive event, combined with its occasional *cult-like* magico-religious aire, has caused a repelling force that in turn has helped to create a decisive opportunity for such gladiator-like sport activities to thrive. Another contributing aspect, it seems, is that for many people today, including numerous aikidoka, the pursuit of *higher consciousness* has more to do with whether or not you're in touch with popular culture or, in general, how to superficially fit in with a prevailing sociopolitical culture than with true, character-probing ontological endeavor. Furthermore, the underlying causes are clearly and quickly identified when the contemplative person puts their thought to determining the etiology of this problem. It emerges thusly: the innate condition of being for human beings is such that they live in some kind of societal structure. The culture and or sub-cultures within which they exist present to their senses a multitude of stimuli and conditions from which they evolve their attitudes and subsequent behaviors. Their attitudes can be considered as *tools,* a tool being a device, be it behaviorally based or material in essence (e.g., a handsaw), that permits the person to construct a personal reality within their group or society. With *attitude tools* a person can construct a behavioral response to their society. With *physical tools* a person may build a house (It is interesting to contemplate the kanji character that represents the Japanese word concept *ai,* as it exists as the form of a house). A person's *behavioral house,* often being affected by certain ignoble cultural values which are plausibly paraded as beneficial, can be built upon deceitful or false premises, upon muddy or infirm ground. This condition of psychological foundational weakness occurs typically when the individual cannot self-initiate unhampered or clear thought concerning the matters of their existence as a sentient being that is subject to the natural phenomenon of *cause and effect.* When such inability to think logically or reasonably occurs, they are likely to pick up and use the wrong attitude tools (those that do not entirely protect, sustain, and enhance life) and thereby construct a behavioral house from which emerges a succeeding generation of one or more individuals who are even more afflicted by the generally wrong cultural attitudes that give rise to further societal distress and turmoil. With just a little contemplation any person can apprehend this valid psychosocial phenomenon and its portent for the individual and their society.

The Competition Dilemma

An example of unclear thinking, or of no thought all, that may result in an action, no matter if it be conscious (a decision) or unconscious (an unthinking response), which in turn may produce a negative outcome (a representation of the condition of one's behavioral house), is exemplified by the following allegorical tale:

"Not too long ago there was a youth of ten years aged. A pellet rifle he shouldered; he aimed at a resting chickadee. It was a snowy winter day, so calm from the silence which only snow seems to bring. You know the feel, where No-sound almost seems to plead for Sound. Pow! Off went the pellet zinging through the cold, crisp air; slow enough to see, fast enough to interfere. Down the small bird fell; and, thrashing about upon the ground, its wings fluttered an answer to No-sound's plea. The youth rushed forward to see. The bird, wings wildly flapping, tried to fly; but alas, in its unbalanced condition -- a leg had been severed -- it could not."

"'For what reason,' the youth thought, 'did I do this' 'I did not need food to eat, the bird was not attacking me.'"

"The cat was close now, quite an opportunist; intensely watching, it crouched and prepared to pounce."

"Feeling guilt and sadness, not knowing what to do, the youth stood still. He thought, 'Should I help the bird? Or, should I finish this which I began?' 'Whoops!' The cat pounced! Thoughts set in motion."

Julian *-- 1990*

One point gleaned by this writer was this: *it was as if the workings of the rifle's mechanics had a certain power, a power to lure the curious person who shouldered it to produce pull upon its trigger.* I am curious (as to what it does); consequences yet to be realized. With weapon in hand you have now become part of the rifles mechanics; and, it beckons, 'Try out this tool' -- for what reason can there be for having shouldered it other than to use it? This is the dilemma. The very tool with which one identifies, be they external (physical, a rifle) or internal (attitude, the willingness to shoulder, to aim, and the responding to the lure to squeeze the trigger), draws your behavior toward carrying out the tool's innate purpose-spirit!

Every tool has its specific function, and it is not unreasonable to propose that when used for its intended purpose it manifests a certain object-oriented quality that could be loosely termed its *spirit*;

e.g., as in *the spirit of the law.* There are true, real world examples of this type of outcome that are present in all human history, both minor and major. Such has occurred to young and old, unaware and aware, unknowledgeable and knowledgeable. A much older example of this phenomenon, which follows, and this is not meant to disparage the noble art of hunting, can be read in the book **The Witchery of Archery**, *Chapter IV*, authored by Maurice Thompson, published in 1878 C.E.

"*It is one of the peculiarities of your true archer that he shoots at anything in the shape of a bird or wild animal that presents itself. With him 'all fish is game' in the broadest sense. Having a bunch of light deal arrows with me, I began practising on the redwing blackbirds that now and then perched within easy shot on the 'bonnets' of the lilies, and so utterly oblivious of everything else did I become, that it was like being startled from a dream when a great blue heron sprang heavily into the air from a little tussock in the midst of a clump of water-growing shrubs, not more than twenty-five feet from me. My arm was in good training, however. Instinctively I let fly at him just as he made a half-turn, and poised himself for a vigorous sweep. The light arrow struck him somewhere about the thigh, and remained stiffly sticking in the wound. The huge bird whirled over and over a few times, and then mounted perpendiculary through the air. Up, up he went. I launched two or three unsuccessful shafts after him, but he heeded them not. Right up he struggled, by a narrow spiral course, till he began to rapidly diminish in apparent size, and finally, after flickering indistinctly on the sky for a time, he utterly vanished. But this was not all. Several minutes afterwards the headless shaft of the arrow came whirling down, and fell near to me. It had been broken off close up to the brazing, and was quite bloody. Where did that stricken, powerful bird go to? Did he continue to mount till, suddenly exhausted, he fell with outstretched wings through a long incline into the merciful bosom of some wild everglade? Or did he go up until his piercing eye discovered that paradise of birds where no archer ever lies in wait? No matter; I lost a beautiful tuft of plumes by his energy and pluck.*"

It can be understood then, that arising from both an individual's extent of experience with life and the force of enculturation that brings the person to an act of choice, no matter if it be conscious or unconscious, the tools they choose to build or remodel their behavioral house have innate properties that may draw them unwittingly to an unexpected, perhaps ignoble or ignominious conclusion.

Thoughtful consideration of how a tool might be or should be used is essential toward achieving an intended good, productive, and humane outcome. Conversely, improper use of the tool can result in a disastrous outcome. Consider the following events of the morning August 1, 1100 C.E. that resulted in the death of King William Rufus of England during a hunt in England's New Forest reserve.

"The king and Walter (Walter Tirel, a French lord) posted themselves with a few others in one part of the forest, and stood with their weapons in their hands eagerly watching for the coming of the game, when a stag suddenly running between them, the king quitted his station, and Walter shot an arrow. It grazed the beast's horny back, but glancing from it, mortally wounded the king who stood within range. He immediately fell to the ground, and alas! suddenly expired..."[5]

And, let us not forget the combative engagement between Atsumori and Naozane related earlier in the preface of this book; though not an accidental occurrence, it was a result of behavior imparted by their culture, unquestioned and accepted by its real-life actors. Attitude tools that lead to a point of mental response usually elicit an act. An act manifests its effect or force in the physical realm, no matter if it is in the form of the spoken or written word or other outwardly expressed bodily action. An example is that of verbal or written social dissent, carried out by one's action when lifting the picket sign and or expelling the spoken word, or through the use of the writing implement to pen the word. Even *a drink of a present-day 'cultural kool-aid'* is an act arising from your attitudinal toolbox.

The significant people who have made decisions concerning that which comprises the philosophical and technical foundation of Aikido have applied their attitudinal tools toward the construction of its ethos. Whether or not that ethos is maximally useful or productive towards protecting, sustaining, and enhancing life is subject to, at any time, probing analysis.

There are reasons, both external and internal, which explain Aikido's limited affect upon the diminishment of violent attitude and behavior in societies around the world. Aikido, its philosophy, is somewhat impotent in a world so full of sensory stimuli and satiation where the individual is coddled from cradle to grave in a cultural environment of distraction by one kind of entertainment or another that is engineered by corporate social engineers (psychologists and linguistic communication specialists). This type of cultural encapsulation is foisted upon the senses of each person by a multitude of media magnates whose techniques include specialized dissimulation, and wherein, each person is urged by their basic drives, innate ignorance, and fear to seek 'nurturing' through involvement with dubious group oriented pursuits (such as those that define our modern era's so-called *culture wars*) or to worship quirky ascetic activities that are socially fruitless. The following are several examples of such a pernicious phenomenon. Consider any of the modern gladiatorial-like sports wherein the aggressive behavior of the participants is praised as a 'glorious' or sometimes 'virtuous' ethos when in fact such leads only to the emergence of a cultural atmosphere that often proposes the ignoble attitude that *might* (i.e., power) equals *right* (the latter being behavior that truly and validly arises from pure-self); or, the misdirected or quirky secular and non-secular organizations that eventually evolve covert or overt violence; and, lastly, escapism or pseudo-asceticism that causes detachment of the individual from productive societal involvement.

Emerging from these aforementioned diverse yet interconnected forces are certain deleterious effects, such as unbridled satiation of nerve-ending desire postulated (either purposefully or unconsciously) as that which produces happiness as contrasted to the view that it is a modicum of self-control emanating from will-power (objectively assessed by the individual embracing the concept of pure-self, recognizing and accepting mortality, and understanding the effects of the indifferent acts of Nature) that strengthens character and minimizes the possibility of harmful excesses. This is a present day social problem in the United States of America that arose prominently during the latter part of the 20th Century after W.W. II. The very circumstance with which the Aikido of today finds itself labeled -- that is, as an ineffectual means of self-defense -- is partially a result of the affect of these deleterious social problems and forces; the other part, discussed earlier, is a result of the ever increasing emphasis that Morihei Ueshiba placed on the spiritual underpinnings and teachings of Aikido as he aged, and after his death, Kisshomaru's interpretation of his father's teachings and how he implemented his perceptions of those toward setting a new direction for Aikido in the post W.W. II era. These maladies have emerged from the failure of Aikido's chief proponents to present to the world a cohesive, dynamic, and functional philosophical ethos, detached from magico-religiosity, which has been unified by a different, newly synthesized competitive event that showcases the social importance of an aiki aligned, real self-defense. From this failure has come the divergence of many competent Aikido teachers, disgruntled for this one reason, each having established different sub-organizations or factions. Fortunately, the maladies that have weakened Aikido's social potency and its effectiveness as a viable means of self-defense could be addressed by its various organizations. If such is done competently, the subsequent efforts should produce some success toward renewing its social potency and restoring its functionality for personal self-defense.

Weaknesses in an organizational structure often result in a corporate body's dismemberment. Organizational fractures result in new, peopled factions; these new factions typically result in a reduction of collective effort, thus emerging a diminished overall affect. Ineffective action typically results in failure to achieve a goal.

Fracture → Faction → Feebleness → Failure.

In spite of the problem of factionalization, those who practice Aikido and take its philosophy outward into daily life are like a diamond in the sand, or water in the desert -- tough and rare, precious and vital; durable and brilliant, fluid of life. Yet, these types of attributes can only produce their possible best societal effect when those of one person are united with those of others into a single force, focusing a cohesive creative potential, laser-like, toward the accomplishment of a goal that is mutually desired, where collective effort is the oasis sustaining life, neither defocused nor evaporated by the heat of humanity's social grittiness. As a fractured crystal is to a laser or disseminated water is in the desert, similarly is the Aikido community as a force for contributing to any further societal improvement.

Though somewhat difficult to assess, it can be said that the maximum benefit that Aikido might have will only occur when events come to pass that regenerate a condition of mutual interaction and cooperativeness that unifies most, ideally all, aikidoka. Until then, an aikidoka's efforts to manifest the mutually accepted pleasant and useful aspects of Aikido, while productive for the individual, will have only a small measurable effect upon minimizing the violence within the larger human realm, and therefore a negligible positive effect upon the collective human condition.

As it relates to Aikido, the ideal goal should consist of unifying its divergent factions through the formation a new dual-aspect cooperative, quasi-competitive event so that the resulting coalition could direct its energy toward the establishment of an ostensibly kinder, situation-appropriate cultural attitude concerning how to resolve conflict as illuminated by the concept of aiki. Such an event is proposed in outline form in Chapter IX.

The Greater Good of Sport

Organized and controlled competition in the form of sport provides a social avenue, or method, through which its participants as well as its spectators can have a largely useful as well as positive affect upon any particular human culture, but only if the code of behavioral ethic serves to promote good human relations. Sport creates camaraderie of one kind or another by offering a purpose comprised of what its participants -- players or spectators -- consider meaningful. For the players, "meaningful" is, at the least, comprised of participation in their society, which results in recognition, self-esteem, and money. For the spectators, "meaningful" is constituted of a sense of community through participation in a shared pastime and probably an idenification (association) with certain behaviors or attributes of a player or a team, which contributes to their self-esteem. There is not at all anything wrong with this as long as it tends to promote good human relations -- this is the greater good of sport. With what might all the millions of people be otherwise involving themselves if not for controlled, organized, and properly directed (non-harmful) sports? Religion? Philanthropy? Science? Outer Space exploration?

Kisshomaru Ueshiba, while considering Aikido's future, in a sincere desire to be true to certain aspects of what he perceived to be Aikido's philosophic foundation, may have erred when he made the statement "... *aikido refuses to become a competitive sport and rejects all forms of contests or tournaments...*"[6] This he said from a deep concern that "*Such things are seen as fueling only egoism, self-concern and disregard for others.*"[5] In fact, these conditions of personality noted by Kisshomaru frequently manifest in one player or another, in one team or another, or in one spectator or another.

Perhaps a little speculative, yet pertinent, is the likelihood that Kisshomaru's attitude arose as a response to the competitive nature of the sociopolitical dynamics evolved from Jigoro Kano's involvement with the Olympic Games Committee to include his Judo in the Olympic Games, for such effort was continued after Kano's death in 1938 C.E. Nevertheless, there are other aspects of the sociopolitical reality of Budo during the post war era which likely affected his attitudinal position regarding competition. Judo was a relatively new discipline distilled from several of Japan's older martial arts (primarily from the Kitō-ryū and Tenjin Shin'yō-ryū Jujutsu disciplines); it was infused with the creativity of Kano, and as a vital creation of Japanese origin it sought not only acceptance as an Olympic Games sport but also, thereby, validation as a new, vital, and ostensibly predominant form of Budo. Both Morihei and Kisshomaru Ueshiba had probably discussed on numerous occasions the possible effect that certain personal and professional relationships might have upon the future development of Aiki-budo, such as with the Japanese government's Greater Japan Martial Virtue Association or Judo's Kodokan. Judo was officially accepted as an Olympic sport in 1954, at a time when Morihei and Kisshomaru Ueshiba (the latter, at that time, being the Aikikai head instructor), Kenji Tomiki (founder of present day Shodokan Aikido), and Gozo Shioda (founder of present day Yoshinkan Aikido) were all involved with the interpersonal imbroglios that set a course for uncertain change in Aiki-budo, the result of which was the emergence of several factions. Each of these identified its martial activities by the new term *aikido*. (Kenji Tomiki was the first to use the term *aikido* in his book, *Judo and Aikido*, 1956). Furthermore, both Morihei and Kisshomaru were uncomfortable with Kenji Tomiki having primary loyalty to Judo, as well as with Tomiki's insistence that any true and valid form of Budo did not disassociate itself from shiai and randori. Lastly, immediately after W. W. II, many more Japanese people than ever before were collectively apathetic toward, even opposed to, some of their own cultural attitudes that spawned the type of nationalistic fevor (a form of competition) that had led Japan to war (discussed at the beginning of this chapter). It is likely that Kisshomaru's statements concerning competition were the method by which he differentiated Aikido from the other martial arts in order to distance the fledgling Aikikai organization from any type of association with Judo and the Kodokan, thereby removing Aikido from any possible consideration as an Olympic Games sport while claiming the moral high-ground in an effort to suppress any Japanese inclination toward a possible future resurgence of ethnocentric nationalism that might have a potential for violence. Aikido was to be an art or discipline through which a practitioner might obtain a higher, keener understanding of life, with a bias intended to impart to the practitioner a kinder, gentler attitude, yet still tough (ideally) when necessary, thereby creating a divergence from the older Bushido attitudes that had typically evolved barbarous strife among individuals, clans, and nations.

Though Kenji Tomiki was correct in his theory that true Budo does not ignore either randori or shiai, his decision to include these important elements for aikido training at a time when Morihei was manifesting a more religious view of his Aiki-budo (and just as Kisshomaru was beginning to shape Aiki-budo into the Aikikai's presentation of Aikido) was destined to arouse interpersonal conflict about who controlled and guided the philosophical and technical basis as well as the future of Aikido. In affect, a multifaceted competition was emerging. Gozo Shioda had already split off to form Yoshinkan Aikido. Tomiki had been urged by Japan's Waseda University to formalize a method of competition. Tomiki, an adept master of both Judo and Aikido, was moving his essential being about within the academic realm. Tomiki, a dynamic man, who was proclaimed by many of his peers as equal to Kano in his ability to perform, inspire, and accomplish, was certainly a formidable sociopolitical force. Tomiki -- who knew that both randori and shiai were essential to prove or maintain the martial or self-defense effectiveness of any technique, tactic, or strategy -- was destined to experience the martial-based sociopolitical dynamics and interpersonal squabbles that resulted from a conflict of ideas with Morihei and Kisshomaru Ueshiba, which, in turn, resulted in separate rather than collaborative efforts. Competition, in the viewpoint of the two Ueshibas, was a manifestation of behavior firmly held to be antithetical to the concept of aiki, an idea that must be rejected.

Interestingly, a competition, be it sport or otherwise, does not have to be structured in a way that results in deleterious individual or cultural attitudes. The ethos by which competition might be defined can be different than that which comprised the type of behavior to which Morihei and Kisshomaru were opposed. Yet, undoubtedly, a society must be cautious, for when some type or another of martial attitude is either unthinkingly or purposefully synthesized with the *idea of sport* (or with sport-like elements that are seemingly characteristic of this) and then subjected to the manipulations of present-day media science by a sport corporation's desire for profit, what typically emerges is a sensational bloodsport; not a Budo.

The shaping, perhaps even cultivation in some cases, of one kind of character trait or another within a person does occur within a sport. The character or quality of personality is largely influenced by a sport's code of behavior and its subsequent interactive effect upon the innate character of each participant -- both player and spectator. Who creates the code of behavior of a sport? Unfortunately, the usual code of behavior, often unproductively affected by the desire to win and earn money, does not often provide the best ground from which one may attempt to grow the most ideal condition of higher consciousness. However, from the overview of general societal well-being, the negative, devolving affect of this anomaly is sometimes or somewhat minimized when compared to the benefit provided by sports in general; i.e., sports provide many people with diversion and relaxation from the stresses of a *controlled reality* that is typically neither completely perceived by them nor entirely of their own making.

Old Jujutsu made use of at least two forms of competition, those being street fight and warfare. Through these methods, though brutishly violent and severe, the effectiveness of any particular martial technique was clearly demonstrated. Let us not forget, the word *martial* refers to fighting, for the purposes of war, and martial arts up to the time of Aikido, perhaps excepting Judo, were combat oriented. Hence, true combat arts were martial in their character and they were comprised of a large body of the various martial disciplines that defined first Bushido, then later, Budo. Competition among the practitioners of any of these was often brutal.

For some aikidoka to exhibit an attitude that sportive competition is a behavior to be shunned is to lose perspective of the good that is present in such. They lose both the opportunity to not only shape the nature of that competition so that it largely exhibits a positive ethos but also to shape the condition of the 'game of humanity' so that any of its obvious negative aspects, when viewed objectively from a personal as well as cultural perspective, may be somewhat or largely diminished, thus affecting a change in the general ethos of both sports and society as a whole. The failure of some forms of Aikido to embrace some type of quasi-competitive event has likely resulted in a lost opportunity to thoroughly seed modern society with the concept of aiki and its attendant usefulness; i.e., harmonized energy, harmonized spirit.

The structural and philosophical challenges that make it difficult for the whole of Aikido to embrace sportive competition reside primarily in the psychological realm of that which comprises our innate human nature and in the sociological realm that instills within any particular human culture its values and mores. Additionally, for the Japanese people, there seems to be a cultural predisposition toward the formation of factions, particularly in religion, possibly conferred from generation to generation by either a memetic transmission or another collective social force process, whereby a faction to which a person may belong helps to establish the raison d'être of their existence through the differences that are perceived between one faction and another.[7] Such a phenomenon also seems to affect the United States of America, and probably other regions of the world, too. For the larger part of the Aikido community to embrace sportive competition, such competition would need to comport fully with the philosophical tenets by which Aikido manifests its unique ideological being. From the standpoint of the individual and life, a person's existence from the time of birth until death is full of natural competition; no example of this need be given herein as any simple thought concerning this matter will quickly produce the necessary proof. The most important aspect to fully consider, though, is that of how the individual projects their personality into life and into the culture within which they reside. The individual, after attaining a certain perceptive ability and maturity, is responsible for assessing the competitive aspects of their environment and how to interact with it in a way that not only results in their survival but also, from the ideal viewpoint, enhances it for the other people with whom they interact. One person and another form a group; many people form a larger group; but the collective will of the group projected outward into life, and the power to affect that arises from such, can lose perspective of that which comprises objective enhancement of their culture, their society, and their geographic environment. Struggle by people, overt or covert, for the purpose of defining cultural or societal values and mores is a form of competition, and when considered from that valid perspective, Aikido has attempted to compete against another set of established cultural and societal values (in which there is a sportive element) which have developed from certain types of *group-think* aspirations and eccentricities (a collective will) that have emerged from innate human nature; or perhaps, from the obfuscation of pure-self.[8] However, this innate condition, that is, the affect of fear (e.g., anxious self-protectiveness, flight or fight, mortality), desire, greed, indolence, sloth, stubbornness, and avarice (but assessing the extent of the affect of these for any one person or group is relative to the circumstances) does not necessarily need to induce the various types of personal or group behavior which result in less than harmonious, unproductive, and sometimes outright per-verse or violent cultural, societal, or environmental outcomes.

Today, though ostensibly internalized as a cultural collective unconscious attribute (largely an outcome of Japan's reconstruction period following W.W. II and of ongoing influence from other cultures), the concordance of an individual's identity with the so-called 'samurai spirit' (which entails technical skill as well as subordination and devotion to a clan, group, or team) is clearly apparent for many Japanese. From the viewpoint of a Japanese collective unconscious, swinging a Baseball bat (a wooden sword of sorts; a bokken) is a cut of the sword (a katana) or a swing of a staff (a jo; a wooden staff of specific diameter and length). The ball itself, though intermittently managed or *played* by man, can be contemplated as a messenger of fate, but sometimes bouncing uncontrollably it certainly represents chance or the inevitability of change. A bunt with the Baseball bat is a tactic to further a certain strategy and can be likened to a parry or feint with the katana or jo -- a sacrifice by the bunter for the benefit of the team -- and team-to-team competition can be somewhat contrasted with clan-to-clan interaction. (Compare Japan's present day corporate structure with the old feudal Han structure). The *catcher* frequently signals through the use of coded hand gestures to the *pitcher* in order to transmit to the latter a suggestion as to what type of ball toss would most likely result in a missed swing by a *batter* of the opposing team; this signaling being representative, to the Japanese, of the obscured workings of life that happen behind the main social scenery (e.g., *ura o miru*). Baseball's rule section 6.02 requires certain behavior from a batter, and if a batter does not abide by these the umpire may call a strike upon the batter even when the pitcher has not thrown the ball; thusly, a batter is required to participate -- i.e., they must step into the batter's box, swing or not, otherwise, outside of the batter's box they can be called "out." The entire game is full of tactic and strategy, which beckons one to contemplate the battles of old through the play of the new. Supportive of this statement as it pertains to Japanese Baseball culture, a very early reference from the *Alumni Association of the First Higher School of Tokyo* relates that "*Sports arrived from the West. In Ichiko baseball, we are playing sports, but we are also putting the spirit of Japan into it. ... Yakyu (i.e., baseball, literally 'field ball') is a way to embrace the samurai spirit. To play baseball is to manifest this spirit. Thus our members are just like the warriors of old with their samurai spirit.*"[9]

A Baseball team is a group of people cooperating during its play to achieve an end goal, i.e, to achieve a win over the opposing team. Ideally, each person within the group organizes their thought and action in a manner that coordinates or merges their behavior with the other members of their team in order to achieve that goal; herein is found a type of harmonious interaction. The individual, a person, determines whether or not they can fit in and harmonize their behavior with other members of their team. A team where the players are well harmonized -- where each member performs their function well (with minimal or no error) as it pertains to the team goal -- will, more often than not, achieve the goal, a win.

Does any individual who subordinates theirself to the collective, a team perhaps, lose contact with or understanding of their essential being? There is evidence that could support the proposition of this as a hypothesis, but the extent to which it occurs and its affect upon the individual is likely dependent upon both the character of the person and that which they value as the basis of their ethos as tugged upon by the dynamic forces of the society within which they exist and the effect of the relevant forces of the group to which they have subordinated theirself (themselves). However, no matter to what extent it may occur, the individual always has some understanding of what comprises their unique essence as a human being, their individuality. An in-depth discussion of this will not be pursued here, as it is a study unto itself. It is sufficient to relate that some degree of aiki (harmonized energy or spirit) occurs not only in the sport of Baseball but in most other team sports, too. Hostility between members of a team, or hostility of one team member toward a member of another team is occasionally apparent, and obviously this is not a *harmonious* interaction. However, it is the nature of the human being to be challenged from time to time with determining how to properly express disagreement with another member or other person in a manner that is unlikely to result in the continuance or exacerbation of disagreement. Within the context just aforementioned, there resides an interesting psychological dichotomy. Disagreement does not always have to be viewed as disharmony, for, it may evolve as a *psychological stimulus vehicle* that presents to the participants a dynamic tension which, when navigated properly and with skill, is more likely to result in harmonious *travel* and a safe *arrival* rather than a *wreck*. Put differently, disagreement might be disharmonious, but with the implementation of the correct process of interaction, disharmony can be metamorphosed into harmony and peace. Discord arises when a person believes that they do not exist within a social structure, that they are separate from the social realm or that they can exist outside of it. Of course, this is an erroneous perception, and a person so believing is often struggling to achieve an unreasonable and less functional sense of *I am*, as considered from an objective viewpoint, within their societal as well as cultural setting. An individual is always contemplating, on some level or another, recognized or not, the extent to which they are the *I am* as contrasted to the extent to which the collective is permitted to affect their being as the *I am*.[10] At some point in life, whether the individual is considering the one-to-one relationship or the one-to-others (group, team, organization, etc.) relationship, they must fall in line, must fit in, must get along to some degree or another; the extent to which any person can be *free* or to *be theirself* is a function of how much freedom is given to each by the societal group within which they exist, and, by the choices they make within the confines of their social reality that, itself, is affected by the world's other societal realties. Much of a person's energy can be directed toward determining how and where they will fit in, their effort directed toward manifesting the shape of their social existence as influenced by harmony. Harmony is omnipresent and urges the individual to find concurrence, *to find their peace*. When a person is unable to determine how and where to fit in, the personal existential angst that results therefrom will typically result in one or another of the various psychological states of anxiety; some of these can be self-destructive. The Japanese have a certain, unique understanding of the relationship of the individual versus society, probably meme related, and from such many of its societal members have an affinity for activities, e.g., Baseball, that represent their collectively held and valued societal ethos.

Though possibly difficult to quantify, a team member, subject to the effect of the forces of both group and established society, retains, to some extent, small or large, their unique essential character. The actual make-up of a person's character (largely dependent on to what extent pure-self is apprehended) may be consciously assessed by the same. Furthermore, it is each person's responsibility to apprehend their essential qualities and existential composition (i.e., the meaning and significance of their being), and to assess how they and life interact. Nonetheless, no matter what the precise condition of self versus team is, the individual who is a team member is still an individual.

Judo is a modern sport, derived from old Japanese martial jujutsu systems, that offers a competitive activity (shiai) but is not primarily a team effort, that is, team versus team. Rather, it is person-to-person physical struggle or contest designed, ideally, to improve each participant's mental and physical qualities toward evolving a state of higher consciousness, thereby producing a stronger and calmer, respectful and kinder personality. There are certain, established rules of engagement and a code of etiquette that guide a participant's interaction during their competitive match with an opponent. Judo is one of many sports that represent a supreme effort of the *I am* to express its position as a unique and powerful force, somewhat distanced from, but still acceptable to, the effect of a society's collective ethos. One may practice Judo and not be required to participate in formal competition; notwithstanding, there is always some type of apparent or hidden competition occurring -- e.g., the practice of Judo technique with another person can exhibit certain aspects of the competitive attitude, and or of self-judgment, usually manifesting as a thoughtful comparison of one's abilities or skill against that of another's. Whether it is a formal or an informal match, such is an outward expression of the participant's curiosity about their ability to overcome a challenge to their *I am* identity. The necessity of instilling good sporting conduct -- i.e., a set of behavioral expectations that govern person-to-person interaction, which are designed to obviate temper escalation and any tendency toward an attitude of revenge -- is of paramount importance in promoting participant camaraderie through harmonious interaction. Currently, two prominent organizations oversee most of the training, competition, and ethos of Judo -- these are the International Judo Federation and, for oversight of the world's Olympic Games, the International Olympics Committee. The rules for competitive Judo are designed to reduce injury, instill good etiquette, and promote spectator interest. The rules and etiquette have evolved from a society's need to find balance between the competitive nature (survival instinct) of the *I am* in contrast to the immutable reality that harmony irresistibly urges an individual to find an equitable outcome with their colleagues; not doing so leads, once again, toward any of the various states of anxiety and conflict -- *Naturem expellas furca tamen usque recurret.*[11] Achieving such a balance is an example of harmony -- of aiki -- in Judo. Reflecting upon the numerous characteristics of Asian martial-art-derived combative sports, such an existential balance is also certainly evident in those styles of Aikido that have developed and embraced a relatively safe competitive shiai; e.g., Shodokan Aikido.

When considered from a learned judoka's position, the best victory is had when their actions and counteractions during a match are designed to bring into play their highly developed perception, strength, and technical abilities in a way that makes use of the opponent's actions. Ideally, aikidoka do the same. The *makes use of* concept is an innate aspect of harmony. In fact, the participant who aligns their behavior most wisely with harmony is more likely to win the match than not; notwithstanding, there are circumstances during a match that might result in loss even when one is attentive to harmony, or accord. Harmony, then, is quite present in Judo and the participant who aligns with it (and it is nearly impossible not to do so) is practicing a valid aspect of aiki. Judoka apply their efforts to harmonize (making use of and fitting in; accord; Wa) in the face of what are truly very difficult and challenging circumstances of person-to-person competition, and from the point of view of that which constitutes valid humanitarian oriented self-defense, even a Judo shime-waza technique (e.g., a carotid artery restriction hold) when applied to incapacitate an aggressor could be considered as a technique to regain control of a difficult encounter carried out for the reason of restoring peace (an aspect of harmony). Does the judoka's creative potential and unique being suffer as a result of aligning with harmony? No.

One rainy day in the state of Washington (where the author resides) I entered the business premises of a favorite coffee house. I visit there frequently, seated in a somewhat secluded corner, contemplating the matters of life and, of course, frequently endeavoring to write the content of one manuscript or another. As it often occurs for any person who regularly visits such a business establishment, one barista or another comes to know a customer's usual preference when ordering a coffee or cup of tea. As it happened, as I was placing my writing gear upon the table, I noticed that a barista who regularly opens the business in the morning was assisting another customer. I continued with the placement of my gear and upon finishing, walked toward the service counter, noticing that he was yet busy at the espresso machine with the previous customer's order. As I approached the order window, what was present before my gaze but a tall, royal blue drink mug placed upon the countertop, already having been warmed with a burst of hot water, then drained, and ready to receive its intended use. As he was yet busy with the other customer, I placed the required recompense upon the counter, walked several yards down toward the other end of the countertop, filled it with the decaf house brew and returned to my table. This interaction is a small example of harmonizing energy in the form of cooperation brought about by the somewhat intuited mental processing of the barista. He is still his unique self, and I am yet myself, yet we united briefly in a harmonious dynamic.

Deleterious Aspects Emerging from Competition

Pertaining to sportive competition, when considering the psychological growth of an individual within a society, Kisshomaru Ueshiba was concerned about the development of an excessively egoistic[12] person whose character manifested as largely arrogant, haughty, and disrespectful; put differently, he was concerned about the loss of the individual to objectively assess the essence of their being in relation to other people and society -- the loss of the ability to see the other as a reflection of oneself (at least in some part or attribute, good or bad) -- to the point where they would begin to lose their sense of humanity, that is, their sense of compassion, equanimity, and fair play. Of equal importance, he was concerned with the degradation of the transmittal of those ethical and philosophical aspects which were, and are yet today, the stimulus in an aikidoka for the development of a spirituality that manifests Aikido's humanitarian oriented qualities. He understood correctly that a lot of what comprised sports (both in the areas of human ego and business organizations) focused on sports as a method of financial gain, frequently producing psychosocial forces within a group or team that tended to distract the individual from efforts of how to evolve a spiritual attitude that manifested values which were good for the development of a human being (e.g., compassion and equanimity).

In sports today there often occurs an occassion where one or more players are elevated to a 'demigod' status by means of their specialized skill, perhaps by Faustian choices made in union with the needs and maneuvers of their team's management and fandom. Each of these individuals will have their personality shaped by their particular sport's corporate business machinery. The modern sport team ethos -- which is crafted by its management personnel (coaches, lawyers, counselors, and media specialists) who make use of behavioral psychology and all forms of media to push forward into public view certain individuals or teams for the reason of attracting spectator attention -- is directed largely toward ticket and merchandise sales, i.e., toward a monetary goal. Today, the commerce activity of the sports industry is a multi-billion dollar business. The implementation of the necessary organizational machinery to accomplish a *profitable* team results in the need for one team member or another to be placed in the public limelight. As this occurs, the values and mores that comprise a player's ethos are reshaped by the individual in response to their *team's needs*, which process then triggers a self-initiated reevaluation about their sense of importance to the team, their family, and society. Such reevaluation is ongoing, occurring little by little and here-and-there, and usually it does not trend toward negative behaviors. However, there can occasionally emerge in a player an insufferable arrogance; and, in an extreme case, such a player may behave in a way that is contrary their society's laws.

In their book *A Primer of Jungian Psychology*, Calvin Hall and Vernon Nordby accurately conveyed that "*If a person becomes too involved and too preoccupied with the role he is playing, and his ego begins to identify solely with his role, the other sides of his personality will be shoved aside. Such a persona-ridden person becomes alienated from his nature, and lives in a state of tension because of the conflict between his overdeveloped persona and the underdeveloped parts of the personality.*"[13] This psychological maladay has affected many people, particularly in those endeavors of life, like sports, that tend to make possible the conditions where an individual, who is one amongst the multitude, may become idolized.

Aikido's Incongruities

Contemplating the whole of Aikido up against the reality of life, and bringing into thoughtful consideration the actual concerns present during a self-defense situation and how that should inform an aikidoka as to whether they may use the word *martial* to describe their discipline, there are both the subtle affects of a sociopolitical uncertainty (e.g., Kisshomaru's considerations about how Aiki-budo would manifest its characteristics in the post W.W. II era) as well as erroneous thought (arising from a mentality that is subject to, or affected by a desire or need) that can lead a person toward embracing the partially errant idea that "*Aikido rejects all forms of violence, justified, or unjustified.*" Idealism carried forth into the battlefield of self-defense always increases the probability of an unnecessarily dangerous or harmful outcome. A simple example of this danger occurs when an aikidoka vows to reject all forms of violence, justified or unjustified, and therefrom refuses to study Aikido in a manner that causes it to be useful for self-defense. At this point, for a person of such attitude, Aikido can no longer be termed either a physio-spiritual self-defense art or a martial art.

When a teacher -- such as the once very knowledgeable, skilled, and well-meaning Kisshomaru Ueshiba -- presents to the world by means of the written or spoken word that *Aikido is a true martial art*, then the very nature of such statement infers a request for proof in technical form, i.e., performance oriented proof to substantiate the claim. If one displays action that looks like a martial art, then to be true to that which it looks like, which is orientation toward fighting and war, one should actually have that kind attitude and skill; otherwise, it is nothing more than dance. So, what is Aikido, a martial art or a dance; or is there an in-between place for it? If its a martial art, then one must align fully with the concept of *martial* and support that alignment with behavior that is disposed to fighting and warfare (i.e., with both attitude and technique suitable for fighting and warfare). If its a dance form, then by all means, divorce it from practicality and perhaps call it aiki-dansu or -taiso (harmonized energy dance or exercise). However, if Aikido can be descriptively placed between these two positions, then one must define it somewhat differently by aligning it with other concepts that do not make use of martial characteristics to define its philosophical and technical foundation. One such concept could be (and for many is) a Budo ethos that seeks to protect, sustain, and enhance life but does not neglect to instill and maintain functional self-defense ability. Do aikidoka really want to identify with the concept of *martial* when that to which they actually aspire is Morihei Ueshiba's definition of Budo, which is, according to him, *the Way of Stopping the Weapons of Destruction?* An aikidoka should not ignore the reality of what is required of them in a situation of self-defense! Aikido should not be considered as martial art; rather, it should be identified as an art derived from or synthesized from a martial art while postulating therefrom that it has transcended the necessity of martial attitude and thereby having arrived as a pure Budo form. Interestingly, today, there are numerous Aikido schools and numerous 'Aikido' styles that are heavily invested in the 'martialness' of that which they teach, practice, and consider as true Aikido; and from such an attitudinal alignment, i.e., with martial characteristics, it seems as if these should not be considered to be Aikido. *There is a careful balancing act that teachers and students of Aikido need to maintain in order for them to be able to legitimately identify their practice as true Aikido.* This "balancing act" can be best realized by not becoming excessively invested in the attitude and behavior that expresses or represents the martial idea (i.e., fighting and warfare orientation).

Conclusion

Any Aikido organization which does not offer a voluntary competitive (shiai) or a mandatory quasi-competitive event (randori), any which has become self-constrained by magico-religiosity that has resulted in a 'divorce' from the difficult, violent, and often ugly reality of self-defense (e.g., when theological mysticism is imprac-tical toward achieving the goal of aiki-aligned self-defense ability), or any which has emerged from errant attitudes a self-imposed and unnecessary philosophic prejudice (e.g., competition is not good for the development of the human being) has contributed to Aikido's self-limiting efficacy, i.e., its distress. Having said this, it is impor-tant to know also that Kenji Tomiki, the main proponent for a com-petitive event in Aikido, failed to present successfully to Morihei and Kisshomaru Ueshiba a convincing argument (format) for com-petition that would reflect concordance with Aikikai Aikido's philo-sophy. For aikidoka, organizational fracturing causes, in one way or another, distraction (perceived or not) from a more productive path of learning that might lead them toward the realization of a higher awareness of the workings of life -- a higher consciousness. The result of this kind of distraction is reduced cooperation between the sensei of the different Aikido organizations -- e.g., those of the Aikikai, Nihon Aikido Kyōkai (Japan Aikido Association), Shodokan Aikido Kyōkai (Shodokan Aikido Association), Yoshinkai (Spirit Cultivation Association), Shin-shin Toitsu Aikidokai (Mind-Body System Aikido Association) -- which contributes to the failed, mal-formed, or slow germination of the idea of aiki within the world's societies.

As long as the majority of the extant Aikido community refuses to embrace some form of unifying competitive or quasi-competitive event that elucidates the concept of aiki (and such does not at all need to be in the general form that exists as the basis for combative sports, such as with Judo or Taekwondo), Aikido is likely to suffer further factionalization, thus moving it, a once vital physio-spiritual discipline, toward further social impotency and obscurity. How-ever, this is only part of the solution for the problem of factional-ization, as there are other aspects of human attitude and contention that give rise to discord. For example, Shodokan Aikido, the only organization that offers a competitive event, suffered a split in the year 2012 that arose from irreconcilable differences. Is there a way to unify Aikido's various primary factions in order to strengthen or reestablish Aikido's social potency?

The Competition Dilemma

[1] See, **Rockets Through Space** by Lester Del Rey. Premier Books, a division of Fawcett World Library, paperback, third printing, 1960, pages 23 - 31. Also interesting, since the beginning of the 21st Century there has been a steady decrease in both traditional Martial Arts and Science Fiction book sales, which is directly connected to a shift in peoples' interests.

[2] See, **The Spirit of Aikido** (Aikido no Kokoro) by Kisshomaru Ueshiba. Translated by Taitetsu Unno. Kodansha International, Ltd.; paperback edition, first printing, 1987, page 16.

[3] See, **Theory of the Essence of Judo** by Minoru Mochizuki, Aiki News magazine #65, 1984.

[4] See, **The Way of the Gladiator** by Daneil P. Mannix. New York, New York, iBooks, Inc., an iBooks paperback book, second printing, 2001, pages 186 & 224.

[5] See, **Life in a Medieval Castle** by Joseph and Frances Gies. Published by HarperCollins, a Perennial book edition, paperback, 2002, page 136.

[6] See, **The Spirit of Aikido** (Aikido no Kokoro) by Kisshomaru Ueshiba. Translated by Taitetsu Unno. Kodansha International, Ltd.; paperback edition, first printing, 1987, page 15.

[7] See the web-tome entitled **Transmission, Inheritance, Emulation** Peter Goldsbury, the chapter entitled **The General Impact of the Pacific War** (WWII) **on Aikido**, section entitled **Conclusion: From Ueshiba Father to Ueshiba Son**; published online at Aikiweb.com, 2008.

[8] See, **A Primer of Jungian Psychology** by Calvin S. Hall and Vernon J. Nordy. Published by the New American Library, Inc., a Mentor paperback book, seventh printing, 1973, page 38.

[9] See **Yakyu Bushi**, an article published by the *Alumni Association of the First Higher School of Tokyo*, February 28, 1903.

[10] The French existentialist philosopher Jean-Paul Sartre proposed the "I am" as a human psychosocial construct to identify that the quality of any person's life comes into existence as a result of choices made in response to circumstances presented, whether or not any particular person makes a conscious choice is irrelevant; thus, a series of choices comes to constitute a person's primary social identity and reality. The Spanish philosopher José Ortega y Gasset also proposed a similar social construct as exem-

plified by his famous maxim "*Yo soy yo y mi circunstancia*" ("I am I and my circumstance.").

[11] "*You can throw out Nature with a pitch fork, but she'll always turn up again*"; translated from the Latin.

[12] **Egoism** is a doctrine which proposes that a person's self-interest is the "*a priori*" (presumptive) motive of all conscious action. **Egotism** is a condition where a person has developed an exaggerated sense of self where such an attitude of being is an unreasonable, unwarranted or faulty projection of their subjective reasoning (not objectively held by others) that emerges from their unique specific personal circumstances of psychological development in response to their existence within any particular group, society or culture thereof.

[13] See, **A Primer of Jungian Psychology** by Calvin S. Hall and Vernon J. Nordy; New American Library, Inc., a Mentor paperback book, seventh printing, 1973, page 45.

Chapter VIII

Kenji Tomiki: History and His Contribution to Aikidō

As an Aikido teacher I have often noticed how the majority of Shodokan aikidoka are acutely and knowledgeably aware of the historical events that are pertinent to Aikido. Yet, just the opposite often exists as a state of knowledge for those practicing Aikikai or Shin-shin Toitsu Aikido concerning knowledge of Kenji Tomiki and his Shodokan Aikido organization, or for that matter, regarding many of the other different Aikido organizations (e.g., Yoshinkan and Yoseikan Aikido). It is not a great surprise, then, that within these other styles, it is rare to find a practitioner who knows that Kenji Tomiki was the first deshi to whom Morihei Ueshiba awarded the coveted Menkyo Kaiden scroll (Total Transmission License). At the time of this conveyance, in 1940 C.E., the martial system that Morihei Ueshiba taught was known as *Aiki-budo*,[1] presented under the legitimate authority of the *Zaidan Hojin Kobukai* organization. In 1941, as Japan prepared to further expand its military action on several different fronts, several factions within its government succeeded in acquiring complete control of all-important indigenous institutions and organizations. In late 1941 C.E., after much political intrigue, General Hideki Tōjō, who had previously been in charge of the Japanese Kantogun Army's operations in Manchuria, was appointed prime minister of Japan by Emperor Hirohito. As part of his plan to further mobilize Japan for a declaration of war upon the United States of America, which had earlier placed a total embargo on oil shipments to Japan, he assumed direct control over the activities of the Dai Nippon Butoku Kai (Greater Japan Martial Virtue Association). Tōjō, having assumed chairmanship of this organization, directed it to make certain changes toward bringing all of the relatively new Budo disciplines into alignment with the Japanese war effort.[2] For Ueshiba, the name for his discipline, Aiki-budo, could no longer include the kanji for *bu*. Instead, it must include the kanji suffix of *dō* and all future advancements must be issued in the *Dan System*[3] of rank identification; all of the previously issued advancements of the older *Menkyo System*[3] would be converted to equivalency in the Dan System. As a result, Kenji Tomiki's Menkyo Kaiden was converted to the equivalence of 8th Dan. In 1942 C.E., after difficult discussions with the Dai Nippon Butoku Kai, which were carried out by Minoru Hirai[4] (the founder of Kōrindō Aikido) who was the emissary sent by Ueshiba to negotiate, the 'negotiated' term of *aikido* was agreed upon. From that point onward, Morihei Ueshiba's discipline of Aiki-budo was understood to be an *aikido* discipline, no matter how disagreeable. Later, after W.W. II, this forced renaming would provide a significant part of the basis for contention between Kenji Tomiki and Ueshiba's Aikikai because *1)* this term *aikido* was a generic classification identifier,[5] *2)* Ueshiba was still annoyed with this forced renaming, and *3)* Tomiki was the first of Ueshiba's top deshi to use the term in a book. Shortly after Japan's unconditional surrender in September of 1945 C.E., the Dai Nippon Butoku Kai, and many other institutions and organizations that had been judged to be supportive of Japan's war effort were entirely shutdown by the occupying military authority of S.C.A.P.

The year 1942 C.E. was replete with interesting events for the development of Aiki-budo/Aikido. *First*, early in the year, *aikido* became the official, government-recognized name for Ueshiba's discipline. *Second*, Japan's Imperial Navy is defeated at the Battle of Midway in June, and shortly thereafter, Morihei Ueshiba returned to Japan and retreated to his residence in Iwama.[6] *Third*, in August, Ueshiba attends the annual Manchuria-Japanese Exchange Martial Arts Demonstration held at Kenkoku University, Manchuria, after having been designated by his government as its official martial arts representative for this event, one which commemorated the 10th anniversary of Manchurian 'independence' from China. Japanese losses at the Battle of Midway were kept quite secret by the top officials of the Japanese military, and only the top echelon personnel of Japanese military and government were fully aware of these and its meaning for the future of Imperial Japanese suzerainity. It is possible that Morihei Ueshiba had gained information about this defeat, for he had numerous social connections with persons well situated in the military and government; e.g., Minoru Hirai (head Jujutsu teacher for the Japanese Imperial Army's Military Police), K. Tomita (Osaka Police Chief and, later, Cabinet Minister of Japan's

Prime Minister Fumimaro Konoe through 1941 C.E. as well as a de-voted student of Aiki-budo), Japanese Prince Kaya (a general in Japan's Imperial Army), and Isamu Takeshita (an influential but re-tired admiral of the Japanese Imperial Navy). It is important to note here that Kenji Tomiki is not without reproach when considering his connection to Japan's actions in Manchuria. However, let us not forget that many of the Japanese 'actors' on the world's stage during that era, having been raised within their particular culture, believed in their cause, no matter how wrong it eventually became; many people who were responsible for Japan's national policies and ac-tions were unable to unwrap quickly enough the deleterious effects of their enculturated veil that obscured the type of cognitive 'vision-ing' that might have prevented Japan's militaristic expansionism and its role in W.W. II. This type of culture driven socio-political phe-nomenon, that of colonization, has affected the nationalistic goals of other countries, too; e.g., in the past two centuries, Great Britain's colonization of India, France's colonization of Southeast Asia, the formation of the Union of Soviet Socialist Republic (U.S.S.R.), and the United States of America's (U.S.A.) policy of expansionism that is typically known as its *Manifest Destiny.* In the year 1934 C.E., Kenji Tomiki accepted a teaching position at the Daido Gakuin Academy[7] in Changchun (Shinkyo), Manchuria, resigned from his teaching position at the Kakunodate Junior High School, Japan, and moved to Tokyo, very near to Ueshiba's Kobukan Dojo. This posi-tion was the result of a recommendation given by Morihei Ueshiba at the request/order of Army General Hideki Tōjō, who had been promoted to the rank of major general in 1933 C.E. and placed in command of the Japanese Army Ministry's Personnel Department.[8] While in Tokyo, Tomiki prepared for his assignment in Manchuria and assisted Ueshiba in the latter's teaching duties at the Kobukan Dojo and elsewhere.[9] Approximately one and a half years later, in 1936 C.E., Kenji Tomiki departs for his assignment in Manchuria as an official bujutsu teacher for Japan's Kantogun Army Kempeitai (Military Police) and members of the Japanese Imperial Household Ministry who were stationed there. In the spring of 1938 C.E., shortly after Kenkoku University's building had been completed, which was also situated in Changchun, General Tsuneo Matsudaira, one of the University's founding members and a student of Morihei Ueshiba's, made a recommendation to the University's president, Soichi Sakuta, that Ueshiba be given a position there as the official bujutsu advisor.[10] After administrative approval later in the same year, Ueshiba then recommended Tomiki as his assistant bujutsu teacher at this relatively short-lived school, which position Tomiki accepted. At that point, Hideo Ohba took over Tomiki's role and duties as the head bujutsu teacher at the Daido Gakuin Academy.

In spite of his position as an assistant professor of bujutsu at Kenkoku University, in July of 1945 C.E. Tomiki was conscripted for service in the Kantogun Army.[11] Toward the end of W.W. II, after Russia had entered the war against Japan, Tomiki was captured in Manchuria and imprisoned in a Russian prison camp in Siberia. After his release in 1948, Kenji Tomiki was repatriated to Japan. In 1948, the newly formed Zaidan Hojin Aikikai organization, which had been approved by S.C.A.P. and the new Japanese government, replaced the prewar Kobukai organization. After limited practice at the Aikikai Hombu Dojo had begun to resume in 1949, the Aikikai, as a result of its new charter, formally designated all of Morihei Ueshiba's previously issued Menkyo System promotions in the Dan System ranks (though such a process had been initiated earlier by Tojo's order). In 1954, Kenji Tomiki was awarded a full professorship at Waseda University and headed the University's physical education department. In addition to his professional endeavors, he taught an occasional Aikido class at Morihei Ueshiba's Aikikai Hombu Dojo in Tokyo from 1949 until 1958 when, due to irreconcilable differences between him and Morihei and Kisshomaru Ueshiba, he officially broke away from the Aikikai Aikido organization.

After his repatriation, Tomiki began a careful analysis of all of Aikido's techniques. Each technique was assigned a specific name, and techniques with a similar implementation basis were grouped together in categories that made possible a quicker-than-before learning process for students of Aikido. For example, the ***Junana hon no kata*** of Shodokan Aikido consists of five different groups of techniques, the first being the ***Atemi waza***, which consists of five techniques that, after performing an irimi movement, can be applied as either a pushing or a striking action. This was a unique insight and formulation because it

1) Provided Aikido students with a range of application that was useful in tempering a defender's actions to the lesser or greater severity of a possible self-defense scenario, thereby creating a practical representation of the concept of aiki;

2) Increased the safety of Aikido practice during both kata and randori practice because there existed a standardized set of techniques with which each student was familiar;

3) Established a well-organized method of learning Aikido that could be taught as a physical education course at the high school or university level; and,

4) Provided the foundation for the development of a possible Aikido competitive event that, if reasonably implemented, would provide all aikidoka with information about the functionality of Aikido techniques for self-defense.

The waza (technique) groups of the ***Junana hon no kata*** (Seventeen basics of the form), successively, are the

1) ***Atemi waza*** (5 striking techniques);
2) ***Hiji waza*** (5 elbow techniques);
3) ***Tekubi waza*** (4 wrist techniques); and
4) ***Uki waza*** (3 floating techniques).

Hiroaki Kogure, 8th Dan Shodokan Aikido, informs us that during the formation of Shodokan Aikido's structural basis, "*The greatest difficulty was how to handle atemi since in aikido it is hard to execute an effective joint technique without using* atemi."[12] Today, beyond the arena of self-defense training, these waza are the technical basis for Shodokan Aikido's competitive event, and are sometimes termed ***Randori no kata***. In Shodokan Aikido, there are numerous other kata, too, which reflect Kenji Tomiki's training under his teacher Morihei Ueshiba; these are categorized under the term ***Koryu no Kata*** (old style forms) and are successively learned as a requirement for advancement to higher *Dan* grades (blackbelt levels). In addition to Morihei Ueshiba's body of techniques and theory, Shodokan Aikido includes certain other techniques that herald from Judo which a student may optionally study, e.g., the ***Goshin Jutsu no Kata*** (self-defense forms), which assists a student to further increase their self-defense knowledge and skill.

During the first several years following 1950, S.C.A.P. began to allow Japan to restart many of its traditional activities that had been forbade since the end of Japan's W.W. II hostilities; as a result, many of its martial arts, after reshaping their governing organizational charters to certain requirements outlined by S.C.A.P., were slowly restarted. Kenji Tomiki began teaching on the average one class per week at the Aikikai Hombu Dojo and did so up until his separation from the Aikikai in early 1959. In 1953, he and other master Judoka from the Kodokan journeyed to the United States of America for the reason of sharing their knowledge of hand-to-hand combat with the U.S. Air Force. In 1954, though Tomiki's specific area of academic expertise was in political science and economics, he was awarded a full professorship to head the physical education department at Waseda University, Tokyo, Japan. The awarding of this cross-profession position was largely due to his experience and knowledge of Judo and Aikido as well as his keen ability to analyze the combative disciplines from a technical as well as historical perspective.

In the year 1958, Kenji Tomiki established Waseda University's Aikido Club. After his separation from Aikikai Aikido early in 1959, he focused on the development of a sportive element for Aikido and with the assistance of Hideo Ohba and numerous others established the Shodokan Aikido Hombu in 1967, in Osaka, Japan. In the year 1974, Kenji Tomiki, Hideo Ohba, and their supporters officially established the All Japan Aikido Association. He worked continuously to improve Shodokan Aikido and supervised the Aikido course as well as other physical education programs at Waseda University until his retirement.

Professor Tomiki authored numerous books and articles pertaining to Judo, Aikido, and exercise. His book *Judo: Appendix Aikido* was the first competent overview of Aikido as analyzed from the perspective of Japanese Budo technical theory, history, and philosophy and, accordingly, begins to hint upon his point of view regarding the need for a competitive event. Also, he was an accomplished Japanese calligrapher. His calligraphic works are well appreciated and, as one might imagine, these are difficult to obtain.[13] Several other books that Tomiki authored are *Judo Taiso* (Judo Exercise), *Aikido Nyumon* (New Aikido), *Shin Aikido Tekisuto: Aikido Kyōgi no Tebiki* (Vital Aikido Textbook: Aikido Sport Manual), and *Taiiku To Budo* (Physical Education and Budo).

As of October, 2012, Shodokan Aikido in Japan has suffered a factionalization event. Tetsuro Nariyama shihan now heads a separate organization called the Shodokan Aikido Federation, while Fumiaki Shishida shihan and chairwoman Masako Tomiki (Kenji

Tomiki's daughter) jointly administer the Japan Aikido Association and refers to their Aikido as Tomiki Aikido. Tetsuro Nariyama and Fumiaki Shishida jointly authored the book ***Aikido: Tradition and the Competitive Edge*** in 1985, which concerns the history, evolution, techniques, and competitive events of Shodokan Aikido.

Shinbuden Dojo at Kenkoku University, Manchuria, 1942 C.E.

Seated, left to right:
Kenji Tomiki, Morihei Ueshiba. **Standing, left to right:**
Unkown, Hideo Ohba.

Kenji Tomiki: History and His Contribution to Aikidō

[1] Prior to Ueshiba naming his martial art *Aiki-budo*, other known names that he used briefly include Aioi Ryu Aiki-jujutsu (~1927 C.E.), Aioi Ryu Aiki-bujutsu (~1929 C.E.), Asahi Ryu Jujutsu (~1933 C.E.), Ueshiba Ryu Aiki-budo (~1935 C.E.), Aiki-budo (~1936 C.E.). The Zaidan Hojin Kobukai was an organization that was an officially recognized Japanese foundation, which had been formed by Ueshiba and numerous people from the Japanese military, police, and Imperial family backgrounds.

[2] Aikido is typically classified as a Budo discipline, as is Judo, Karatedo, Kendo, Jodo, and Iaido. Budo are the modern Japanese quasi-martial, self-defense, or combative sport disciplines created during and after the Meiji Restoration (beginning in 1868 C.E.). Bujutsu are those earlier Japanese disciplines with an unequivocal martial aire, i.e., military disciplines for the purpose of killing an enemy during war. Jujutsu and Kenjutsu, for example, are classified as Bujutsu (martial art) disciplines. See *How Aikido Was Named* by Stanley Pranin; article from the Aikido Journal Bulletin Board, November 22, 1999.

[3] The *Dan System* was originally conceived and used by a Japanese Go (a game of strategy) master player during the Edo Period (1603 C.E. to 1867 C.E.). The particular Japanese word 段, in rōmaji written as *go*, means *stage* or *step* (as in a step of a staircase). Jigoro Kano, while creating Judo, refined and instituted this Dan System to reflect a judoka's achieve-ment level during their successive stages of progression; essentially, it is an academic system of classification designed to reflect a recipient's know-ledge, experience, and position. Kano, being politically active, promoted the Dan System for use nationwide. The *Menkyo System* was an older sys-tem that indicated the extent of transmission of knowledge to a student. Up until the Dai Nippon Butokukai was required to make certain changes by Prime Minister's Hideki Tojo's directives of 1942 C.E., there was no Japanese Ministry of Education requirement for a bujutsu teacher or bujutsu school to issue promotions in accordance with the Dan System.

[4] In January of 1942 C.E., Minoru Hirai was appointed by Morihei Ueshiba to act as the Director of General Affairs of Ueshiba's Kobukan Dojo. In late 1945 C.E., after Japan's surrender of W.W. II, he established Korindō Aikido's first dojo. During the war he was head of the Jujutsu department of the Japanese Imperial Army's Kempeitai (military police) School.

[5] During Minoru Hirai's discussions with the Dai Nippon Butoku Kai, it was decided that the term *aikido* expressed best the Japanese traditional philosophy of "michi" (path towards achievement or the path of behavior leading toward the achievement of proper behavior) and would serve well

as an all-inclusive term for the classification of any new budo, including Ueshiba's, that had characteristics similar to Ueshiba's Aiki-budo. See *Interview with Minoru Hirai* by Stanley Pranin; Aikido Journal online, article #100, 1994.

[6] Stanley Pranin, in an article entitled *How Aikido was Named?* (Previously entitled "What is the origin of the term aikido?," November 22, 1999), posted online at the Aikido Journal Bulletin Board, indicates that Morihei Ueshiba was perhaps ill from some sort of gastrointestinal malady.

[7] The Daido Gakuin Academy, transliterated as *United Front* or *Great Unity* Academy, founded in 1932 C.E., was an institute designed to further Japan's Asian agenda, i.e., the Greater East Asia Co-Prosperity Sphere.

[8] Though the Kobukan Dojo had been established in 1931 C.E., the non-profit entity governing it, the Zaidan Hojin Kobukai, was not officially established by registration with the Japanese Ministry of Education until April 30, 1940 C.E. The Zaidan Hojin Kobukai was initially organized by several retired high-ranking military men. Isamu Takeshita, a retired Japanese Imperial Navy Admiral and friend of Ueshiba, was the organization's chairman; among the other board members were retired Army General Katsura Hayashi (vice chairman), Count Fumimaro Konoe, Count Toshitame Maeda, Takuo Godo, Kinya Fujita, Kozaburo Okada, and Kenzo Futaki. Ueshiba was in charge of the teaching at the Kobukan Dojo. There is the possibility that both Takeshita and Ueshiba conferred about who to recommend for this position in Manchuria. Tomiki was recruited by General Hideki Tojo upon a request presented to the Kobukan Dojo. A year later, in 1935 C.E., Tojo was placed in command of the Kempeitai (Military Police) of the Kantogun Army of Manchuria. See *Interview with Shigenobu Okumura* by Stanley Pranin; Aiki News magazine, article #203, 1983.

[9] There are a very few reports that Kenji Tomiki actually accepted a commission in the Japanese Imperial Army. His move to Tokyo might have been for the reason of receiving basic army training. This might seem reasonable as he was there for at least one year before making the trip to Manchuria. See, *Timeline*, a web article concerning the historical development of Hapkido at www.midwesthapkido.com/timeline.htm, and *History of Aikido*, a web article by Central London Shodokan Aikido at www.centrallondonshodokanaikido.co.uk/about-central-london-shodokan-aikido/history-of-aikido/#.UnL3m1PueSo. Additionally, there is the article *Interview with Shigenobu Okumura* by Stanley Pranin (Aiki News magazine, article #203, 1983) that indicates Tomiki was recruited by then

General Hideki Tojo, and if this is accurate, then it is possible that Tomiki's "preparation" in Tokyo was a typical preparation for any higher administrative or military person for the possibility of combat; according to the *Hideo Ohba Biography* by Fumiaki Shishida, Tomiki was conscripted by the Kantogun Army in 1945 C.E. as Japan's military control of Manchuria was collapsing. Wouldn't it have been reasonable for Tomiki to have had, at the least, military training prior to leaving Japan in order to be expected to fight effectively in a military engagement if or when such became necessary? Tomiki's academic and martial credentials at that time were of a high level, and it would seem unreasonable to situate such an educated man in a military campaign zone with no basic army training; therefore, to be conscripted as an ordinary recruit does not make sense. As the Russian Army invaded Manchuria in 1945 C.E., Tomiki was captured and interred in a Siberian prison for nearly three years; this length of interment probably reflected his value to the Russians as a captive soldier with respect to his role in Manchuria.

[10] See, *Interview with Aikido Doshu Kisshomaru Ueshiba* by Stanley Pranin; Aiki News magazine, article #81, 1989.

[11] See, *Hideo Ohba Biography* by Fumiaki Shishida; Aiki News magazine, article #85 (Part 1) and #86 (Part 2), 1990.

[12] See, *Interview with Hiroaki Kogure* by Stanley Pranin; Aiki News magazine, article #82 (1989).

[13] *Hirafuku Hyakusui*, 平福百穂 (1877 - October 30, 1933 C.E.), was a Japanese Painter who embraced the "Western" oil painting method, in addition to the traditional Japanese art methods, in many of his later artistic endeavors; he was an uncle of Kenji Tomiki. For information about Kenji Tomiki's calligraphy works see http://tomikiaikido.blogspot.com.

Chapter IX

Aikido Competition: A Reformed Shiai

Of all the present day Aikido organizations only one, Shodokan Aikido, offers competition events where two participants engage each other in a controlled contest for the reasons of *1)* proving and improving the functionality of any purported self-defense technique, tactic or strategy, *2)* testing of each participant's underlying character for the reason of improving their general integrity and attitudinal alignment with the concept of aiki, and *3)* providing a unique social atmosphere of camaraderie that further enhances the participants' understanding of their proper and best role in humanity. This event is entirely voluntary. The primary focus for a novice aikidoka who practices under the auspices of the Shodokan is largely concerned with training that has some similarity to the traditional training promulgated by the Aikikai, but with a few important technical, categorical, and terminology differences imbued by Judo's influence upon Aikido. The shiai of Shodokan Aikido is an adjunct activity in which only a small percentage of its aikidoka participate. Nearly all other systems of Aikido do not have a shiai event (See Chapter VII for details). Also, there are aikidoka who cross train; for example, a Yoshinkan practitioner may decide to experience competition by training in Shodokan Aikido in order to prepare for the latter's competitive events.

To transcend the discord that has emerged from Aikido's two opposing philosophic stances as well as provide a different path by which a person may develop pleasant attitude and productive behavior within the framework of a competitive event, where there arises no undesirable self-adulation and haughtiness, or where little or no disrespect manifests toward another person who exists with a different attitude or ability, and whereby the underpinnings of all Aikido is elucidated and validated, there must be an additional event that occurs alongside of *physical shiai* (a meeting to test) in order to create what could be described as an *evolution event* for all Aikido. Such evolution would exhibit a synthesis that would arise from the combination of physical shiai with some type of philosophically oriented *verbal contest* (a shiai unto itself) that could serve to unify the interaction of the participants during their contentious efforts to elucidate the principles, workings, and significance of the concept of Aiki. Two aikidoka would participate in a non-physical struggle to elucidate the meaning and truth of *ai* or *wa, ki,* and *aiki*. This new *philosophic shiai* could be designed around a dialectic process, where such a process would consist of a guided, spoken, purposefully contentious dialogue between the two participants who hold a different viewpoint about a subject and want to glimpse, derive, or reveal its innate truth or reality through a reasoned, logical argument. The goal of a philosophic shiai would be that of the resolution of a challenge, disagreement, or problem that is relevant to all Aikido through rational yet piercing verbal discourse toward the development of a an objectively discerned truth or reality. Its purpose would be to seek the transcendence of opposing positions in order to arrive at that truth or reality by

1) Providing justification for rejecting both alternatives as false; and,
2) Helping to elucidate a real but previously veiled integral relationship between apparent opposites that have been kept apart and regarded as distinct (e.g., opposing attitudes concerning competition).

The dialectic method considers, ideally, the whole of reality as an evolving phenomenon and attempts to provide a functional solution to any problem that emerges therefrom. When considering how to associate properly the usefulness of a philosophical shiai with physical shiai for Aikido, or to understand fully the various forms of the dialectic method, the Socratic Method, the Hegelian Method, the Buddhist dialectic method, and the Indian Jain dialectic should be reviewed. The Hegelian dialectic method proposes a thesis, opposes it with an antithesis, and then arrives at a resolution through synthesis. In his work *The Science of Logic*, for example, Hegel describes his dialectic of existence where, first, existence must be posited as pure *Being*; however, pure *Being*, after careful examination, is found to be no different than *Nothing*. When it is realized that what is coming into being is, at the same time, also returning to nothing (for example: a person's life is a progression toward dying), *Being* and *Nothing* can be united as *Becoming*.

In itself, Shodokan Aikido's physical shiai is obviously a type of dialectic method -- a physical dialectic that certainly requires of its participants good physical prowess as well as focused mental effort. However, its present form does not include a sufficient philosophical impetus that can provide a solution to the problem of Aikido's *great divide*, i.e., the problem of its two opposite philosophic stances concerning the usefulness and validity of competition.

In Buddhism, including Zen, there is a dialectic method that illustrates the usefulness of formulating a means through reasoning by which a prevailing attitude, either personally or culturally held, may be challenged and possibly transcended to achieve a new condition of thought that is enlightening toward assessing the possibility of a new balance, where more than two attitudes, positions, or points on *the fulcrum of Reality* (i.e., Nature's fulcrum) is considered. (For information about the idea of *Nature's fulcrum* and a person's interaction upon it see page 246 of this chapter.) This method is typically termed *Upaya-kaushalya*, which transliterates approximately as *skill in means*. Upaya-kaushalya presents that Buddhist adherents (but usually a monk) may use their own specific methods or techniques in order to ease suffering and introduce others to the concept of *Dharma*.[1] The implication is that even if a technique or viewpoint (for example, a competitive event) is not ultimately *true* or *valid* in what might be considered as the highest sense or goal, it may still be an expedient practice to perform, or view, or to hold; that is, it may bring the practitioner closer to true realization anyway in spite of its lesser truth or lesser validity. However, this must be done skillfully, as to do otherwise is likely to result in the further entrenchment of the very characteristic that is undesirable, unproductive, or not humanitarian. Is it not possible to find or develop in shiai a suitable basis of performance that would be acceptable to all Aikido styles while elucidating the principles of Aikido?

As a companion to the proposed philosophic shiai, the present physical shiai of Shodokan Aikido would probably require a little reshaping in order to produce a slightly different but enhanced physio-philosophical ethos; such an improvement would be designed to nurture or further enhance benevolent qualities in each participant while yet instilling functional, reality oriented self-defense ability.

Outline of a New Dual-Event Shiai

How might such an event, a new shiai, rather, a dual-event shiai look? Below is an outline.

1) No awards given, no privileges bestowed, because such an event is for the purpose of elucidating Aikido's truths, which are to be ascertained by the efforts of all who participate (i.e., the two participants and those oversee the event and contemplate the outcome of their interaction);

2) Philosophic shiai, where participants cooperate by contesting the validity of an ethical problem, or a spiritual conundrum, or ascertain an immutable truth as such pertains to the elucidation of aiki through an interactive verbal dialectic discourse that is overseen by a moderating panel and referee;

3) Physical shiai, where the interaction could be similar to that of Shodokan Aikido's shiai, but with an emphasis guided by a moderating panel towards the achievement or implementation of aiki theory that is functional for self-defense as outlined by the *Budo-hiketsu: Aiki no Jutsu*[2] (1899) and by the *Goshin-jutsu Ogi*[3] (1917), and as modified by Jigoro Kano's three concepts of

   a) *Seiryoku zen'yō* (精力善用 {maximum efficiency, minimum effort}),

   b) *Jita kyōei* (自他共栄 {mutual welfare and benefit}),

   c) *Jū yoku gō o seisu* (柔よく剛を制す{gentleness controls hardness}{soft and fair goes far}), and

by Morihei Ueshiba's three attitude reminders[4] to

   d) Train to harmonize one's mind with the activities of all things in the Universe,

   e) Train to harmonize one's mind with the activities of all things in the Universe (this he purposefully repeated),

   f) Train to direct the ki that connects the mind and

body to harmonize with the activity of all things in the Universe;

4) No declaration of a winner;
5) Each entrant issued a certificate that acknowledges their participation; and, lastly,
6) Participation in such an event is voluntary.

Philosophic Dialectic Interaction

Philosophic shiai should be voluntary and not necessarily following or preceding physical shiai; it can be presented as a standalone event. However, if it is presented as connected to the physical shiai, the same participants who engaged in physical shiai are necessarily scheduled to engage in philosophic shiai. The philosophic shiai consists of an active verbal discourse that is representative of the dialectic method. Guided and maintained by a body of referees, emphasis should be placed upon those philosophical aspects that, in combination with physical technique, comprise the foundational ethos of Aikido. Dialectic topics generally conceived or derived from pertinent questions such as *What comprises the essence of Budo?, What are the technical principles of Aikido?, What is the philosophic essence of Aikido?*, and *How does an aikidoka manifest aiki in daily life?* must be organized and presented in a valid dialectic form. Also, it may be useful to have each participant argue from the other's perspective, switching their argumentative stance.

Mohandas Gandhi's *Satyagraha* is an Indian dialectic procedure for discerning various kinds of social truth. Though most often employed as a means of non-violent civil protest to overthrow governmental oppression, Satyagraha[5] (truth-struggle) might, in a modified form, serve as a model for such a dialectic event. A possible name for Aikido's philosophic shiai could be *Aiki-no-Satya*, meaning *Truth of Aiki*, thus noting the contribution of Ghandi and India.

In Satyagraha, means and ends are inseparable -- the means employed are attached to the end result or goal and affect the quality or nature of the resulting truth. In other words, an *unjust means* that is employed to obtain supposed justice toward supposedly obtaining peace and harmony is contradictory and can only result in further disorder. This can be observed in the cyclic reoccurrence of violence when revenge is taken, and therefrom arises the necessity of clearly understanding how to properly and skillfully use Aikido as an art of peace rather than as an art of fighting.

Satyagraha can proceed toward an incorrect conclusion. This occurs when the two participants are mentally focused on being the 'last man standing.' In this circumstance, both participants hold an attitude that projects or exhibits victory as their goal; this typically prevents the attainment of objective truth, i.e., the ideal goal of the this particular dialectic process. Therefore, a skilled referee and a moderator, whose sole purpose is to keep the truth-struggle focused on the collective pursuit of the truth of technique and the truth of character (the shaping of a character that manifests a sincere benevolent self-aware higher consciousness) is of great importance to the philosophic shiai's dialectic integrity. Regarding a generalized form of Satyagraha for Aikido, F. G. Bailey's conceptualization, from his book **The Prevalence of Deceit,** where "*It, Satyagraha, requires one to state a thesis, oppose it with an anti-thesis, ..., ..., so as to produce a new and better strain, a synthesis.*"[6] is probably a good starting point.

Philosophic Dialectic Guidelines

Purpose

The purpose of this particular dialectic is to investigate as well as elucidate the essential, undisguised meaning of Aikido's pshysio-spiritual tenets -- e.g., the physical and spiritual characteristics of aiki, the hypothetical workings of kotodama, the philosophic basis of reasonable and lawful self-defense action as shaped by a person's society -- by testing the extent of their validity in order to improve their functionality, thus furthering in each participating aikidoka a continuing interest in seeking a higher understanding of the workings of life.

Interactional Format

A two-person, or perhaps two teams where each team consists of two members, verbal truth-struggle, which is overseen by one referee, one moderator, and a panel of seers. The following is a list of possible participatory requirements and rules by which a participant in Aiki-no-Satya could be guided.

1) Must be a practicing aikidoka;
2) Must give time (service) to their dojo's mundane matters of maintenance;
3) Must be willing to be completely responsible for any position stated which they have initiated during the dialectic, rather than attempting to or actually pushing that responsibility onto their fellow participant(s) or partner(s), thereby avoiding alienation of the partner where loss of their portion of the truth may occur;
4) The participants must always provide a face-saving method of situation-dependent escape for their partner(s) because the specific purpose of their dialectic engagement is to validate Aikido's truths; victory over one's partner (or the opposing team) is not the goal, as the very word "victory" is antithetical to the goal;
5) Must manifest a consistent non-violent attitude;
6) Must manifest a consistent respect for all creeds and all religions;
7) Must show consistent respect for elders;
8) Must show a consistent belief in the importance of seeking truth;
9) Must show faith in, or consideration of, the inherent capacity of the human being to act with understanding, compassion, flexibility, and grace, which qualities they will attempt to evoke during the dialectic;
10) Must manifest law-abiding behavior;
11) Must harbor minimal or no resentment or anger;
12) Must suffer the anger of his partner without responding in kind;
13) Must not curse, swear, or use purposefully insulting or demeaning speech;
14) Must behave courteously;
15) Must heed the directives of the referee and moderator; and, lastly,
16) Must, overall, show commitment to the usefullness of this process.

Role of the Referee (Suisensha, 推薦者)

The referee, or *suisensha*, acts when necessary to make judgment as to whether or not, and to what extent, certain of the above conditions are met before and during the dialectic, ready to call foul when necessary. The goal of the referee is to keep the discourse on subject, and to ensure that interaction of the participants occurs in a manner that does not engender contempt for each other. The conduct of the participants is regulated by the referee according to 3), 4), 5), 6), 7), 8), 9), 10), 11), 12), 13), 14), and 15) above.

Role of the Moderator (Shikaisha, 司会者)

In order to properly direct the *aiki truth struggle* toward a productive conclusion, that is, an endpoint to the dialectic, the moderator, or *shikaisha*, must organize its course by preparing one or several philosophic propositions that will be presented to the two participants. The moderator is a member of the Seers (see below), and each seer would rotate through this role. In addition to setting the *tone* of the dialectic by providing its topic, the moderator has also the function of directly overseeing the referee's role during the dialectic, and may interject when necessary if the referee errs.

Function of the Seers (Senkakusha, 先覚者)

The information provided by the focused discourse of the two participants engaged in the *aiki truth struggle* will be recorded by a group of either three or five seers known as senkakusha (enlightened person, or seer) and from this information will be gleaned specific information that will permit verification of or enhancements to the philosophical and working technical underpinnings of Aikido. One member of this oversight group will act as the moderator during the dialectic (see above).

Officiating Guidelines

1) Must meet the criteria outlined above in the Participatory Guidelines.
2) Must be of Dan grade in Aikido.

3) Must be thoroughly knowledgeable of Aikido history, technical theory, and philosophic foundation.
4) Must be knowledgeable of the dialectic method.

Physical Dialectic Interaction

The technical physical shiai, a form of dialectic itself, should consist of Shodokan Aikido's basic shiai guidelines, with subsequent improvements to follow as suggested and implemented by a new directional board of supervisors that could be comprised of members from both the Aikikai and Shodokan Aikido organizations and should be structured where no award, no trophy, no personal award or privilege is given. The participant's reward, if one needs such, is that of individual knowledge gained as well as that of knowing that their collective effort has resulted in contemplation by each member of the overseeing panel (seers) as to how the participant's (a truth-struggler) performance has contributed to proving the foundation of Aikido to be valid, or how it has improved Aikido's technical and philosophical underpinnings. This style of shiai could include various self-defense scenarios, designed with soft obstruction fixtures positioned to setup variation in situational circumstances, where the tori (the "performer" of a technique--termed "nage" in some other styles but meaning "thrower") makes use of both verbal and physical skill to resolve in an acceptable *aiki* manner the situation of mock discord. Considering the types of self-defense situations that occur for women in life beyond the dojo, it is reasonable to suggest that they be permitted to engage in mock situations where a man is their opponent.

Philosophic and Physical Shiai Summary

Thusly constructed, a new dual-event shiai would be comprised of a philosophic event and a physical event. Together, rather than a being considered as 'competitive,' these would be understood as a Satyagraha-like endeavor, with, perhaps, *Aiki-no-Satya* as its name. It should be noted here that the number of people who participate in Shodokan Aikido's present-day shiai is small in comparison to those who study Shodokan for its self-defense or health benefits, or to those who study other Aikido styles derived from Kenji Tomiki's teachings, e.g., those descended from the Fugakukai or European Tomiki Aikido organizations. This number is even smaller when compared to those who study Aikikai Aikido, or when compared to the number of participants of all Aikido styles worldwide that object to competition. Keeping this in mind, an *Aiki-no-Satya* shiai could exist as a relatively minor subdivision under the guidance of a panel that would consist of senior sensei from both Aikikai and Shodokan Aikido, thus embracing both cooperation and unity, i.e., *wa* (和). Whether or not such cooperation occurs, it could be useful for the Aikikai to consider an 'investment' in such an idea anyway, for, at the very least, it could create the 'shape' of a shiai of its own origin, counter-positioning itself as an intercessor against another legitimate style of Aikido that has its own unique form of shiai, thereby resisting any move toward the inclusion of an 'aikido' event in the Olympic Games, or, most disturbingly, a 'Pro Aikido' sport organization. Either way, such organizational action, which could provide a respectable but difficult path toward unification, would need to be conducted carefully, making certain to clearly consider all its ramifications so as not to further alienate large numbers of aikidoka.

Cross-Organizational Cooperation

Toward this end -- i.e., increased inter-organizational activities or unification of Aikido's many factions -- it would be a good achievement, expressive of *wa*, if the world's numerous Aikido organizations could agree to convene regularly an international convention for the reason of establishing a definitive agenda for creating cross-organizational cooperation, perhaps to include cooperative training activities that not only demonstrate the technical principles common to all Aikido styles but also share as well as validate the unique perspectives of those organizations. To identify such a cooperative event, perhaps a name like "All Aikido Friendship Convention" or "International All Aikido Convention" might be useful. The first gathering for this purpose could be held in Tokyo at the Nippon Budokan Center, then once every four years or so held at different locations around the globe. Interestingly, a gathering of this type occurred in November, 1972 at the *Second Japanese Budo Festival*

(Nippon Budosai), where Aikikai Aikido, Shodokan Aikido, and Yoshinkan Aikido cooperated in an Aikido demonstration. Over a decade later, Stanley Pranin, an author and biographer of Aikido, as well as an aikidoka, organized the *Aikido Friendship Demonstrations* (first held in the year 1985, the last in 1988) but these did not apparently include participation by any Shodokan Aikido group. After these ended, there was an event called the *Aiki Expo*, which brought together many practitioners of aiki based martial arts, but this too has ceased to exist. The *Multi-discipline Aiki Seminar* was held at an Aikikai associated dojo in the city of Seattle in March of 2011, but this, also, is not a regularly occurring event. Most recently, in May of 2014, Aikikai Aikido's 52nd *All Japan Aikido Demonstration* (under the authority of the Zaidan Hojin Aikikai, i.e., the Aikikai Foundation) was held at the Nippon Budokan Center in Tokyo, while for Yoshikan Aikido (under the authority of Zaidan Hojin Yoshinkai, i.e., the Yoshinkai Foundation) its own *All Japan Aikido Demonstration*, the 59th such event, was held in November, 2014 at the University Olympic Park Gymnasium in Komazawa. Neither of these demonstrations included officially sanctioned, cooperative interaction between the many Aikido organizations that represent the numerous different Aikido styles of today, i.e., these two demonstrations are separate, held at different times and locations, and are held as an event to bring together their own style's aikidoka while strengthening each organization's raison d'être. Note also that both the organizations aforementioned use the same name to advertise their own event, "All Japan Aikido Demonstration," but this does not mean that all styles of Aikido throughout the world demonstrate at either of these events. *Does this not indicate a condition of competition between these two organizations?* Today, some Aikido organizations hold "bridge" training seminars, but all too often such an event only attracts participants from the same or a similar style from distant locations rather than cross training aikidoka from different styles.

In 1991, Takashi Kushida shihan broke off from the Yoshinkai Foundation when he objected to changes in Yoshinkan Aikido's advancement standards that were promulgated by its founder, Gozo Shioda. In 2006, Kyoichi Inoue shihan of Yoshinkan Aikido resigned from the Yoshinkai Foundation, which was a result of unresolvable attitudinal differences. As one can imagine, both of these 'splits' resulted in the emergence of several more Aikido factions.

Due to differing perspectives regarding the future of Shodokan Aikido, Tetsuro Nariyama shihan resigned from the Japan Aikido Association (J.A.A.) in 2012. Masako Tomiki, Kenji Tomiki's daughter, and Fumiaki Shishida Shihan remained with the J.A.A. Tetsuro Nariyama shihan heads up the newly formed Shodokan Aikido Renmei (Shodokan Aikido Federation). The Aikido of the J.A.A. is referred to as either "Tomiki Aikido" or "The Aikido of Tomiki"; practically though, I refer to it as Tomiki-ryū Aikido, at least until the J.A.A. comes up with another name. Each organization has a separate competitive event that will supposedly be held every two years. This is a further weakening of that which could have otherwise directed a collected, spirited effort toward a necessary revisiting of the idea of future cooperation between different Aikido organizations. It is important to know that not all Tomiki-ryu aikidoka are competition oriented; in fact, most are not. Now more that ever before, Aikido's evolution will be best realized through the good efforts of aikidoka who establish and maintain cross-organizational cooperation for the reason of protecting, sustaining, and enhancing life.

The Idea of Non-contention: An Impediment to Cooperation

Realistically, it's unlikely that the suggestions of this chapter will produce such cooperation. You might ask, Why? *First*, its a bit impertinent, but someone needs to directly address all aspects of *Aikido's Distress.* Then, *secondly*, there is the problem where *spirituality* -- no matter what its quality   is considered by many people to be a personal psychological phenomenon that originates exclusively from or is possessed uniquely within an individual (though actually it is a psychosocial phenomenon), which, when conceived in this manner, is impenetrable (from a believer's perspective) by analytical scrutiny. In addition, people who are thusly inclined to believe usually maintain that when analysis is convened to determine the nature of spirituality, the very application of such tends to besmirch its metaphysical (spiritual) quality. Spirituality for these individuals is a subjective experiential condition, a sense or sensing of a particular way of being or essence in being, which exists in a mental place where objectivity either cannot enter or must not be permitted to enter. When considering *the first*, "cannot enter," it is assumed that there exists an inviolable metaphysical construct -- separate from a possible *soul* -- which for any person so aligned is usually attributed to the workings of a supernatural force or realm (e.g., a 'spirit world') and is accessible only through the rejection of the type of objectivity (analytical scrutiny) that would expose its weaknesses; this type of rejection is termed *faith.* When considering *the second,* "must not be permitted to enter," it can be understood that scrutiny of any configuration of spirituality is considered a violation of its sanctity and must be avoided so as to not destabilize its desired or perceived metaphysical quality. Interestingly, from the standpoint of some past as well as present social engineering proponents, there can be usefulness in maintaining a certain degree of societal discord based upon attitudinal differences, a type of purposefully instigated culture-dependent societal 'unreality,' if you will, which is brought about through the implementation of certain methods of psychosocial manipulation. At the micro-societal level, this is particularly true in any Aikido school, style, or organization where magico-religiosity is prevalent; there, reality is something other than the real, the actual, i.e., the objectively revealed. In contrast, isn't it pleasant and encouraging when there 'blossoms' a spirituality that manifests peace without imposing peace? Magico-religiosity is a form of *gen* (幻), i.e., illusion.

Kisshomaru Ueshiba in his book *The Spirit of Aikido* suggests that *ki* and *aiki* -- metaphysical concepts that are the foundation of true Aikido study and which help to the develop an aikidoka's sense of spirituality whether nor not they embrace competition -- should be investigated from a scientific, i.e., analytical, viewpoint.[8] Does not the technical analysis of Aikido's physical principles as they pertain to crafting a relatively safe form of competitive shiai -- which process would obviously necessitate a serious consideration of its 'spiritual' nature (i.e., the constituents of its philosophic ethos) -- produce a useful effort toward the scientific investigation of ki and aiki? I think it does. Notwithstanding, in Chapter 1, page 15, and Chapter 7, page 166, Kisshomaru Ueshiba lays out his problems with competition and tournament. It seems that he is concerned primarily about the following three points.

1) Egoism and disregard for others is encouraged or heightened by involvement with competitive events;
2) Aikido and its philosophy, having risen up from Japanese

culture and its unique spiritual disciplines, is comprised of much more than physical strength, technical cunning, and the winning of a contest -- to move it toward competition would move it away from any semblance of spirituality; and,

3) The possibility that Aikido could be divorced from the very spirituality (i.e., its Japanese philosophic ethos) that keeps it centered in the realm of *non-contention*[9] (the character of which has been proposed as a repository of love and peace) by the effect of a deleterious force; in this case, the typical formulation of any sport 'budo' competitive event. In such a scenario, Aikido (Aikikai in particular) is pressured to re-make itself as a sport (e.g., with characteristics similar to that of Shodokan Aikido Renmei), which then requires a sportive event that results in a winner and a loser. Later, this scenario 'spins off' (emerges) an aikido-like professional sport, *Pro Aikido* if you will, with all the typical markings, such as violence, brutality, and profit.

He proposed that when in the typical winner/loser formulation, 'sport budo' competitive events (where the term *budo* has been used loosely to describe a combative but sportive interaction) give rise to a certain brand of prowess that, in the process of achieving such, instills within a competitor a certain *kill'em all, let God sort'em out* urge to win. Kisshomaru Ueshiba considered this, from the stand-point of traditional Japanese philosophy, to be a spiritual blight.

So, if the ideas of *love* and *peace* (which are often variable) are proposed as that which comprises the psychosocial 'spiritual vessel' within which the idea of "non-contention" resides, does it follow that a "competitive spirit" is contained within a psychosocial 'anti-spiritual vessel,' which is constructed of *hate* and *conflict*?

The *idea of non-contention* is a valid proposition *as only a part* of a hypothetical psychological concept that can be applied toward obtaining accord or peace. In the case of humankind vs. Nature, non-contention might be somewhat realized, but never completely. Then, in the case of person vs. person, it is even more difficult to re-alize because some mental conditions (e.g., unresolvable anger-in-the-moment, self-indoctrination, and various mental disorders) and societal forces (e.g., societal indoctrination and its use in a manner that invariably results in social strife) often result in a tumultuous outcome no matter what is done to avoid it. In some Aikido styles, "non-contention" is supposedly accomplished by 'channeling' from one person to another the power of "creative love," which had been claimed by Morihei Ueshiba to be the primary force of Budo. An aikidoka who embraces such an idealistic and sentimental metaphysical proposition will typically experience a pervasive self-indoctrination that blocks the learning of the technical skill that is necessary to develop functional self-defense skill.

When the *idea of non-contention* is mistakenly valued as being 'spiritually' superior to *the process* of *learning how to achieve and maintain a condition of oneness with actual non-contention*, there creeps up from the shadowy haunts of a practitioner's mind a little psychic glimpse of mortality, which, deceivingly, 'speaks' of avoidance. It whispers to each, *Avoid, oh, please avoid the inquiry and effort that will emerge from deep within me the mortality-awakened-mindset where thoughts of the disconcerting matters of self-defense torment my consciousness.* Thus, one glimpse at a time, a student of Aikido avoids a difficulty right here or that problem over there and soon, little by little, feeling 'nourished' by their 'non-contentious' practice, they suppress their *inner truth-mirror* as they happily communicate the love and peace of their aiki 'self-defense,' sword or stave in hand;[10] but, all the while, unable to contemplate how sport competition might actually provide information about a functional type of aiki self-defense and a complete, i.e., valid, aiki spirituality.

From this author's experience, though *the first* of Kisshomaru Ueshiba's concerns above can occur, the large majority of people who participate in a competitive event are either unaffected or only slightly affected by this type of psychological difficulty; and when it is the latter circumstance, most who experience this eventually mature toward kindness and respect. Regarding *his second concern*, I'm grateful to Kisshomaru Ueshiba for his dedication to expressing the part of Japanese philosophy that embodies a unique aspect of spiritual culture in Japan, i.e., his family's Aikido. Why not put Aikikai's 'mark' on shiai, but in a way that aligns with its philosophical underpinnings -- e.g., *Aiki-no-Satya Shiai* -- where the 'win' acts to seed society with Aikido's philosophy? Addressing *his last concern*, *stage one* of this possible scenario has already occurred within the Shodokan Aikido organizations, and it is possible that something similar to this style's competitive shiai could become an event in the Olympic Games. However, in order for this to occur, Shodokan

Aikido would first have to prove that there is a significant difference between it and the other Asian sport 'budo' events that are presently included in the Games, such as Judo and Taekwondo. Is a *Pro Aikido* professional 'sport' possible? Probably not, for we all know that it would end up looking just like the U.F.C. event. So, the Aikido of today will be the Aikido of the future; and, the Shodokan Aikido organization with their relatively safe, carefully structured, competitive shiai event, which, interestingly, was intentionally designed to elucidate as well as stabilize both the technical and philosophical principles that underpin all Aikido, will continue to exist. Cannot such an endeavor be considered as contributing positively to the spiritual quality of the entire Aikido community? I think so, but *the spirit of cooperation* would enhance such a contribution.

When the underpinnings of the *idea of non-contention* are carefully analyzed, as it may be applied to or by a person, there is found that there exists, primarily, two preexisting conditions. These are

1) A person in relation to the indifferent acts of their natural environment, i.e., Nature; and,

2) A person in relation to or responding to the acts of another person.

In *1)*, a person will experience conflict or struggle in the form of Nature's acts directed toward them. For example, you are walking upon a hiking trail in the Olympic National Park in the state of Washington when suddenly, from the brush on one side, a mountain lion appears and attacks you. (This type of encounter actually does happen to people.) The mountain lion is not at all concerned as to whether or not you want to be involved in this engagement; and, you're not going to be able to have conversation with the animal about the *why* of its attack. The only vocalizing you'll be able to do will be your various shouts and groans as you try to keep from being eaten. In *2)*, we must consider that *there are two primary types of conflicts or struggles* that a person may experience with other people. *First*, there is the situation of the personal non-physical conflict; this is where one must engage verbal conversation to either explain or defend attitudes or behaviors. Such explanation or defense may arise in normal everyday life when one experiences discord with another person, typically a result of misunderstandings or resolutely held sociopolitical viewpoints; and, when laws are breeched, some people may find themselves civilly engaged in a court of law to redress a grievance or wrong. *The second important situation* that concerns us is that of harmful physical conflict (battle, struggle, fighting, etc.) with another person. Within this type of conflict, there are numerous circumstance-dependent subtypes that can be identified as belonging here. However, the most important of these, which I'll discuss because of its relevance to the discussion about the use of the concept of non-contention in Aikido, is that of the situation of an unwarranted and unrelenting physical attack from which you cannot escape except by mounting a successful self-defense. In this type of attack, no matter the *why* of it, the aggressor is never concerned about the idealistic concept of non-contention; he or she is only focused on immediately injuring, or killing you. If one is the type of person who wants to maintain their bodily well-being, one cannot afford to be thinking about engaging an aggressor with conversation about Aikido's teachings concerning non-contention; especially when the option of tactfully withdrawing, a form of avoidance, has passed (possibly because it was a surprise attack or your withdrawal path was blocked). In the final analysis, if you are unprepared or unwilling to repel the all-out and unremitting violence of such an attack -- i.e., unwilling to contend -- the outcome would likely be injury or death. As an aikidoka, are you so much a pacifist that you would suffer unnecessary bodily injury or death? If so, so be it. If not, then I suggest you take a careful look at your relationship with the concept of non-contention. *Oneness with non-contention does not mean that you need to suffer injury or death.* Rather, it means that you do your best to have good relations with people. However, it also means that you must learn how to defend yourself against an aggressor, because in *the knowing of how to do so* you find new information about how to maintain your condition of *oneness with non-contention.* Competition, such as in shiai, provides a person with another method or way by which they may assess and improve their *know how.*

Aikido's philosophic ethos (of which its technical principles are part) can easily be imagined as one of the numerous parts of a *psychosocial plank* (i.e., a person and their constructed mentality as they exist within a society and Nature) whose totality (its length, breadth, and depth) is precariously balanced at the keen edge of a fulcrum base, where the latter represents Reality (which is the foundation of Nature). Among the numerous psychosocial pairings that reside on or within a plank, e.g., known or unknown, unoblivious or oblivious, concern or unconcern, and safe or unsafe, *non-contention* resides on one side of the beam while *contention* resides on the other side. Sportive competition, natural competition (struggle to achieve harmony with Nature's forces), and personal self-defense skill are among other constructed pairings that could be included here. When a person's psychological constitution or response is such that it is weighted too far in either (or any) direction, their existence within the realm of what is certainly known as harmony with Reality (aiki), as given by Nature, which is ideally character- ized by a plank in perfect balance, is disturbed. Such a relationship with Nature's harmony can be accidentally, unknowingly, or pur- posefully disturbed -- possibly to a point where, in the worst case, a plank begins an wild gyration that unseats it from the keen edge of Nature's fulcrum. Too much non-contention or too much conten- tion is undesirable because one or the other will unbalance the plank. Why? Nature seems to insist upon a balance of forces. *Con- tention* goes against the prevailing forces of another person, or those of a family, a society, or Nature, which typically results in a certain amount of friction, resistance, or struggle. *Non-contention*, which goes along with a prevailing force, though producing little or no friction or resistance while in-stream, proceeds to an outcome that is dependent upon the direction of the prevailing force; but, any change to a person's direction as they are in-stream only occurs if they can oppose (to some extent or another) the prevailing force (i.e., they must contend with it). For example, a person who falls in- to a river can go along with the current, hoping to have a safe re- turn to its bank at some point; but, to reach the bank before they are dashed against the rapids or skewered by the protruding branch ends of a submerged log, they must usually swim skillfully as well as strongly at a down-current angle (~45 degrees or less) in the di- rection of the river's flow -- such action is representative of a type of *useful contention* for the purpose of attaining the river's bank and safety. It is unlikely the person will set foot on the bank if they are unskilled in swimming, of insufficient strength, or panic. As it per- tains to people, a prevailing force can be defined as a person's ex- pressed attitude or act, a group's attitude or act, a government's at- titude or act, a society's attitude or act -- i.e., social forces -- or an act of Nature that is directed toward the individual upon whom it is applied -- i.e., natural forces. A somewhat modified envisioning of this proposed contention/harmony/non-contention model, one that is a little more complex, is that of a *psychosocial disc* that is balanced upon a cone base whose apex is the fulcrum (but a point rather than an edge) at the center of the bottom of the disc, which is shown in *Figure 3* below.

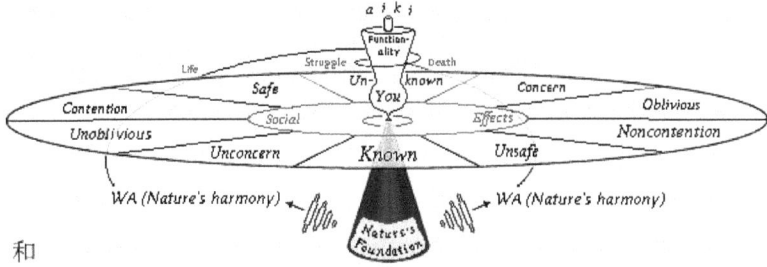

Figure 3

An illustration of the hypothetical **Psychosocial Disc**: *WA* (*Nature's harmony*) is the innate force in life that upholds balance and provides many opportunities for the polishing of a person's truth-mirror and the rediscovery of their pure-self. Envisioned as a spinning balanced *top*, which can sometimes wobble, a person's condition of balance as well as the state of their functionality moves about on this disc. A *top* (person) that wobbles can remain on the disc but will also dissipate its (their) energy unproductively. All movement upon this disc is a result of the 'shape' of their mentality as affected by the forces of Nature. Social effects are those such as familial, cultural, and social indoctrination, and culturally and or socially influenced information filtering and reshaping. You (the *top*) can make excursions from the center to experience life and learn. However, there is a point of no return, where upon moving too far from center the disc tilts to a degree where you can find yourself sliding toward a premature reunion with Nature's Foundation, which is disintegration and eventual reconstitution into something other than your former conscious corporeal state.

Many people who participate in a sport, perhaps a majority, do not consider its competitive aspect as a matter of contention or that it is especially contentious; rather, they consider it as a useful activity by which one's character attributes may be revealed or improved and where overall skill can be tested. As an inherent aspect of most sports, competition absent of contention can and usually does exist, but this type of quality most often occurs when such an attitude, i.e., non-contention, is instilled in the participants by a society's teachers. When you engage in a contest with another, you must not behave badly toward the other, neither in thought nor act, for in truth, the competitive event is a test of your own character. Remember, from the *Preface* of this book, *"the recognition of the innate human qualities in the other person is not only the preeminent meaning of what it is to be human but, in fact, it is an authentic revelation of pure-self unto self."* No matter how the contest goes, you learn because you discover more about your character and determine more about the weak and strong points of your skill.

Conclusion

In asking *"Isn't what matters [is] that we continue the process of evolution through experimentation?,"*[7] Professor Fumiaki Shishida, a Tomiki-ryu shihan, presents thereby an idea similar to that presented by Kisshomaru Ueshiba in his book **The Spirit of Aikido** when the latter requested research into the metaphysical idea of ki.[11] If ki is real, then it must have some type of affect upon the physical nature of world, of the Universe. The phyiscal nature of the world includes an inherent dynamic of, at the very least, transitory contention, i.e., a temporary condition where the interaction of forces may sometimes conflict until a merging or dissipation has resulted in a harmony. The study of violent conflict (a type of contention) between two people is essential so that we may understand the best methods by which it may be resolved in accordance with The Three Precepts -- protect, sustain, and enhance life. When properly structured, competition should not be found to be antithetical to a valid Aikido. Also, since Aikido presents itself generally as a physio spiritual discipline derived from, but different than martial arts, it must, out of necessity, be very careful to maintain a clear definition of the interrelationship of the physical (exercise, health, self-defense practice) and the spiritual (psychology, metaphysics, social responsibility), otherwise, it might just as well become a Shinshukyo (a new religion).

I hope that this chapter, though a little idealistic, will serve to 'awaken' aikidoka and inspire them to ameliorate their differences in a way that will shape a cooperative, productive, and realistic future for all Aikido styles and organizations. Is it possible to construct a solution that could overcome the differences between the competitive and non-competitive 'camps' of Aikido? Yes, I think so!

Aikido Competition: A Reformed Shiai

[1] *Dharma*, loosely, is the effort that a person directs toward seeking an understanding of any phenomenon and/or its properties in order that one might attain a higher consciousness (awareness of self and its relationship to society and life) and promote harmony.

[2] **Budo-hiketsu: Aiki no Jutsu** (Secrets of Budo, Aiki pertaining to the Art) -- a small treatise concerning the ancient secrets of Japanese martial arts; published in 1899. The topic entitled *Aiki no Jutsu* discusses the characteristics of aiki and its importance toward achieving success when performing martial techniques.

[3] **Goshin-jutsu Ogi** (Defensive art secrets) -- another small treatise concerning the secrets of Japanese martial arts; published in 1917. "... aiki-ho is a technique used to halt the enemy's attack by taking the initiative."

[4] See, **The Spirit of Aikido** (Aikido no Kokoro) by Kisshomaru Ueshiba. Translated by Taitetsu Unno; Kodansha International, Ltd., paperback edition, first printing, 1987, Chapter 4, page 75.

[5] See the book entitled the **Prevalence of Deceit** by F. G. Bailey; Cornell University Press, paperback, 1991, page 25.

[6] Ibid, page 24.

[7] See, **The Process of Forming Aikido and Japanese Imperial Navy Admiral Isamu Takeshita: Through the analysis of Takeshita's diary from 1925 to 1931** by Fumiaki Shishida, 8th Dan, Shodokan Aikido, Waseda University, Tokyo, Japan.

[8] See, **The Spirit of Aikido** (Aikido no Kokoro) by Kisshomaru Ueshiba. Translated by Taitetsu Unno; Kodansha International, Ltd., paperback edition, first printing, 1987, chapter 1, page 25.

[9] The use of this word "*non-contention*" as a 'tool' to construct a description of Aikido's philosophic ethos has, in my opinion, emerged serious confusion or misunderstanding about what Aikido is, or is not. Perhaps this translation is somewhat skewed, off the mark, or not quite right, a result of its transliteration from Japanese to English. Whatever the case may be, its effect as derived from its printed meaning in English, which occurred in 1984, has allowed American *New Age Movement* advocates and devotees to partially shape Aikido's philosophic ethos in a direction suitable to their conception or visualization of life; this is why I mentioned earlier that Aikido might one day become a Shinshukyo, i.e., a new reli-

gion. Examples of how this particular movement's quirkiness has seeped into Aikido's ethos can be perceived when one sees or hears so many oxymoronic statements from aikidoka -- e.g., *Aikido is a peaceful martial art, As a martial art; Aikido's essence is love*; and one more, *Aikido is a non-violent martial art.* Also, Morihei Ueshiba's oral *douwa* (mythical tales), which he recorded and later were published, have been interpreted by many of these New Age advocates with a meaning shaped to fit this needs of their movement. See the article entitled *The Founder Morihei Ueshiba, a God? Reflections on the Anniversary of Japan's Surrender to the US Coalition* by Gyaku Homma; published online by the Nippon Kan, August 15, 2005. http://www.nippon-kan.org/senseis_articles/05_uishiba-god/05_ueshiba-god.html.

I admire Kisshomaru Ueshiba for his magnificent work toward defining Aikido as a unique physio-spiritual discipline while also including in it the basic technical aspects that a person needs when 'faced' with common self-defense scuffles. His discord with Kenji Tomiki in the late 1950s and later with Koichi Tohei in the early 1970s was shaped by his concern about what would constitute the identifying aspects of Aikido's philosophic ethos; Tohei's Shin-shin Tōitsu Aikido of today is probably what Aikikai Aikido would have looked like if Tohei had become its Doshu. For Kisshomaru, Tomiki and Tohei's view of Aikido were at opposite ends of the spectrum; he attempted to place and keep his conceptualization of Aikido somewhere in the middle. However, in spite of Kisshomaru Ueshiba's efforts to find that middle -- a place between life's physical reality and a person's natural tendency toward forming or embracing a spirituality -- his conception of *non-contention*, which I'm sure he formulated with good intent, has either been misunderstood or not fully understood; either way, in my opinion, it has been 'hijacked' and misapplied.

See, *The Spirit of Aikido* (Aikido no Kokoro) by Kisshomaru Ueshiba. Translated by Taitetsu Unno; Kodansha International, Ltd., paperback edition, first printing, 1987, Preface, page 12. See the **Glossary** for a definition of the word "contend."

[10] Typically, Aikido's use of the sword is in the form of a *bokken*, which is a wooden version of a number of different Japanese cutting blades, e.g., a katana, a tantō. However, some schools do use real, i.e., steel, blades to clarify certain technical points; occasionally a real katana is used in certain types of demonstrations. Also, sometimes, distinct Kenjutsu disciplines are intermixed with standard Aikido training, though this is usually discouraged because it negatively impacts Aikido's philosophical ethos. Bokken training, typically referred to as "*aiki-ken*," is not a thoroughgoing aspect across all Aikido; some Aikido schools use weapons unrelated to aiki-ken, which makes use of bokken and stave only. The primary purpose of such training is to point out to the practitioner any error in their performance

of 'empty-handed' Aikido. See the *Glossary* for a definition of the word "truth-mirror."

[11] See the book *The Spirit of Aikido* by Kisshomaru Ueshiba. Translated by Taitetsu Unno. Kodansha International, Ltd., paperback edition, first printing, 1987, pages 27 and 30.

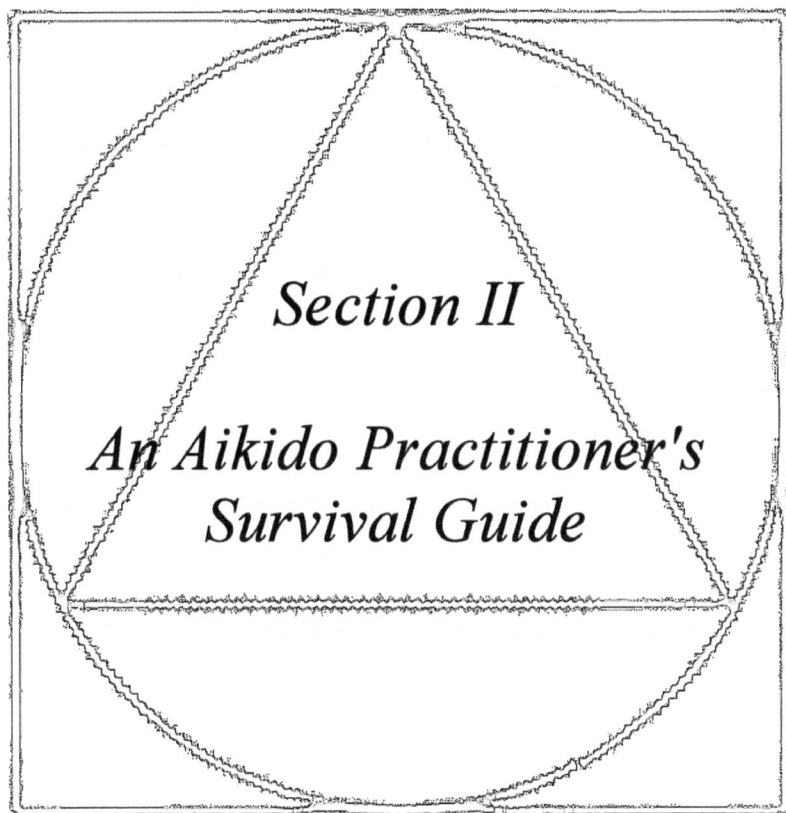

Section II

An Aikido Practitioner's Survival Guide

Chapter X

Finding a Suitable Aikidō School or Style

There are numerous different Aikido styles, today. The differences that set one apart from another are a result of each style's presentation of the reason for and the performance of Aikido's techniques, tactics, and strategies, which is somewhat teacher dependent. It is from the dynamic interaction of the teacher and his students with Aikido's philosophy that the emphasis or character of that which comprises each style's unique essence is evolved. Nevertheless, all true Aikido styles share a common philosophical and technical basis in that, when correctly aligned with the concept of aiki, they seek to align with and make use of the forces of Nature toward the goal of protecting, sustaining, and enhancing life.

Whether any particular style's ethos is experienced as weighted toward self-defense training or as a path of spiritual development, or a combination of these, depends primarily upon the nature of a head teacher's personal attitudes as shaped by Aikido's philosophy to the extent permitted by their personal inclination or needs in relation to the acquisition of skill in self-defense. This effect develops in any teacher a certain level of interest in one aspect (e.g., self-defense) or another (e.g., spirituality) and, as they teach, the summation of all the student's attitudes exerts an approval and affirmation effect (though some may dissent) of the attitudes and methods of the teacher; thusly, a closed-loop teacher-student/student-teacher feedback relationship emerges. Those who dissent often go off to seek another style of Aikido. The sense or feel that an observer might experience when viewing the training at a particular Aikido dojo as well as that which they may determine about the characteristics of any particular student's training are a result of the head teacher's attitudes intermingled with those of the students. This type of interaction results in an emphasis that shapes the content of the body of Aikido techniques taught.

Finding a Suitable Aikido School or Style

A person who seeks to learn Aikido should consider well that a little bit of personal effort applied toward determining the general philosophy of the Aikido school where they might participate in training is an essential first step toward choosing a school that is suitable. Therefore, a prospective student must ascertain the stated or unstated, well-defined or ill-defined philosophical essence of the school from which they might learn. Aikido schools or organizations can be generally categorized as having a

1) Spiritual emphasis, physical fitness a secondary concern or incidental, with a minimal or vague self-defense concern;
2) Spiritual commune emphasis, often with cult-like characteristics, physical fitness a secondary concern or incidental, self-defense incidental;
3) Self-defense emphasis, with either a murky or well-defined philosophical ethos, physical fitness oriented;
4) Combative sport emphasis, typically guided by a sport ethos that is clearly defined (e.g., rules of play and regulations), physical fitness inherent; or
5) Trilateral balance emphasis between the elements of physical fitness, philosophical ethos, and self-defense, where its philosophy can make possible a characterization of its activities or teachings as behavior, when consistently expressed, that could be termed as 'spiritual.'

When a purported school of Aikido, which associates the term *aikido* with its activities, presents attitude, behavior, and technique that is unnecessarily aggressive and continuously harsh, it is likely that it is not true Aikido, but rather, it is a martial art. To be truly Aikido, a school's technical aspects and the performance of them by its students must be shaped by and exhibit completely the concept of Aiki while seeking to embrace the Three Precepts. A school of Aikido will manifest in its collective attitude and demonstrate in its techniques both of these ideas. Today, most schools of Aikido that are members of a well-guided Aikido organization will have teachers that have met certain well-established, basic, organization-wide technical requirements that generally provide a student with safe, interesting, and useful training toward this end.

The most well-known presentations of Aikido today are

1) *Aikikai* (Aiki Association) -- the basis of which was established by the progenitor of Aikido, Morihei Ueshiba, but further developed by his son, Kisshomaru Ueshiba;
2) *Tomiki-ryu* (Japan Aikido Cooperative Association) -- founded by Kenji Tomiki;
3) *Shodokan* (Shodokan Aikido Cooperative Association) -- founded by Kenji Tomiki and Hideo Ohba;
4) *Shin-shin Toitsu* (Mind-Body School of Thought Aikido Association) -- founded by Koichi Tohei;
5) *Yoshinkai* (Spirit Cultivation Association) -- founded by Gozo Shioda; and,
6) *Yoseikan* -- founded by Minoru Mochizuki.

Secondary and tertiary styles as well as cooperative associations are many. Some of the styles include Kihara, Korindo, Shinei Taido, Manseikan, and Tendoryu Aikido. Included in the secondary organizations category are the Fugakukai, Jiyushinkai, Keijutusukai, Zantoppakai, British Aikido Association, American Tomiki Aikido Association, and the International Aikido Alliance.

Facets of Aikido: Differing Emphasis

A characterization or emphasis can be reasonably applied to identify how an Aikido organization and its associated dojo (schools) may manifest that which is embraced as its philosophy and technical aspects. Generally, this can be perceived and understood as a

1) Movement emphasis -- Movement with an emphasis on the artistic value of Aikido;
2) Spiritual emphasis -- Mystic pursuit of certain ephemeral concepts drawn from Aikido's aiki basis, with potential for cult-like characteristics;
3) Self-defense or police emphasis -- Engenders ability to successfully defend against attack as well as control aggressor, physical fitness attendant; or a
4) Philosophical emphasis -- Recognition of the chaos arisen from the inequities in life. Practice in this kind of school

seeks to achieve a functioning tri-lateral balance of 1), 2), and 3) above in order to achieve a curriculum that may develop in the student a certain productive spirituality and unique self-defense ability.

When seeking to pursue a study of Aikido, a person should determine the condition or nature of their own being in life. Thusly self-aware, one may determine which style of Aikido is suitable to their personality and need. An issue that may arise for any student is that of a slowly unfolding recognition that the organization in which they are participating is something other than that which they had once thought it to be, or desired it to be. This type of situation may arise from the student's perception of their school's ethos becoming in their thought less vague after having experienced the school's teachings and interpersonal dynamics, this latter constituting its philosophically derived ethical spirit. Those "interpersonal dynamics" are the person-to-person dynamic interactions, i.e., the student-to-student and student-to-teacher attitudes and behaviors that an aikidoka experiences during training.

Chapter XI

General Aikidō Technical Considerations

The many experienced authors who have written about Aikido have produced detailed analysis and information of that which comprises its technical performance. Another such work is not necessary. Notwithstanding, a good general review of its technical basis, in keeping with the guidance of O-sensei's sixth reminder[1] in aikido training, is worthwhile.

Prior to this discussion, it is quite important for any practitioner of self-defense or martial art to clearly apprehend that their discipline exists in accordance with its philosophy, stated or not. The evident or unclear, the ambiguous, the ethical or unethical principles comprise a discipline's philosophy. A discipline's philosophy affects the behavior of its adherents, and the behavior of the adherents creates the formation and ultimate essence of their discipline. Therefore, the technical foundation of a particular discipline is affected first by the attitudinal position held in the thought of each of its proponents, and second, by the behavior that arises from that thought.

Aikido's technical foundation has been influenced by its proponent's philosophical dispositions, with Morihei Ueshiba's efforts to identify the initial aspects of that foundation serving as the initial *sacred seed*, and Kisshomaru's Ueshiba's efforts to shape and clarify its character. Kenji Tomiki, from the perspective of ensuring that Aikido's technical aspects would remain functional for self-defense, made his contribution to the refinement of Aikido's philosophy, too.

In this chapter, the basic technical aspects of space-condition (engagement distance), directions of off-balance, balance breaking, timing (fall and rise, following and leading, entering and merging), mental fortitude (in training and in combat), awareness, strategy and tactics, and body conditioning (including diet and exercise) will be briefly discussed.

Space-condition is a certain distance between tori (a *performer* of a technique -- termed *nage* in some styles but meaning *thrower*) and uke (a *receiver* of a technique) where uke must take a single, deep step forward in order to begin an attack directed at tori. Practice scenarios in Aikido include solo, paired, and one opposed by several. When an uke moves they do so in an energetic way that represents the basis of an attack upon tori, i.e., energetic, directed movement that shows commitment to making contact with tori. However, the attacking methods are slightly modified in order to reduce the possibility of injury to either tori or uke when an error in performance occurs. For example, the typical attacks are hand-blade strikes derived from traditional Japanese sword movements rather than fists, but at a higher level of experience a tori is frequently required to practice defense and counterattack against an uke who attacks with fist and foot.

A clear understanding that the physical stability of the human being, when standing or in motion, is easily disturbed, and that, in fact, its movement in any direction is a series of controlled off-balance and recovery movements, is essential knowledge for a good performance of Aikido, particularly for minimal effort self-defense. There are four primary and four secondary directions of off-balance as viewed from the static, standing condition -- a total of eight directions. Tori can initiate off-balance (mental or physical) in an uke through indirect or, in certain limited circumstances, direct action, or, typically, may make use of uke's off-balance that results from their own movement.

As tori, timing of your movement with that of uke (or an assailant) by giving keen attention to uke's body fall and rise as well as direction of movement, developing the ability to enter or turn to merge, and to follow or lead at the most opportune moment is indispensable in taking advantage of their intention and energy. A precise, internalized understanding of timing is necessary to transition successfully from a parry to a strike, throw or control technique. It is very important to ensure, typically through proper timing, that the momentum of your entering movement is not employed against you by your opponent.

Mental attitude, a form of posture, which has been evolved out of apprehension or fear into a calm condition of respectful strength, emanates increased confidence. This condition of being increases the safety and comfort of all.

Mental alertness (awareness) that causes a person to be keenly perceptive and understanding of the circumstances of their situation, be it self-defense or otherwise, as well as completely aware of their surrounding environment is of great importance; the latter may be employed toward securing a tactical advantage. It is also important to thoughtfully grasp that an opponent can be an agent of vicious destruction, free to suddenly move in any direction for any reason in order to launch their attacks toward controlling or destroying you. The mental resolve to protect oneself must be calm and unwavering, and such strength in attitude must arise from skill that itself has developed from practice, contemplation, and then more practice.

Strategy and tactics, an important consideration when in engaged in defense of self, is a matter not to be neglected. Flanking, in its various forms, is an essential tactical skill. A dominating attitude that is not overly confident is useful in defense of self. Aspects of timing are often useful in tactical performance toward the achievement of an overall strategy. A clear mental grasp of the human being's dynamic body movements and how to make use of these (the concept of *aiki*) is essential to accomplishing minimum exertion and successful self-defense. A clear understanding of how to make use of the human body's fall and rise that occurs as a result of its foot movement is essential to effective following, leading, entering, turning, merging, striking, throwing, and pinning.

The development and internalization of techniques, strategies and tactics must occur long before any eventual self-defense encounter, for situations requiring self-defense arise unexpectedly, sometimes without warning. The time for self-defense is not the time for thinking about tactics and strategy; rather, it is time for spontaneous learned action in defense of self.

A healthy diet and aerobic exercise is essential to maximize the productiveness of one's training as well as one's longevity.

The Basic Technical Principles of Aikido

Kamae (構え), a specific body alignment (posture or stance) is an essential technical element in the practice of Aikido. Though any particular stance is largely transitory during randori or a situation of self-defense, one stance or another facilitates a practitioner's learning of any of Aikido's subsequent techniques, strategies, and tactics. A full understanding of and proficiency in kamae helps a practitioner to internalize Aikido relatively quickly. The basic solo (tandoku) kamae in Aikido are

1) *Shizen-tai* (natural body posture) -- each foot side by side pointed very slightly outward and approximately hip-width apart, toe line even;

2) *Hidari-hanmi* (left half-body stance, an oblique stance) -- left foot forward and straight, right foot rearward and pointing outward (to the right) at a 45 to 90 degree angle in relation to the alignment of the forward foot. This stance is also know as *hidari gamae*; and,

3) *Migi-hanmi* (right half-body stance, an oblique stance) -- right foot forward and straight, left foot rearward and pointing outward (to the left) at a 45 to 90 degree angle in relation to the alignment of the forward foot. This stance is also know as *migi gamae.*

The basic paired (sotai) kamae in Aikido are

1) *Ai-hanmi* (or ai-gamae) -- the two persons who are facing each other are positioned in the same hanmi stance, e.g., both with their left foot forward; and,

2) *Gyaku-hanmi* (or gyaku-gamae) -- the two persons who are facing each other are positioned in an opposing hanmi stance, e.g., one person with their left foot forward, the other with their right foot forward.

Ma-ai (間 合 い {space-condition}{space-fit}{space-harmony}{fitting into the interval} (間, where *ma* = {interval}{space}; 合, *ai* = {fit}{merge}{unite} hence, a fitting in or harmony is established through the observance of a distance or interval), is an essential tactic for maintaining the space that will make possible a better assessment of how to respond to a possible threat before it becomes threatening. It is a term that refers to the space between two opponents in combat; specifically, the engagement distance.[2] Ma-ai incorporates both the distance between opponents and the time it will take to cross the distance as well as the angle and rhythm of interaction. In Aikido, initial ma-ai is judged to properly exist when both aikidoka in ai-hanmi (ai-gamae) stance, facing each other, touch fingertips from the arm corresponding to the lead foot, then drop the arm. In training, when paired up to practice any particular technique, it may feel right, comfortable, or less intimidating to make a very slight tsugi-ashi step forward or backwards to adjust the space condition. There are three important uses of maai. *First*, it provides a viewpoint beyond the reach of an attack where the defender might discern and mentally process more about the intentions and actions of an aggressor; *second*, it reduces the possibility of escalation the situation by maintaining a distance that is not dangerously close, where if such existed, an aggressor might quickly initiate a successful attack upon the unaware or unprepared defender; *third*, it requires an aggressor to make a sudden and committed action to break or reduce that distance in order to launch an attack, giving the defender just enough time (if alert and skilled) to counterattack. Concerning defense against an opponent, the three basic distances of ma-ai are

1) *Tō-ma* (long interval);
2) *Ittō-ma* (middle interval); and,
3) *Chika-ma* (short interval).

Ittō-ma is the distance where each person may step one step forward and deliver a strike; this varies somewhat depending on the size of each person and whether or not either person is armed with any weapon other than a ballistic one (e.g., a rock, a throwing star, a bow with arrow, a javelin, a pistol). Reiterating, in order for Aikido to work effectively as a body of self-defense technique, and in fact to actually look like classical curvilinear aikido, careful attention must be given to the function of ma-ai; specifically, the maintaining of ittō-ma ma-ai at the outset of a situation of self-defense is essential to achieve the performance of functional, safe, and ideal technique. When ittō-ma is breeched or reduced to chika-ma, direct grappling, as in Judo, is necessary. Many Aikido schools do not address the difficulty of close-quarters hand-to-hand self-defense scenarios; but, in those that do, if practice is primarily for the reason of inculcating self-defense ability, special attention must be given toward always maintaining ittō-ma or greater. Many people who are not trained in self-defense frequently experience a breech of a safe space-condition (ma-ai) when faced with certain uncomfortable social circumstances, e.g., personal boundary violations, irregardless of the institution of civil law and presence of police forces. This type of occurrence is sometimes viewed by an incidental observer who is knowledgeable of the importance and use of ma-ai. Proper, unconsciously maintained ma-ai for any given moment of engagement in a rapidly changing randori or self-defense situation tends to induce in an uke or an opponent the necessary energetic off-balance condition that facilitates the timing required to deliver counterattack techniques that typically result in a successful aiki-oriented defense of self.

Kuzushi (崩し or 崩す{corner breakdown}{pull off balance}), is a term denoting the unbalancing of an opponent by moving their body in a manner that momentarily disturbs their center of gravity. Specifically, it refers to the process of moving an opponent into a position where their stability is compromised in order to more easily apply a defensive technique. The combative (martial-art-derived) sport and self-defense art of Judo considers it as an essential first maneuver of a three-step strategy in accomplishing a successful throw of an opponent: *kuzushi* or *tsukuri* (fitting or entering) and *kake* (execution). Judo, Shodokan Aikido (Tomiki-ryū Aikido) and Wadō-ryu Karate as well as many other Japanese martial arts and sports make frequent and strong use of kuzushi. The methods by which a disturbed condition of balance is achieved in uke or an opponent are dependent on the conditions of *ma-ai* (interval, space condition), *tai-sabaki* (body positioning and weak lines of balance), and or *atemi* (strikes, including *kiai*), or a combination of these. The three primary methods to accomplish kuzushi are

1) Direct initiatory action -- any *direct initiatory action* that quickly, in one direction, disturbs an opponent's balance from which he cannot recover a useful condition of balance; e.g., a quick push backward, forward, or sideways;

2) Direct initiatory counteraction -- any *direct initiatory counteraction* that results in the overextension of an opponent's action of attack and thereby disturbs his condition of balance; e.g., pull when pushed, push when pulled, or, turn

when pushed, enter when pulled; and,

3) Eliciting an opponent's counterproductive action -- any *misleading or wily initiatory action*, with or without physical contact, that is designed to elicit from an opponent a response which positions them in an unbalanced condition and or disadvantageous position; e.g., a feint or other purposeful distraction, or a combination attack specifically designed to bring about a condition of unavoidable off-balance in an opponent.

Sen, 先 (before, lead, ahead, previous, future, precedence) describes initiative and timing when in a combative situation. Sen is derived from the word *sente* (先手, beforehand).

In the midst of a situation of self-defense where you have momentarily been caught off guard, *Ato-no-sen* (後の先, where 後 means late, behind, delayed) means to retake the initiative just after the opponent's attack. If you've not already been defeated, sometimes it is possible to act with this kind of initiative to regain control and accomplish a successful defense.

Go-no-sen (禦の先), of which the far left kanji sinogram is on occassion confusingly represented by 後 (meaning {late}, {behind}, {delayed}; kunyomi reading of *ato*), is better described with 禦, *gyo* or *go* (onyomi reading), meaning {ward off}, {defend}, or {resist}, which through an analysis of all the parts (known as *bushu*, both root and radical) that comprise it implies the implementation of *ai*, 合, linguistic root *au*, {fit}, {merge}, {come together}, or {unite} in order to accomplish a successful defense. Understanding that hand-to-hand fighting is a situation where the opponent is attempting his own offensive, this type of *sen* is a dynamic responsive initiative where the defender's action rebounds off of, merges with, or redirects the energy of the opponent's attack in order to thereby initiate a superior offensive toward suppressing any further attack, often utilizing the opponent's mental and or physical off-balance. Examples from Aikido are any of its pertinent immobilization or projection techniques. The implementation of this kind of sen points to skill in perception, timing, counterattack, and suppression or neutralization. The ki (energy and or spirit) of aiki (harmonized energy or harmonized spirit) is primarily Go-no-sen, for in most circumstances when one is pitted against a competent opponent who is equally capable (person-to-person and not armed with a ballistic or explosive weapon), defeat is the usual outcome if one makes the first move; typically, the first strike.

A careful study of *ato* and of *go* will reveal that there is an important difference between these two words, for within the specific meaning of each there exists certain identifying attributes that define their respective roles toward determining the actual definition of the tactical concepts of Ato-no-sen and Go-no-sen. It is interesting to note that some martial art teachers have, and have had, different explanations as to the meaning of these two types of sen, with some describing their meaning in one way and others in another way, often in opposition. No matter what a teacher may present as the essential meaning of these two forms of sen, it can be perceived that there is an important difference that arose from the Japanese usage of Chinese sinograms during the past cultural exchanges between these two societies. Over time, the Japanese people developed some of their own sinograms (kanji) as well as separate readings (pronunciations) of the sinograms that had been borrowed from the Chinese language.[3] This difference needs some clarification.

To begin, a number of different kanji have the pronunciation of *go*, and others have parts (bushu, or brushed stroke radical or root sets) in common with those pertinent to the discussion of Ato-no-sen and Go-no-sen. The following are examples.

禦 -- onyomi reading of *gyo* or *go* (kunyomi reading *fusegu*), meaning {ward off}, {defend}, {protect}, or {resist};

拒 -- onyomi reading of *kyo* (similar to pronunciation of *gyo* above) (kunyomi reading of *fusegu*, also), but specifically meaning to {ward off with hand} or {defend};

防 -- onyomi reading of *hou* (kunyomi reading of *fusegu*, also), but with a more general meaning of {defend} or {prevent};

後 -- onyomi reading of *go* (kunyomi readings of *okureru, nochi*, or *ato*) {behind}, {back}, or {later};

徼 -- kunyomi reading of *kyou* (similar to pronunciation of *gyo*) {go around} or {seek} (this kanji is no longer in general use);

很 -- kunyomi reading of *kon* {contrary to} or {to go against} (this kanji is no longer in general use);

徂 -- kunyomi reading of *so* {go} or {to go} (this kanji is no longer in general use);

往 or 徃 -- kunyomi reading of *ou* {let go}, {going}, {chase away}, {journey}, or {travel} (this kanji is no longer in general use);

冴 -- onyomi reading of *go* (kunyomi readings of kuuru, hieru, saeru) {be clear}, {serene}, {cold}, or {skillful}; and,

五 -- onyomi reading of *go* (kunyomi reading of itsutsu) {five}.

The following pertinent analysis of 禦 provides more information about its meaning.

彳 -- *gyōninben*, kunyomi reading meaning {step}, {step with left foot}, or {a stepping man};

卩 -- *fushizukuri*, kunyomi reading meaning of {join}, {stamp}, or {seal};

止 -- *tomaru*, kunyomi reading meaning {stop} or {halt}; and,

示 -- *ji*, *ki*, or *shi*, onyomi reading meaning {energy}, {force}, or {spirit}.

The meaning of 禦 then is: step, join, stop spirit. That is, step and join to stop the spirit or step and merge to stop the spirited attack. This suggests action that makes use of an opponent's movements and would tend toward minimizing the use of unnecessary force as through the use of technique carried out in an aiki manner, that is, through movements like irimi and tenkan. This *stepping* (getting off the line of attack) *and joining* (going with or merging) is that aspect of purposeful timing that must include physical actions like *irimi* (entering), *tenkan* (turning), and kuzushi (balance breaking) toward quickly achieving *ai* (fitting in). These types of movement are refinements of the actions necessary to successfully ward off an attack.

Continuing, the following analysis of 後 provides more information about its meaning.

彳 -- *gyōninben*, kunyomi reading meaning of {step}, {step with left foot}, or {a stepping man};

幺 -- *chiisai*, kunyomi reading meaning of {short}, {little}, {one}; and,

夂 -- *suinyū*, kunyomi reading meaning of {go slowly}.

The meaning of 後 then is: step short (or step little) and go slowly. This has the meaning of *moving cautiously*. Think about this, is *aiki* movement performed cautiously or tentatively? No. Instead it is a quick response that is designed to fit in or merge with an opponent's attack in order to make use of their movement to achieve a successful defense or victory. Sureness or confidence is the primary psychophysical aspect of *aiki* movement. Therefore, it is reasonable to think that 後 is better spoken as *ato* (later, behind) rather than as *go* in order to remove confusion, and that 禦, *go* or *gyo*, as described above is a much better fit to represent that kind of Sen where Go-no-sen is identified by and accomplished through *aiki* movement.

Other than the specific types of action which exclusively represent it, such as irimi and tenkan, 禦 is the most probable linguistic brushed act or sinogram construct, basis or reason, that *aiki* is considered by many aikidoka as Go-no-sen timing.

From this point of difference it is reasonable to think that those Japanese people of different clans who were involved in traditional martial arts eventually evolved a situation where there arose different meaning and pronunciation for this kanji, thus making possible confusion about which utterance meant what, and a confusion as to whether or not there was any difference between Go-no-sen and Ato-no-sen. In languages that use sinograms, this type of linguistic flexibility makes possible over the course of time the emergence of occasionally different meaning as well as different pronunciations.

Go-no-sen and Ato-no-sen attitudes are different, as 後 inaccurately or insufficiently represents Go-no-sen of Aikido. Though both include a different element of later timing, Go-no-sen includes the conscious design element of rebounding off of or merging with energy, somehow making use of the direction and energy of the opponent's attack, in order to accomplish a successful counterattack, whereas Ato-no-sen is action to attempt a recovery after being surprised and nearly overwhelmed. The difference resides in the response that a defender creates through the attention to which they will give toward how to respond to or rebuff an opponent's attack. Specifically, will a defender's counterattack include the skillful use of the direction and energy of the opponent's attack (Go-no-sen), or will it be a blunting of the attack with a momentary pause (Ato-no-sen)? Aiki movement is Go-no-sen. In offering some support of this idea, Tokimune Takeda, the second doshu of Daito-ryu Aikijujutsu, tells us that "*If you move first to cut your opponent, you will end up being beaten. So we should always use go-no-sen.*"[4]

Sen-no-sen (先の先) means to make your defensive action at the very instant that the opponent begins his movement of attack, i.e., strike as the opponent mentally commits to an attack but before he moves. In other words, the defender attacks during that instant between the opponent's decision to attack and his actual movement to attack. Sen-no-sen means to take the initiative with a preemptive action, and under certain limited circumstances such a way of acting can be successful; it is during this brief moment that a defender may make an action to elicit a counteraction from an opponent, which may in turn be utilized by the defender and taken to a successful self-defense conclusion.

Through astute perception, intuition, tactical speech, and perceived body language one may be able to achieve the *Sen-sen-no-sen* (先々の先) condition, i.e., anticipate the attack/danger. For example, that dangling tree branch that you previously discerned is an evident concern, but now, because you've identified it as a risk to your bodily integrity, you can take a slightly different path of travel, but if altering course is not possible, your awareness of the threat, i.e., the lucid attention that you have given to the threatening circumstance, will more likely than not prepare you to agilely move to avoid it if it falls. Thusly, you've utilized astute perception to anticipate the danger. Another example. You've deescalated a confrontation with another person who takes offense easily because you managed to sincerely present an equitable proposition; but this assumes there exists sufficient flexibility in the reasoning ability of the other person, or that you have somehow been able to connect to a part of the other's mentality that itself finds agreement with your proposition. The ancient Chinese philosopher *Laotse* reminds us that "*It is the way of Heaven to prevail without contention.*"[5] Thusly, through the use of tactical speech, you've "*prevailed without contention.*"

Irimi (入り身), enter body at the side, is generally the same in both styles. Irimi means to enter forward toward the opponent at some lesser or greater angle (preferably to the outside) in order to gain either a shared-in-common temporary tori/uke rotational point or entrance to uke's side or back (shikaku); this facilitates a tori's (defender's) command over an uke's (aggressor's) attack by situating them in a position where they may easily apply a technique to counter and defend. When an opponent initiates a strike -- such as a punch, kick, or, sometimes, a visible moving projectile -- irimi can only become a viable maneuver if

1) Proper ma-ai exists, or, if not, an adjustment is immediately made to achieve it; and,
2) The movement to enter is made at the approximate midpoint of attack, i.e., a point where an opponent cannot stop

their attack due to their condition of dynamic movement extension (which will become the attacker's overextension if the defender is no longer in a position to receive the attack's energy).

No matter what, an irimi movement is most successful when the opponent has committed to their attack, cannot change their attack, and will unavoidably arrive at grabbing or hitting only empty space (because you are not there to receive it). Knowledge and proper use of ma-ai, i.e., proper timing, as well as the other technical aspects mentioned in this chapter, are essential toward achieving skill in the use of irimi movement; otherwise, late timing (Ato-no-sen) typically necessitates a tenkan or ushiro (backward) tsugi-ashi movement. Pertinent here, Kisshomaru Ueshiba relates to us that after a defender has performed an irimi movement, "... *you have sidestepped his attack, and can hit his side with your left fist and his face with your right.*"[6] while Shigenobu Okumura, 9th Dan Aikikai, tells us that in "*Not 'conflicting', Aikido enters with Irimi and settles things in an instant, without pairing up like Judo. If it's Irimi-nage then you throw them, but if you strike them with the heel of your hand (in the instant of the Irimi) then it's all over.*"[7]

Tenkan (転換), turn and convert/merge, is a pivot to one's rear on the lead foot, typically 90 to 180 degrees. That is, if the left foot is forward, the pivot is clockwise, and if the right foot is forward, the pivot is counter-clockwise.

Aiki (合気), fit in or join with energy or spirit, is any movement by tori (the defender) that results in a purposeful merging of their movement with that of uke (the opponent) in order to make use of the uke's direction of movement and energetic actions toward accomplishing a successful self-defense that requires less expenditure of tori's energy than would be otherwise experienced by not merging. Whether in Aikido practice or for a situation of self-defense, the technical actions of *irimi*, *tenkan*, and *kuzushi* as well as the use of *ma-ai* are essential if a person is to manifest *aiki* oriented attitude and movement. Pertinent here, Tokimune Takeda relates to us that "*Aiki is to pull when you are pushed, and to push when you are pulled. It is the spirit of slowness and speed, harmonizing your movement with your opponent's ki. On the other hand, kiai is to push to the limit, while aiki never resists.*"[8]

Tai-sabaki (体捌き) is a term that describes a repositioning of a tori's or defender's body. It can be best conceived as a type of *balanced-in-the-moment management of body movement*. Tai-sabaki is often used to avoid an attack by an angular or sometimes curvilinear body movement, such that the receiver of the attack ends up in an advantageous position and may proceed to control and subdue an aggressor. Tai-sabaki often includes both centripetal and centrifugal forces produced by a tori's quick rotational movement that draws in and temporarily maintains the aggressor's off-balance condition that was produced by tori's initial evasive action. A good example of tai-sabaki occurs when a defender moves off-the-line-of-attack through the use of *irimi* or *tenkan* movements rather than conflicting with the attack by blocking and brute strength; this quickly provides tori with an opportunity to merge (a primary form of aiki) because uke is unbalanced and momentarily unable to initiate any type of counterattack. *Ki no nagare* (flow of body energy) and *chikara no dashi* (extension of power) are integral with tai-sabaki. The various *Ukemi* movements (break-falls) are examples of tai-sabaki, too, but these are special techniques of falling and rolling designed to prevent or minimize injury to either tori or uke, or to a defender when in a self-defense situation.

Ashi-Sabaki (足 捌き or 足さばき) or *Unsoku* (运足) are terms that refer to stable, functional body movement through specific foot movements, i.e., footwork. Aikido footwork is typically performed on the ball of the foot. Ashi-sabaki is the foundation of tai-sabaki, for without proper footwork the basic Aikido movements and timings are found to be difficult or nearly impossible to perform From either hanmi, the basic Aikido techniques of unsoku are

1) *Tsugi-ashi* (shuffle foot movement) -- a sliding, following-foot stepping movement, either forward or backward;
2) *Ayumi-ashi* (walking foot movement) -- lead foot steps forward and the other following similarly to pass that foot, with the toes of each foot pointed slightly to the outside, this being similar to regular walking but a little more stable;
3) *Tenkai-ashi* (rotation foot movement) -- an on-the-spot pivot performed simultaneously on the ball of each foot to end facing in the opposite direction;
4) *Kaiten-ashi* (revolve and turn foot movement) -- a step for-

ward with the rear foot, then an inward pivot on the ball of
each foot to end facing in the opposite direction; and,

5) *Tenkan-ashi* (transition foot movement) -- forward foot begins a pivot on ball of foot with heel moving outward while
   rear foot slides in a curving step backward to end facing in
   the opposite direction.

Tai no Tenkan (体の変更) means to turn the body to any compass
point, as required, by pivoting on one foot while quickly sliding the
other foot rearward in a curvilinear movement. The effect of this is
that one's body turns in a circular manner in order to facilitate a
proper technical response to uke's attack.

Zanshin (残心) is a term used in the Japanese martial arts that
refers to a state of awareness, of relaxed alertness. The literal translation of zanshin is *remaining mind.*

Tactics and Strategy

This book is not for the purpose of revealing specific physical
technique, strategy, or tactics. However, a general consideration of
some of pertinent aspects will assist an Aikido practitioner to form
their thought around how to train and how to prepare for a possible
scenario of self-defense. Ideally, strategic and tactical considerations should occur before, during, and after a situation of self-
defense.

Typically, the *five opportunities to seize* an opponent during a
self-defense situation are

1) Immediately after parrying an opponent's strike;
2) Immediately upon being grabbed by an opponent;
3) During or immediately after merging with an opponent;
4) Immediately after a performing a successful feint; and
5) Immediately after delivering a strike to an opponent.

Typically, the *seven opportunities to strike* an opponent
during defense of self are

1) At the beginning instant of an opponent's action;

2) As the opponent nears the end of his action of withdrawal;
3) Immediately after parrying an opponent's strike;
4) Right after slipping (a form of irimi) an opponent's strike;
5) Quickly after merging with an opponent's action;
6) Immediately after seizing an unbalanced opponent; and
7) Immediately after a performing a successful feint.

Important Technical Principles

Ma-ai no Ri (間合の理) -- space and timing principle.

Kuzushi no Ri (崩しの理) -- breaking opponent's balance principle.

Kokyu no Ri (呼吸の理) -- breath control principle.

Kaeshi no Ri (返しの理) -- returning energy principle.

Hanashi no Ri (離しの理) -- letting go principle.

Tsuiteiku no Ri (ついて行くの理) (stick to and go with) -- sticking to or following principle.

Ridatsu no Ri (離脱の理) -- separating (from) the grasp of an opponent principle.

Iri no Ri (入りの理) -- entering principle.

Tenkan no Ri (転換の理) -- diverting or turning principle.

Ju no Ri (柔の理) -- gentleness principle; that is, push when pulled; pull when pushed.

Aiki no Ri (合気の理) -- merging with energy or fitting in with spirit principle; that is, enter when pulled, turn and merge when pushed.

The last two above can be understood somewhat by contemplating the circumstances of two people, one on each side of a door, each not knowing that another person is standing on the other side. The person on the inside of the door begins to pull it open at a instant before the person on the outside begins to push, but the latter is surprised and stumbles forward slightly before recovering their balance. This type of situation reveals to a perceptive observer the beginning phase of what is termed the *off-balance and recovery cycle* (*kitō*, 起倒 -- rise and fall) as it applies to human movement, where such is the functional technical basis of *kuzushi* from which Ju-no-Ri as well as Aiki-no-Ri have been developed. However, these two principles are different in their technical performance and as a result each infer or exhibit a slightly different innate character. Ju-no-Ri, where the defender (tori or nage) creates action in a specific direction to affect a purposeful off-balancing in order to setup the opponent (uke) for a throw and pinning technique, exhibits a somewhat offense oriented character. In contrast, Aiki-no-Ri exhibits a *lets-see-what-develops-in-order-to-use-it* or *non-oppositional* characteristic and therefore can be considered as a slightly more ethical embodiment of self-defense philosophy -- that is, to the extent that such is possible without the defender suffering bodily injury, let the opponent defeat themselves through their own actions. A good understanding of the technical aspects of these two principles and skill in using them during practice is essential toward developing competency in functional self-defense ability.

Some Methods of Practice

1) Solo and paired practice (kata practice).
2) Resistant-uke (an 'unmovable' uke) drills (balance breaking).
3) Varied-space-condition drills (ma-ai observation).
4) Following-movement-and-speed drill.
5) Offering-lure drill.
6) Striking-parry entering drill.
7) Close-encounter parrying drill.
8) Dodge-duck-slip drill.
9) One-two and one-two-three punch defense drills.
10) Kick defense and counterattack drills.
11) Strengthening forearms exercises.
12) Line drills.
13) Surrounded drill.
14) Controlled sparring (*randori*, 乱取り) practice.
15) Hand-to-hand ('push-hands') randori practice.
16) Lead-and-merge to flow drill (*ki-no-nogare,* 気のれ流).

An improper implementation of the last two of these practice methods (15 and 16 above) can result in the emergence of a mindset within an aikidoka where they expect that a certain cooperative, minimally resistant, often predictable interaction between tori (nage) and uke will occur. If tori has not sufficiently practiced how to respond to the dynamic (quick, strong, and sometimes erratic or unpredictable) attacks of an aggressive opponent, the mindset that is necessary to respond to a real attack will not be properly developed.

Self-defense Considerations

Though typically an indication of misjudgment, inexperience, or simply being caught off-guard, it may be useful or necessary to quickly *duck* (in place), *twist* torso (in place by rotating hips, knees ankles), *sway* (in place by quickly leaning from hips), *slip* by (in place by head movement from neck with or without a slight body movement forward), *dive* or *roll* (using ukemi), or *jump* (in place upward or over) in order to avoid an opponent's attack. However, when doing any one of these movements, maintain body stability and integrate quickly with it an element of a counterattack. Do not lock (through overextension) arms at the elbow or legs at the knee. When caught up in a situation requiring self-defense, a defender will experience bodily injury when they cannot avoid an opponent's attack; therefore, when faced with an aggressor of equal or greater skill, it is essential that you make the best possible use of ma-ai while quickly implementing any maneuver that achieves victory. When a person finds theirself unavoidably involved in a situation that requires justifiable self-defense action, victory can be lost as a result of an error in position, technique execution, or from being surprised by the relentless brutality and skill of an aggressor. When there are only two combatants, lengthy self-defense engagements -- those over one minute -- typically benefit the person who has more endurance; such is to be avoided. Since Aikido is the discipline that an aikidoka practices, ideally, an aiki-oriented defender should wait for the aggressor to initiate an attack; thereby, the latter commits to a breaching of ma-ai while exposing the 'vehicle' (e.g., their arm), energy, and direction of their attack to the possibility of control by the defender. However, there can occur a circumstance that would necessitate a preemptive intercession (strike to stun, grab, followed by an immobilization or neutralization technique); this occurs when an aggressor is or seems to be reaching for a hidden or visible weapon. Practical self-defense includes skill in the techniques of atemi.

Shoji Nishio, 8th Dan Aikikai, informs us that "*In a real situation we use atemi.*"[9] When the typical Aikido ma-ai is breeched, it is essential that the aikidoka defender know how to implement aiki during the use of grappling techniques. When faced with more than one aggressor, control the energetic body of the first aggressor in a way that permits its use as a momentary shield that facilitates the attainment of useful tactical positioning from which you can defend against the second aggressor, and so on; unfortunately, even though you are an aikidoka with an evolved behavioral ethos, you should, ideally, incapacitate the first aggressor that you engage in order to make certain that they cannot reenter the fight and do you harm. *An aikidoka defender must act to protect their well-being in a way that results in an outcome for the aggressor that is dictated or given by the level of danger that might be present in a fight's particular set of circumstances; in this way it is possible that a defender as well as the aggressor will arrive at the end of their altercation with an outcome attended by little or no injury.* Skill in self-defense results from a conscious decision to practice self-defense techniques, strategies, and tactics. The ability to keep calm and make safe decisions when faced with a possible or actual attack by an aggressor is a result of having attained that skill. Skill and preparation represent a key that unlocks a reasoning, functional confidence while locking up a whole lot of fear. When in a self-defense situation, it is almost never possible to "*keep your wits about you*" if you have not developed the necessary skill to confidently defend yourself.

Lastly, it is important to mentally apprehend that the majority of people in civilized societies infrequently experience a situation that requires self-defense skill and action. Therefore, an aikidoka should not get so concerned with the matters of fighting that they begin to emanate a harsh, "*kill'em all and let God sort them out*" attitude or spirit. In fact, if you have taken a turn toward such attitude and behavior, this can only result in further mental unbalance that is neither good for you nor for your friends and family. Many who emerge this type of harsh attitude are found to be frequently dysfunctional in a civil society, and, at that point, they are actually better suited for a military-like combat role. A person who practices Aikido and later goes out into their community with a secret or open desire to engage in fighting will certainly attract the conflict that they seek; however, this person is not a true aikidoka, for they have rejected harmonious human relations as well as Aikido's

Three Precepts. Practice Aikido as part of a regimen for maintaining bodily health, where self-defense ability takes on a productive role because a proper perspective of its role in relation to civilized society has been objectively achieved and maintained. When in doubt, return to the fundamentals.

[1] See **The Spirit of Aikido** by Kisshomaru Ueshiba. Translated by Taitetsu Unno. Kodansha International, Ltd.; paperback edition, first printing, 1987, page 85.

[2] In Kendo, *ma-ai* is the usual term that refers to the proper combative distance. In his treatise entitled **Heiho-kadensho** of 1632 C.E., Yagyū Munenori, a samurai and Kenjutsu master, used the term "suigetsu" when referring to the combative distance between two warriors.

[3] Chinese characters include ideograms, but many of these characters also have logographic qualities. However, Chinese language characters and character sets derived from Chinese characters are neither wholly ideographic nor logographic. Typically, a character set is separated into pictograms, semantic-phonetic compounds, simple ideographs, logical aggregates, associate transformations, and phonetic loan characters. A term inclusive of all the aforementioned is *Sinogram*, emphasizing the Chinese origin of the characters as well as their Han period origin; Chinese *hanzi* and Japanese *kanji* are examples of this category.

[4] See **Tokimune Takeda** by Stanley Pranin; Aiki News magazine, article #88, 1991.

[5] See **The Wisdom of Laotse** by Lin Yutang. Random House, Inc.; hardcover, first edition, 1976.

[6] See the book entitled 合気道 (Aikido) by Kisshomaru Ueshiba. Hozansha Publications, Ltd.; over-size paperback, twelfth printing, 1985, page 21.

[7] See the Internet's online article entitled **Interview with Aikido Shihan Shigenobu Okumura** by Christopher Li.

[8] See **Tokimune Takeda** by Stanley Pranin; Aiki News magazine, article #88, 1991.

[9] See **Interview with Shoji Nishio**, by Stanley Pranin; Aiki News magazine, article #60, March 1984.

Chapter XII

Safe Aikidō Practice and the Practitioner's Demeanor

Dojo Practice Dynamics

Unsafe practice, behavior that either purposefully or unknowingly produces the circumstances that result in injury, is an intolerable condition that Aikido's philosophy does not uphold. It is the sensei's important responsibility to provide Aikido instruction that is free of injury. Consisting partly of minimized physical injury risk and secondarily of minimal inappropriate mental apprehension, a productive learning environment is that which provides progressive internalization of techniques, tactics and strategies with few hindrances.

The Aikido student's safety and progression are two important aspects of training. Safe training attitude is a technical consideration for three reasons. *First*, it helps to reduce the specific concern a student may have regarding the possibility of injury during practice. *Second*, it reduces the time required to internalize any given technique, tactic, or strategy. *Third*, safe practice is a manifestation of Aikido's philosophy -- protect, sustain, and enhance life.

Group dynamics in an Aikido school will cause a certain collective attitude to manifest. No matter what the collective attitude may be like, safety during training must not be compromised by the sensei, by the individual practitioner, or by the social force of the collective, i.e., the class. When practicing Aikido, one must say "No!" to any activity that seems to be or is indeed unsafe, or for which one is unprepared. Do not permit the force of the group (peer pressure) to induce you into action that is likely to result in injury to yourself or your partner. If circumstances permit, proper dojo etiquette should be observed when refusing to participate in what you perceive to be activity for which you are not prepared or might be otherwise unsafe.

Prior to enrolling for Aikido instruction or training discuss with the teacher (sensei) that which comprises the proper behavior when refusing to participate in an uncomfortable or unsafe activity, as proper dojo (way place, school) etiquette should be observed. Do not enroll in an Aikido school when you determine that the sensei is unapproachable regarding matters of safety and general guidance.

The interaction between a tori (performer of technique; nage in some other styles) and an uke (receiver of technique) when practicing Aikido is of special importance when considering the creation and sustention of a productive learning environment. Physical injury and unproductive mental turmoil during practice is unacceptable. Interpersonal relational turmoil as well as physical injury can occur in a dojo, particularly during randori (taming disorder, or free play) when the dynamics of differing individual personalities mingle. The desire to possess power over another person or to be victorious[1] is often the stimulus for such on-the-mat discord. This type of discord can be minimized if each aikidoka nurtures the development of an attitude that embraces true and unflagging respect for the other person's need for bodily safety. One task of the sensei is to ensure that such respect is present in the behavior of each student.

The condition of relationship that exists between tori and uke is defined by the actions of these two participants. Each has their motivation for training in Aikido, known or not (see Chapter XIV teacher responsibility here), but the essence of the tori-uke relationship is dependent upon how the characteristics of their motivation dynamically intertwine. When all is said and done, are they not partners in a quest that seeks to determine truth?

Typically, a sensei provides to all students a set of rules that regulate and guide the condition of the tori-uke relationship during practice. Those rules should be such that they promote and establish productive practice. These rules assign a specific responsibility to tori for uke's bodily integrity and to uke for a specific aspect of tori's mental comfort, when together in practice. Additionally, each student when acting either as tori or as uke is held accountable to the sensei for their ability to perform accurately and safely in either role. When a sensei is remiss in his duty to ensure safety, the student must act to ensure his or her own safety.

Over the course of life, the knee joints of a person's legs receive a lot of wear. Aikido's kneeling techniques, practiced from a kneeling position (seiza) and frequent walking on the knees (shikko) can have deleterious effect upon the knee and toe joints over a long period time. Many of the Aikido techniques that require such position can be practiced from the seated position in a chair.

General Overview of Tori's Responsibilities

While in training, to never intentionally perform a technique in a manner that may result in injury to uke. This includes the negative conditions of practice of going so fast or severe that uke cannot possibly perform ukemi to preclude injury, or performing a technique upon uke with which they are unfamiliar.

Learn to know when and how to abort safely applied techniques (where such is possible) that may have gone askew in order to help uke preclude injury.

General Overview of Tori's Accountabilities

1) Continuous safe performance of all Aikido exercises, techniques, and randori in a manner devoid of harmful intent or outcome.
2) Full understanding of one's own attitudes toward others when in a dynamic of power.
3) Full understanding of one's functional level of compassion toward and protectiveness of others.
4) Full understanding of one's own issues with control, anxiety, and fear.

General Overview of Uke's Responsibilities

1) Continuous progressive and safe performance of Aikido's ukemi waza (receiving techniques) with a springy lightness of body movement.
2) Achievement of the ability to preclude injury to oneself when an applied technique evidences that an injurious out-

come is inevitable if preventative action is not instantaneously taken. From the viewpoint of uke's safety, uke should take care to give only the action energy necessary for tori to competently and safely execute the technique being practiced, but not with such abandon (i.e., unnecessary or excessive intensity of action) that it leaves uke vulnerable to misuse by tori.

3) Rarely to resist tori's application of technique, except when required by the exercise or technique, or as directed by the teacher.

General Overview of Uke's Accountabilities

1) The continuous progressive and safe performance of ukemi waza.
2) The verbal expression of any mental discomfort concerning anxiety about their ability to safely act as an uke, or their concern about any overzealous or abusive application of technique by tori during training.

General Interactional Considerations

Tori, typically, is responsible for uke's safety up to the point where uke is responsible for the performance of functional ukemi. Good, functional, and safe ukemi is where uke's ukemiship precludes uke injury. As before, uke is responsible for that specific aspect of tori's mental comfort in that uke's ukemi must be well internalized so that they might pass safely through tori's application of technique. If uke's performance wanes during tori's application of technique, not matter what the cause, uke may become injured.

During their mutual practice of Aikido, tori and uke are together for the benefit of each other. The role that an aikidoka plays during Aikido training reverses, i.e., at one time a tori, later as an uke; thus, the abovementioned responsibilities and accountabilities pertain to all aikidoka. Participation as uke helps a practitioner to become a safe acting and respectful tori (nage); having been an uke one realizes that when it is time to perform as tori, one will make one's best effort toward ensuring safe practice for uke, thus avoiding injury of uke. What tori does affects uke, and what uke does affects tori; therefore, it is essential that each know and carry out their respective responsibilities.

Each aikidoka must always act with respect for the kind of practice, i.e., safe practice, which engenders non-destructive learning.

Six Reminders Regarding Attitude during Practice

First, for the reason of safe and efficient practice as well as respect of the supervisory authority, a true and reasonable aikidoka subordinates their ego to that of the teacher. Such behavior demonstrates that the student possesses one type of control over self, thereby helping to engender a functional and pleasant atmosphere of training for all.

Second, since the techniques of Aikido include bending and twisting of the joints as well as throws, an aikidoka must not engage an attitude that demonstrates a competitive behavior where the well-being of one's uke or 'opponent' (partner or fellow contestant) is subordinated by the desire for victory. Such a mindset will likely result in injury.

Third, a thorough understanding of Aikido techniques and how to instantly and usefully implement any one of them in real-life or self-defense circumstances can only be achieved through constant and varied practice, whether that practice be in the dojo or elsewhere.

Fourth, Aikido that is practiced as a holistic fitness art is functionally different than practiced as a self-defense art. It is important that the aikidoka differentiate between these two useful practice modes because confusion as to what one or the other actually is can develop a false sense of skill in the realm of that which is required for defense of self. No matter which of these two a student chooses to emphasize, a relaxed and complete awareness of one's surrounding dynamic environment is an important aspect of training and being. However, when training for self-defense it is of utmost importance to develop your skill in Aikido such that there is no vulnerability to an aggressor's actions of attack; Aikido is largely a response driven self-defense form (initially a defensive rather than an offensive self-defense) that is susceptible at certain moments during an attack to weaknesses or penetration that, if not mitigated by careful awareness and training, can result in an opening of which the aggressor may make use.

Fifth, considering self-defense, if an attacker against whom you must defend knows techniques and strategy that are derived from the same root as Aikido, it is likely there will be no decisive outcome, or if there is it may not favor you. Therefore, be wise in considering to whom you'll transmit your Aikido knowledge. Careless dissemination of knowledge that could be used by corrupt individuals to harm you or others is a grave error in judgment.

Sixth, when physical action is required, whether in practice or self-defense, withhold your temper. When your temper flares, withhold physical action if possible.[2]

Remember, as uke, you have the right to say *No!* to any practice for which you are unprepared or you deem unsafe. Many uke have unnecessarily experienced injury that occurred because of their inability to recognize dangerous circumstances of practice or because of apprehension about the resilience or toughness of their spiritual and physical constitution in relation to both conscious and unconscious response to their Aikido group's expectations concerning that which comprises a "good uke." Practice toward the development of knowledge and skill in Aikido is best realized when no injury occurs.

"When you overlook the rude mannerisms of others because of your own unpreparedness, or when your reasoning guided by selflessness wanes, there occurs the situation where Might subordinates Right; Might becomes Master, justice serves Might, and right is what Might likes."

Julian -- 1992

[1] See **The Spirit of Aikido** by Kisshomaru Ueshiba. Translated by Taitetsu Unno. Kodansha International, Ltd.; paperback edition, first printing, 1987, page 8.

[2] See, the philosophy of Gichin Funakoshi, founder of Karatedo.

Chapter XIII

The Abatement of Fear

"Thus, when confronted by an enemy, you are awakened to self, and, further, on going through the gateway of death, you come to view death in the light of life, and regard life and death as one."[1]

Kenji Tomiki - Shodokan Aikido Founder
8th Dan Aikikai Aikido, 9th Dan Kodokan Judo

Who knows how to quiet the nerves when you feel those gut twisting, body shaking, spine tingling emotions that are a manifestation of fear? Oh, fear!

It might be the fear of meeting people because you feel, in some way, inadequate; or, the fear of failure, because you feel inadequate. Perhaps it is the fear experienced during a confrontational encounter. Though, no difference here, it's fear; and its arrival beckons unto Chaos.

Each time anxiety or fear grips you is yet another time that your own true inner self critically judges the essence of your composure, your very being as you. All cover-up, any delusion is swiftly stripped away, your mental composure shaken. Perhaps *the emperor's 'clothed' nakedness* is revealed.

When involved in a confrontational situation that has the potential for physical violence, what comprises your fear? Here, your fear resides in your quick and likely unconscious recognition of that which you may lose, typically manifesting as increased heartbeat, inconsistent or rapid breathing, skin flushing, abdominal fluttering and uneasiness, body trembling, etc.; but, notice that the psychological condition of what anxiety, concern, worry, or fear is comprised is that which *may* occur, not that which is occurring. Nevertheless, if a physical engagement occurs you may receive bodily injury, suffering perhaps some minor bodily discomfort, or, if a truly violent encounter, serious bodily damage that may require special attention from a doctor and weeks or months of convalescence to recover. Also, when unprepared to properly respond with defensive movements, you may be somewhat stunned at the onset and throughout the entirety of such an assault, which in actuality is a quickly emerging and violent disruption of your personal space-time reality, thus causing the well-known default nervous system response of *freeze, flee,* or *fight.* Quivering thought and inaction is demonstrative of a freeze response; a typical flee response is demonstrated by turning and running; while a typical fight response is demonstrated when two adversaries engage in some type of hitting (fisticuffs, kicking, clubbing, etc.) and or wrestling. Worse yet, you could lose your life, thus leaving your family subject to the affect of your demise. Is this acceptable?

After you have minimized any negative effects that life can bring to bear upon your psyche, your fate is largely what you make it to be. You must acquire the ability to perceive and respond to all attempts of connivery and skullduggery as well as the preliminary positioning that likely signals an impending assault. A good place to begin your self-assessment is to consider your psychological conditioning pertaining to the strong utterance of the words *No* or *Stop.* When faced with a creepy, contentious, threatening, or otherwise portentous encounter, even though you might be experiencing anxiety, can you calmly yet firmly say *No!* or *Stop!,* then, wary of the other person's response, remain firm in your decision to oppose?

So, what do you do about it, your fear? This may be difficult to ponder, but with a little careful thought one can find the answer. Many a person ignores these soul-shaking events, ignores those opportunities to investigate their response, for their own manifestation of fear is so unnerving that they block reasoning, block productive action toward a useful outcome. For many of this personality type, the immediate meaning of their psychologically disturbing event passes quickly enough, and, if alive, they dismiss their indicator for change, *'clothing'* again their inadequacy (covering it up). However, sometimes a fear event does not pass until a change for the better or worse occurs.

What, then, is the method for quieting the nerves, relieving the tension and vanquishing your fear in order to become a calmer, stronger and more productive person?

Understanding Aikido

The Abatement of Fear

First, you must accept that you, only you, are responsible for your responses to the various events or forces that life directs toward you. You must act calmly. You must act from a place of knowledge. You must act with skill. But, how to accomplish these? Astonishingly simple, the answer is found in the learning of knowing how to meet with courage any unnerving event in order to proceed toward changing it into relative calmness!

Second, to discover the "knowing how" you must train yourself in the very circumstances that gives rise to your fear with the idea of resolving it to a condition of confidence. Can you do this? In so doing you gradually reduce or eliminate the thoughts of what may occur, a result of your preparation and developed abilities -- your skill.

Third, when you experience fear, stop, silence your noisy actions, listen, look, and assess; then, respond appropriately, without panic. No panic will occur if you've taken steps to prepare yourself to meet with calmness and strength the various tumultuous situations that may arise in life. If unprepared, run toward that place or circumstance that you consider to be safe. Unfortunately, running away may not result in safety. Seriously, sometimes it may be a good day to die, for no person will escape their physical demise -- at some point, life is terminal.

Though not for in depth discussion within this writing, it is useful to mention that various convoluted aspects of fear can produce in a person behavior that slowly weakens their focused life force and diminishes their overall energy and creativity. One who is apprehensive of conflict avoids it and thusly creates a psychological body of being within and around themself that represents the effect of their fear. The shape of that body, a condition of anxiety, depends upon that of which it is comprised in relation to the person's unique psycho-spiritual being.

Heijo-shin, mental composure, is calmness under the pressure of unnerving circumstances. Such mental skill is essential to successful defense of self. Though not a martial artist, Samuel Clemens (a.k.a., Mark Twain), a late 19th and early 20th Century writer, stated that "*Courage is resistance to fear, mastery of fear, not absence of fear.*"

The Abatement of Fear

[1] See, *Judo: Appendix Aikido* by Kenji Tomiki, page 158.

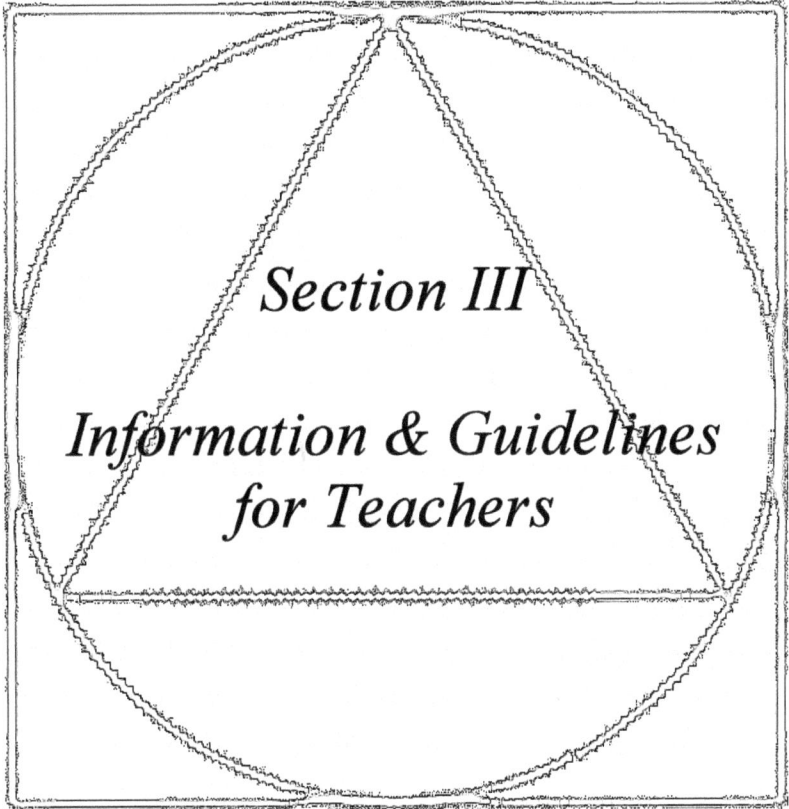

Section III

Information & Guidelines for Teachers

Chapter XIV

Teaching Considerations and Methods

Teachers should embrace and adhere to a step-by-step, grade-to-grade teaching program that provides a student with a goal-oriented program of study. Assuming that a student of Aikido is desirous of learning aiki-self-defense, such a proper program of instruction presents to a beginning student an organized practice that helps a student to quickly learn and thoroughly integrate the ideas and techniques of Aikido while also promoting safety. No injury is acceptable; if such occurs it could be an indication that insufficient attention has been given to safe practice methodology.

Guidelines

A student is usually aware of their general desire or need that is motivating their enrollment in an Aikido school. However, many students have either undisclosed or unconscious secondary motivations for studying it. The teacher is responsible for discerning each and every motivation of a student in order that the best decisions regarding the student's training can be made.

After taiso (warm-ups), show waza (techniques) or kata (a specific series of techniques) first, corresponding to the student's level of training, using the help of two previously trained students to demonstrate. If this is not possible, use the most limber, resilient, and wiry student who is trained in that which you will be demonstrating. Following demonstration, have the students practice repeatedly and slowly. When you, the teacher, know that your student has the ability to act safely, then you may decide to move into randori practice. Initially, randori must be performed slowly, too. You must ensure that randori practice is productive, and an important part of that is the aspect of safety. Toward this end, beyond the obvious self-defense training reasons, solo and paired kata practicing are excellent intructional methods that help a new student to become familiar with the movement and energy dynamics of randori while improving their proprioception. Do not present advanced technique and methods to a student who is not prepared to receive or perform such.

The individual attitude of both a student and teacher is extremely important in the maintenance of safety during Aikido practice; that of a student must be neither timid nor aggressive, while that of a teacher must be fully supportive of each gender, neither timid nor harsh, yet appropriately challenging. You must be alert to all of the various aspects of the dojo's environment as well as to the differing interacting physical and psychological dynamics that exist among the practicing students.

The teacher must recognize that some male students, depending on the culture or sub-culture from which they come, may tend to consider the female student as less capable due to her different musculature and gender-specific upbringing. Seek to overcome this bias by ensuring that the male student perform technique as he would when training with another male student, i.e., properly and safely, and by requiring the female student to become physically strong and resilient in her musculature as well as technically skillful. Notwithstanding, the physical strength disparity that exists for most women in relation to men must be recognized, acknowledged, and reasonably addressed by the teacher. Any deleterious affect that may arise from such a disparity upon the training of a less physically powerful student can be minimized by deemphasizing the use of force through the implementation of technical principles that are designed to utilize the energy and movements of an uke; for example, the emphasis of ma-ai and kuzushi. Work with the female student to increase her overall prowess. Remember, the primary concern of Aikido is harmonized energy.

As a teacher, it is not acceptable for you to allow a stronger person to *muscle their way through* a technique (the use of unnecessary or excessive strength) that is being applied to uke, no matter what gender. Considering what comprises self-defense when engaged in a physical conflagration with another person, the performance of ideal Aikido is exhibited when the defender makes use of an aggressor's energy and direction of movement to their own advantage;

such action being a true representation of aiki. The use of superior muscular strength should be kept to a minimum in order to focus on the learning of maximum efficiency through minimum effort; however, when in training the teacher may request that an uke apply forcefully their strength in order that tori may better learn how to make use of that dynamic toward improving their aiki oriented self-defense ability.

When teaching, be appropriate and respectful yet justly firm in all matters and decisions, as the people who you teach are your students, your responsibility. Teachers should not become emotionally involved with any of their students; a teacher's prime and only involvement with a student is for the reason of their education in the discipline of Aikido. The following additional guidelines are sometimes useful.

1) Require all students to perform hand washing before class;
2) Require all students to keep finger and toe nails clean and short;
3) Do not permit a student who has obvious *cold* or *flu* symptoms, or other communicable illnesses, to practice;
4) As a teacher, learn and be able to perform basic first aid for injuries that might be likely to occur during practice;
5) In the event of a bleeding injury be cautious about contact with blood while making the appropriate medical response because some diseases are blood born;
6) Be alert to the indications or signs of over-heating or exhaustion of students, particularly during randori practice; and,
7) Emphasize safety.

Character Evaluation

The evaluation of the character of a person is essential toward *1)* a sensei making a decision as to whether or not accept a person as a student and *2)*, if the person is acceptable as a student, how the sensei will shape his teachings to achieve the best possible outcome for them. A person's personality is shaped from and around their basic psychological character, of which the innate pure-self is part. A careful evaluation of the student's personality, either of a retrogressive design or a test-and-response design, in order to understand their character is useful for this purpose. According to the ancient Chinese sage Confucius, *"Man's mind is more treacherous than mountains and rivers, and more difficult to know than the sky"* [1] because he *" ... hides his character behind an inscrutable appearance."* [1] Confucius continues by outlining his *nine tests for judging a person's character*, which are to

1) Send a man on a distant mission to test his loyalty;
2) Employ him nearby in order to observe his manners;
3) Give him a lot to do in order to apprehend his mental composure and understand his abilities;
4) Suddenly put a question to him in order to test his knowledge;
5) Make a commitment with him in order to test his resolve to live up to his word;
6) Trust him with money to test the essence of his ethical fortitude;
7) Announce to him a coming change in order to perceive his integrity;
8) Participate with him in a social occassion where alcohol is served and consummed in order to gain insight into his character; and, lastly,
9) Put him in female company to see his attitude toward women.

Confucius ends his outline by saying, *"Submitted to these nine tests, a fool always reveals himself."* [1] These nine tests work equally well for the feminine gender. Though a teacher may apply this method, there are other, modern methods of character testing available to teachers. One such method employs a long series of questions that evaluates various aspects of the human personality based upon a person's responses. These methods of personality screening may be useful for the teacher who desires to ensure that a safe and productive learning environment exists for all students in their dojo .

Koans

A test employing a number of koans may be useful as a method for the teacher to assist a student's learning of Aikido, particularly if that student is interested in teaching certification. The development of this particular linguistic perception tool is attributed largely to both Chan (Chinese) and Zen (Japanese) Buddhism. Koan curricula, such as those of the Rinzai or Soto schools of Zen Buddhism, exist for the purpose of assisting a Buddhist devotee toward enlightenment. A study of koan should direct a student toward *kenshō* (an initial insight or awakening arriving into consciousness through momentarily "seeing nature," i.e., seeing the nature of a thing or an event), then further training toward achieving *satori* (clear and full understanding of an aspect of Nature), and finally *nirvana* (Buddhist enlightenment where aversion, delusion, anxiety, desire, etc., are, literally, "blown out," i.e., extinguished).

The definition of what constitutes koan arises from that which it requires of the person who embraces it -- specifically, keen, perceptive thought. However, the usual cognitive processing that a student may use to resolve other types of questions or problems in their normal circumstances of life are likely not those that must be discovered and used to unlock the lesson of a koan. Lateral or out-of-the-box thinking is typically required; a solution can be either astoundingly simple or intriguingly complex. Some koan have no solutions, and some solutions are student dependent. One definition of koan is that of a linguistic or pictorial presentation of some type of abstract concept (typically in the form of a dialogue, story, question, or statement) that requires from the student new cognitive processing in order to achieve different insight or knowledge about the workings of life. A few examples pertinent to this discussion, which may be employed to this end, without possible answers, follow.

A man guards a book year after year. Which is more important, the man or the book?

The name of names from which you must be freed is what?

What has a beginning has an end. Therefore, that which has no beginning has not an end. Who knows the end of the beginning connected to the beginning of the end?

"Kyosei asked a monk one day, 'What is that noise outside?' The

monk answered, 'That is the voice of the raindrops.' Kyosei said, 'All living things are upside down, deceived as to their true nature and pursuing objects.' The monk then asked, 'What about you, sir?' Kyosei answered, 'I am near to not being deceived about myself.' The monk asked, 'What does 'near to not being deceived' mean?' Kyosei replied, 'Talking in the abstract is easy enough, but explaining reality with words is difficult.'"[2]

A Teacher's Purpose and Duty

Self-esteem seems to be based upon the knowledge of how to do, upon where one fits in society, and upon one's usefulness to humankind. The usefulness of one's knowledge is seldom fully realized if kept within, unrevealed, or ineffectually communicated. In fact, upon death, one's ability to transmit knowledge is, likely, forever gone. Furthermore, of what significance is one's life when after living and learning if all that which is self is not at some prior time presented to, and in some part, if not wholly, accepted by, another person?

You must transmit your skill as well as that portion of your knowledge that is immutable truth! To present one's knowledge to the receptive person, and then to do so in a manner that will assist that person to develop useful skill and valid ethical behavior is the purpose and duty of the teacher; and this is that which is the significance or usefulness of the teacher's life. When pursuing "*the purpose*" (i.e., the transmission of skill that is hinged to ethical behavior) a teacher must embrace selflessness and truthfulness so that when performing "*the duty*" (i.e., the responsibility to convey that skill in the best possible way that is ethically useful) they will be able to guide a student towards ethical accomplishment without retarding the students' process of integration (i.e., a combining of that which is sensed with useful, systematic action in order to develop skill in doing) and self-realization.

When performing "the duty," a teacher must be appropriate; meaning, they must be respectful of the student's need for bodily integrity. Often, at first, a teacher knows little of the intrinsic attitudes and abilities of their student and therefore should proceed slowly with the presentation of Aikido in a manner that encourages progress. Of equal importance, a teacher must emphasize appro-

priate and effective self-defense action in accordance with the philosophy of *aiki,* the precept of *tomaranu kokoro* (spirit that knows
no stopping), and humane ethics.

Multiple Intelligence Theory

While instructing, many teachers have experienced the student
who is less adept at learning the physical movements of Aikido. Ex-
cluding any physical motor function disability, this kind of person
may benefit from an educational approach that is based in the relatively recent theory of learning types termed *Multiple Intelligence
Theory* (M.I.). Viewed from a perspective of teaching evolution, this
theory helps to establish a new psychological basis for identifying
different learning styles (modalities) that exist for people. The importance of this for the teacher is that they could have one or a-
nother student in their dojo (or classroom) who do not necessarily
learn in the same way as the majority therein. At its core, M.I. proposes that human cognitive operation occurs with varying natural
ability in specific and differing cognitive areas (innate modalities),
rather than only a single general intelligence. Those areas[3] are

1) Linguistic intelligence -- a capacity to employ language effectively, in both speaking and writing;
2) Logical intelligence -- a capacity to infer or deduce with
   minimal error and use numbers effectively;
3) Spatial intelligence -- the capacity to apprehend the characteristics of the visio-spatial realm and make productive use
   of them;
4) Bodily intelligence -- a capacity to use the coporeal body to
   express ideas and feelings or facility in using one's hands to
   produce, transform, or accomplish;
5) Musical intelligence -- the capacity to apprehend, discrimi-
   nate the characteristics of, transform, and express musical
   forms;
6) Interpersonal intelligence -- a capacity to perceive and
   make distinctions in the moods, intentions, motivations, and
   feelings of other people;
7) Intrapersonal intelligence -- self-knowledge awareness and
   the capacity to adapt on the basis of that knowledge;

8) Naturalistic intelligence -- a capacity to understand the workings and importance of the natural enviroment, i.e., Nature, and humankind's relationship to it; and,
9) Existential intelligence -- sensitivity to the characteristics of the human condition (e.g., birth, death, possibility of soul) and a capacity to reason out an understanding about it that can serve as a foundation for a useful, acceptable existence.

Other intelligences that have been proposed for consideration are spirituality, moral sensibility, creativity, and humor.

Considering the present Multiple Intelligences Theory, the nine intelligences are innate in each person. These intelligences interact complexly and there are many paths that one may take toward a-chieving a higher functioning in each. Most people can develop each of these intelligences toward a certain higher level of compe-tency. There are currently four developmental stages typically re-cognized for people, ranging from early childhood through adult-hood.[4]

The benefit to the teacher when employing the understanding of M.I. theory is that of being able to know how one student or a-nother perceives and responds to life. In knowing this, the teacher can better structure their instruction to meet individual or group needs. Many books concerning M.I. theory have assessment tests included therein.

People can have mentally *awakening* or mentally *inhibiting* ex-periences in life.[5] *Awakening* experiences are those momentus e-vents in time where a person's developing innate abilities become clearly enhanced. *Inhibiting* experiences refer to those that slow down, stop, or even retard the functioning of the intelligences. I-deally, an Aikido sensei is ethically bound by Aikido's philosophy, as shaped by the Three Precepts, to guide their students upon a pro-ductive path of training; therefore, they should ensure that no in-hibiting experiences, either mental or physical, occur. The two mental attitudes of a sensei that are of paramount importance when teaching are

1) Discerning a student's unique character and affirming it in a productive way that manifests the Three Precepts; and,
2) Upholding the student's need for safe practice, especially when practising Aikido with a self-defense emphasis.

　　　　Understanding Aikido

[1] See the book entitled ***The Wisdom of Laotse*** by Lin Yutang. Random House, Inc.; hardcover, first edition, second printing, 1976, page 250.

[2] See the book entitled ***Zen Koans*** by Gyomay Kubose. Henry Regnery Company; hardcover, first edition, 1973.

[3] See article entitled ***Theory of Mulitple Intelligences*** at Wikipedia.org. http://en.wikipedia.org/wiki/Theory_of_multiple_intelligences; 2014.

[4] See the book entitled ***Seven Ways of Teaching: The Artistry of Teaching with Multiple Intelligences*** by David Lazear. IRI/Skylight Publishing; paperback, 1991, pages xxiv and 110.

[5] See the book entitled ***Multiple Intelligences in the Classroom*** by Thomas Armstrong. Published by the Association for Supervision and Curriculum Development; paperback, 1994, pages 2 and 11.

Chapter XV

An Aikidō Master's Personality Attributes

What comprises the personality of an Aikido sensei or master teacher? What will a master of Aikido exhibit as behavior when having arrived at a higher condition of skill, awareness, and understanding of Aikido as well as of life? Generally, a master of Aikido

1) Is never neglectful of the need to inculcate in his or her students honest and functional self-defense ability that is useful toward protecting their lives and sustaining their overall well-being;

2) Always seeks to find in the other person the human quality that helps to awaken and maintain his or her humaneness;

3) Seeks to align his thoughts with the concept of "rightmindedness"[1] as outlined by Takuan Soho;

4) Has the ability to discern those aspects that characterize and make different a martial or police art, a self-defense art, a combative sport, and a spiritual art;

5) Acts to ensure the safety of their students, whether in practice in the dojo or in the effectiveness of techniques, strategies, and tactics of self-defense;

6) Practices and teaches for the reason of discovering universal immutable law, not imbuing such process with subjective magico-religiosity, while maintaining vital health and mastering fear, thereby calming and strengthening their own psychological composure;

7) Has the ability to properly brush the kanji characters which comprise the word Aikido, as such ability exhibits the development of a contemplative artistic skill that helps him or her to appreciate and connect with that part of the Japanese culture that has evolved the discipline of Aikido; and

An Aikido Master's Personality Attributes

8) Acts to protect, sustain, and enhance life, because such a way of acting is a reflection of having truly evolved a higher consciousness.

Kisshomaru Ueshiba reminded us that "*Both Aikido instructors and students must dedicate themselves to truly mastering the art, plumb its depths, dispel its distortions, and present its authentic form.*"[1]

[1] See ***The Spirit of Aikido*** by Kisshomaru Ueshiba. Translated by Taitetsu Unno. Kodansha International, Ltd.; paperback edition, first printing, 1987, page 20.

Chapter XVI

Primary Techniques Comparison
of Aikikai and Tomiki-derived Styles

Generally, the physical technique body of Aikido consists of pins and holds (immobilizations), and throws (projections). Immobilizations terminate with uke being pinned or firmly controlled. Projections end with uke being thrown.

Immobilizations (Pins & Holds)

Aikikai schools	Tomiki-derived schools
Ikkyo	Ude Osae
Nikyo	Kote Mawashi
Sankyo	Kote Hineri
Yonkyo	Tekubi Osae
Gokyo	Gyaku Ude Osae
Shiho Nage	Shiho Nage
Kote Gaeshi	Kote Gaeshi

Table 1

Projections (Throws)

Aikikai schools	Tomiki derived schools
Kokyu Nage	Kokyu Nage
Irimi Nage	Gyaku Irimi Nage
Kaiten Nage	Kaiten Nage
Koshi Nage	Koshi Nage
Aiki Otoshi	Aiki Otoshi, or Mae Otoshi variant

Table 2

Atemi (hitting body techniques) is also taught, but emphasis on this is minimal until the aikidoka proves that their understanding of Aikido's philosophy is well embraced. Atemi is often modified for safety reasons, e.g., shomen-ate performed as a push rather than in a striking or thrusting manner. Practical self-defense includes skill in the techniques of atemi. Atemi practice is largely the same in all Aikido styles. Morihiro Saito, 9th Dan Aikikai, reminds us that *"Aikido includes atemi, although of course training is not the same as reality so we do not apply atemi fully in the dojo."*[1]

[1] See **Interview with Morihiro Saito by Stanley Pranin**; Aiki News magazine, article #88, 1991.

Chapter XVII

Teaching Children:
Considerations and a Course Outline

A child's physical and psychological conditions are in a continuous state of growth, becoming stronger and taller in body, and in mind more self-aware as well as learned of the matters of life. Recent neurological studies show that the developing female brain stops physical growth at around 24 years of age, while the developing male brain not until approximately 27 years. Prior to 18 years of age, a young person's joint plates (jointed areas between the bones of the body) are still growing; improper stress on these can cause injury that may result in bone malformation. Therefore, it is necessary that an Aikido program for children be structured in a way that does not interfere with this growth, but rather, only does that which imparts skill, understanding, compassion, resolve, and strength. A program of training that includes ukemi, unsoku, irimi and tenkan, atemi waza, nage waza without joint pressure, randori, and various other non-joint oriented exercises is appropriate.

> **Joint locks should be avoided as part of a program of Aikido for children.**

A program for children should be designed to begin at the very basic beginning foundational underpinnings of Aikido, progressing to a point where the older, more skilled child student can perform certain basic atemi and nage waza in kata and randori. Such a program should begin around 10, 12 or 14 years of age and culminate at 14, 16 or 18 years of age, whereupon the youthful student can transition to an adult program. These different beginning and ending ages are hinged to the actual program of Aikido developed by the sensei (teacher) or organization.

All youthful students should be thoroughly prepared by means of progressive (step-by-step) training so as to reduce the possibility of injury to them. For example, when presenting how to perform a forward roll, first present it from a kneeling position. After they learn how to do a kneeling roll, then present the stand-up (up-right) version. This kind of progressive training should also exist for any grouping of atemi or nage waza. *Kata* (practice movements, i.e., forms, arranged in groupings that consist of specific techniques) can be taught to children as long as such does not include joint locks. Also, proper respect for other aikidoka and elders, dojo etiquette, and safety during practice should not be neglected.

The transition between a children's program and an adult program should be well thought out, should be an easy entry point where, essentially, culmination of the exercises and techniques of the children's program are simply the beginning aspects of the adult program.

The children's Aikido program taught by the Zantoppa Kai is constructed in the following form.

1) Rei (a greeting to express respect);
2) Short discussion concerning safety during practice;
3) Stretching, aerobic warm-up, and strengthening exercises;
4) Break-falling and rolling methods practice;
5) Entering, turning, and merging methods practice;
6) Reminder about safety during practice;
7) Self-defense techniques, presented in several different kata, which are not joint-pressure oriented;
8) 3-step partner kata practice that is appropriate for each kata group;
9) Object proximity and threat awareness drills;
10) Reminder about safety during practice;
11) Situational self-defense practice, including how to verbally minimize tension, deescalate confrontation, and how to escape or retreat calmly and orderly; and, lastly,
12) Slow hand-to-hand (te-tai-te) randori (similar to Taichi's push-hands drill).

The Zantoppa Kai Children's Program Course Outline

This program consists of two 75-minute class sessions each week for approximately 2 years. Generally, its content consists of various Aikido exercises (*taiso*), basic movement patterns (*undo*), beginning defense techniques (*waza*), both slow and fast hand-to-hand practice (*randori*), and situational awareness instruction. It begins at the arbitrarily denoted point of Jukyu (tenth level) and proceeds to its completion point at Yonkyu (fourth level) step 3. The time-in-grade requirement before testing for advancement to the next level is given the table below.

Level of Proficiency	Obi Color	Training Hours
Jukyu	White	0
Jukyu to Kukyu	White with one yellow stripe	24
Kukyu to Hachikyu	White with two yellow stripes	36
Hachikyu to Shichikyu	Yellow	36
Shichikyu to Rokyu	Yellow with one blue stripe	48
Rokyu to Gokyu	Yellow with two blue stripes	48
Gokyu to Yonkyu, step 1	Blue	64
Yonkyu, step 1 to Yonkyu, step 2	Blue with one red stripe	64
Yonkyu, step 2 to Yonkyu, step 3	Blue with two red stripes	64

Table 3

Such a program of study is designed to help the child learn how to control and organize their movements in order to develop a state of increased harmony (aiki) between self and the world. It is an effective method for improving endurance and strength. Furthermore, it offers the child a social environment of cooperation and camaraderie where they will be guided toward accomplishment in Aikido with respectful firmness. Lastly, this program can help the student to understand how to resolve some apprehension or fear into relative calm, thus helping to develop a more relaxed as well as confident youthful person.

The child must be from 10 to 14 years of age, must be of sound mental and physical health such that reasonable performance of the program may occur, must be interviewed by the sensei to ascertain their basic character and attitude toward life before registering for the class. The child must have completed a physical exam carried out by a competent physician with permission to participate given by his or her parent(s).

In order to cause a relatively pleasant and productive relationship between the sensei and the student, and between student and student, you must always have in mind the welfare of all students. The following directives for the sensei will help achieve the aforementioned.

1) Go slowly;
2) Be accurate with attention to safety in your presentation;
3) When presenting new material, demonstrate it with an assistant sensei or senior adult student so that your less experienced students can see a good visual example;
4) Emphasize atemi waza as throws, not strikes;
5) Ensure that NO joint pressure techniques occur;
6) Practice emphasis should be placed on child-to-child interaction during practice, and maintain adult-to-child interaction to a minimum because size differences (mass in motion) can cause injury quickly;
7) Be very attentive to all actions occurring during practice;
8) Know first aid, and remain calm if ever an injury situation does arise;
9) A sensei should always allow the parents of children to watch training and advancement tests; and, lastly,
10) A sensei should always respectfully receive a student's or parent's comments or concerns.

The following information for students and parents is useful.

1) Before joining a particular school of Aikido, observe its

classes and direct your pertinent questions toward members of its administrative and technical staff;

2) Students should become aware of the exact nature of dojo etiquette (social manners) by asking the school's teacher or administrative interviewer of its specifics before participating in training, and, if this etiquette is acceptable to the student it should be followed when presenting their comments or concerns to the teacher; and,

3) Parents should, ideally, wait until a water break, the end of the class, or the beginning of the next class to present any comments or concerns.

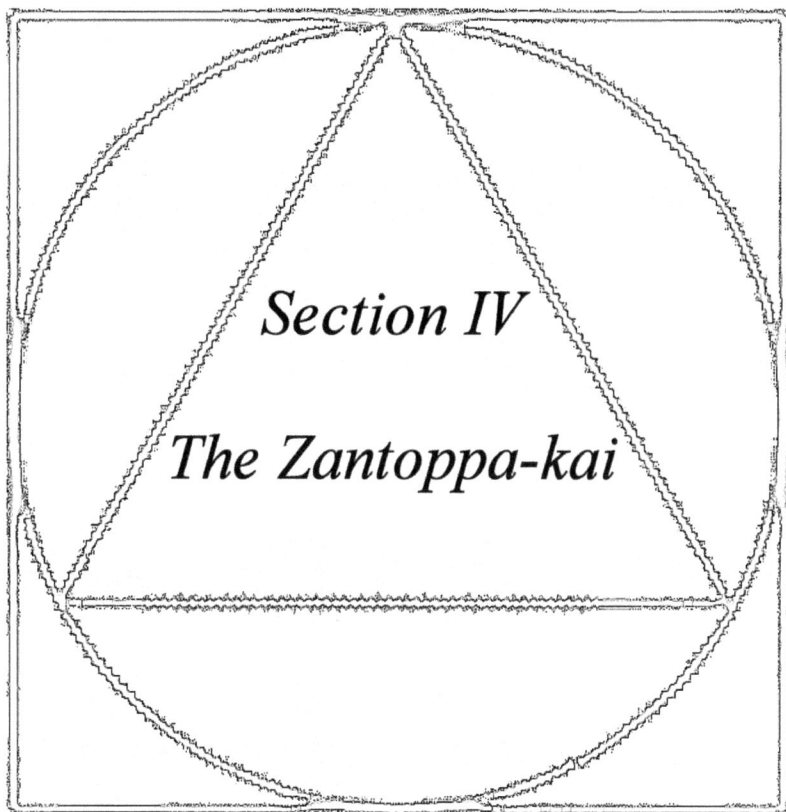

Section IV

The Zantoppa-kai

The Reason for the Zantoppa Kai (斬突破会)

There are quite a number of different disciplines of martial, self-defense, fitness, and sport endeavor that are based upon learned and organized human physical movement under the most difficult of circumstances, the pitting of one person or group of people against another in a physical struggle. Each of these has a some type of attendant philosophy, stated or not. Depending upon the person's need and psychological predisposition at the time of starting practice of a discipline from any of these general categories, one or another may be considered, from a subjective viewpoint, to be more suitable than another. When contemplating martial or self-defense disciplines, it will be found upon comparison that some elements of one discipline are a functioning aspect of another. For example, considering the general characteristics of *self-defense* as compared to those of *martial art*, there are a finite number of actions or methods that one can use to hit, twist upon, throw, hold down, knockout, or kill -- i.e., subdue or neutralize -- an opponent, with the difference between these two combative attitudes being largely a result of the characteristics of a society's collectively-held philosophical ethos. There is always technical similarity between disciplines that can be ascribed to a particular general category regarding the principles of movement, as applicable to the human being. For example, you'll find some basic elements of Judo as well as some of Taichi in Aikido; and, you'll find many of the technical aspects of Judo and Aikido in a military, combat oriented martial art where the object is to kill an enemy. The manner in which combative actions are implemented by combatants will impinge upon an observer's thoughts, and from this interaction there emerges a certain collectively held attitude that serves to identify a discipline's unique characteristics. This type of relationship is that which causes the emergence of the *'public face'* of a discipline; and the interaction between the participants (combatants) of any particular discipline and its observers or promoters is the primary reason for the eventual assignment of one particular 'spiritual aire' or another to it. (Let's not forget that the term *spiritual* can possess either a negative or positive characteristic.) When a discipline is oriented to address certain self-defense or martial needs, an effect of this type from the public arena (the outcome of the interactions between its participants, observers, and promoters) can have a deleterious affect upon its technical functionality. This type of social problem affects the character of civilian self-defense reality. For example, today in the U.S.A., civil actions via lawsuit in courts across the country by an aggressor (the one who initiated a violent act) against the reasonable defense of a defender (who acted in defense of self against the unwarranted attack are sometimes won by the former. Frequently, opposite to sensible reasoning and previously established case law, many government prosecutors are, especially in the so-called 'progressive' states, regularly persecuting people who acted to defend themselves lawfully and reasonably. Indeed, such prosecutors often make use of every trick and wile at their disposal to squash a person's right to reasonable self-defense action. Of course, there is an explanation for such an upending of the balance of justice, but such is not a topic for discussion herein. Suffice it to say that one's self-defense actions must be done carefully if one wishes to avoid a problematic social aftermath.

Valid Aikido styles manifest certain physio-philosophical teachings (physical techniques hinged to, attended by, or combined with philosophical principles) that provide, if one chooses to embrace the real concern of self-defense, an unparalleled path of study directed toward the development of a person who is *ideally evolved* through the attainment of a higher understanding of life (toward a higher consciousness) and who is neither *consumed* nor *outcast* by society. The practical meaning of this is that an aikidoka seeks to embrace a condition of being that upholds true Aikido self-defense behavior as evidenced by their alignment with the concepts of Ai Nuke No Kyoukun, the Three Precepts, and Aiki rather than the martial attitude that evolves the less noble (i.e., less justifiable) self-defense outcomes; the distinction here is that the latter is purposefully disposed to the attitude of fighting and warfare whereas the former is not. This *true self-defense* aspect of Aikido can be understood by acknowledging that a physical technique has associated with it a certain innate and inseparable philosophy, that is, it is imbued with a certain basic meaning, a meaning that emerges onto the stage of life by the performer's decision to use it, and in what manner they will use it. For example, a punching technique with a fist results in a collision with an opponent, perhaps resulting in unnecesary damage for a given situation of defense; whereas an Aikido iriminage technique (entering throw) results in a merging of movement and energy and can come to an undamaging conclusion, which is better for some situations of self-defense. *Technique ethics* for combative disciplines is infrequently taught, and often the martial degree to which a technique can proceed improperly informs and then misguides a student's thinking to the point where martial attitude is wrongly considered as reasonable self-defense.

Specifically, *ideally evolved* means that an aikidoka has balanced selfishness with selflessness, has inculcated within their being a sincere goodwill toward all people, and never neglects the need for self-defense prowess. Achievement of this attitudinal condition requires years of self-discipline in the study of the matters of life in order to wean a person from the misdirection of one's ego as well as from any inculcated untruths presented by society. This can only be accomplished by making a conscious study of cause and effect and by consciously acting to resolve disorder into a condition that is inclined and ordered toward harmony. Aikido is an enabling system that helps a person, an aikidoka, to discover a path toward attainment of an ideally evolved condition of being, of proper relation to life. Explaining even further the meaning of *ideally evolved*, a person studying Aikido should learn how to defend against both verbal and physical attack with courage and skill, being mentally sturdy yet flexible, of calm demeanor, firm and decisive in physical action but never excessively forceful, and sincere yet respectful in all encounters with other people.

Aikido is one of but a few disciplines that present the *most-right approach* toward achieving a higher awareness and understanding of the matters of life -- a higher consciousness. What is meant by *most-right approach*? It is that a person seeks to protect, sustain and enhance life. Aikido techniques and strategies are among those that embrace such a philosophy as well as permit the transformation of disorder to relative order, ideally toward harmony, i.e., good relations. Most people prefer happiness to misery; a discipline such as Aikido is that kind of activity that manifests the *most-right approach* to life when studying a physio-spiritual discipline. What is the reason for the existence of the Zantoppa Kai Aikido Association? (See Section VII for its translated meaning.) Aikido, as an identifier or container for the concept of aiki, has suffered much factional divergence. The often-sensed spiritual aspects of Aikido are at the core of this problem, for in being largely of a subjective nature, a-greement as to that of which those aspects may consist cannot be easily realized or agreed upon by those people involved in establishing inter-school cooperation. Another factor leading to divergence has been the lack of an inter-school practice structure or cooperative event, like shiai, that would tend to bring its practitioners together. Modern Judo, and now more recently Shodokan Aikido, have provided such an inter-school event for their practitioners. These two points, which comprise part of Aikido's somewhat dys-functional social dynamics, have given rise to the disappointing increase of the many styles of Aikido. The Zantoppa Kai came into existence for the reason of tending to these problems.

As Kyuba-no-michi eventually evolved toward the codification and establishment of Bushido, Bushido was later reconstructed to form the identifying foundation of Budo. Today, Aikido has ostensibly become the preeminent modern identifier of this evolutionary process of Japanese Budo because of its aiki-oriented philosophy and how that philosophy informs its practitioners to make use of its respectable self-defense technical capabilities. Though Judo may have at one time imparted its philosophic force toward dominating as the preeminent modern philosophic identifier of that process, while not diminishing here its physio-technical uniqueness and large participant base worldwide, its sole reliance upon shiai in this new millennium to exemplify the possibility of a continuing evolution of higher consciousness is self-limiting. On the other hand, Aikido's physio-spiritual philosophic thrust is sometimes found to be faltering because of its dabbling in magico-religiosity, this being a problem particularly in the U.S.A. Today, Japan's people consider Judo as their most important national form of Budo; and its position as the premier combative sport in the Olympic Games heralds its physio-technical superiority worldwide. The International Olympic Committee's decision in February of 2013 C.E. to remove the Greco-Roman and Freestyle Wrestling events from its upcoming 2020 C.E. Olympic Games was partly a result of the popularity of Judo (and other combat sports of the Olympic Games), and partly a result of several of the criteria that the I.O.C. used to evaluate whether one sport or another could be included in the Olympic Games; these criteria include *1)* to what extent the sport's own internal attitudes allow full participation by both genders and *2)* the sport's general spectator popularity. Greco-Roman Wrestling had been included in the Olympic Games since its reestablishment in the year 1896 C.E. However, soon thereafter, many strong complaints from around the world lodged with the I.O.C. concerning its removal have succeeded in reestablishing the historic position of Greco-Roman Wrestling as an active sport in the Olympics Games. F.I.L.A. (the International Federation of Associated Wrestlers), an organization that guides and governs sport wrestling worldwide, quickly reworked its administrative rules to *1)* give all its wrestlers a role in decision-making, *2)* added two weight classes for women, and instituted rule changes to make wrestling competition *3)* easier to understand and *4)* more interesting for spectators by permitting more aggressive wrestling by increasing the possibility of a decisive win. Note that change number *4)* is one that arises from the affect of spectator interest, and it is likely that this very athlete/spectator phenomenon is the other aspect that both Morihei and Kisshomaru Ueshiba knew could affect the truth of their discipline.

Though Judo today is likely the preeminent *combative sport* of the Olympic Games, with the number of its practitioners worldwide surpassing that of Aikido by a ratio of approximately 5:1, its present collectively expressed philosophic ability (created by Jigoro Kano's principles of *seiryoku zen'yō* {maximum efficiency, minimum effort} and *jita kyōei* {mutual welfare and benefit}) to produce a further e-volution toward the type of philosophically inspired physio-spiritual evolution that Aikido has embraced is unlikely. Why? Judo's sport ethos is essentially combative, i.e., technical cunning merged with physical prowess directed toward a goal of victory over an opponent, frequently with an award given that exalts the primacy of such victory. Though made relatively safe by the keen insights of Jigoro Kano and his successors, and while instilling a comaraderie amongst judoka as well as a general respect for life, there is occasionally sensed by an impartial observer an aire of haughty egoism concerning that which is considered a judoka's superior ability to dominate any possible situation of physical contest; this dysfunctional aire is by no means limited to Judo, or to the martial arts. This author has experienced this type of egoism on a number of occasions, and two that come to mind that represent it best are these: On *one occasion* while teaching an Aikido course at a college (approximately twenty-five years ago), the training sessions were conducted in a small secondary gymnasium where from time-to-time an observer could view any class that was occurring there. Other classes officially scheduled consecutively by the college were also held therein, e.g., Fencing, Dance, Aerobics. When the gymnasium was not scheduled for an official class it was permitted by the college to be used by any enrolled student, and such was clearly stated with signage at the three entrance points to this gym. During one of my scheduled classes, there entered the gymnasium a young adult male in what looked to be a uniform of a Korean martial discipline; and soon thereafter, several other people in similar garb entered. They began to practice; this was distractive for my students. Not knowing whether this was the result of errant scheduling by the college, or just some fellow from another discipline who decided it would be 'ok' for him to practice there, I excused myself from the presence of my students and approached the young man, a black belt, who was beginning to instruct. I neared to the distance of approximately seven feet, reasonable ma-ai for this circumstance, and said to him, "Pardon me, sir. Are you aware that the gymnasium is scheduled at this time for an Aikido class?" At this point he turned to face me (having ignored my approach while continuing to teach his people). He replied, "It doesn't matter." From his response I immediately suspected that there was not a scheduling error and that he had simply taken it upon himself to hold unauthorized and impromptu training sessions with his people in the gymnasium. My Aikido students were attentively watching our interaction. I said, "It does matter, sir, as you and your people are interfering with the scheduled events of this class. If you do not have permission of the college to hold training here, then you should withdraw from the premises and return later." He postured briefly, seemingly readying himself for an attack, but a brief moment of reason seemingly entered his thought, as he responded with a stern voice saying, "I'd like to talk with you off the mat." I agreed and cautiously moved with him to the edge of the mat. All people were attentive. After a short and tension filled walk to the edge of the mat, which was near to a water fountain that was situated in an "L" shaped area of the wall, he turned quickly toward me and cornered me in this area. As I attempted to quickly to move out of the corner, he would position himself in front of me upon each turn to one side or the other, which were attempts on my part to effect a regaining of ma-ai. Several times he thumped me upon my chest with his forefinger, exclaiming quietly, "I should kick your ass right now." At this point, I was mostly out of the sight of my students due to the obscuration effect of the "L" shaped wall. I briefly contemplated taking the wrist of his hand with my left hand while performing a Shomenate technique with the other, but decided not to as the encounter would then be escalated into something more ugly. Instead, I told him with an assertive voice that "it is likely that the campus police was on the way, and that he would be a wise man indeed if he made the decision to depart." During this episode of finger thumping, I noticed a patch reflecting his association with a well-known Korean discipline. He threatened me several more times with offensive language of various 'flavor' as well as informing me that he was "a U.S. Navy officer and has never been so ordered to vacate a premise by a civilian underling." I suspect that out of his other thinking he knew that his own people, at the least, were viewing the events and that he could not reasonably justify actually "kicking my ass" if I did not act first. This unfortunate engagement lasted for a duration of about five minutes before he finally relented and decided to withdraw. He called his people to follow him out, all of them departing with various facial expressions. I returned to my students. A few of them were visibly shaken, as several of them had actually approached closer so that they could see what was occurring around the corner of that "L" shaped wall. I advised all of them to depart immediately to the college's student center through an opposite doorway while I notified the campus police (as they had not arrived). The next day I filed a complaint with the college's administrative office. Several days later the campus police contacted me with further details, including that this wayward teacher was in fact a U.S. Navy officer, that they had filed a complaint with the U.S. Navy, and that I could pursue further redress in civilian court. I chose not to do so. The class continued with no further interruptions. The exact reasons for this man's response, either evident or veiled, will never be known, as such an occurrence often erupts quickly from a place of submerged attitude or stress that has been conveyed upon the individual as a dysfunctional mental imprint by the very discipline or developmental circumstances in which the he or she has been nurtured. He never returned to apologize. A *second occurrence* that characterizes this type of egoism was one that emerged from the personality of a well-known U.S. teacher of both Aikido and Judo, who is now deceased. During an Aikido seminar that this author attended in the mid nineteen-eighties, when two important Japanese Aikido senseis had been invited to travel to the U.S.A. to teach, this aforementioned U.S. teacher while discussing the importance of recognizing how to use the movement theory of *"off balance and recovery,"* digressed for several minutes from his presentation to inject numerous comments about the superiority of Judo over Aikido, and that a judoka in contest with an aikidoka of a similar ranking (i.e., belt level) would "whoop and clean the mat with" the latter. This occurred in the presence of some seventy or so Aikidoka as well as the Japanese senseis. Understandably, I was taken aback and disappointed by such comments, as rather than being perceived as a stimulus to thoroughly understand how to make use of an aggressor's off-balance and subsequent recover attempt, Aikido's usefulness as a functional and valid means of self-defense was being besmirched, and, in fact, as I learned later during this seminar, a certain extent of embarrassment as well as uncertainty about the functionality of their discipline was experienced by many of its attendees. From this latter incident and several others like it, one of which is briefly discussed in the *Autobiographical Sketch* at the end of this book, I began to understand that it might be necessary to find a different Aikido organization with which to associate. Obviously, even in people who make what outwardly seems like the proper behavioral gestures toward embracing a pursuit of higher consciousness, combative disciplines can *sometimes* imbed counterproductive bias, appalling haughtiness, and a willingness to commit illegal aggression; this is likely the main problem that both Morihei and Kisshomaru Ueshiba considered when they decided not to embrace a competitive event for Aikikai Aikido. Notwithstanding, this is not to imply that a practitioner of Aikido is without flaw, and, also, this is not to say that a competitive or cooperative event cannot be organized where few or no such behavioral problems emerge (ideally). The *first* and *second* of these negative behaviors can also emerge for an aikidoka, but arising typically from a spiritual self-deluding. The *third* behavior manifests only rarely because Aikido's techni-philosophical approach to self-defense is aligned with non-aggression. Remember, Jigoro Kano at one time, upon viewing Aiki-budo at Ueshiba's dojo in Ayabe, declared that this forerunner of Aikido was indeed an embodiment of Kano's ideal martial philosophy. Egoism of the type outlined previously, and where the martial, self-defense, or sport discipline permits, either carelessly or purposeful by the means of its activities and awards, the expression of such, is counterproductive toward further personal and societal evolution. When considering that which is necessary for a successful self-defense outcome, a self-defense discipline must embrace a balance between an individual's bodily integrity or safety and the actual mental and physical techniques employed to achieve the former. For a marital discipline (only to be used in a theater of war) there should be only one concern, that of opponent or enemy elimination or capture; but, for a self-defense discipline (to be used in the theater of everyday civilian life) there is a need to temper a defender's response in accordance with their prevailing cultural mores and given civil laws. In the civilian realm, those disciplines that have a tendency toward implementing harsher methods to accomplish defense against an aggressor, and where these exhibit more of a martial attitude as their collective aire rather than a reasonable concern (in relation to the nature of violence during a self-defense encounter) about excessive or unnecessary force and injury to an aggressor, are unsuitable for bringing about further evolution toward a higher, collectively realized, human consciousness, i.e., less human strife and suffering.

Other Japanese martial arts or martial derived sport activities that have been popularized in the U.S.A. and Europe are Karatedo (focusing on the use of fist, foot, and weapons, e.g., nunchaku, sai, kama, bō), Kendo (with a focus on striking with a wooden sword, both shinai and bokken), and Jodo (with its focus upon the use of a wooden staff, the jō, and bokken). All these would have a difficult problem to overcome if the leading proponets of each attempted to moderate sufficiently their martial aspects to somehow represent a further evolution of higher consciousness. Why? Because the obvious intent of the use of one or several weapons (including the use of many harsh and often unnecessary fist and foot techniques) is to severely incapacitate or kill an opponent. Why? Because the martial empty-hand (kara-te) techniques and weapons were designed specifically for warfare combat. Contrast this, then, to the method of *appropriate-for-the-circumstance* self-defense behavior, like that conveyed by the principles of *jita kyōei* (mutual welfare and benefit) and *aiki* (harmonized energy and spirit). For example, a katana's purpose as a tool is directly attached to severely damaging or quickly killing an opponent -- its use is not like that of a machete's, the primary purpose of which is that of cutting through tough vegetation or brush. Martial weapons and techniques are designed to facilitate a specific warfare combat purpose, and martial attitude and technique is rarely suitable for the non-military or non-police citizen, who are the large majority of people. To carelessly disseminate martial attitude and technique within a society is to inseminate the minds of its people with wrong mental attitudes and skills, the outcome of which can only be citizens who are in some way or another psychologically edgy and quite disposed to take offense at the slightest provocation. Remember, from Chapter VII, "*Every tool has its specific function, and it is not unreasonable to propose that when used for its intended purpose it manifests a certain object-oriented quality that could be loosely termed its 'spirit.'*" It is important to note, however, that Karatedo and the design of its weapons emerged largely as a defensive response by the people of Okinawa to defend their lives, property, and land from marauding Japanese warriors during Japan's feudal era. Notwithstanding, Karatedo's linear techniques (punch, strike, kick), combined with its weapons use, in spite of a definitive code of behavior[1] that cautions its practitioners against offensive use of these, is somewhat problematic as a torchlight that could light the path toward further development of an even higher collective, not personal, human consciousness or societal awareness. One can ascertain the validity of this assessment by evaluating the effect of a purposefully or accidentally well-delivered punch, kick, or strike with or without a weapon, especially when employed as a first line of 'defense' toward self-protection without considering other options or being trained in other self-defense skills that make possible other options. This type of 'self-defense' response can result in the unnecessary injury or death of an aggressor, where such an outcome during the threat neutralization process can be viewed by an incidental observer, a family member, or a court as wrong and or unjustifiable. The problem is evident when taking a close look at the unnecessary injuries and deaths which result from person vs. person fights or citizen vs. police encounters where, when scrutizing these, many show that this type of harmful outcome is often the result of only one strike to the head, neck, or chest. However, this is not to say that there might not be a valid situation where such techniques or weapons are justifiable. Even in Aikido there is taught atemi; but, the use of such should only occur rarely, e.g., when there arises a situation where several aggressors attack. After careful scrutiny and contemplation, it can be realized that the martial arts of Judo (or Jujutsu),

Karatedo (all its styles), Kendo (or Kenjutsu), though respectable in the context of their martial heritage and usefulness in combat or combative sport, cannot offer quite the same type of personal behavioral or spiritual achievement and or societal progress as Aikido because the techni-philosophical characteristics of these other disciplines have a built-in effect that limits the extent to which a practitioner thereof can further move toward the refinement of self in way that is useful for the further strengthening of a peaceful as well as productive civil society; this being a result of the time period in which they evovled. Shoji Nishio, 8ᵗʰ Dan Aikikai, informed us that *"O-Sensei's methods were completely different compared to those of the classical martial arts. His way was completely the opposite of the direction of other Japanese martial arts. If these arts don't change their direction, I think they will end up becoming useless."*[2] However, I'm not saying that these have not made significant contributions toward higher personal or collectively valued societal awareness, for they have. And, yes, it could be argued that Aikido might not be that torchlight either, because it is not positioned well on the philosophical high ground due to the fact that it also uses weapons (primarily bokken and jo) during training sessions. One of the difficulties in aligning with a position of philosophical loftiness is that an aikidoka (or a practitioner of another discipline) must develop a certain proficiency with certain weapons and methods of attack in order to learn how to skillfully defend against an aggressor who may make use of such; the difference is, of course, that the weapons used in Aikido are largely for the reason of learning necessary fundamental body movements, and later, secondarily, to learn how to defend empty-handedly against an aggressor who wields them. As contrast, for example, Kenjutsu makes use of a sword with a martial purpose to immediately incapacitate or kill, typically a severe and obscene outcome. Of course, even an edged weapon can be used to control or chastise without seriously injuring or killing an aggressor, but, this is not the weapon's primary purpose. Ideally, when demonstrating Aikido's technical connection to Kenjutsu or Kendo with a bokken or katana in hand, a master aikidoka sensei (particularly those who have Kenjutsu expertise) should not teach their students in a way that is approving of its use for offense and killing; when demonstrating Aikido to the public, care should be taken only to show empty-hand evasion and defense against these or other weapons. In our modern era where high-speed ballistic weaponry is so prevalent, it is essential that an aikidoka learn how to defend against this threat, too; though in some Aikido schools defense a-gainst guns is taught, this type of defense should not include the use of a gun as the primary method of defending against the threat of a gun. These are difficult considerations.

If Aikido as considered in the mind of the reader does not fail on the account that it too makes use of a few weapons, or, more to the point, does not fail to provide the necessary philosophical as well as technical backbone to act as that torchlight, there is cer-tainly yet another problem that could cause it to further disconnect itself from this particularly important role. When all those Aikido factions that claim the principle of aiki as their underlying prin-ciple[3] are not unified as a cohesive force, that which constitutes Aikido's guiding light may flicker, die out, and fail to light the path of truth.[4]

I suppose that a "Vulcan nerve pinch," if such were possible, could serve as the best example of self-defense evolution. Interest-ingly, perhaps Judo's Shime-waza (breath and or blood flow con-striction techniques) are the best example of such technique that can be used against an active, ever-moving aggressor whose intent is the perpetration of violence upon a defender; any aikidoka who is serious about self-defense should study these. Though a single fist or other strike to the head of an aggressor can completely incapa-citate them, it can also, either intentionally or accidentally, perma-nently damage the organs of the head or kill. Most truculent ag-gressors are very difficult to subdue because they are unwilling to resign themselves to the fate of surrender or retreat and therefore will not cease and desist until physically made to do so. Study this problem diligently.

The Zantoppa Kai exists as a small gathering of Aikido practi-tioners who are dedicated to maintaining a clearly perceived and commonly held understanding of those aspects of the martial, self-defense, philosophical, and social realms that, when brought prop-erly together, elucidate exactly the unique foundational essence of Aikido while neither neglecting nor refuting the need for functional self-defense in order to provide an aikidoka with a unique path to-ward further self-improvement, thus contributing to a higher, i.e., humanely oriented, social consciousness. Differing emphases occur from one Aikido group to another, largely a result of both personal need and cultural values. In this writer's opinion, *the most egre-*

Understanding Aikido

gious error of emphasis in an Aikido course of study occurs when its core philosophy is so skewed toward *magico-religiosity*, typically by the sensei, that what emerges is nothing more than spiritual fakery, often associated with the characteristics of cultism. *Second* to this are those groups that practice quasi-aiki with the idea of developing a *holistic* approach to life while feigning realism in their performance of self-defense technique. *Lastly*, some groups practice without systemization of Aikido's basic techniques, thus frequently obscuring its basic technical principles. A result of this latter problem can be partial group-to-group incompatibility when there arises an opportunity for a group of one style to practice with that of a different style; and, for the aikidoka in training, another is the slower apprehension of how to make its techniques work functionally in a self-defense encounter. Aikido groups with characteristics that place them wihin any of these three categories can obscure or partially negate Aikido's usefulness as a unique self-realization path toward a higher understanding of life; such realization, which only occur when there is an elevation of consciousness, requires serious consideration and treatment of functional self-defense. Of course, there are those Aikido groups and persons, indeterminate in number, who do much better than this. It is important to recognize that Aikido's factionalization is a type of discord that is, of itself, contrary to its own lofty philosophical ideals.

Zantotsu is an older martial precept from a past age in Japanese Bushido. However, this precept's martial significance is yet part of the technical basis, along with that of *datotsu*,[5] of modern Budo, or Bujutsu; especially in Kenjutsu, Kendo, and some Aikido styles that take a careful look at the importance of functional self-defense ability. However, interpreted from a viewpoint of non-martial philosophy, zantotsu can also mean to *remain and engage* life, never to become 'shackled' by the challenges in life, rather, always facing these with vigor and resolve in order to forge ahead and overcome.[6] A good part of the guiding philosophy of the Zantotsu Ryu and the Zantoppa Kai is based herein.

The Zantoppa Kai is an attempt, as promulgated by its adherents, to greatly diminish the several aforementioned problems that exist within the realm of Aikido today, yet remaining steadfast in a clear understanding of the foundational essence of Aikido -- to Protect, Sustain, and Enhance life.

Karl Geis Seminar at Poulsbo Dojo ~ 1985
Poulsbo, Washington U.S.A.

Standing, left to right:
E. Patricia Alden (Ikkyu), Michael Spiller (Ikkyu), Jån J. Sunderlin
(Shodan, Tomiki Ryu Aikido), Karl Geis Shihan (Fugakukai Aikido),
John ? (Rokkyu)

Kneeling, left to right:
Allen Schaffer (Ikkyu) and Thomas Sheehy (Ikkyu).

(Mr. Thomas Sheehy sensei, today, is ranked 6th Dan Kihara
Aikido, a derivation of Shodokan Aikido, by Fugakukai International)

(Photographed by Becky Morey, Gokyu)

Raab Park Mid-Sommerfest Aikido Demonstration ~ 1987
Poulsbo, Washington, U.S.A.

On deck left to right:
Jån Sunderlin (Nidan, Tomiki Ryu Aikido), Tom Sheehy (Shodan),
and children.

Raab Park Mid-Sommerfest Aikido Demonstration ~ 1987
Poulsbo, Washington, U.S.A.

On mat:
Jån Sunderlin as tori (Nidan), Tom Sheehy[7] as uke (Shodan).

Zantoppa Kai Aikido Directors ~ 1990
Bremerton Dojo, Washington, U.S.A.

Standing, left to right:
Jolene S. Cantrell (Shodan) & John White (Yondan).

Seated, left to right:
Jån J. Sunderlin (Shidosha, Z.T.K.A.) & William Gregory (Shodan).

Bremerton Dojo Children's Class Demonstration ~ 1998
Bremerton, Washington, U.S.A.

On mat left to right:
Jån Sunderlin (Shidosha, Z.T.K.A.), Chris Mills (Shodan, Z.T.K.A.).

Children seated on the mat left to right, front row:
Bracken B. & Lauren H.

Children seated on the mat left to right, rear row:
Michael B. & Jennifer P.

(Mr. Chris Mills, today, is also ranked 3rd Dan
Aikikai style by the United States Aikido Federation)

Zantoppa Kai Aikido Formal Sitting ~ 2007
Illahee Dojo, Washington, U.S.A.

Standing, left to right:
Shannon Rauch (Ikkyu) and daughter, Donna Clayton (Gokyu),
Larry Clayton (Yonkyu), Omar Liripio (Ikkyu), Curtis Cameron
(Ikkyu), Lachlan S. (Rokyu).

Seated, left to right:
Sijer Harder (Nidan), Mark Niebuhr (Nidan), Max Sadtler (Shodan,
both Aikido and Jodo), Jån J. Sunderlin (Shidosha), John Copeland
(Shodan), and Hunter Morrigan (Shodan).

(Photo by Mr. Terry Harder, Shodan)

The Reason for the Zantoppa Kai

[1] Importantly, "Karatedo is not only the acquisition of certain defensive skills but also the mastering of the arts of being a good and honest member of society," "The great virtues of karate are prudence and humility," "If your hand goes forth, withhold your anger. If your anger goes forth, withhold your hand," and "The ultimate aim of karate lies not in victory nor defeat, but in the perfection of the character of its participants." Also, see the *Twenty Principles (Niju Kun)* of Karatedo as stated by Gichin Funakoshi.

[2] See the article entitled *Interview with Shoji Nishio* by Stanley Pranin. Aiki News magazine; Article #91 and #92, 1992.

[3] That is, the definition of *aiki* collectively given by the statements and actions of Morihei Ueshiba, Kisshomaru Ueshiba, and Moriteru Ueshiba through decades of evolution arising out of the efforts of the Zaidan Hojin Aikikai. See Chapter III.

[4] Gichin Funakoshi, founder of Karatedo, recognized factionalization as a problem, too. See his book, *Karatedo: My Way of Life*.

[5] See the *Glossary* for a definition of *datotsu*.

[6] See the book entitled *Fighting to Win* by David J. Rodgers; Double & Company, Inc., Garden City, New York, hardcover, first edition, 1984.

[6] Today, Tom Sheehy is 6th Dan Kihara Aikido, bestowed by the Fugakukai.

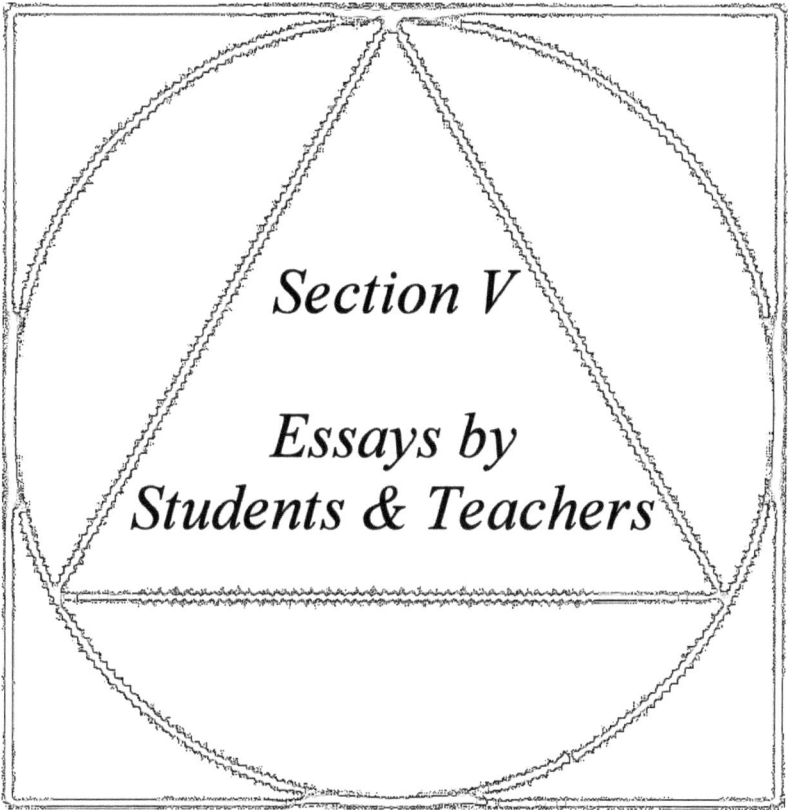

Section V

Essays by
Students & Teachers

Student & Teacher Essays

The short essays found in this chapter may be useful for the reader because they express varied Aikido knowledge and perceptions. The first essay has been written by a Zantoppa Kai advanced Aikido student of Dan grade who has entered the Zantoppa Kai Teaching Program, while the second and third essays have been written by Dan grade students who have chosen the Zantoppa Kai Self-Defender Program path of study. The use of quotation marks in this section is different than that outlined in the Preface.

Gozo Shioda & the Development of Yoshinkan Aikido

by Mark Niebuhr, Nidan
Zantoppa Kai AikidoTeaching Program

Yoshinkan Aikido is considered to be a "hard style" by many who practice Aikido. The methods of training and practice are closer to the pre W.W. II style teaching of Morihei Ueshiba, founder of Aikido. This essay is a brief look at the founding and development of Yoshinkan Aikido.

The founder of Yoshinkan Aikido was Gozo Shioda, born on September 9, 1915, in Shinjuku, Tokyo. Gozo Shoida's father, Seiichi Shioda, was a prominent pediatrician at this time, and he had constructed a dojo at is home in Yotsuya, Tokyo; his father's dojo was named Yoshinkan. Shioda senior had invited various teachers to demonstrate as well as teach there, in his dojo. It was here that Gozo Shioda became interested in the relatively new discipline of Judo. Shioda caught on very quickly and soon he had advanced to 3rd dan. The young Shioda like to challenge police judo teachers in order to test his technique, to push his learning and skill to the limit. Gozo also studied the sword art of Kendo.

In 1932, at the age of 17, Gozo was sent by his father to watch a class taught by a man named Morihei Ueshiba. Ueshiba's Kobukan dojo was a unique endeavor as practice there occurred only by invitation. Some martial artists considered practice at the Kobukan dojo "exclusive."

During Shioda's first visit he watched Ueshiba throw his opponents around easily and seemingly without effort. He was "certain" that what he'd seen was a fraud, little more than choreography. Ueshiba invited the young Shioda to come up and try out his Judo skill on him. Shioda found himself flying through the air and hitting the ground headfirst -- he was immediately convinced that this was not choreography.

The next day, May 24, 1932, Shioda joined the Kobukan dojo and began training under Ueshiba as an uchi deshi (resident disciple). Shioda would end up assisting Morihei Ueshiba in teaching Aiki-budo at the Nakano and Toyama military schools. Shioda studied under Ueshiba until 1941, when he also graduated from Takushoku University.

1941 was a year that contained several important events in his life. Shioda would be married to Nobuko; he would uke for Ueshiba in a demonstration before the imperial family. Also, he would leave the Kobukan dojo to go to work as a [*military*] secretary to General Hata, in China; Japan was preparing to enter W.W. II. At this point in time, Aiki-budo was being shaped, not yet Aikido but not exactly Daito-ryu Jujutsu. Aiki-budo would not fully evolve into Aikido, thus officially named, until the follow year, 1942.

In November of 1942, Shioda traveled on [*military*] business from China to Taiwan, Celebes, and Borneo. In January of 1943, Shioda arrived in Pontianak, Borneo. Here, by happenstance, he met an old college classmate, Nobuo Nishi, who had already been in Pontianak for about a year. Nishi showed Shioda around the area. Shioda had traveled to Borneo to take part in a joint corporate endeavor and he was to fill the position of Director of General Affairs & Accounting Management of the Taiwan Colonization Company. The other end of this endeavor was the Taiwan Tanning Company. [*Taiwan had figured prominently in Japan's colonization effort as both an economic resource and military base, with many thousands of non-Japanese Taiwanese fighting for the Japanese cause during W.W. II. See history of Taiwan, 1895 thru 1945. J.J.S.*] Two days after arriving, Shioda became infected with Dengue Fever. Dengue has similar symptoms as those of Malaria. No medication, other than aspirin, was available, and it took only about one week for Shioda to recover from this illness. After recovery, he set himself to the necessary task of finding housing, which was under the control of the Japanese Naval Civil Administration. The president of the company for which Shioda worked, a Mr. Omori, introduced him to two people, a Mr. Shigeeda, Director of Naval Civil Administration, and a Mr. Masaki, Director of Public Law in Pontianak; these two officials later were instrumental in providing circumstances that per-mitted Shioda to begin teaching Aikido there. Later, while having friendly conversation with Shigeeda and Masaki, Shioda learned that Masaki held a 5th Dan in Judo. During this conversation he mentioned Aikido and his training with Morihei Ueshiba and gave a short demonstration. Masaki was duly impressed and indicated that he would like to begin learning this Aikido. They set a time for the next day. Shigeeda wanted also to join the lesson. Now, Shioda had his first two students since leaving Ueshiba's dojo. After becoming acquainted with these two government officials, matters of life went well. Shioda's request for housing was promptly met.

After the end of W.W. II, in May of 1946, Shioda returned to Japan and spent a couple of months at Ueshiba's country residence, the Iwama dojo and farm, to regain his composure and strength. During this time he continued to teach Aikido for Ueshiba at many different police departments. Since the war, Aikido had changed considerably, a result of Ueshiba's changing attitude as to how to present it in the new post-war era. Shioda was uneasy with these changes and wanted to teach the "old ways," those of Aiki-budo.

Shioda sensei returned to Tokyo in order to work for the Kokan Steel Company, where he was invited to teach Aikido to its employees. During this period of his life, he remained in close contact with the police martial art teachers from his younger years. Naturally this led to traveling around demonstrating to various Japanese police forces the effectiveness of Aikido technique for the control in apprehension situations. Of course, this evolved, of functional necessity, a specific police oriented Aikido-like curriculum. Included among the many police agencies which engaged his expertise were the Tokyo Metropolitan Police and the Kidotai (Riot Police).

In 1954, after a ban on the general teaching of martial arts was lifted (This had been implemented after W.W. II), the Nippon Sogo Budo Association sponsored the first post-war martial arts demonstration. Shioda was awarded the grand prize for best performance.

This demonstration and award was given in the presence of approximately 15,000 spectators.

In 1955, Yoshinkan Aikido was officially established. Shioda sensei was awarded 9th Dan in 1961 by Morihei Ueshiba. In 1965, the Yoshinkan dojo was built. In 1984, the International Martial Arts Federation awarded Shioda sensei with 10th Dan along with the title of Meijin (Grand Master). On July 17th, 1994, Gozo Shioda passed away. He was 78 years old, survived by his wife Nobuko and by his three sons, Tetsutaro, Takahisa, and Yasuhisa. Yasuhisa was born November 15, 1952 and is now the Director of the Yoshinkan Aikido Dojo, located at Kami Ochiai near the Shinjuku district in central Tokyo.

Gozo Shioda saw the need to systematize[1] and name the techniques of Aikido. This is one important distinguishing aspect of Yoshinkan Aikido. Another is that the *hakama* garment is only worn after reaching 4th Dan. When teaching, he was known for always taking an active roll in his classes.

Yoshinkan Aikido is one of the largest and strongest sub-styles of Aikido. It is used by many law enforcement agencies for its non-injurious restraint and apprehension techniques. During Yoshinkan training, the emphasis is on basic fundamental movements, timing, and solid basic techniques as well as gaining philosophical insight about how one should best conduct himself in life. Another important point of emphasis is that of learning defense against all other martial arts through the study of their various types of techniques and attacks. Atemi waza (hitting body techniques) figures prominently in the study of Yoshinkan; this includes the use of kicks, elbow strikes, back-fist strikes, and punches.

Yoshinkan Aikido retains Aikido's general philosophy of minimal violence by focusing study toward determining what comprises improper or unwarranted physical interaction during a self-defense or police apprehension scenario. An approximate translation of the term *Yoshinkan* is a *house to cultivate spirit*.

[1] He was not alone in understanding the need for this. Kenji Tomiki did similarly.

Does Aikidō Really Work?

by Curtis Cameron, Shodan
Zantoppa Kai Aikido Self-defender Program

In today's world of televised combative sport, MMA (mixed martial arts) and cage fighting have brought a new level of violence and savagery into the public sphere. The use of weight training for enhanced strength and body mass, kickboxing in the standup game, and the "grind and pound" aspects on the mat have created a truly vicious spectacle of violence. In truth, it is obvious that the attitudes and techniques used by the participants in these spectacles can function well for real-world aggression or self-defense encounters.

With the sophistication of today's training methods and the incredible revenues generated, a portion of which is used to finance new fighters with even more enhanced training, MMA is evolving into a commodity of ultra-violence for "entertainment" that is being perpetrated upon, consumed, and absorbed by many people, thus emerging a new sociological facet of the public's collective "consciousness." If a regular "Joe" happened to be assaulted by an aggressor who was skilled in executing this type of violence (and there are more of this type out there than ever before), he would find it necessary to defend with attitude and techniques that would result in bodily damage to the aggressor in order to realize a successful defense. For those people who attempt to maintain civility, and here I'm speaking mostly about men and to men, this is part of the ugliness of today's street fight. But, how does this negative-trending, probably deleterious social phenomenon affect Aikido?

Aikido, the *harmonized energy way*, suffers significant disrepute amongst numerous practitioners of other martial arts because so many of Aikido's teachers have rendered ineffectual the self-defense quality of many of its techniques with misunderstood perceptions and applications of the difficult-to-qualify idea of "ki." Claiming to be able to teach people to defend themselves with wishful or feel-good thinking, they attract all types of people who are not violently inclined, yet who may have a real interest in self-defense, but are, unknowingly, led down a path that is likely to end in defeat if ever confronted with real malice and violence. They mistakenly believe that they can defend themselves because they are unaware that what they learned is either technically weak or missing something entirely; but suppressed somewhere in their mentality they still have insecurity about their self-defense ability, and from time to time via a momentary glimpse into their psyche they wonder, "Does Aikido really work?" Today, the innumerable discussions that concern the effectiveness of Aikido as a self-defense art all seem to revolve around this question. Aikido's main purpose is to provide a student with a path of learning that makes use of the concept of aiki (harmonized energy) toward the development of functional yet humanely oriented self-defense ability.

Morihei Ueshiba, the founder of Aikido, was a skilled martial artist who had spent a lifetime studying and teaching Daito-ryu Jujutsu as well as other martial arts. He had gained plenty of experience from competitive and oppositional situations as well as from teaching his students how to control or neutralize an aggressor through striking, kicking, and throwing techniques; yet, he was ever searching for his ultimate Budo. After years of training, teaching others, and experiencing conflict, he realized that the only way to stop violence is not to engage in or teach violence. In the end, Ueshiba incorporated techniques from several Jujutsu and Kenjutsu martial disciplines in order to create his own mixed, ethics-based self-defense discipline of stunning grace and power.

Over his lifetime, Ueshiba had several spiritual experiences which helped him transform his ideas of Budo; it was after one of these during W.W. II when he realized that *"To smash, injure, or destroy is the worst thing a human being can do. The real Way of a Warrior is to prevent such slaughter -- it is the Art of Peace, the power of love."*[1] The import of this quote is that it conveys a social idea with which any truly civilized person can agree. In the majority of civilized communities, both past and present, real violence is shunned, the perpetrators are feared, and lawful action taken to rid the community of such anti-social behavior. Why then does it occur that Aikido is often ridiculed in the martial arts world when presenting this very reasonable and obvious ideal? The ignominy that such ridicule may, from time-to-time, impart to those who practice Aikido emerges from the collective summation of the inability of those who practice to connect its philosophy with functional self-defense ability; i.e., when faced with the difficulty of a self-defense encounter, the failure to implement the philosophy of aiki so that it produces a successful self-defense outcome!

Aikido is not a martial art. Aikido is an art of peace. But, this does not mean that the technical underpinnings of Aikido are weak. When embracing the study of a philosophical lofty discipline such as Aikido, it is necessary to develop a thorough understanding of the influence that its philosophy has upon its technical curriculum in order to develop the correct attitude and functional skill that, when brought into action, can ensure a defender's safety during a self-defense incident. As a comparison, a police officer carries a pistol, but he/she may first use tactical conversation, pepper spray, a taser, or a baton rather than shooting someone; meaning, he/she doesn't often go to the point of drawing their pistol and shooting unless the circumstances require it. It is obvious that the vast majority of police officers do not deploy a gun as their first action toward maintaining law and order and keeping the peace. Ideally, police officers are trained to bring to bear the least amount of force necessary in the performance of their duty toward maintaining law and order in civilized society. Though officers of the peace do have conferred upon them by law a certain authority to use deadly force, the theory of law enforcement proposes a minimum use of force, ideally, and only to move toward the use of deadly force when a situation specifically indicates the need to do so. For example, an errant citizen is brandishing a weapon and is about to or is using it in a death-dealing manner. A police officer responding to such a situation would certainly quickly assess the dynamic circumstances, take cover while deploying his gun, and probably neutralize the threat.

Remember, Morihei Ueshiba stated in his Aikido training rules that *"Aikido decides life and death in a single strike, so students must carefully follow the instructor's teaching and not compete to see who is the strongest.*"[2] Doesn't this suggest that Aikido techniques, if executed properly, are effective in defending against an aggressor's attack? I think it does! Aikido techniques are ultimately, but ideally, the most effective techniques because they propose making use of the laws of physics while guided by a certain set of ethics.

Yes, some Aikido styles incorporate "atemi" or strikes that are absolutely devastating, these being similarly made us of by a wide variety of other self-defense disciplines or martial arts. The difference being that the atemi used in these styles is emphasized as a method of creating off-balance in an aggressor in order that a technique can be applied more easily toward the goal of neutralizing the attack and subduing him less violently, rather than visiting upon him unnecessary bodily damage at the very first opportunity. Palm strikes to the chin or nose, fist strikes to various sensitive body areas, hand-blade strikes to the neck or face, trips and low kicks, joint locks, throws, and chokes and strangles, all are part of Aikido's technical repertoire and may be used a self-defense situation if the circumstances require it; all these are used in MMA today in one form or another. However, several of the mainstream Aikido styles do not train their students to become competent in the use of atemi or how to respond to the physical and psychological energies that erupt during a self-defense encounter. Ironically and sadly, *many aikidoka have been seduced by Aikido's message of peace to the point where relatively few of them could successfully defend themselves.*

When presented with a situation of violence, and arising out of the need to arrive safely at the end of a self-defense encounter, a person may find it necessary to employ techniques that result in damage to an aggressor in order to stop the latter's attack. If the circumstances of the self-defense situation permit, one object that should be inculcated in an Aikido-trained defender is to not damage the aggressor unnecessarily. Rather, an aikidoka should be trained with the specific intent to defend in a manner that visits only minimal bodily damage to an aggressor; that is, to do no more than is necessary to protect one's own bodily integrity.

One trouble with Aikido in today's world is not a question of the functionality of its techniques, rather it is with the perception held by martial artists and street-wise fighters as to the value of its philosophical basis when an improper understanding of that basis weakens or invalidates its technical prowess and thereby misleads its practitioners. Those people who understand the importance of maintaining civility and peace in a society frequently lean toward training in the types of schools whose ideas embrace or have a feeling of humanitarianism and creativeness, which latter part makes possible the emergence of certain brands of spirituality. It is here, in this type of school, that they hope to find kindred folk who embrace a similar attitude toward life; believing that this or that "humanistic" approach will tend to dissipate human concerns about fear and violence. People who are thusly disposed are never entirely able to remove themselves from awareness of social violence. As a result, they will attempt to manage this part of their personal reality by engaging practice in the "softer" self-defense disciplines (such as Aikido or Tai Chi) but will seek out among these only those schools that tend to be divorced from the hard reality of what is required to defend against an aggressor's attack. Much of mainstream Aikido has been slowly transformed (by people with such an attitude) from a viable, dynamic, humane form of self-defense into what seems to be a discipline that is most suitable for subjective spiritual excursions or dancing and has little to do with or concern about self-defense. The aikidoka who are mentally inclined in this way seem to believe that the study of their *Aikido* will magically confer upon them a functional inculcation of self-defense skill without having to embrace the hard training conditions that are necessary to develop it. If a supernatural conference of self-defense skill is not their expectation, then it can be said that they are studying for other reasons, such as physical fitness, comaraderie, or to experience that part of aiki, separated from self-defense concerns, that might emerge for them a gathering of non-self-defense derived esoteric knowledge. These latter are not necessarily to be frowned upon. However, true Aikido does not neglect the development of functional self-defense skill.

When subjected to violent encounter, force is involved, and that force must be controlled. Sometimes when in a fight-or-flee situation, one cannot easily flee and the only option is to fight and defend. When doing so, it's often necessary to actually hit and hurt someone to get them off balance so that they can be more easily thrown or subdued, thus neutralizing the aggressor's ability to continue their attack. People who exist in a civil and peaceful environment, where life is supposed to be, ideally, with relatively few violent incidences, often mentally push aside the evidence of violence within their society. It is out of this type of behavior that a new but weaker breed of aikidoka have emerged, one that seems to require little or no consideration of how to handle a truly violent self-defense situation. For such aikidoka, only soft, flowing movements -- where through a projection of a difficult-to-prove quantity called *ki energy* is an aggressor magically thrown, where never again does the aggressor rise up to reinitiate yet another attack -- are acceptable to them. Self-deceived in a fantasy environment where they can 'defend' themselves without having to experience the hard training circumstances necessary to develop functional self-defense skill, such aikidoka are programmed for failure if they are ever confronted by an aggressor who physically attacks them. Is such a condition to be considered as practice and skill development that represents true Aikido? Unfortunately, this is often the perception of Aikido that is held in the thoughts of many martial artists and other observers.

Ai-ki-do, the "harmony spirit way" or the "harmony energy way" means something specific, but something other than the sole pursuit of a quirky spirituality. In a defense situation, one has two choices:

1) Meet violence with equal violence and compete to see who is strongest; or
2) "Harmonize" with, i.e., merge with the aggressor's movements and make use of their energy to ensure your victory.

However, if someone attacks with great force, a defender cannot often send him gently on his way to contemplate the error of his ways because the intensity of the aggressor's attack must be met, controlled, and dissipated in such a way that it can be entirely neutralized; this typically ends up requiring that the defender damage the aggressor using techniques of unique conception and effectiveness. Aikido has such techniques, but depending on the style and dojo, the necessary teacher/student attitude and technical skill that is required to implement them effectively for a self-defense encounter might not be taught.

Generally, the goal of training in Aikido should not only be to create a person who can successfully defend against another person's attack but also to transform the student into a person who acts to protect, sustain, and enhance life; where the latter is represented by the internalization of aiki-aligned teachings and techniques that produce a more humane self-defense behavior. In the words of my sensei, Jån Sunderlin, this can be summed up, ideally, as:

"By the means of aiki-aligned self-defense skill, when you find yourself in a self-defense encounter, do no unnecessary harm to the aggressor while ensuring your safety."

It is this philosophy, innate in true Aikido training, that over time creates a true aikidoka -- someone who is fit and uniquely strong, flexible and fluid, who when in a self-defense encounter has the ability to block or parry and merge with the energy of any attack thereby avoiding injury, and, if necessary, to strike and apply technique toward subduing the aggressor, all performed instinctually, without an intent to commit unnecessary harm.

Yes, Aikido concerns self-defense; and yes, it can be astoundingly effective when properly performed. Nonetheless, it's also about self-realization. It's about facing up to weaknesses and diminishing or removing the affect of these by developing new strengths; it's about creating better people who act out of a slightly better set of ethics (more humane); and, in doing so, create a better world one person at a time.

Does Aikido really work for self-defense? When considering its technical functionality for self-defense, a conditional "Yes"; the caveat being that an aikidoka must embrace the development of skills that are useful toward achieving a certain functional defense ability that can, when in a situation where they must protect their life from an aggressor's attack, ensure their safety while not doing unnecessary harm to an aggressor.

[1] See, **The Art Of Peace** by John Stevens; published by Shambhala Publications, Inc., paperback, sixth printing, 1992.

[2] See, **The Spirit of Aikido** (Aikido no Kokoro) by Kisshomaru Ueshiba. Translated by Taitetsu Unno; Kodansha International, Ltd., paperback edition, first printing, 1987.

My Personal Development

by Hunter F. Morrigan, Shodan
Zantoppa Kai Aikido Self-defender Program

I first sought training in Aikido in 1993 at the urging of a friend. I had heard on the news that several children had been shot by a gunman while swimming in a community pool and in that same year the country saw unprecedented violence as a result of shootings that took place in schools. I was nearly paralyzed by fright at the thought of allowing my eleven year old daughter go to school in the morning and endured heightened anxiety for most of the day until she was home safely. I shared with a friend that my mental situation was threatening to develop into something of an obsession, and I feared giving in to the desire to keep my child home from school indefinitely. My friend suggested I seek out an Aikido class. I knew very little about martial arts, although a fellow student in college had attempted to teach me some Judo moves at one time. My friend was hoping to give me some sense of control over my own safety and to overcome the sense of helplessness and victimization of individuals, particularly women, which often develops in a violent culture.

I looked in the telephone book for an Aikido class and there were only a couple to be found among the adverts for Taekwondo, Karate, and Kung Fu. I investigated the school nearest my home and signed both myself and my eleven-year-old daughter up for classes. The concept of taking the energy of the attacker and using it to deflect or transform the attack appealed to my karmic sense. The skills were fairly slow to emerge, as I discovered I did not have a highly developed sense of proprioception (concept of one's position in space arising from stimuli in one's own body); I also am not a very visual learner and copying complex movements that were demonstrated by other people was a challenge. I did slowly develop some skills, both physical and mental. I became more visual and learned how to move my body through space and know where my limbs were. These skills have benefited me in many ways, other than on the practice mat. Now, I learn any physical discipline -- such as swimming, dancing, playing the drums -- more efficiently than before because I believe the study of Aikido forged new neural pathways in my brain. Although my daughter only stayed with the class for about a year, she was able to learn some important lessons about how to notice the important changes in the environment that signal trouble, and how to maintain a space condition and to move with a force coming toward her. I, on the other hand, stayed with the program until I became pregnant with my second child, later to earn a first-degree (Shodan) black belt. The school, due to a severe economic downturn, disbanded shortly after my second daughter was born.

I learned many things from my experience as an Aikidoka. For example, I learned that there is a "red zone," which is a concept with more than one use, including that in any given environment; there is a zone created when a threat arises, and one must learn to be aware of the threat in front of oneself, to the sides and behind. The concept of "red zone" can also be used to identify the location of the highest level of threat or danger. This is one of the more valuable lessons I learned in that a lot of danger comes to fruition before the victim knows what hit him or her. Seeing the attack coming, or understanding the signs to look for before an attack begins, is one of the best ways to be prepared to take protective action.

The concept of a "space condition" (ma-ai) has been a very helpful tool for me. A lot of unpleasantness can be avoided by controlling how close others are allowed when one so chooses. The person who is not allowed within the grappling or striking range loses much of the element of surprise and the concomitant shock response of the victim. The attacker has to decide to commit himself or herself to an attack, giving the very energy that will be used by the defender to neutralize or thwart the attack. I also learned that women can succeed against an attacker, even if the attacker is larger and stronger, if the woman knows how to use the attacker's energy against him or her. I learned that the best course of action is to minimize the threat, then clear the area as soon as possible. I had always had the notion that practitioners of martial arts (though I don't understand Aikido to fit the concept of "martial," it is usually designated as such by popular convention) would be fighting the aggressor to the bitter end...much like in the movies. It was a shift in understanding for me when I realized that Aikido does not teach a course of action of fighting to the death unless there is no other solution. Minimal response to maximize safety is the better course.

Do what has to be done to address the immediate threat, then cautiously retreat! This way of looking at things allows me to maintain my non-violent beliefs, while also allowing me to protect myself and those under my protection. Learning to give a commensurate response is a useful skill at work, in parenting, in navigating relationships with other people -- not just in the event of an attack.

The joint locks and stressors that are among the fundamentals in Aikido are painful and debilitating to an attacker. When applied properly, these joint locking techniques cause the arms and legs of an attacker to become temporarily inoperative or to cease to function at all, allowing the defender an opportunity to get away. In the course of one of the jobs I have held in the correctional system, I have found that a very large, angry attacker can be taken down and held in place while help is on the way by use of such techniques.

The study of Aikido has given me many responses to danger that I can choose to make other than the responses of fear and victimization. Having the repetoire of tactical body movements and techniques of Aikido that are scaleable to any given self-defense scenario allows me to quickly determine an appropriate response; such has made me stronger and more self-confident. A couple of years ago in my present job in Child Welfare Services, I found it interesting when a supervisor requested me to go with one of the men in the office to remove children from a potentially dangerous situation, thus acting as his bodyguard. It is unusual, even in this day and age of "equality," for a woman to be seen as sufficiently competent to provide protection for a man.

I still become concerned when I hear of violence in the schools, the work place or in the streets where my family lives, but my response is quite a bit different. Recently a high school student stabbed two other students at random in the bathroom at a local high school, nearly killing one of the students. These students are the same age as my daughter, who is now in high school. I did my best to give my daughter the tools to be aware of her surroundings, to notice signs of impending danger and protect herself with parries, strikes, and arm control techniques that are simple but elegant in their effect. The skills that I've learned from studying Aikido may not completely prevent me or my loved ones from being harmed, but it gives us something to do other than freezing -- paralyzed by uncertainty -- and becoming a victim.

The study of Aikido has improved my life situation in many ways other than confidence through self-defense skill. I count this experience as one of the more valuable educational experiences I have had. I wholeheartedly advise women to seek out Aikido as a discipline that confers important mental as well as physical and self-defense benefits. Aikido has most certainly empowered me.

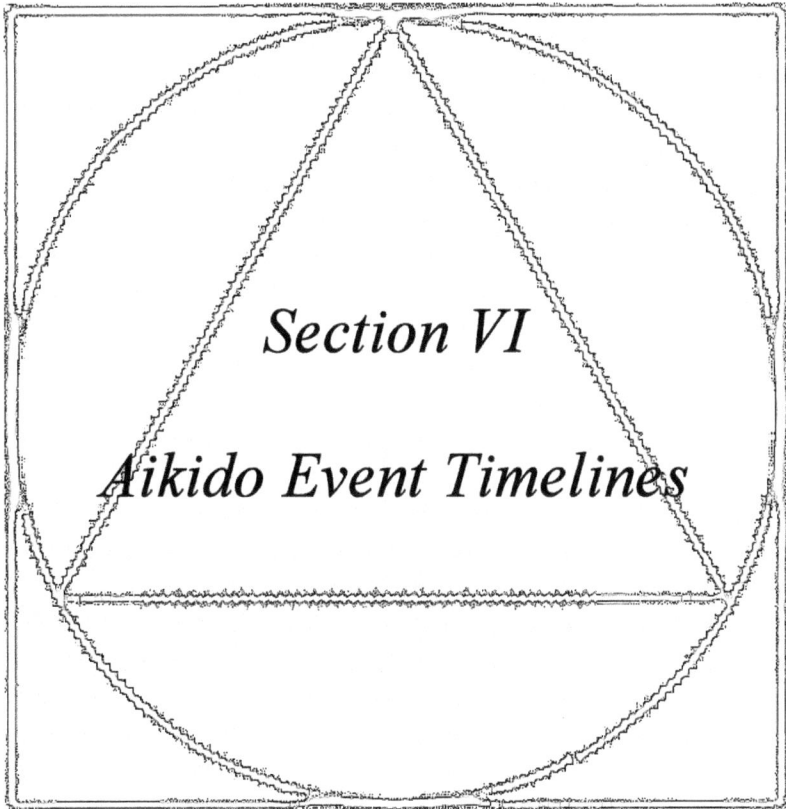

Section VI

Aikido Event Timelines

Aikido Event Timelines

Timeline #1 -- Comparison of Morihei Ueshiba and Kenji Tomiki

Morihei Ueshiba	Kenji Tomiki
1883 - Birth in Tanabe, Japan.	**1900** - Birth.
1895 - Morihei's father is attacked by thugs. **Morihei** realizes the need for self-defense training.	
1901 - **Morihei** studies Tenjin Shin'yō-ryū Jujutsu for a short period of time.	
1902 - **Morihei** studies Shinkage-ryu Kenjutsu for a short period of time.	
1903 thru 1906 - Japanese Army duty. Honorably discharged. While in the army, in 1903, **Morihei** begins study of Yagyū Shingan Ryū Taijutsu from Masakatsu Nakai, Sakai, Japan.	
	1906 - **Tomiki** begins bokken training at 6 years of age.
1908 - **Morihei** receives a menkyo kaiden certificate of completion in Yagyū Shingan-ryū Taijutsu from Nakai Masakatsu and Masanosuke Tsuboi.	
1911 - **Morihei** studies Kodokan Judo under Kiyoichi Takagi in Tanabe for a short period of time.	**1910** - **Tomiki** begins judo training at 10 years of age.

1915 - **Morihei** meets Daito-ryu Jujutsu master Sokaku Takeda and begins training. Between 1915 and 1922, **Morhei** receives Daito-ryu's Hiden Mokuroko, Hiden Ogi, and the Goshin'yo te transmission scrolls from Takeda.	
	1919 - **Tomiki** receives Shodan grade in Judo.
1920 - **Morihei** meets Deguchi Onisaburo, founder of the Shinto-derived O-moto Kyu religious sect, in January. Morihei's father dies while visiting with Onisaburo. First and second sons die in August and September, respectively. Morihei experiences great angst and a spiritual quest with Onisaburo as his guide follows soon thereafter. First Ueshiba dojo built.	**1920** - **Tomiki** succumbs to illness: may have been tuberculosis or influenza.
1922 - Morihei's mother dies. Under strained relations with Takeda sensei, **Morihei** receives a Kyoju Dairi (teaching certification) in Daito-ryu and a Kashima Shinden Jikishinkage-ryū (swordsmanship transmission scroll) from Sokaku Takeda. Later that year, Morihei proclaims "Aiki-budo" as the name of his discipline.	
	1923 - **Tomiki** enters Waseda University after recovering from a long illness. Elected secretary of the University's

	Judo club and meets Jigoro Kano.
1925 - Admiral Isamu Takeshita of the Imperial Japanese Navy makes first visit to meet **Ueshiba**, viewing a demonstration of his bujutsu in Tanabe, Japan.	
	1926 - **Tomiki** independently seeks out Morihei Ueshiba, a meeting occurs, and, in the summer of 1927, he begins study of Ueshiba-ryu Aiki-budo. This meeting is of his decision but arranged by Hidetaro Nishimura, a judoka as well as a Waseda University functionary. Nishimura was an Omoto-kyo follower and became aware of Morihei Ueshiba via this religious sect's activities. From 1927 through 1936 Tomiki intensely studies with Ueshiba.
1927 - **Morihei** begins teaching Aiki-budo classes at the Japanese Naval Staff College (the *Kaigun Daigakkō*, i.e., the Naval War College).	**1927** - **Tomiki** graduates from Waseda University with a degree in political science, enrolls in the masters program for economics.
	1928 - **Tomiki** is promoted to Godan (fifth degree black belt) in Judo.
1930 - **Morihei** demonstrates his bujutsu to military and government officials; Jigoro Kano (founder of Judo) is among these.	
1931 - **Morihei** Ueshiba establishes headquarters of his	

bujutsu in Wakamatsu-cho prefecture, Japan, and names it the Kobukan. Japanese government declares the foundation of the nation of Manchuria in March of 1932.	
1932 - Dai Nippon Budo Sen'yokai (Society to Promote Japanese Martial Arts) is established, with Onisaburo Deguchi as president and **Morihei** Ueshiba as chairman.	**1932** - **Kenji Tomiki** acts as the "Permanent Secretary" (Jonin Kanji) for the Budo Sen'yoka organization.
1933 - **Morihei Ueshiba** publishes his Aiki-budo technical manual entitled ***Budo Renshu***. *The compilation of this manual is organized and edited by Kenji Tomiki.*	**1931** until 1934 - **Tomiki** is employed as a teacher at Kakunodate junior high school. Meets Hideo Ohba with whom he begins a lifelong friendship.
	1934 - In preparation for a job change, **Tomiki** resigns from his high school teaching position. Moves to Tokyo in order to prepare for move to Manchuria. The securing of this position was facilitated by a recommend-ation provided by Morihei Ueshiba.
1936 through 1942 - **Morihei** visits Manchuria in successive autumn visits to continue teaching Tomiki and to supervise the bujutsu training programs. Awards Tomiki a Menkyo certification and advances him to 8th Dan in 1940. Also, he continues teaching at the Kobukan Dojo.	**1936** - **Tomiki** moves to Manchuria to take up a teaching post at the Japanese founded Daido Gakuin Academy. His job there is to teach bujutsu to the Japanese Kantogun Army, the Military Police, and the Imperial Household Agency.
1937 - **Morihei Ueshiba** formally enrolls in Kashima	**1937** - **Tomiki** continues teaching bujutsu at the Daido

Shinto-ryu in order to study further ken and jo techniques.	Gakuin Academy.
1938 - **Morihei** publishes another technical manual entitled ***Budo***; continues with his teaching assignments at various military institutions. Accepts position as head bujutsu advisor/teacher at the newly founded Kenkoku University in Manchuria. **Morihei** recommends Tomiki as his assistant teacher there.	**1938** - **Tomiki** continues teaching bujutsu at the Daido Gakuin Academy. During this year he is awarded an assistant teaching position at the newly founded Kenkoku University in Manchuria. Later in this year, **Tomiki** begins teaching bujutsu at Kenkoku University. **Hideo Ohba** takes over teaching the bujutsu programs at the Daido Gakuin Academy.
1939 - During this year, **Morihei's** first official visit as a bujutsu advisor/teacher to Kenkoku University occurs.	**1939** - **Tomiki** continues teaching at Kenkoku University.
1940 - **Morihei Ueshiba** visits Tomiki in Manchuria for a martial art demonstration, further instructs Tomiki and Ohba in Aiki-budo, and promotes Tomiki to 8th Dan. In this year, Ueshiba establishes the legal identity of the Kobukan dojo with the help of retired naval admiral Isamu Takeshita and registers the name Zaidan Hojin Kobukai as the organization governing Aiki-budo with the Japanese Ministry of Education.	**1940** - **Tomiki** continues teaching at Kenkoku University. Tomiki is promoted by Morihei Ueshiba to 8th Dan in Aiki-budo.
1941 - **Morihei** continues to teach at various military instututitions in Japan. The Greater Japan Martial Virtue Association, under the direction of then Japanese	**1941** - **Tomiki** continues teaching at Kenkoku University.

Primer Minister Hideki Tojo, orders Morihei to join its ranks and suggests several different names for renaming his Aiki-budo.	
1942 - **Morihei** travels again to Kenkoku University to advise and teach. Further disgruntled with the Japanese government's attempt to unify all budo under its control, Ueshiba distances himself from the Greater Japan Martial Virtue Association and retreats to his residence in the Iwama prefecture to contemplate the matters of life and the exact essence of his Aiki-budo and its meaning. At this time, he appointed **Minoru Hirai** as his representative to interact with the Greater Japan Martial Virtue Association. **Minoru's** discussions with this official political body resulted in an eventual agreement, sometime between 1942 and 1945, that Morihei Ueshiba's Aiki-budo would be considered to be the progenitor form of a new discipline termed *aikido*. To date, it is unclear whether Morihei Ueshiba was pleased or unpleased with this decision.[1] His reticence to embrace directly and openly the political will of this juridical body caused him, obviously, much discord; it is quite reasonable to think that	1942 - **Tomiki** continues teaching of bujutsu at Kenkoku University.
	1942 (cont.) - **Tomiki** continues teaching of bujutsu at Kenkoku University.

the term *aikido* which today identifies Aikido might have been an entirely different one had he acted differently, or had the war not occurred. During these war years he establishes the Aiki Shrine. **Kisshomaru Ueshiba** becomes director of the Kobukai Foundation.	
1945 - The Greater Japan Martial Virtue Association (Dai Nippon Butoku Kai) is dissolved by the post W.W. II occupation authoritative body, S.C.A.P.	1945 - In July, **Tomiki** is drafted into the Japanese Army. As Russian troops move into Manchuria, Tomiki is captured, imprisoned, and placed in solitary confinement near Lake Balkash in Siberia.
1945 through 1950. S.C.A.P. bans the practice of all martial arts.	1945 through 1948. During **Tomiki's** imprisonment, he further refines his ideas about how to implement a competitive aikido event.
1948 - The Japanese government officially recognizes the name Zaidan Hojin Aikikai as the new organization under which Morihei Ueshiba's Aikido will be presented. **Morihei**, by this time, has decided that his son, Kisshomaru, will be the Doshu [inheritor of the tradition and ways] of Aikido. Iwama dojo is completed in this year.	1948 - **Tomiki** is released from Russian incarceration and returns to Japan.
1950 - Regular practice resumes at the Aikikai's Tokyo dojo. Morihei restarts teaching but on a limited basis.	1951 - After repatriation to Japan, **Tomiki** is admitted as a member of the teaching staff at the Aikikai Hombu Dojo.
	1953 - Tomiki travels to the U.S.A. as part of a delegation to

	instruct Judo to certain members of the U.S.A.F.
1954 - Morihei's Omoto-based spirituality remains steadfast. He continues to formulate a metaphysical basis for Aikido, which he eventually presents to aikidoka as "Takemusu Aiki."	**1954 - Tomiki** receives a full professorship to head the newly formed physical education department at Waseda University, Japan. Later in this year he publishes *"Judo Taiso."*
	1955 - Tomiki continues teaching occasional Aikido classes at the Aikikai Hombu Dojo.
1956 - Hombu Dojo is moved from Iwama to Tokyo.	**1956 - Tomiki** publishes his book *"Judo appendix: Aikido"* that helped to introduce the West to both Judo and Aikido and is considered the first book to incorporate in the title the term *aikido*, giving serious treatment to the meaning of aiki.
1957 - Kisshomaru Ueshiba's book entitled, *Aikido*, is published.	
1958 - Morihei and Kisshomaru Ueshiba disagree with Kenji Tomiki's ideas regarding a competitive event for Aikido.	**1958 - Tomiki** establishes Waseda University Aikido Club, authorized by the university. Also, he publishes the book *"Aikido Nyumon"* and begins research for the development of competitive Aikido. This is the beginning of the discord between Kenji Tomiki and Morihei Ueshiba, as well as with Kisshomaru Ueshiba.
	Early, **1959 - Tomiki** officially breaks away from Aikikai

	hombu.
1960 - First public Aikikai spon-sored Aikido demonstration oc-curs. **Morihei Ueshiba** receives the Japanese *Medal of Honor with Purple Ribbon.*	**1960 - Tomiki** teaches regularly both Judo and Aikido at Waseda University. He continues his research toward establishing a competitive event for Aikido.
1961 - The All-Japan Student Federation is established with Morihei Ueshiba as its head. Honolulu Aikikai dojo opens.	
1963 - First All-Japan Aikido Demonstration is held.	
1964 - Morihei Ueshiba receives the Japanese *Order of the Rising Sun, 4th Class* award for his ef-forts toward founding Aikido.	**1964 - Tomiki** becomes the senior professor of Physical Education at Waseda University and was in charge of the post-graduate course in physical education. University, in charge of a post-graduate course in physical education. Tomiki publishes the text entitled "***Shin Aikido Tekisuto***" (New Aikido Textbook).
	1967 - Tomiki, Ohba, and others establish the Shodokan Aikido hombu.
1968 - Morihei Ueshiba receives the Japanese *Order of the Sacred Treasure*, which recognizes him as a national person of import-ance.	
1969 - Morihei Ueshiba gives final demonstration in January. Dies in April of liver cancer.	
	1970 - Tomiki retires from Waseda University. He

	publishes the book "*Taiiku To Budo*" (Physical Education and Budo). Completes foundation research for competitive aspects in Aikido.
	1971 - **Tomiki** receives 8th Dan in Kodokan Judo.
	1974 - The Japan Aikido Cooperative Association (Nihon Aikido Renmei/Kyokai) is established with Tomiki as first president. Also, Tomiki is elected to position of vice president of Japan's Budo Society.
	1976 - The Shodokan Aikido hombu is designated as the headquarters of the Japan Aikido Cooperative Association with **Tomiki** as director.
	1977 - **Tomiki** visits the Australian Aikido Association and teaches a seminar.
	1979 - **Kenji Tomiki** dies of intestinal cancer.

Timeline #2 -- Major Events: Kisshomaru Ueshiba and Kenji Tomiki

Kisshomaru Ueshiba	Kenji Tomiki
	1900 - Birth.
	1906 - **Tomiki** begins bokken training at 6 years of age.
	1910 - **Tomiki** begins judo training at 10 years of age.
	1919 - **Tomiki** receives Shodan certificate in Judo.
1921 - **Kisshomaru** is born (3rd son of Morihei Ueshiba).	
	1924 - **Tomiki** enters Waseda University after recovering from a long illness (may have been tuberculosis). Elected secretary of the University's Judo club and meets Jigoro Kano.
	1926 - **Tomiki** independently seeks out Morihei Ueshiba, a meeting occurs, and Kenji begins study of Aiki-budo in the summer of 1927. This meeting is of his decision but arranged by Hidetaro Nishimura, a Waseda University functionary. Nishimura was an Omoto-kyo follower and became aware of Morihei Ueshiba via this religious sect's activities. From 1926 through 1936 Tomiki intensely studies with Morihei.
	1927 - **Tomiki** graduates from Waseda University with a degree in Political Science,

	enrolls in the masters program for economics.
	1928 - **Tomiki** is promoted to Godan (fifth degree black belt) in Judo.
	1931 thru **1934** - **Tomiki** is employed as a teacher at Kakunodate junior high school. In 1934 Assists Morihei in teaching Aiki-budo classes at the latter's dojo in the Wakamatsu-cho prefecture.
1937 - At 16 years of age, **Kisshomaru** begins serious training of his father's Aiki-budo.	**1936** - **Tomiki** moves to Manchuria to take up a teaching post at the Japanese founded Daido Institute. Teaches Aiki-budo to the Japanese Kantogun Army and the Imperial Household Agency.
1938 - **Kisshomaru** appears as uke in his father's book entitled "Budo."	**1938** - **Tomiki** is awarded an assistant professorship at the Kenkoku University in Manchuria. He continues teaching Aiki-budo.
1940 - Morihei establishes the Zaidan Hojin Kobukai organization, officially recognized by the Japanese government as a non-profit entity. The first chairman was retired admiral Isamu Takeshita, with General Katsura Hayashi as vice chairman. The other board members were Count Fumimaro Konoe, Count Toshitame Maeda, Takuo Godo, Kinya Fujita, Kozaburo	**1940** - **Kenji Tomiki** is advanced to 8th Dan by Morihei Ueshiba. He continues teaching at Kenkoku University.

Okada, and Kenzo Futaki and other well-known people.	
1942 – At 21 years of age, **Kisshomaru** Ueshiba becomes director of the Kobukai Foundation, appointed by his father, Morihei.	**Tomiki** continues teaching at Kenkoku University.
	1945 - In July, **Tomiki** is conscripted by the Japanese Army. As Russian troops move into Manchuria, Tomiki is captured, imprisoned, and placed in solitary confinement near Lake Balkash in Siberia.
1946 - **Kisshomaru** graduates from Waseda University with a degree in Economics. Note that Waseda University was the alma matter of both Kisshomaru Ueshiba and Kenji Tomiki. Also, both he and Kenji majored in economics.	**1945** through **1948**. During his imprisonment **Tomiki** further refines his ideas about how to implement a competitive aikido event.
1948 - **Kisshomaru** officially oversees the formation of the Aikikai which replaces the Kobukan organization. Legally recognized by the Japanese government as the Zaidan Hojin Aikikai.	**1948** - **Tomiki** is released from imprisonment in Russia and returns to Japan.
1949 thru **1955** - **Kisshomaru** is employed by Osaka Shoji Company, a business involved with securities trading. Resigns this position in late 1955 to head up the reorganization of his father's Aikikai organization.	**1953** - After repatriation to Japan, **Tomiki** travels to the USA as part of a delegation to instruct Judo and Aikido to the USAF. Karl Geis (founder of the Fugakukai) meets Tomiki during this visit.
	1954 - **Tomiki** receives a full professorship at Waseda

	University, Japan as head physical education department. Later in this year he publishes "Judo Taiso."
	1955 - Tomiki continues teaching an occasional class as a guest sensei at the Aikikai Hombu.
1956 - Kisshomaru akes decision to devote all his effort to the development of the organizational aspects of the Aikikai and to "modernize" certain aspects of the teaching of his father's Aikido by clarify its philosophical underpinnings and introducing a standardized curriculum, all this requiring an effort over several decades. Hombu Dojo moves back to Tokyo from Iwama.	**1956** - Tomiki publishes his book *Judo: Appendix Aikido* that helped to introduce the West to both Judo and Aikido and is considered the first book to incorporate in the title the word *Aikido* that gives serious treatment to the meaning of aiki.
1957 - Japan Publications Trading, Ltd. publishes **Kisshomaru's** book entitled *Aikido.*	
1958 - As Kisshomaru continues to formulate his curriculum, he and his father (Morihei) begin to have disagreements with Kenji Tomiki as to what the modernized form of Aikido should manifest. Key among the disagreements is whether or not Aikido could embrace a competitive event, such as existed in Judo. He strongly believed that any competitive event formulated for Aikido	**1958 - Tomiki** establishes Waseda University Aikido Club, authorized by the university. Also, he publishes the book *Aikido Nyumon* and begins research for the development of competitive Aikido. This is the beginning point of Tomiki's discord with the elder Morihei Ueshiba and his son Kisshomaru.

would only further entrench the the primacy of superior physical skill in martial arts in a way that would detract from the true meaning of Budo, thus 'wrongly' maintaining the idea of "martial" therein.	
	Early, **1959** - **Tomiki** officially breaks from the Aikikai.
1963 - **Kisshomaru** makes his first international tour to promote Aikido worldwide. Several other subsequent tours occur for the same purpose.	**1964** - **Tomiki** becomes the senior professor of Physical Education at Waseda University and was in charge of the post-graduate course in physical education. Tomiki publishes the text entitled *Shin Aikido* **Tekisuto** (New Aikido Textbook).
1967 - **Kisshomaru** officially oversees the teardown of the old Kobukan Dojo building. Authorizes construction of the new Aikikai Hombu on same site.	**1967** - **Tomiki, Ohba**, and others establish the Shodokan Aikido hombu.
	1970 - **Tomiki** retires from Waseda University. He publishes the book ***Taiku To Budo*** (Physical Education and Budo). Completes foundational research for competitive aspects in Aikido.
	1971 - **Tomiki** receives 8th Dan in Kodokan Judo.
	1974 - The Japan Aikido Association (Nihon Aikido Renmei/Kyokai) is established with **Tomiki** as first president. Also, Tomiki is elected to position of vice president of

	Japan's Budo Society.
	1976 - The Shodokan Aikido Hombu is designated as the organizational body of the All Japan Aikido Association with **Tomiki** as director.
	1979 - **Kenji Tomiki** dies of intestinal cancer.
1987 - Kodansha International, Inc. publishes **Kisshomaru's** book entitled "***Aikido no Kokoro***" (*The Spirit of Aikido*). Herein he presents formally his controversial and faction-producing idea that "Aikido rejects all forms of violence, justified, or unjustified."	
1995 - **Kisshomaru** receives the prestigious Zui Hosho Medal from the Japanese government.	
1999 - **Kisshomaru**, while in hospital, dies of respiratory failure.	

Timeline #3 -- Comparison of Judo and Aikido Formational Events

Jigoro Kano	Morihei Ueshiba	Kenji Tomiki
1860 - Birth	**1882** - Birth	**1900** - Birth
1882 - Kano establishes his Juku School.		
1879 - Kano demonstrates Judo for United States of America president Ulysses S. Grant.		
1906 - Kano begins to introduce Judo to the Japanese school system. His effort continues through at least the year 1917.		
1909 - Kano establishes the Kodokan Judo hombu. **Kano** serves as the first Asian member of the International Olympic Committee from 1909 until his death in 1938.		
	1920 - Ueshiba establishes his Ueshiba Juku dojo.	
1922 - Kano establishes the Kodokan Bunkakai		

(Kodokan Cultural Society).		
		1926 - Tomiki meets Ueshiba for the first time. This meeting is of his decision but arranged by Hidetaro Nishimura, a Waseda University functionary. Nishimura was an Omoto-kyo follower and became aware of Morihei Ueshiba via this religious sect's activities.
		1927 - Tomiki begins training from Ueshiba in the summer of this year.
1928 - Kano establishes the Nada High School.		**1928 - Tomiki** is promoted to Godan (fifth degree black belt) in Judo.
1930 - Kano, upon the invitation of Japanese Naval Admiral Isamu Takeshita, attends a demonstration in October given by Ueshiba in Mejiro, Japan.	**1930 - Ueshiba** demonstrates his Aiki-budo to Jigoro Kano and other Japanese officials. Following the demonstration, Kano reportedly announces something similar to 'This is my ideal	

	Judo.' Some report that 'Budo' was the word actually spoken.	
Early 1931 - Kano sends Minoru Mochizuki and another top judoka to study with Ueshiba (Mochizuki is later awarded two Daito-ryu Jujutsu scrolls by Ueshiba in 1932).	**Late 1931 - Ueshiba's** Kobukan organization, a corporate-like entity for the furtherance of his discipline of Aiki-budo, is established. (Note similarity of this name, Kobukan, to Kodokan.)	
1931 thru 1938 - Kano was one of several prominent spokesmen for Japan's bid to have Judo included in the 1940 Olympics.		**1934 - Tomiki** assists Ueshiba in teaching Aiki-budo classes at the latter's hombu dojo in the Wakamatsu-cho prefecture.
1938 - Kano dies of probable pneumonia infection; but a few historians theorize possible assassination by poison (**Kano** was strongly opposed to the militarism that led up to W.W. II, many others who similarly held this view were, in fact, murdered).	**1936 through 1942 - Morihei Ueshiba** visits Tomiki to continue teaching him. Awards Tomiki a Menkyo certification and advances him to 8th Dan in 1940.	**1936 - Tomiki** relocates to Manchuria to first teach at the newly established Daido Institute, then later at Kenkoku University. Teaches Aiki-budo to members of the Japanese Army and the Imperial Household Agency.

	1940 - Ueshiba establishes the legal identity of the Kobukan with the help of naval commander Isamu Takeshita by registering the name Kobukai Foundation with the Japanese Ministry of Education.	**1940 - Tomiki** is advanced to 8th Dan by Morihei Ueshiba and admitted as a member of the Kobukai Foundation's board of directors.
		1945 - In July, **Tomiki** is drafted into the Japanese Army. As Russian troops move into Manchuria, Tomiki is captured, imprisoned, and placed in solitary confinement near Lake Balkash in Siberia.
	1942 – The term *aikido* is registered by the Greater Japan Martial Virtue Association, a Japanese governmental agency, as the official term for that which Ueshiba's Kobukai Foundation teaches. Kisshomaru Ueshiba becomes director of the Kobukai Foundation.	**1950 -** After repatriation to Japan in 1948, having spent approximately three years in a Russian prison camp after the end of W.W. II, **Tomiki** assists Kisshomaru Ueshiba in teaching at the Kobukai hombu dojo from 1950 until his break from the Aikikai in 1958.

1958 - Judo's Kodokan hombu moves to its present location (as of 2011).		**1958 - Tomiki** founds the Waseda University Aikido Club, serving as the locus for the development of his aikido ideas.
1960 - Judo is demonstrated as an exhibition event during the Olympic Games.		
	1961 - All-Japan Student Federation established with **Ueshiba** as first president.	
1964 - Judo is finally introduced as an Olympic sport in the Tokyo Olympics.		
		1967 - Tomiki establishes the Shodokan Aikido hombu.
	1969 - Morihei Ueshiba dies.	
		1974 - The *Japan Aikido Coopertive Association* (Nihon Aikido Renmei/Kyokai) established with **Tomiki** as first president.
		1979 - Kenji Tomiki dies.

Timeline #4 -- Comparison of Attitudes & Events leading to
Factionalization

Kisshomaru Ueshiba Born - 1921	Kenji Tomiki Born - 1900	Koichi Tohei Born - 1920
	1906 - Tomiki begins bokken training at six years of age.	
	1910 - Begins Judo training at ten years of age.	
	1919 - Tomiki receives Shodan certificate in Kodokan Judo.	
1931 - Kisshomaru begins training in Aiki-budo, taught by his father.	**1928 - Tomiki** is promoted to Godan (fifth degree black belt) in Judo.	**1929 - Tohei** begins Judo training under father.
		1934 - Tohei receives Shodan certificate in Judo from father at age fourteen.
1937 - Kisshomaru resolutely commits his efforts to the learning of Aikido.		
1938 - Appears frequently in pictures as uke in his father's book ***Budo***.		
1939 through **1942** - **Kisshomaru** continues training	**1940** - Kenji **Tomiki** is advanced to 8th Dan by Morihei	**1939 - Tohei** Begins Aiki-budo training with Morihei

and is frequently Morihei's uke.	Ueshiba.	Ueshiba.
1942 - Morihei Ueshiba ceases most of his teaching duties and withdraws to his home in Iwama; **Kisshomaru** takes over leadership of the Kobukan dojo at this time, though practice is difficult due to bombing. It is in this year that the term *aikido* is arrived at by negotiations between an emissary sent by Morihei and the Dai Nippon Budokai for not only Aiki-budo but for other similar martial arts.	**1942** - Kenji **Tomiki** continues teaching in Manchuria.	**1942** - **Tohei** is inducted into the Army.
By directive of S.C.A.P., from **1945** until **1950** no martial arts are allowed to be practiced. During this time, **Kisshomaru** and Morihei Ueshiba focus on creating an Aikido suitable for the dawn of a new age.	**1945** - In July, **Tomiki** is drafted into the Army. As Russian troops move into Manchuria, Tomiki is captured, imprisoned, and placed in solitary confinement near Lake Balkash in Siberia.	
	While imprisoned,	**1947** - **Tohei** begins

	Tomiki begins to develop his ideas for a competitive Aikido event.	training with Tempu Nakamura, Japanese yoga teacher and founder of *Shin-shin Tōitsu-dō*, the Way of Mind and Body Unification.
	1948 - Kenji **Tomiki** is released from imprisonment by the Russian Army and repatriated to Japan.	
1950 - With S.C.A.P. restrictions on martial arts training beginning to be lifted, **Kisshomaru** begins a restart his father's Aikido organization; he continues training and teaching.	**1950** - **Tomiki** assists Kisshomaru Ueshiba in teaching at the Kobukai hombu dojo from 1950 until his break from the *Aikikai Aikido* organization in 1958.	After W.W. II, around **1950**, **Tohei** resumes Aikido training and begins teaching at the Aikikai hombu dojo as head instructor until **1971**. Continues training with Tempu Nakamura.
		1952 - **Tohei** is promoted to 8th Dan by Morihei Ueshiba; Kisshomaru has not yet accepted his possible role as the next doshu of Aikido.
1953 - **Kisshomaru** continues the Aikikai's reorganization efforts, training,	**1953** - **Tomiki** travels to the U.S.A. along with a group of other adept judoka to teach the	**1953** - **Tohei** travels to the U.S.A. state of Hawaii after receiving an invitation from the

and teaching.	United States Air Force's service members Judo; a few also learn Aikido (Karl Geis was one of these service members).	Hawaii branch of the Japanese Nishikai health system, stays for one year to establish Aikido there in order to assist not only in dissemination of the art but also to earn money for the rebuilding of the Aikikai hombu dojo.
	1954 - Tomiki receives a full professorship at Waseda University, Japan as head of the physical education department. Later in this year he publishes "*Judo Taiso*" (Judo Exercises).	
1955 - Kisshomaru resigns from his position at the Osaka Shoji Company, Ltd., then his full-time employment, in order to devote all his efforts to the strengthening of *Aikikai Aikido*. Also, he probably senses that Tohei is beginning to threaten his role as	**1955 - Tomiki** begins to approach both Morihei Ueshiba about developing a standard Aikido curriculum that could reduce the time needed to learn it.	**1955 - Tohei** returns to Hawaii for further teaching and visits the continental U.S.A. to begin an expanded effort to disseminate Aikido. (Gozo Shioda breaks from the Aikikai, causing concerns about the continued existence of Ueshiba's art.) Late in the year,

Understanding Aikido

successor doshu to his father's creation, Aikikai Aikido.		**Tohei** returns to Japan in order to bolster the *Aikikai* position as the progenitor of Aikido.
1956 - Kisshomaru begins to express objections about Tomiki's idea to include Aikido training at the university level. He strongly believed that any competitive event formulated for Aikido would only further entrench the the primacy of superior physical skill in martial arts in a way that would detract from the true meaning of Budo, thus 'wrongly' maintaining the idea of "martial" therein.	**1956 - Tomiki** approaches both Morihei and Kisshomaru Ueshiba about a standard curriculum as well as a competitive event for Aikido. Informs the Ueshiba's of his intent to develop a program of Aikido at Waseda University. Authors the book "*Judo: Appendix Aikido*" that helped to introduce the West to both Judo and Aikido and is considered the first book to incorporate in the title the term *aikido* that gives serious treatment to the meaning of *aiki.*	**1956 - Tohei** accepts officially the role of chief instructor at the Aikikai hombu dojo upon the request of Kisshomaru Ueshiba, the later is now fully responsible for the advancement of the Aikikai's further development.
1957 - Kisshomaru informs Kenji Tomiki that he should not use the term *aikido* to describe the discipline that he would be teaching	**1957 -** In spite of both Morihei and Kisshomaru Ueshiba's request that Tomiki not use the term *aikido,* **Tomiki** decides to retain *aikido* as the	**1957 - Tohei** begins, very gradually, to infuse Aikido with his formulation of the concepts of ki.

when he begins teaching an *Aikido* course at Waseda University. Japan Publications Trading, Ltd. publishes Kisshomaru's first book entitled ***Aikido.***	name by which he will identify the discipline that he will teach as a physical education activity/sport at Waseda University.	
1958 - **Kisshomaru** continues training and teaching.	1958 – In April, **Tomiki** founds the Waseda University Aikido Club that serves as the locus for the further development of his aikido ideas; begins teaching the University's first Aikido course. In order to obtain the permission of the university to do this, it requires Tomiki to structure Aikido in a way that would permit the teacher and academic review board to discern the progress of each Aikido student; the method of analysis required to accomplish this necessitated the inclusion of a shiai event. Retains use of the term *aikido* to identify his	1958 - **Tohei** continues to infuse Aikido with his ideas about ki.

Understanding Aikido

	teachings/discipline. Authors the book *New Sport of Aikido.*	
1959 - Kisshomaru continues training and teaching.	**1959 -** Early in the year, due to un-reconcilable viewpoints, **Tomiki** officially breaks away from the *Aikikai Aikido* organization. De facto, the name *Tomiki-ryu Aikido* is then used to identify Tomiki's Aikido.	**1959 - Tohei** returns to Hawaii to further reinforce his methods of Aikido amongst his students there.
1960 - Kisshomaru continues his training and teaching, and begins to formulate his ideas about how the concept of *ki* should be fit into Aikido, if at all.		**1960 - Tohei** begins the publication of a series of books that presents a technical curriculum fused with his ideas about *ki.* Though these are not the officially sanctioned curriculum of the Aikikai, they are well received by many top aikidoka of the time, but not all. Authors the book *Aikido, The Arts of Self-Defense.*
		1961 - As a result of arrangements made by **Tohei**, Morihei Ueshiba visits the

		Honolulu Aikikai dojo in Hawaii for its dedication and opening ceremony. Authors the book *"What is Aikido?"*
1963 - **Kisshomaru** visits Los Angeles, California, U.S.A to teach Aikido and establish a beginning Aikikai Aikido basis there.		
	1964 - **Tomiki** authors the book *The New Aikido Textbook.*	
		1965 - **Tohei** returns to the continental U.S.A. to further establish Aikido in several states.
		1966 - **Tohei** authors the book *Aikido in Daily Life.*
	1967 - **Tomiki** with the help of Hideo Ohba, other top students, and financial backing officially established the *Shodokan Aikido* hombu (headquarters). The name *"Shodokan"* replaces the name of Tomiki as the	

	identifier of this Aikido style, though many teachers around the world of Tomiki's style of Aikido continue to use the name *Tomiki-ryu Aikido* (even today).	
1969 - Upon his father's death, **Kisshomaru** assumes traditional role as doshu of *Aikikai Aikido*. However, there had previously been serious discussion among the top Aikido teachers and the elder Ueshiba of passing this role on to Koichi Tohei. There was soon to begin a definite struggle for this leadership role. This struggle would revolve around to what extent *ki* would figure into the further development of *Aikikai Aikido's* philosophical and technical foundation. Kisshomaru wins role as doshu of *Aikikai Aikido*.		1969 - **Tohei** again returns to the continental U.S.A. to continue establishing Aikido in several states. In January, **Tohei** is advanced to 10th Dan by Morihei Ueshiba just before the latter's death. This advancement was probably an act by Morihei to recognize Tohei's significant *ki oriented contributions* to *Aikikai Aikido*, which Morihei recognized as a shared, kindred psychological attribute, but also an act that would permit Tohei to 'strike out' on his own in the event of an unresolvable political struggle between he and

		Kisshomaru for the role of doshu.
1970 - Kisshomaru begins to formulate his ideas about a standardized curriculum for Aikikai Aikido. Continues teaching at hombu dojo.	**1970 - Tomiki** authors the book *Physical Education and Budo.*	**1970 - Tohei** has already formed his version of a standardized curriculum influenced by his interest in ki, and has been teaching it in Hawaii and other states of the U.S.A. He probably reasoned that as Kisshomaru shaped his curriculum there would likely be significant ideological differences between the two competing curriculums. Observe that this is one form of competition, i.e., differing ideas; one will win out over the other.
1971 - Kisshomaru and Tohei disagree as to what extent *ki* (ostensibly ethereal, difficult-to-quantify energy of one type or another) and its possible characteristics and effects should be included in Aikikai Aikido teaching	**1971 - Tomiki and Ohba** continue to promote and work toward a competitive event for Aikido.	**1971 -** While yet head instructor at Aikikai, after his initial disagreement with Kisshomaru Ueshiba, **Tohei** forms the independent *Ki no Kenkyukai* (Ki Society) outside of the organizational boundaries of the

curriculum (Kisshomaru later terms this difficult-to-quantify phenomenon "*magico-religiosity*").		*Aikikai.*
1972 to 1974 - Within the Aikikai organization, tensions between **Kisshomaru's** supporters and those of Tohei's increase.		**1972 to 1974** - During further evolution of his discipline within *Ki no Kenkyukai,* **Tohei** infuses Aikido with *Shin-shin Tōitsu-dō* (Japanese yoga) concepts.
1974 - May, **Kisshomaru** Ueshiba accepts Tohei's resignation from *Aikikai Aikido.*	.	**1974** - In May, **Tohei** submits a letter to the *Aikikai* organization and officially resigns; names his new discipline *Shin-shin Tōitsu Aikido.*
	1975 - *Japan Aikido Cooperative Association* (J.A.A) is established with **Tomiki** as first president.	
1977 - **Kisshomaru** authors the book *Aikido Founder: Morihei Ueshiba,* published by Kodansha, Ltd.		
	1979 - December 25,	Between 1974 and

	Kenji **Tomiki** dies of cancer.	2011, **Tohei** authors numerous other books and articles.
	1980 - Hideo Ohba becomes the second president of the Japan Aikido Cooperative Association.	
1984 - Authors the book *The Spirit of Aikido*, a good yet overdue effort that states what Aikido is (or is not) and serves well to strengthen Aikikai Aikido's role as the progenitor style.		
	1985 - Tetsuro Nariyama and **Fumiaki Shishida**, top shihan of Shodokan Aikido, jointly author the book *Aikido: Tradition and the Competitive Edge*.	
1999 - January 4, **Kisshomaru Ueshiba dies**. His son, **Moriteru Ueshiba** accepts the role as third doshu of *Aikikai Aikido*.	**1986** - Hideo **Ohba** dies. **Nariyama** and **Shishida** accepted a joint administrative directorship of the Japan Aikido Cooperative Association.	
	1986 thru 2011 - Gradually,	**2011** - May 19, Koichi **Tohei dies**.

	differences in Aikido technical theory and the future direction for the *All Japan Aikido Association* create disagreements between these two shihan.	His son, **Shinichi Tohei**, succeeded him as the director of the Shin-shin Tōitsu Aikido-kai, the organization that oversees *Shin-shin Toitsu Aikido*.
2012 Since 1955, numerous significant Aikido teachers have broken off from the Aikikai organization and formed different styles of Aikido; notable are: *Yoshinkan Aikido, Shodokan Aikido, Yoseikan Aikido, Shin-shin Toitsu Aikido,* and *Shin-shin Aikishuren Kai Aikido (Iwama dojo Aikikai Aikido descendent).*	**2012** **Nariyama** and **Shishida split** in 2012, effectively creating two organizations. Those are: *Shodokan Aikido Federation* (referring to their aikido as *Shodokan Aikido*), and the *Japan Aikido Cooperative Association* (referring to their aikido as *Tomiki Aikido*).	**2012** Since the formation of *Shin-shin Toitsu Aikido* in 1974, several significant factions have split off; notable are: *Yuishinkai Aikido, Shin Budo Kai, Kokikai Aikido,* and *Seidokan Aikido.*

It is important to mention here that the viewpoints of Minoru Mochizuki, who was the founder of *Yoseikan Aikido* (which later was reorganized and renamed *Yoseikan Budo*), and to some extent those of Gozo Shioda, who was the founder of *Yoshinkan Aikido*, are sometimes found to be in agreement with Kenji Tomiki's ideas. All of these individuals sought to ensure the effectiveness of Aikido techniques for real-world use, both for civilian self-defense use and police work. Therefore, I have not included these two significant Aikido shihan in this timeline. Also, I have not included Noriaki Inoue (a.k.a, Yoichiro Inoue, Morihei Ueshiba's nephew), who, soon after W.W. II, would teach his martial discipline using the name *Aiki-budo* (later renamed *Shin'ei Taido*); this being yet one more significant faction that emerged as a result of Inoue's exasperation concerning his uncle's response to the Japanese government's second and last suppression of the Omoto religion.

Wisely, Kisshomaru Ueshiba placed the Aikikai Aikido organization between *combative sport* (e.g., Shodokan Aikido) and the subjective, difficult-to-prove psycho-spiritual wanderings that are present in some Aikido styles and numerous dojos, where the *first above* was philosophically objectionable to both him and his father, while the *second above* was objectionable solely to him. Morihei Ueshiba's inclination toward religiosity, especially the type of religious mysticism that arose in him as a result of the Omoto-kyo's teachings and its various social movements and escapades, provided Kisshomaru with a different perspective about the function of *ki* in the formulation of a reasoned and functional Aikido philosophy that would maintain its viability over time. Helpfully, Kisshomaru Ueshiba believed that idea of personal *ki* -- i.e., a dynamic interaction of a person's unique physio-spiritual expression of *pure-self* (of whatever degree) and their *behavioral vitality as affected by the other naturally occurring external forces of life* (e.g., the action of another person or the acts of Nature) -- arises naturally as well as productively from within a person as they practice Aikido and, therefore, does not need to be specially cultivated.

Timeline #5 - Names Used to Identify Ueshiba's Evolving Martial Art

~1920 through ~1926 -- *Daito-ryu Jujutsu.*
~1927 through ~1929 -- *Aioi-ryu Aiki-jujutsu.*
~1930 through ~1937 -- *Aioi-ryu Aiki-bujutsu.*
~1938 until early 1942 -- *Ueshiba-ryu Aiki-budo.*
Early 1942 until 1957 -- *Uncertain.* (Morihei Ueshiba was still contemplating the possible use of the generic term "aikido.")
1957 until present -- *Aikikai Aikido.*

During his life, Morihei Ueshiba used many different names for various reasons to identify his ever-evolving martial discipline. The above names reflect those he used the longest, seemingly with an intent to keep them. The term *aikido* was heavy-handedly assigned by the Dai Nippon Budokai in 1942 C.E. when this organization came under the influence of General Hideki Tojo. The martial discipline of *Yagyū Shingan-ryū Taijutsu* was sometimes taught informally by Ueshiba for a short period of time prior to his initial exposure to and training in Daito-ryu Jujutsu in 1915 C.E.[2]

Legend

~ = approximately

Table 4 -- Names of Northeast Asia's Villages, Towns, and Districts

The following is a list of names of Northeastern Asian places through which Onisaburo, Ueshiba and the others of the wayfaring Omoto-kyo group traveled after arriving in Manchuria in February, 1924 C.E. Listed in order of first visited, then succeeding.

Chinese Name	Japanese Name
Antung, Manchuria -- a town located just northwest of the mouth of Yalu River. Korea (Chosen), is to the southeast on the other side of the Yalu river. Sometime after 1945 C.E. it was renamed *Dandong*.	Unknown
Fengtian, Manchuria -- a town, sometimes romanized as *Mukden*. in southern Manchuria, just north of the Liaodong Peninsula. Also referred to by the older names of *Shengjing*; today it is known as *Shenyang*.	Hoten
Changtu, Manchuria. A town located south of Sipin.	*Shotofu* Also, sometimes abbreviated as *Shoto*.
Ssupingchien, Manchuria -- a town situated just southeast of today's Sipin. Then, also known as *Sipingjie*.	*Old Shiheigai*
Sipin, Manchuria -- a relatively new town then, situated approximately halfway between the town of Changchun to the north and Shenyang to the south. It is here that a railway traveler would depart the train station in order to travel north to Changchun, or west to Chengchiatun and eventually to Tongliao in Inner Mongolia, or north to Taonan.	*New Shiheigai* This town, very near to Old Shiheigai, came about as a result of the railway installation and its subsequent locomotive transportation services.

Chengchiatun, Manchuria -- a town just south of today's town of Shuangliao, east of Tongliao, and located in Inner Mongolia.	*Teikaton*
Changchun, Manchuria -- a town situated centrally in the geographic area of Manchuria.	*Shinkyo*
Taonan (Zhaonan), Manchuria -- a village and military/bandit conflict zone where there was situated a fortified Fengtian Army outpost. The railway line ended here.	*Tonan*
Guanghetun, Manchuria -- a geographic location just southeast of Taonan.	*Gongyefu* (also sometimes referred to as Koyafu)
Suolun District -- this was a district separate from Chinese and Russian control that had been wrested from Russian control by the Mongols. This locale served as headquarters for Zhankui Lu's and Onisaburo's newly formed *Neiwai Menggu Dulijun* (Inner and Outer Mongolian Independence Army). This is where their army first came under attack, which caused them to hurriedly depart and head south toward the village of Bayantala.	*Sakura District*
Bayantala, Manchuria -- a village just northwest of Chengchiatun where Onisaburo, Ueshiba and the others of their group came under attack again.	Unknown
Tongliao, Inner Mongolia -- a town west of Chengchiatun. It is here that the members of the Omoto group were captured.	*Paintara*

Table 4

[1] See the **Spirit of Aikido** by Kisshomaru Ueshiba; published by Kodansha International, Ltd., paperback edition, first printing, 1987, pages 100 and 101.   Between 1925 C.E. and his final acceptance of *aikido* as Aikido's identifying name sometime around 1957 C.E., Morihei Ueshiba used numerous different names to identify his discipline.   Three prominent names used were *Aiki-budo, Ueshiba-ryu,* and *Aioi-ryu.*

[2] For details of the names that Morihei Ueshiba to identify his aiki-budo, see **The Process of Forming Aikido and Japanese Imperial Navy Admiral Isamu Takeshita: Through the analysis of Takeshita's diary from 1925 to 1931** by Professor Fumiaki Shishida (Waseda University, Tokyo, Japan).   See also, **How Aikido Was Named** by Stanley Pranin; Aiki Journal, from the Aiki Journal Bulletin Board Forum, November 22, 1999.

Section VII

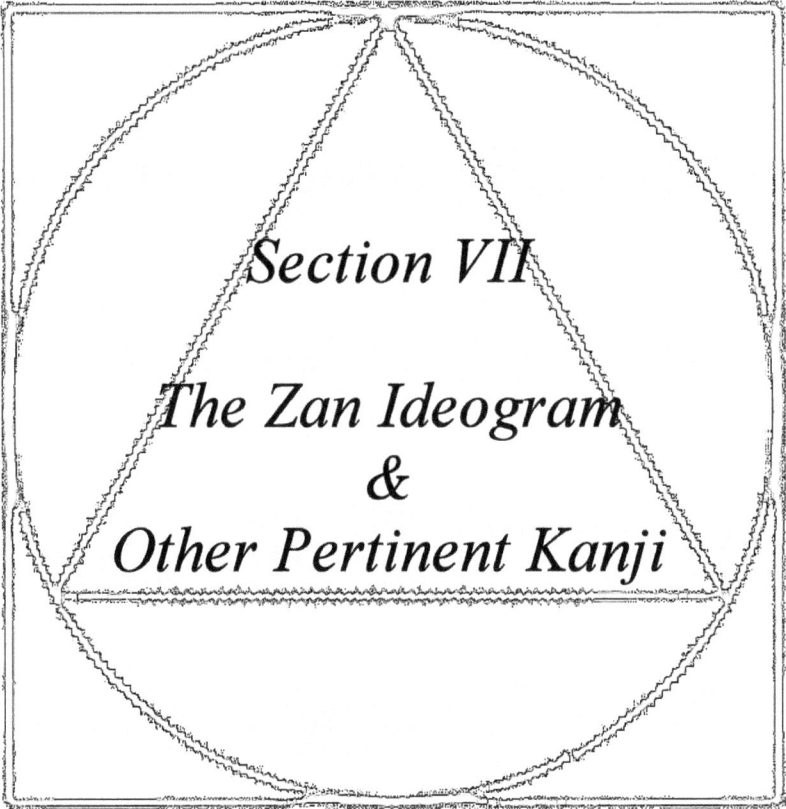

The Zan Ideogram
&
Other Pertinent Kanji

The Zan ideogram & other pertinent kanji

斬, *zan* (onyomi reading)[1] or *kiru* (kunyomi reading) -- meaning of {cut}{cut through}{chop}{sever}{kill}{behead}. An example of the use of this kanji can be seen in the verb *kiru* (斬る) {to cut through}, e.g., as used in the phrase *katana de kiru* (斬るで刀) {to cut through with a sword}.

突, totsu (onyomi reading) or tsuku (kunyomi reading) -- meaning of {attack}{stab}{thrust}{pierce}{jab}{lunge}{sudden}{unexpected}. Examples of this kanji's use can be seen in the verbs tsukinuku (突き抜く) {to pierce}{to shoot through}{to penetrate}, tsukinukeru (突き抜する) {to pierce through}{to break through}, and toppasuru (突破する){to break through}{to overcome}{to surpass}{to exceed}.

破, *ha* (onyomi reading) or *yaburu* (also *yabureru*, both are kunyomi readings) -- meaning of {defeat}{destroy}{break}{rend}{rip}{tear}. An example of this kanji's use is in the verb *toppasuru* (突破する) {to breakthrough}{to overcome}{to surpass}{to exceed}.

Zantoppa-kai and the Zantotsu-ryū kanji analysis

斬, *zan* -- a combination of 車, *kuruma* (symbol meaning *cart*) and 斤, *ono* (symbol meaning *axe*) -- infers a cutting by any kind of implement or by any means. The ancient symbolic meaning of this kanji is an inferred image of something severed from its life-giving source (animal or plant) by the cut of an axe (or other edged implement) and placed upon a wheeled cart.

突, *totsu* -- a combination of 穴, *ana* (symbol meaning *cave* or *slit*, i.e., an opening), 心, *kokoro* (symbol meaning *heart*), and 一, *ichi* (symbol meaning *one*). The basic meaning of this is either "one heart slit," i.e., a physical act of attack, or "one heart opening," an opening to the heart of the matter. Considering the physical being of an animal or human this is an action to immediately terminate life by *piercing to the heart*. Notwithstanding, considering from the viewpoint of overcoming a difficulty or problem, this kanji also means *getting to the heart of the matter* or *pointed and purposeful action*.

To illustrate linguistic flexibility, consider the linguistic construct *toppasuru* (突破する {to breakthrough}{to overcome}{to surpass}{to exceed}. The literal sense of the kanji 突, *totsu* {attack}{pierce}, is shifted to the figurative sense (attack a problem), and when associated with the kanji 破, *ha* {defeat}{destroy}{break}{rend}{rip}{tear}, has the combined literal meaning of *attack and defeat*, but a presently accepted figurative sense of *breakthrough, overcome, penetrate* or *surpass*, i.e., 突破, *toppa*. 会, *kai* (association, society).

斬突破会 合気道, meaning *Zantoppa-kai Aikido*, is an association of aikidoka devoted to learning and maintaining the aiki behavior and skill that is necessary to protect and sustain life when faced with a situation of self-defense. Supportive of this idea, the kanji 斬 is focused toward meaning *cut* or *cut through*, the kanji group 突破 is defined as meaning *overcome* or *penetrate*, and the three kanji, 斬突破, collectively impart a meaning of *cut through to overcome* or *overcome by cutting through*, i.e., survive, the difficult situations that emerge or erupt in life.

斬突流 合気柔術, with a meaning of *Zantotsu-ryū Aikijujutsu*, is a manner or style of performing aiki techniques with an emphasis on maintaining a functional and technically correct self-defense basis, a *truth-mirror*, for the tactics and techniques of Aikido.

When combined, their ancient Bushido meaning of *cut and thrust* is derived out of the context of Japanese feudal clans or armies who were engaged in warfare. This meaning was an inference as to how the warrior (samurai) should engage the opponent while in the midst of battle -- that is, cut and thrust, cut and thrust. At some later point it took on a second meaning, in addition to its martial meaning, a sense of *remaining steadfast and engaging the problems of life in order to gain victory.*

The martial technical meaning of the precept of *zantotsu*, along with its companion precept *datotsu*, is yet employed in the Kenjutsu and Kendo of today.

Note the use of the kanji radical *ono* (斤) in the word *shinshukyo* (新興宗教) {new religion}. The kanji 新 means {new}{fresh}{modern} {recent}, but it refers to a *separation from the old,* i.e., a *cutting of a branch from the established tree.*

Other informative kanji

戦 or 戰, sen (onyomi) or tatakau (or *ikusa* or *ononoku*, all kunyomi) -- meaning of {battle}{fighting}{war}{a war}{warfare}{a battle}{a fight}{combat}{a match}{a game}{a race}.

闘, tatakau (or *tatakai*, both kunyomi) or tou (onyomi) -- meaning {struggle}{grapple}{contend}{compete}{strive}{fight}{battle}{combat}. An example of usage is 闘志, toushi {fighting spirit}, or 健闘する, kentou suru -- meaning {to fight bravely}{to make strenuous efforts}.

掴, tsukamu (or *tsukami*, both kunyomi) or kaku (onyomi) -- meaning {slap}{box the ears of a person}.

槍, yari (kunyomi) or sou (or *shou* both onyomi) -- meaning {spear}{lance}{gun}{rifle}.

鑓, yari (kunyomi only) -- meaning {spear}{lance}{javelin}.

刃, ha (also *yaiba* or *kiru*, all kunyomi), or jin (onyomi) -- meaning {blade} {edged tool}{cutlery}{knife}.

刀, katana (kunyomi); or tou (onyomi) -- meaning {a single-edged sword}{saber}.

剣, ken (onyomi); or tsurugi (kunyomi) -- meaning {two edged sword}{sword}{blade}{clock hand}.

箙, ebira (kunyomi); or fuku (onyomi) -- meaning {quiver}.

笂, utsubo (kunyomi only) -- meaning {arrow quiver}.

後, ato (also *okureru* or *nochi*, all kunyomi); or go (or *kou*, both onyomi) -- meaning {behind}{back}{rear}{later}{descendants}.

逾, go {pass}{go beyond}; 邁, go {go}{excel}; 踰, go {go beyond}; 迴, go {go around}; 戻, go {return}{revert}{resume}{restore}{go backwards}; 旋, go {rotation}{go around}; 囬, go {go around}; 罷, go {quit}{stop}{leave}{withdraw}{go away}; 本, go {advance quickly}{to go back and forth}. **Previous are kunyomi. Following are onyomi.** 禦, go {defend}{protect}{resist}{ward off}; 後, go (ato) {behind}{back}{later}; 冴, go {be clear}{serene}{cold}{skillful}; 忤, go {go against}{be contrary to}; 五, go {five}.

会, kai (or e, both onyomi) or au (or *atsumaru*, both kunyomi) -- meaning of {assembly}{meeting}{meet}{meet together}{party}{an association or a society}{interview}{join}.

流, ryuu (ryū, as in Tomiki-ryū) (onyomi) -- meaning {a current}{a school of thought}{a style}{a mode}{a way}; for example, 起倒流,

Kitoryū (a school of jūjutsu).

大, O (kunyomi) -- meaning {large} {big} {great}.

本, moto (onyomi) -- meaning {origin} {source}{to go back and forth} {advance quickly}.

本, hon (onyomi) -- meaning {main}{true}{real}{book}.

教, kyou (onyomi) -- meaning {doctrine}{faith}{teach}.

心, shin (onyomi) or kokoro (kunyomi) -- meaning {mind}{heart} {spirit}.

合, au (also *ai* or *awaseru*, both kunyomi) or gou (also *katsu* or *gatsu*, both onyomi) -- meaning {fit}{suit}{join}{combine}{meet}.

気, ki (or *ke*, both onyomi) or iki (kunyomi) -- meaning {air}{gas}{steam} {vapor}{spirit}{mind}.

道, dou (also *dō* or *tou*, both onyomi) or michi (also *iu* or *michibiku*, both kunyomi) -- meaning of {journey}{course}{path}{road}{street} {method}{way}{moral}{teachings}.

退, tai (onyomi) -- meaning {retreat} {withdraw} {retire} {resign} {repel} {expel} {reject}.

逮, tai (onyomi) -- meaning {apprehend} {chase}.

撃, geki (onyomi) -- meaning {beat} {attack} {defeat} {conquer}.

撃退 , gekitai -- meaning {beat and repel, or colloquially, to repel or repulse an enemy or opponent}.

拒, kyo (onyomi) -- meaning {repel}{refuse}{reject}{decline}.

斫, kiru (kunyomi) -- meaning {cut with sword}{chop}.

祈, inoru (or *inori*, both kunyomi) or ki (onyomi) -- meaning {pray}{entreat}{beseech}.

斥, shirizo (kunyomi) -- meaning of {reject}{retreat}{recede}{withdraw}{repel}{repulse}.

斥く, shirizoku; verb intransitive (a combination of kanji and hiragana) -- meaning of {step back **or** move back}{leave (the presence of a superior)}{withdraw}{retreat}{concede}{resign}{retire}{quit}.

斥ける, shirizokeru; verb transitive (a combination of kanji and hiragana) -- meaning {repel}{drive away}{repulse}{reject}.

斬殺, zansatsu; noun or participle which takes the auxiliary verb *suru* -- meaning {put to the sword}{death by cut}.

刺し通す, sashitoosu -- meaning {stab}{pierce}{run through} (e.g., with a sword).

斥, seki (onyomi reading) -- meaning {reject}{retreat}{recede}{withdraw}{repel}{repulse}. An example of the use of this kanji is the verb 排斥する, haisekisuru -- meaning {drive out}{oust}{expel}{ostracize}{reject}.

和, wa (or *ka*, both onyomi) or yawaragu (also nagomu or nago-yaka, both kunyomi) -- meaning {harmony}{peace}{peaceful}{soften}.

倭, wa (onyomi) -- meaning {Yamato} {ancient Japan}.

柔, juu (jū, as in Jūdo) (onyomi) -- meaning {gentleness} {softness} {tender} {weakness}.

从, ju (onyomi) -- meaning {two people}.

木, ki (kunyomi) -- meaning {tree} {wood}.

合気道家, aikidoka -- meaning {practitioner of Aikido}.

The Zan ideogram & other pertinent kanji

[1] In Japan, Chinese characters (sinograms, a type of ideogram) are used to represent many of their native words, but ignoring the Chinese pronunciation. Onyomi refers to a much older Chinese derivation yet used in modern Japanese language, this showing the influence of the Chinese language upon Japan. Kunyomi refers to Japanese indigenous derivations either uniquely created or uniquely employed; the latter being a situation of the older Chinese kanji with their traditional meaning being commonly used with that meaning by the Japanese people but with a different vocalization sound (pronunciation). An example here is that of the kanji 斫 given above: the romaji utterance of *kiru* (Japanese kunyomi) and the romaji utterance of *shaku* (older, or Middle Chinese/Sino-Japanese onyomi pronunciation) are rendered or represented by the same Chinese hanzi/Japanese kanji character. Incidentally, the modern Chinese Mandarin (pinyin) pronunciation of this character is *zhuó* (chop).

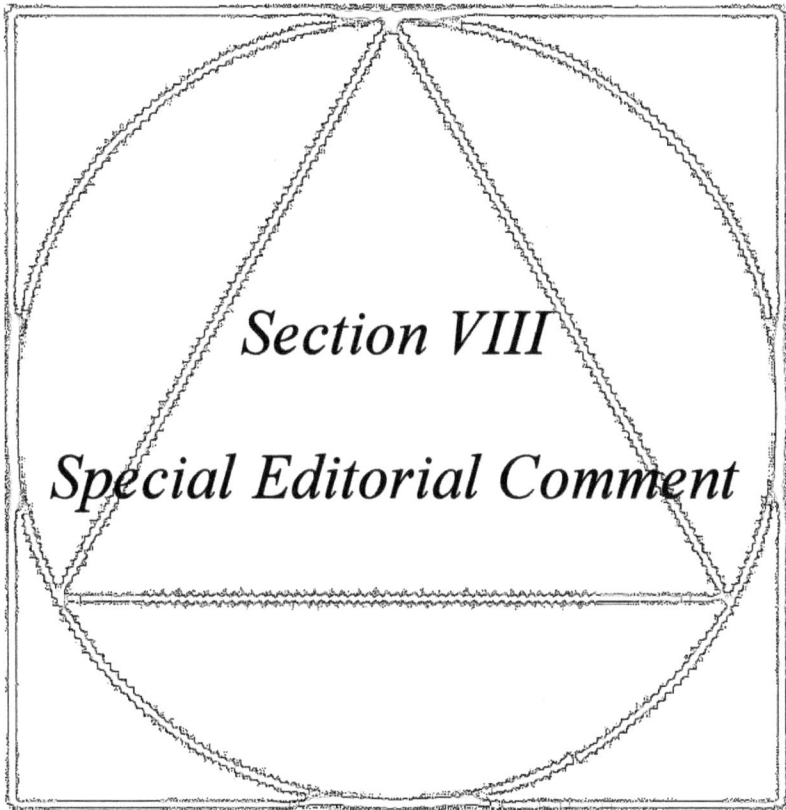

Section VIII

Special Editorial Comment

Special Editorial Comment

In reference to the author's discussion on page 33, the question of the role of spirituality or religious sense in the discipline of Aikido is complex and worth sorting out. Lack of understanding in this area leads to wrong assumptions and practice. Aikido is not a religion, *per se*, if religion is defined as a set of beliefs concerning the cause, nature and purpose of the universe, or belief in and worship of a supernatural controlling power (dictionary.com). There seems to be as many definitions of the term "religion" as there are people who are practitioners of religion. The term originates from the Old French or Latin *religio*, meaning obligation, bond, reverence, and perhaps from the Latin verb *religare*, to bind. These origins have given the term "religion" its uncomfortable connotation as a system of beliefs, or supernatural entity that is "bound" to the system or entity in a dynamic of worship, obedience in behavior and judgment of inadequate practice. Aikido does not have a specific cosmological system that is advanced, more a code of awareness and behavior. The concept of Budo, stopping the weapons of destruction, is a behavioral code based on the belief that destruction and the weapons that bring it about are inconsistent with the beliefs concerning the harmony of human beings with each other and with nature. While many would characterize this as a religious belief, it does not have to be, depending on the definition. The term "spirituality" has come to denote a pursuit of understanding of things pertaining to the human spirit that does not necessarily carry the burden of bondage to a specific system of beliefs, worship of a specific supernatural entity or agreement with any institutional religious sense. The term "spirituality" comes from the Latin *spiritualis*, meaning of breathing or of wind. It is a term not easily unpacked, but seems to suggest concern with things not specifically physical or of the body, and things not easily understood by the mind or intellect. Spiritual things are more ethereal ; there but unseen, felt but not understood. This is another term that is loaded with cultural history and various associations, but is useful, in that it is less offensive, while being at the same time somewhat ineffable. The concept of Budo, can be considered a spiritual concept, in that it is based in a belief about a particular intrinsic worth of the human being and of the forces of nature. These beliefs are not tangible like muscles and cannot be arrived at by reason alone.

Aikido is a discipline that would have its practitioners become holistic in their approach to life, in its embrace of fitness of the mind, body and spirit. Morihei Ueshiba's statements about "walking the spiritual path" as it relates to training the mind and body indicate that he is considering such a holistic understanding of the human being. While there is little evidence that Aikido was engineered to be a religion in itself, or even a specific spiritual path in exclusion of all other paths, it has naturally been informed and influenced by the specific beliefs of its founder and successive practitioners, most of whom are Native Japanese. Most of the questions posed about the "religious" or "spiritual" nature of Aikido come as a result of the discipline becoming available to other cultures, which must then struggle to fit the discipline to their society's particular *weltanschauung* or world view, but influenced by their cultural, religious, or spiritual influence, whether or not they are practitioners of a specific faith. To use an example taken from Western culture, Aikido needs a *Universal Translator*, like the one posed in Star Trek that converts the Star Trek crew's language into something understood by any species they encounter, in effect, putting the message in the species' own language. It seems clear to me that Ueshiba intended Aikido to be a way to draw together and make fit all aspects of an aikidoka, which would include the mind, body and spirit. Aikido has an obvious physical component. What is less obvious is the training of the mind and the aspect of the student that correlates to his or her spiritual sense. The fact that Aikido's origins rise from the Shinto religion with its belief that the Kami are only available to Native Japanese does not mean that with the use of the Universal Translator other cultures cannot bring the discipline to bear fruit for their own spiritual journeys. The Universal Translator in this metaphor would consist of seeking to relate the core or "spirit" of the Shinto beliefs to one's own set of beliefs. This can even be done for a person with a minimum of "beliefs." Practitioners of a spiritual path who have particular values that rise out of their spiritual sense, often do not belong to a particular religion, church, synagogue or temple, but have based their values on cultural mores that are taught through family practice and cultural adherence (often expressed in codes of law). Shinto spirits inform the Japanese through history and cultural practice just as do the "spirits" of Western culture have informed Europeans and as the "spirits" of other cultures have informed their descendants.

Aikido's physical practice is more easily transmitted across cultural lines. The sharpening of the intellect is slightly more difficult to transmit, but has been aided by translation of Aikido texts into other languages, and through the intellectual pursuits and documentation of aikidoka from these other cultures. The spiritual path is the most inscrutable and for good reason. Despite the fact that there are numerous religions and organizations with codes, rituals and doctrines, each spiritual path is unique to the traveler. Unavoidably, this makes it more difficult to understand the precepts laid out by the Shintoist Morihei Ueshiba insofar as the "spiritual path" is concerned. Fortunately for us non-Japanese aikidoka, we are able to translate (with help from both the intellect and the body via the consistent practice of the kata) these precepts into what can be recognized by our own individual sense. Although there is no way to prove it, some things are thought to be universal -- that is, cross-cultural. Ueshiba's concept of the harmony of mind, body and spirit is widespread among cultures. Ueshiba's belief in the intrinsic value of the human being and Nature as evidenced by his value of stopping the weapons of destruction can be understood as one of those spiritual precepts that is universal in its acceptance (if ever such a universality is possible). To use yet another Science Fiction analogy, the protagonist from the movie K-Pax, an extraterrestrial being named Prot, asserts that "*Every being in the universe knows right from wrong.*" Human beings tend to believe at an early age, and perhaps from birth, that harm is not good, and shouldn't be done. Harmony feels good. Creation is positive, within limits or depending on perspective. Moderation in all things makes sense. A minor key seems to beckon for resolution into a major key. Destruction can only be good when it concerns the removal of an impediment in order to recreate without harming life. (We're starting to get into unsure footing here!) Destruction that brings harm to humans or to the Natural world that provides our living environment is not to be done. Harm none. Stopping the weapons of destruction seems to be a worthy goal, says Ueshiba about the true meaning of Budo. If I believe this, value and practice it, I'm walking on this path, too!

Ueshiba was not suggesting that Aikido be a religion or that he should be seen as a God. This is a mistake commonly made by those who do not reflect true harmony in mind, body and spirit. It's like worshipping the vessel instead of what it contains, or worshipping the process rather than the content. Human beings are hard-wired to appreciate ritual; it is a function of our "reptilian" brain (Carl Sagan, *Dragons of Eden*). This is what gives us the desire to practice adherence to what we consider sacred. Aikido provides a well-grounded vehicle for human beings to embrace and practice the harmonizing of all human characteristics and qualities.

A final note is necessary to sort out Morihei Ueshiba's concept of Budo, which proposal seems to render Aikido a non-martial practice, with the fact that it is obviously a practice that also teaches the overcoming of an aggressor with actions that could potentially bring harm or even death to an aggressor. In an ideal world, people might like to live in a collective harmony of mind, body, and spirit where there would not exist contentious behavior, self-defense, or defense of borders. We live in our present world, however, where people with many different conditions or levels of physical, emotional, and spiritual health must contend with the possibility of an attack on our person or family by any of a number of misguided or mentally ill societal members. My personal core values include protecting my family and myself. This seems to me to be one of those universal values (although there are many good Quakers who might attempt to prove me wrong). Aikido provides a method to address a personal physical attack with an appropriate physical response, which offers a chance of survival. The behavioral attitude that is necessary to ready an aikidoka for such a response comes from a place of intellectual commitment that is merged with consistent physical practice while embracing Morihei Ueshiba's ideal philosophy of Budo, i.e., stopping the weapons of destruction (and other values relevant to the aikidoka's spiritual journey). Aikido teaches a proportional response that is the minimum necessary to achieve one's safety when attacked -- i.e., with the least harm to the other person. If a person can distance himself or herself from the attacker, deescalate through conversation or tactfully retreat, these choices are consistent with the practice of Aikido. If the attacker cannot be avoided or dissuaded then, well, "rock and roll." The lack of spiritual responsibility falls mostly on the attacker in such an event, although the defender may later experience some compassion and concern for the necessary damage done. Self-imposed guilt in this instance is unwarranted. The goal is to bring yourself back into harmonious relationship with the circumstances of your existence, and in a larger sense, ideally, with the world. If physical action is required, then the Aikido practitioner must rise to the occasion and defend. In holding such a personal worldview, the necessary physical response of an aikidoka defender is consistent with Budo's ideal tenets as elucidated by Morihei Ueshiba as well as with spiritually proper or right action.

Hunter F. Morrigan
Editor

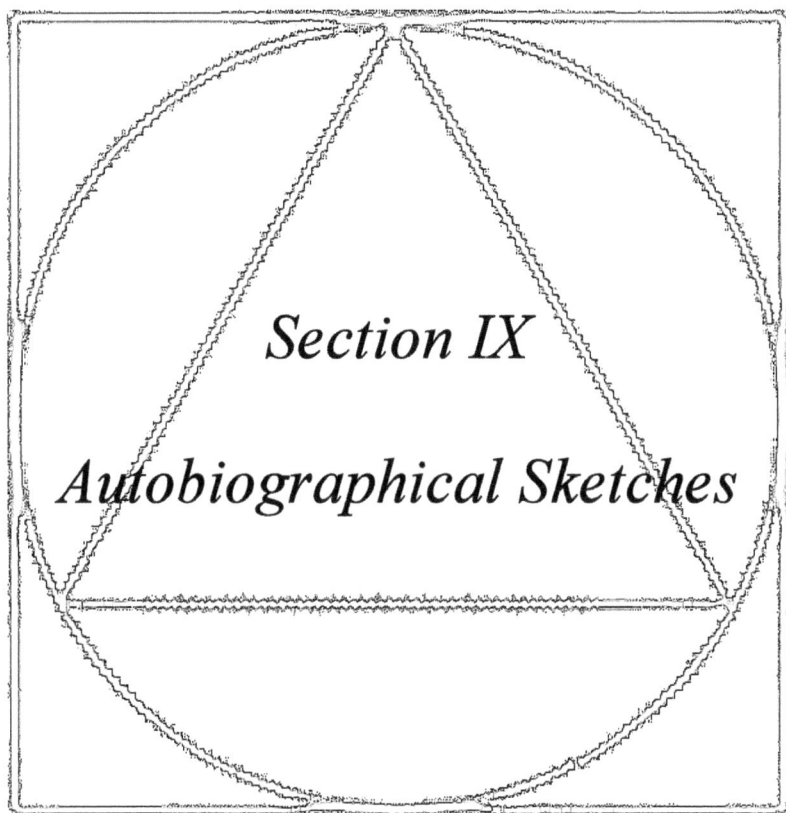

Section IX

Autobiographical Sketches

Autobiographical Sketches

Jån J. Sunderlin, Aikidoka

The author believes that a short overview of his progression toward Aikido as well as his historical experience therein would be a useful body of information that a reader could use to further their own understanding of life.

Public high school is sometimes an odd and tumultuous time for certain developing youth, even more so for one who is an introverted personality, as was I. During my youth, I sought out activities and work that involved few people. Sport activities that were not team oriented were ideal for me. As a physically active youth, I enjoyed track and field sports, but determined that I was most comfortable with track -- relays and distance running. Running, in particular distance running, provided a certain or definite self-introspection process that provided some good information about the inherent aspects or features of my character, elucidating both mental and physical strengths as well as weaknesses. Another sport activity that I engaged was that of wrestling, both in my physical education classes and, for a brief period of time, on the high school wrestling team. Of course, like many boys of that time, I had gained a little natural but unstructured experience at "wrestling" in the form of physical tussles with my younger brothers and neighborhood friends, which had occasionally occurred during various kinds of adventure play.

During the public school era within which I grew and became more largely aware (the 1950s through the 1960s), an occurrence of bullying or of violent physical interaction was, given the community within which I existed, somewhat rare. Yet, disconcertingly, incidents of this type seemed to be increasing in number as time passed. As I later came to understand, this increase was not necessarily a result of more such events occurring in relation to the population, but rather, a perceptual one that was a result of myself becoming more alert to the fact that uncomfortable and sometimes difficult or violent person-to-person interaction was quite more likely to occur than I had ever before realized.

While in high school, several bullying and physical altercations occurred in which I was an unwilling participant/target, and after each such episode, little by little, I began to evolve a maturing attitude as to what could be done as well as to what had to be done in order to minimize such conflict. (This is not to infer that I was able to produce a high level of skill toward resolving this type of human contention, as I was young and yet largely inexperienced.) Of first importance to me at that time was the improvement of my awareness of the various peopled environs within which I found myself as I pursued life. High school was one such environment, bringing together a large number of people, ostensibly for educational reasons. Secondly, but not of lesser importance, was that of developing the skills necessary to recognize the signs of possible or potential conflict in order to avoid or diffuse it, or if that was not possible, to be able to ward it off, i.e., defend against, an aggressor's attack. Consciously awakened, I slowly yet surely engaged Western Wrestling, Boxing, and Fencing, and later, respectively, Judo, Aikido, Jodo, Shiatsu, and Jujutsu, and Hung Ga Kungfu.

Immediately following my graduation from high school in May of 1970, I enrolled in college. In addition to the academic subjects that I had engaged to study, I also enrolled in several successively offered Western Boxing courses that were taught by a boxing coach that had once been associated with the Golden Gloves organization. All students therein participated in learning the movements and techniques of Boxing and put this knowledge to test in many sparring sessions, and later, several boxing matches. I learned well and was an above average boxer. Later, during the Vietnam War era I joined the United States Coast Guard (U.S.C.G.). During my service, I engaged in some required combat and fire-fighting training as well as further Boxing; most people today are not aware that the U.S. Coast Guard had a few of its cutters and numerous armed small boats operating in the coastal areas of what was then known as South Vietnam. At my last duty station, the U.S.C.G. L.O.R.A.N C base that was located at Carolina Beach, North Carolina, I engaged in numerous boxing matches against members of a local amatuer boxing club in Wilmington, North Carolina. These were unofficial 'smokers' (fights) that were hosted by a local wrestling and boxing promoter. By 1976, I had made the decision that I was not going to reenlist in the Guard and in September of that year was officially released from active duty. After release from active duty, I moved back to my home state, Washington, and soon thereafter married a woman who had recently enlisted in the United States Navy. Her first duty station was in Hawaii and naturally I followed. While living in Hawaii, I continued my studies toward a college degree and found a local boxing gym where I continued to maintain my boxing skills. Later, in September of 1978, after having served two years in the U.S. Coast Guard Reserve, I was honorably discharged. After approximately one and a half years in Hawaii, my wife was transferred to Ford Island Naval Base in the north San Francisco Bay area and naturally, again, I followed. While there, I continued my academic studies at a nearby college, and it is during this time that I also began training in Judo, and later Aikido.

During the time up to the point where I began Judo, I was becoming slowly aware of the cognition disorders that many professional boxers were suffering due to repetitive head trauma; the reasons for such was less understood then than it is today. Since I was not a professional boxer and did not intend to go there, I reasoned that repetitive jiggling or shaking of the brain might cause over a long course of time the emergence of some type of cognitive disability; so, I began a search for other combative disciplines in which a person could paticipate in order to maintain physical vigor while also retaining or improving self-defense ability. One day, I came across a flyer on a bulletin board that advertised Judo. I studied Judo for a short period of time, about 8 months, at a small dojo near Vallejo, California. This initial study of Judo was short because of several reasons. *First*, it was oriented toward required competition in order to advance to each successive level of study (*kyu* level or *dan* grade). *Second*, because of its competitive orientation, one's struggles in training or shiai against a partner or opponent often ended in the envitable and frequent outcome of harsh impact with mat; and even though I was prepared by the study of ukemi to properly receive impact with the ground, any such impact shook my body, which meant it also rattled my brain. In addition, such a transition from an active upright position to a ground impact by means of an opponent's success in throwing you would occasionally result in an awkward fall, which itself could and sometimes would injure various parts of the body, e.g., shoulder, neck, knee, ankle. This is not to say that Judo is dangerous, but it is rough and tumble and is best suitable for those with the 'right attitude.' Though I learned quite a lot from my short experience with Judo -- such as balance breaking, ukemi, throwing, and how to better control a struggling opponent with various control techniques -- it was not a combative sport discipline that I could imagine myself doing as I aged because I believed that the harsh impacts would emerge both bodily and cognitive harm (brain injury) over time. As a result, I informed the Judo sensei that I needed a different type of combative disicpline and he recommended that I check out Aikido.

Within several months of ending my Judo study, I was able to find an Aikido sensei who was teaching regular sessions in a small gymnasium. Coincidently, it was located on the Ford Island Navy Base, but I had not previously seen this sensei's advertisement flyers for his instruction. Soon after, sometime in the autumn of 1980, I began training in what was then called Tomiki-ryu Aikido. From that beginning point until now I have been studying and teaching Aikido, Aikijujutsu, and Jodo. During my initial Aikido training, from 1980 through 1988, which provided me with a thorough foundation, I trained under the Tomiki-ryu Aikido shihans Carl Geis, Tsunako Miyake, Takeshi Inoue as well as several other American and British Tomiki Aikido sensei. Tsunako Miyake Shihan took a particular interest in my training because she witnessed and sat in judgment of my Nidan advancement, later commenting to me in the presence of some of Shihan Geis' senior instructors that "*Your performance of your Nidan advancement requirements was so excellent that it surpassed anything I've ever seen, even of our many students in Japan.*" An accurate retelling of this event by the senior instructors who were present at that time could substantiate not only her comment but also that which occurred shortly thereafter, which was that Miyake Shihan presented to me her own obi (her black-belt). As you might imagine, Tsunako Miyake's act sent ripples of unwarranted egoistic concern through the minds of several of these instructors, and the inter-dojo social discord that resulted required the intervention of Carl Geis Shihan, who resolved the problem in the best way possible. It is sufficient to say that Aikido sociopolitical dynamics are sometimes challenging to the point where they turn out unsatisfactory for some. This type of negative-trending social dynamic, of which there were numerous instances, eventually caused me to decide to split off from the Fugakukai. In 1989 I officially separated from the Fugakukai and formed Zantotsu Ryu Aikijujutsu, an organization that serves today as a technical *truth mirror* for the Zantoppa Kai, i.e., for Zantoppa Kai Aikido.

Almost all of my teaching of Aikido has occurred in the state of Washington. Though I have personally taught over 3,200 people in both Aikido and Aikijujutsu, only a little more than one percent of these achieved the coveted Shodan grade or higher, as my methods of teaching demand both commitment and excellence from a student. Presently I'm retired, meaning, I no longer teach either Aikido or Aikijujutsu to members of the general public, but I do maintain my skill and physical fitness by training with several of my teachers who are closeby. When asked, I will consider holding an Aikido seminar, but this occurs infrequently.

To end, I'd like to relate to the reader the best condition of my relationship with Carl Geis Shihan, who was a sensei with a keen technical insight.[1] Upon this author's attendance of one particular Aikido seminar held in 1987 at the headquarters of Fugakukai International Aikido in Houston, Texas, Carl Geis Shihan inscribed the following in a copy of his book entitled *A Book of Twelve Winds* (See photo below), which the author had earlier purchased, thus expressing the condition of his relationship with me:

"You have gone to great lengths to study Aikido in the proper manner. I am proud that a person such as you chose me as a colleague and friend. You grow each time we meet and are a true martial artist, aikidoka, and friend."

Carl Geis, June 22, 1987
Tomiki/Kihara Aikido Shihan
Fugakukai International

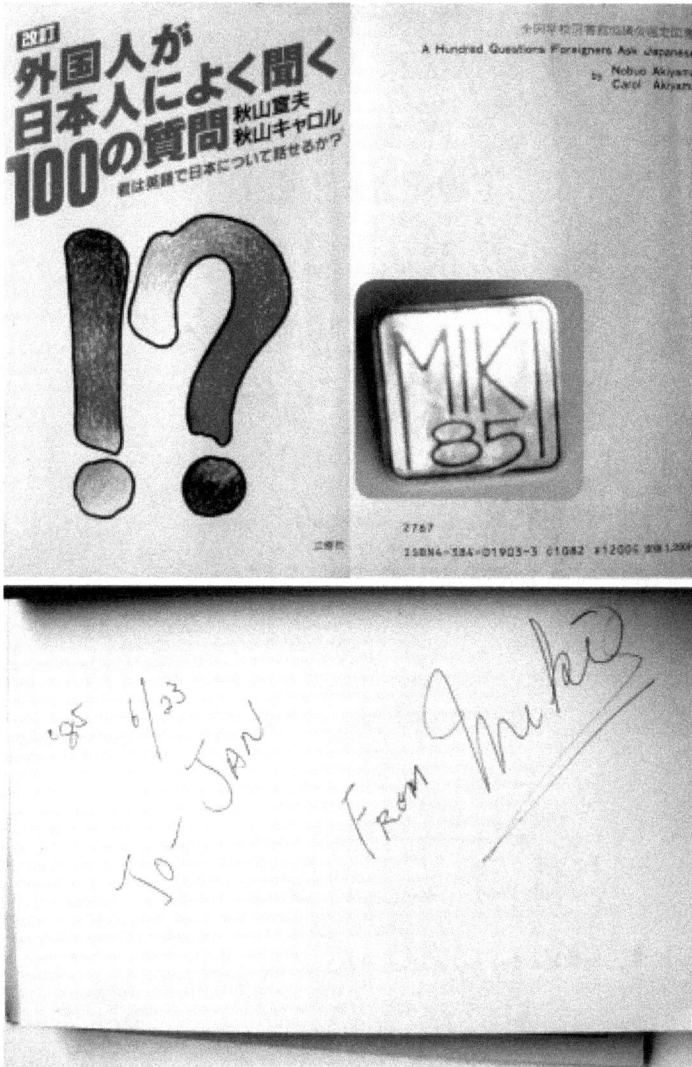

A Hundred Questions Foreigners Ask Japanese book
(Author's *Miyake Seminar* gold pin digitally inset on back cover.)

Given by Tsunako Miyake Shihan (nickname of "*Miki*")
to Jån Sunderlin in 1985.

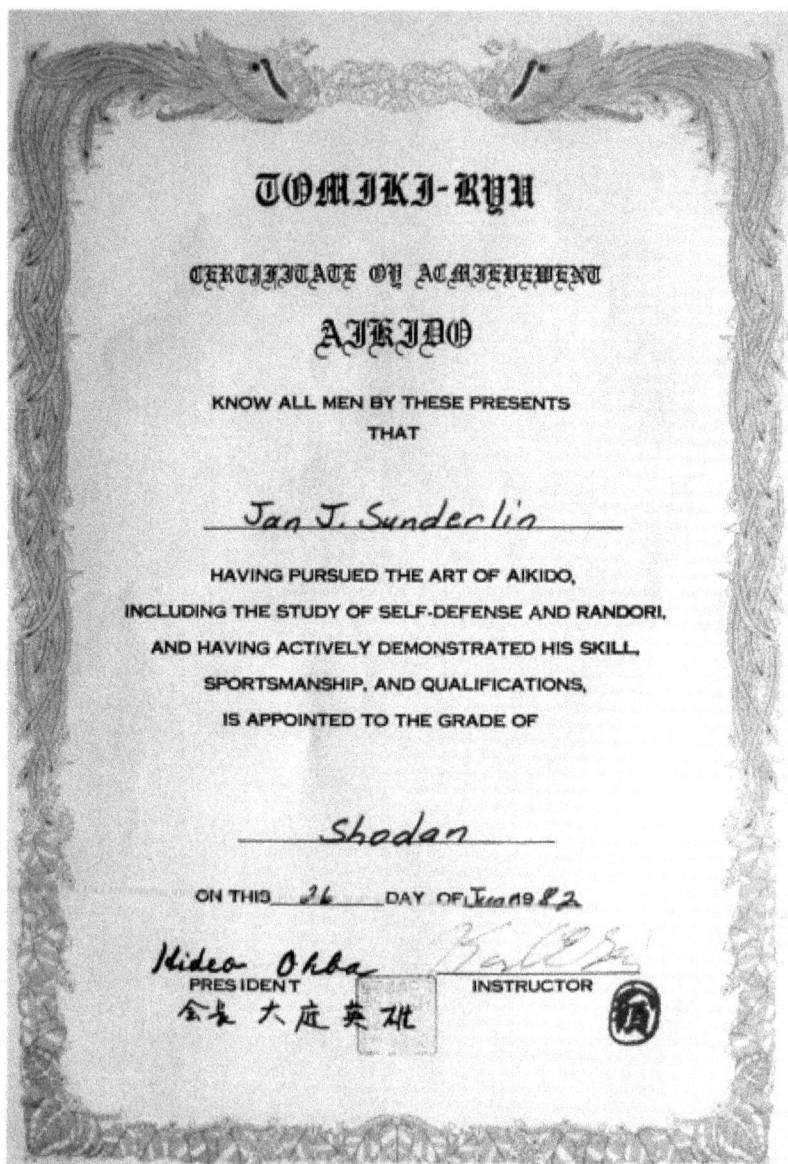

Author's Tomiki-ryu Shodan Certificate -- 1982
(Japan Aikido Association/Shodokan Aikido)
Signed by **Hideo Ohba** (Shihan) and **Karl Geis** (Sensei).

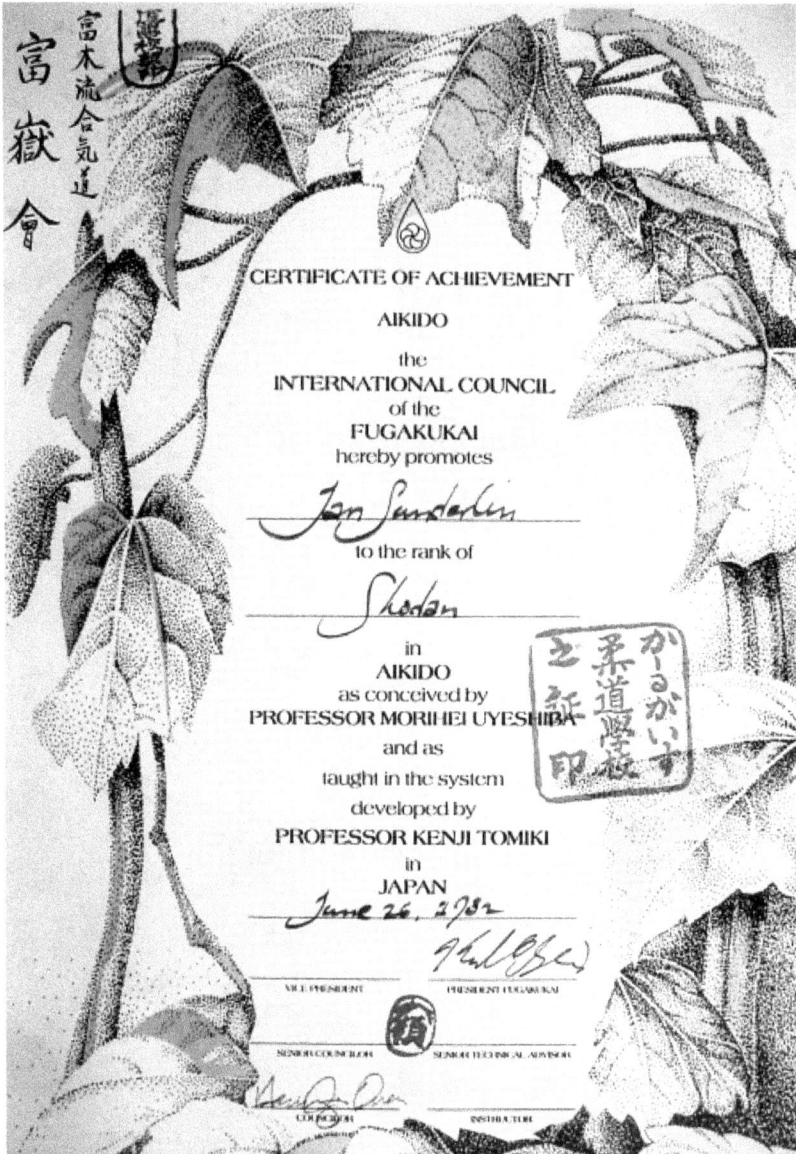

Author's Fugakukai Shodan Certificate -- 1982
(Issued by Fugakukai International.)
Signed by *Karl Geis* (Shihan).

Author's Nidan Certificate -- 1985
(Issued by Fugakukai International.)
Signed by
Tsunako Miyake Shihan, ***Takeshi Inoue*** Meiyo Shihan,
and ***Karl Geis*** Shihan.

The
Zan - totsu Ryu
promotes

Jan Sunderlin
to the rank of
Godan
in the discipline of
Aikido

Author's Godan Certificate -- 1989
(Issued by the Board of Advisors, Zantotsu-ryu Aikijujutsu, following
separation from Fugakukai.)
Signed by Advisors
William E. Gregory (Shodan, Z.T.R.A.), ***Jolene S. Cantrell*** (Shodan,
Z.T.R.A.), and ***Patrick K. Jones***[2] (Nidan, Z.T.R.A.; Shihanke, Tenjin
Shin'yō-ryū).

Dedication penned by Karl Geis, Aikido shihan, in a
copy of his work, *A Book of Twelve Winds*,
owned by the author -- *June 22, 1987*.

DECLARATION

We, the undersigned instructors of the Zan Totsukai Aikido Schools, in recognition of our Shidosha's years of dedicated effort in the refinement and promulgation of this system hereby unanimously and unreservedly appoint Jan Sunderlin to the Honorary rank of KUDAN, thereby encouraging the further development and direction of Shidosha, the Zan Totsukai instructors, and all students in the discipline of Aikido, and in the concepts of Tomaranu Kokoro.

Dated this __1ST__ Day of ___March___ , 1996.

Alan L. Chiswell
NIDAN Z.T.K.A.

John B. Copeland
Shodan Z.T.K.A.

Jason Stacy
SANDAN Z.T.K.A.

Chris Mills
Shodan Z.T.KA

C. Robert Davis
Sandan Z.T.K.A

FB McMullin
Shodan Z.T.K.A.

Declaration of support by the Zantotsu-kai Aikido senseis

(Mr. Chris Mills sensei, today, is also ranked 3rd Dan Aikikai style by the United States Aikido Federation.)

Autobiographical Sketches

[1] Karl Geis Shihan passed away on April 8, 2014.

[2] This sensei and Zantotsu Ryu advisor passed away on February 4, 1997.

Hunter F. Morrigan, Editor in Chief

Hunter Morrigan trained in Aikido to the level of Shodan. She received her Bachelor's degree from James Madison University, a Master's in Counseling Psychology from the University of Puget Sound, and a Master's of Divinity and a Master's of Theological Studies from the Methodist Theological School in Ohio. Hunter is a social worker in the area of Child Welfare and does professional writing for the State of Washington, authoring home studies for a-doption candidates and candidates for relative placement of children. She holds a Shodan grade certificate (first-degree black belt) in Zantoppai-kai Aikido.

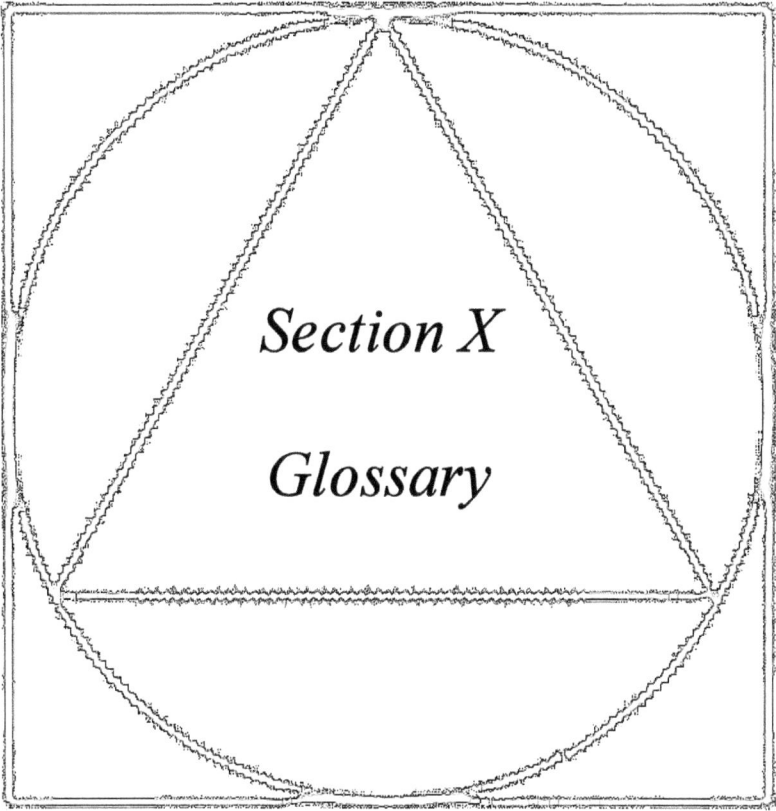

Section X

Glossary

Glossary

Aiki (Japanese) -- Harmony of energy, harmony of spirit, uniting energy, meeting spirit, etc.

Aikikai Aikidō (Japanese) -- A prominent Aikido style that is considered to be technically and philosophically most similar to or aligned with the teachings of the founder of Aikido, Morihei Ueshiba. Other significant styles of Aikido are ***Shōdōkan*** founded by Kenji Tomiki, ***Shin-shin Tōitsu*** founded by Kōichi Tōhei, ***Yōseikan*** founded by Minoru Mōchizuki, and ***Yōshinkan*** founded by Gōzō Shioda.

Aikidō (Japanese) -- The way of harmonious spirit, the way of meeting spirit, the way of harmonized energy, or the way of uniting spirit is a unique physio-spiritual discipline which offers a path of study that can lead a person toward a personal refinement of consciousness while inculcating appropriate and functionally protective self-defense skill that, if applied out of necessity during a situation of self-defense, can be minimally injurious to an offender.

Ai Uchi No Kyoukun (Japanese) -- The Japanese martial precept of mutual striking.

Ai Nuke No Kyoukun (Japanese) -- The Japanese martial precept of mutual escape.

Ākāśa, or ***Akasha*** (Hindu/Buddhist Sanskrit) -- A Far East Indian and Asian conceptualization of that which comprises the underlying motive and connective forces that make possible all that exists in any form or non-form, inanimate or animate -- a cosmic aether. Hinduism, Buddhism, and Jainism each have a slightly different theory of Akasha. Cārvākism, though, holds that it is impossible to perceive or to prove (even through inference) the existence of such an aether. Historical and traditional Asian metaphysical theory consists of five supreme interactive manifestations or phenomenon that have arisen from the infinite; those being, and in order of their occurrence, *1)* Aether (Akasha), *2)* Air, *3)* Fire, *4)* Water, and *5)* Earth. Modern science denies an aether, but, what are we to think of zodiacial dust, radio waves, high-energy particles, gravity, light, dark matter. etc.? Collectively, could these not be considered as an aether?

Ākāśagarbha (Hindu/Buddhist Sanskrit) -- A mythical boddhisattva conception derived from the Far East Indian Sanskrit word *Akasha* that expresses the idea of intergalactic space, aether or ether, difficult to quantify connective and creative force(s), void, etc., that is prominent in Hinduism, Buddhism, and Jainism.

Bodhisattva (Hindu/Buddhist Sanskrit) -- A person who seeks and manifests an awakened or enlightened existence.

Budō (Japanese) -- A Japanese word that is general used to categorize any Japanese martial art. Since the two kanji ideograms that represent this word are somewhat subject to the personal bias of the person rendering its meaning, there is sometimes disagreement as to its best, normalized meaning. Morihei Ueshiba, founder of the discipline of Aikido interprets it to mean "Stopping weapons of destruction way" because it pertains to limited martial interdiction for the reason of restoring order, harmony, and peace.

Bushi (Japanese) -- Refers to the Japanese warrior of antiquity; typically, a retained warrior during Japan's feudal era before World War I.

Bushidō (Japanese) -- Refers to the archaic Japanese Warrior (martial) Way, partially consisting of a certain era-dependent ethical code.

Buddhism -- An Asian religion that proposes that through the acceptance of four evident human truths (the Four Noble Truths) that suffering experienced by any person can be moderated, reduced, or eliminated by the proper implementation and regular practice of eight guiding tenants (the Eight Fold Path), and that through careful mental attentiveness (utilizing both moving and still meditation) the transcendence of misery can be realized, eventually leading to the ultimate spiritual ascendance termed Parinirvana (the final stage of Nirvana), a non-corporeal state of ultra-enlightened being that is merged with the boundless supreme workings of Akasha (aether), the basis of which is the occurrence of sound.

Consciousness -- The innate, ongoing cognitive (mental) processes within the human brain that function to develop, maintain, and re-configure a 'working' model of the world that uses multiple neural feedback loops, neuron meme groups, and interactive neural net-works in relation to various parameters (such as in temperature, vi-brations, space, time, interaction with other people) with the object of attaining a goal (such as in food, shelter, clothing, tools, a mate), which includes self-awareness as well as awareness of things, other living organisms, and all objectively ascertained phenomenon (via the senses). *As soon as a model of the world is formed, self-aware-ness in relation to that model arises by the brain's biased 'force-of-model' phenomenon that incessantly simulates the future in which you will, rather than might, appear. Specialized psychological meth-ods, such as meditation, can temporarily halt the brain's force-of-model imagining or projecting into the future.*[1]

Contend; contention; contentious -- ***Contend***, verb, means *1)* to struggle against or surmount a problem or a danger, or *2)* to assert a certain position in opposition to another, as in argument. ***Contention***, a noun, means *1)* an instance or occurrence of strug-gling against or surmounting (overcoming) a problem or danger, *2)* an instance or occurrence of assertion, particularly one (a position in opposition to another) maintained during argument. ***Conten-tious***, an adjective, means *1)* causing or likely to result in con-troversy or argument, *2)* quarrelsome, sometimes with an aire of belligerence.

Datotsu (打突) -- meaning of *attack and pierce* or *strike suddenly* (unexpectedly).

Delusion -- a false belief or opinion held, often exhibiting resist-ance to reasoning or confrontation with actual fact.

Dharma (Hindu/Buddhist Sanskrit) -- Generally, a proper or righteous existence in accordance with Natural Law. Its linguistic root is the Sanskrit word *dham,* meaning to *uphold* or *support.* Depending on its culturally evolved use in various Asian religions, it may have a slightly different meaning. In Buddhism, its meaning pertains to that which upholds or supports the Buddhist devotee's quest to a-chieve the state of Nirvana.

Dōshu (Japanese) -- Meaning of *Master of the way.* Morihei Ueshiba was the first dōshu of Aikikai Aikido.

Esoteric -- *1)* Knowledge that is <u>dependent or inside</u> of any person's experiential mentality and or cognitive control, and where such is either <u>unascertainable or irreproducible</u> by any other person and is therefore of a subjective quality. For example, feelings, dreams, and imaginings, which are always internal to or inherent in a person's organic and electrochemically enlivened mind; *2)* A body of know-ledge that is typically subjective in quality, but not necessarily exclusively so, and known only to or held secret by a relatively small group of people.

Etheric -- In esoteric cosmology, hypothetically, a plane, other than the Earthly physical plane in which a human being is rooted by the effect of their body's characteristics, that is envisioned or exper-ienced as a subtle state of altered consciousness, difficult to achieve, which transcends the usual functioning of the human senses to thereby reveal ethereal, supernatural, or other unknown phenom-enon.

Exoteric -- Knowledge that is <u>independent or outside</u> of any given person's experiential mentality and or cognitive control, and where such is <u>ascertainable or reproducible</u> by anyone and therefore is of an objective quality. For example, on planet Earth, the chemical element known as Carbon is present in all natural forms of life; this fact is demonstrable to anyone by anyone.

Filial piety -- Respect for one's parents, family, and ancestors.

Gen (Japanese) -- Illusion, illusory.

Gen'yōsha (*Dark Ocean Society*) -- A Japanese secret ultranational organization.

Hyperphysics -- The study of supernatural phenomena.

Intuition -- A perceiving or knowing that arrives into conscious-ness without active sensing or thinking. Some people consider in-tuition to be a mystical phenomenon; however, a majority under-stand it as an unconscious mental (cognitive) processing of uncon-sciously operating cues, which latter are unconsciously fabricated from the influence of previous experiences or learning, in order to provide a possible solution to or useful assessment of an in-the-present situation or circumstance.

Jūdō (Japanese) -- Meaning of {*gentle way*}; a Japanese 'gentle' (thoughtful and tactical) personal self-defense method and sport way.

Jujutsu (Japanese) -- Meaning of {*gentle art*}; a Japanese gentle (thoughtful and tactical) martial art.

Kamae (Japanese) -- Meaning {posture} or {stance}; in translation, the letter *k* sound changes to a letter *g* sound when combined with another word, e.g., *hidari gamae* (left stance).

Kami (Japanese) -- A term used to identify any phenomenon that was unexplainable or any object or phenomenon that was deemed to have extra-human power by the era-dependent reasoning of any particular person, which ability was shaped by the prevailing norms of acceptable thought and often characterized by a lack of analytic thought, i.e., objectivism. Any particular kami is believed to be divine in Nature and therefore can be considered as a god or, when with female attributes, a goddess.

Kenjutsu (Japanese) -- A Japanese knife and sword (martial) art.

Kokuryū Kai (Japanese) -- Black Dragon Society, a Japanese secret ultranational society.

Kyuba-no-michi (Japanese) -- The Japanese way of the horse and the bow.

Magic -- *1)* the use of means -- such as chants, charms, spells, etc. -- that are believed to have supernatural power over the forces of Nature, *2)* an extraordinary power or influence that seems to arise from an unexplainable source, 3) the skill of a person who can produce illusions by sleight of hand and tricks.

Magico-religiosity -- of or having the character of a body of magical practices that are intended to cause a supernatural being to either produce or prevent a specific outcome.

Mantra (Hindu/Buddhist Sanskrit) -- Specific vocalization from the human voice of certain Sanskrit syllables, words, or group of words that are considered by some Asian religions (e.g., Hinduism and Buddhism) to have the capability of effecting aethereal or material change. For example, ॐ (Aum, Om), a single syllable mantra, believed to be the primordial sound of the creation of our universe. The Japanese Buddhist monk Kukai, founder of Shingon Buddhism, was a significant proponent of the hypothetical concept of kotodama (word-spirit), this being the Japanese connection to Far East Indian Mantra theory.

Meta (Greek) -- A prefix with the meanings of {adjacent} {after} {among} {behind} {beyond} used to indicate that a concept is an abstract derivation, i.e., an abstraction from another concept. It typically suggests a "going beyond" or "transcending" of the original idea, argument, or experiential condition.

Metaphysical -- Of or relating to phenomenon or a reality beyond that which is directly perceivable by the senses; hyperphysical, supernatural.

Metarealism -- The study, pursuit, attainment, or expression of a hypothetical phenomenal realm that is beyond normal cognitive reality, i.e., beyond objective reality; or, somewhat more vague, the hyperphysical (supernatural) nature of things.

Metareality -- A cognitive but subjective phenomenal realm or condition of inwardly directed mentality within the mind of a person that has been arrived at through the invocation or implementation of esoteric behavioral processes, which result in, hypo-thetically, the transcendence of normal cognitive reality, i.e., objective reality, and wherein there is believed to exist a realm of here-to-for unknown phenomenon that is valid and or useful to the individual.

Mysticism -- Generally, the idea that a person can, through the im-plementation of certain esoteric processes that are comprised of specialized cognitive or other behavioral techniques, *1)* experience and understand the meaning of here-to-for unknown phenomenon that are inaccessible in normal cognitive reality and or *2)* achieve a 'oneness' with the Absolute, the Infinite, or the Divine, and where such a metaphysical argument has accrued 'validity' over the course of time by the presence of a vast collection of distinctive practices (e.g., rituals, methods of attaining ecstasy, etc.), oral transmissions, and written records that attest to its <u>relative</u> 'truth' within the context of an individual-dependent <u>subjective</u> reality or meta-reality rather than objective reality.

Nasadiya Sukta (Hindu Sanskrit) -- The 129th hymn of the Hindu Rig Veda that provides clues concerning *1)* the general qualities of the forces that could have emerged the Creation event and *2)* how to mentally conceptualize or grasp these.

Nirvāna (Hindu/Buddhist Sanskrit) -- Generally, a person's trans-cendence of both the naturally occurring and self-induced aspects of suffering or misery experienced in life where upon they achieve a unique and supreme psycho-spiritual enlightenment that evolves a condition of perception and stable being where the conscious mind is fully aware of the nature and meaning of its physical containment (the body), is at ease with this, and establishes a correspondence with *pure-self* as the best possible course in life toward achieving complete nirvana, that is, parinirvana.

Nominal -- performing as expected within design parameters; nor-mal and satisfactory.

Norito (Japanese) -- the ancient Japanese Shinto ritual prayers.

Ōmoto-kyo (Great Origin or Great Source Religion)(Japanese) -- A

Japanese new religion derived partially from the Japanese religion of Shinto.

Pious -- Earnestly willing and compliant in the observance of religion or, having and expressing religious reverence; or, generally, aligning with a strict or traditional sense of virtue and morality.

Piety -- The psychological condition of being pious. For example, a religious devotion to and reverence of God, a devotion to and a reverence of parents, family, and ancestors (filial piety), or a devout thought or act.

Physio-spiritual (adjective) -- that which has or consists of both physical and spiritual qualities or phenomenon. In *defining physical phenomenon,* that which is evident and repeatable phenomenon perceived by the human senses and whose actuality or reality can be objectively ascertained and validated. In *defining spiritual phenomenon,* that which is solely a subjective experience, specifically, a reported happening (event, occurrence, experience, etc.) or sensory generated perception that is subject to or a result of the cognitive variations, deviations, or imaginings of the mind (e.g., Platonic phantasma) of any given person where no physical residue or other non-ephemeral evidence of said experience remains to quantify or substantiate its actual occurrence and, also, where such is unrepeatable and cannot therefore be established or verified as a phenomenon of objective reality; other terms related to such are given by the words *paranormal* (event), *metaphysical* (in quality), *spiritual* (experience or quality), *religious* (experience), etc. The definition of *physio-spiritual* contains, then, elements of both the physical and spiritual aspects of the human experience. For further explanation, see the entry for "spiritual" below.

Pure-self -- A naturally present mental core predisposition of a human being as conferred by Nature (i.e., genetic code) or possibly, by a supernatural entity (e.g., a god); meaning, the inherent trait that predetermines an infant's gradual and typically invariable development toward a mentality that reveals through acts (sensory input preferences, thought, speech and other physical actions) a predisposition to comprehend and embrace their genetically (or perhaps supernaturally) bestowed potentiality to be of beneficial significance in humanity as well as their membership responsibility to the humane betterment of the shared human condition.

Rig Veda or ***Rigveda*** (Hindu Sanskrit) -- a collection of ancient Indian Vedic Sanskrit hymns that constitute the basis of Hinduism. Among these hymns are mythological accounts of the origin of the world.

Rōnin (Japanese) -- *1)* A samurai whose lord was socially and economically disenfranchised, *2)* a samurai with no lord to which he might pledge his loyalty, or *3)* a masterless, vagabond warrior.

Sanskrit -- An ancient and historical Indo-Aryan spoken language (not a writing system), indigenous to the country of India, yet in use today. Sanskrit of today is typically expressed in the written manner using various abugida scripts such as Indian Devanagari.

Satyāgraha (Indian Sanskrit) -- A dialectic method developed and practiced by Mohandas Ghandi for the reason of determining social truths. *Satya* means *truth*; while *Graha* means *struggle*.

Shamanism -- Generally, a personal behavioral conceptualization that gathers together a uniquely enlivened person's experiences and knowledge into the form of a self-conceived spiritual vocation -- ostensibly for the reason of helping other people to quiet anxiety or allay fear, guide curiosity, cure ill health, reveal life's workings, or solve the mysteries of life -- and where this person, who is known as a shaman, *1)* offers theirself as a knowledge source to their community with a set of typically esoteric practices or skills (e.g., rituals, healing methods, sometimes ceremony, etc.) that can seem magical or mystical, *2)* performs services for people in accordance with the general social characteristics of a given community, *3)* acts as a 'spiritual connector' to an alternate but hypothetical realm through the practice of ecstasy (e.g., rapture, trance, separation of the soul from the body, visioning), *4)* has structured rituals that are used to carryout the services, affect a change, or achieve ecstasy, and, *5)* when mentally 'visiting' their alternate realm (i.e., ecstasy mode), is dependent upon a 'transcended spirit' or 'transcended be-ing' to attain the insight, understanding, or information which they seek.

Glossary

Syncretism -- As it pertains to this book, a partial or complete fusion of differing systems of belief, as in philosophies or spiritual traditions.

Shinshukyo (Japanese) -- a new religion; typically with some elements of Shintō.

Shintō (Japanese) -- The indigenous Japanese polytheistic religion. Morihei Ueshiba, founder of Aikido, practiced both Shinto and Buddhism.

Spiritual (adjective) -- a subjective approach or inclination toward characterizing the phenomenal events of life that are processed by the mind as immaterial or ethereal in character, often commensurately assigned a religious-like or religious quality. ***Spirituality*** -- a personal state or condition of being "spiritual."

Sūtra (Hindu Sanskrit) -- An ancient Far East Indian literary form that employs concise aphorisms with the intended purpose of facilitating relatively easy human memorization that would permit an accurate restatement of the information when necessary at a later date.

Taijūjtsu (Japanese) -- Skill in marital or self-defense body movements, or, skilled body movements. The Japanese kara-te (empty hand) martial or self-defense disciplines place differing techni-philosophic emphasis upon the activities that comprise their definition; accordingly, it can be observed that Aikido focuses on throwing and joint locks, Jujutsu focuses on throwing and striking, Judo focuses on throwing and pinning, and Karatedo focuses primarily on striking.

Truth-mirror -- As it relates to a person, 1) an 'uncurtained' or 'unfiltered' (typically stark) mental grasp of Reality (Nature) and, in their relationship with it, the degree of willingness to accept its truth, which includes awareness of *pure-self;* 2) an unsullied recognition and acceptance of the pure, actual, and complete workings of all events and phenomenon in Nature and one's interrelationship with it, which includes awareness of *pure-self.* A person may believe that they have a particular appearance, but

454   *Understanding Aikido*

when facing a mirror, they have an opportunity to see the details of theirself; though laterally inverted and termed a "mirror image," the details are exact in the sense that they duplicate your shape. A single mirror cannot return to your eyes a non-inverted image, but it can give you an exact but virtual two-dimensional view or outline of the various features of your body. This phenomenon is also useful in explaining the mental construct of the truth-mirror in that its 'truth' might not be the 'ultimate' truth, but at least its a beginning point.

Truth-seeking -- a state of cognition where a person, after realizing the effect of their society upon shaping the characteristics of their present state of cognition, has removed bias or predisposition concerning any activity, event, movement, occurrence, phenomenon, or perception, no matter how disconcerting, and, unwilling any longer to dogmatically hold onto a certain perception, idea, or ideology, has mostly if not entirely moved their cognitive processing outside of their personal enculturation shell in order to seek either unvarnished (i.e., candid, straightforward, unembellished) or immutable truth.

Ueshiba, Morihei (Japanese) -- The Japanese man who founded Aikido, a Japanese physio-spiritual discipline.

Ueshiba, Kisshomaru (Japanese) -- Son of the founder of Aikido who significantly shaped mainstream Aikido's modern technical foundation and clarified its philosophical concepts.

Ueshiba, Moriteru (Japanese) -- The grandson of Aikido's founder who currently leads mainstream Aikido's organizational entity, the Aikikai (officially termed the Zaidan Hojin Aikikai).

Véda (Hindu Sanskrit) -- Meaning {knowledge}. Composed in Vedic Sanskrit and exclusively an oral tradition until after the firm establishment of Buddhism sometime between 300 B.C.E. and 1000 C.E. However, the oral tradition seems to have predominated until around 1000 C.E. As a result of the deterioration of the manuscript materials used in ancient times, the oldest written form of the Vedas that exist have been dated to around the 11th century C.E.

Vedic (Hindu Sanskrit) -- Descendent from or referring to the ancient Far East Indian Vedic Period (~1750 B.C.E. to ~500 B.C.E.), or Vedic Civilization.

Zaidan Hojin Aikikai (Japanese) -- Meaning, the Foundational Corporate Entity (of the) Unified Energy/Spirit Society.

Zantoppa (Japanese) -- Meaning, to overcome or survive by cutting through or penetrating the difficult situations that emerge or erupt in life.

Zantoppa Kai (Japanese) -- An association of aikidoka (practitioners of Aikido) devoted to learning and maintaining the aiki (harmonized energy, harmonized spirit) behavior and skill that is necessary to protect and sustain life when faced with a situation of self-defense.

Zantotsu (Japanese) -- Combat (warfare) tactical meaning is to *close and strike*; combat (warfare) technical meaning is to *cut and pierce*; every-day-life meaning -- i.e., the *non-combat/non-martial* interpretation -- is to *remain steadfast and engage* life.

Zantotsu Ryu (Japanese inspired) -- A method or style of performing aiki techniques with an emphasis on maintaining a functional and technically correct self-defense basis, a *truth-mirror*, for the techniques, tactics, and strategies of Aikido. A style of Aikijujutsu.

[1] For scientific information about the concept of human and animal *consciousness*, see the book by entitled **The Future of Mind: The Scientific Quest to Understand, Enhance, and Empower the Mind**, by physicist Michio Kaku; Doubleday, NY, 2014.

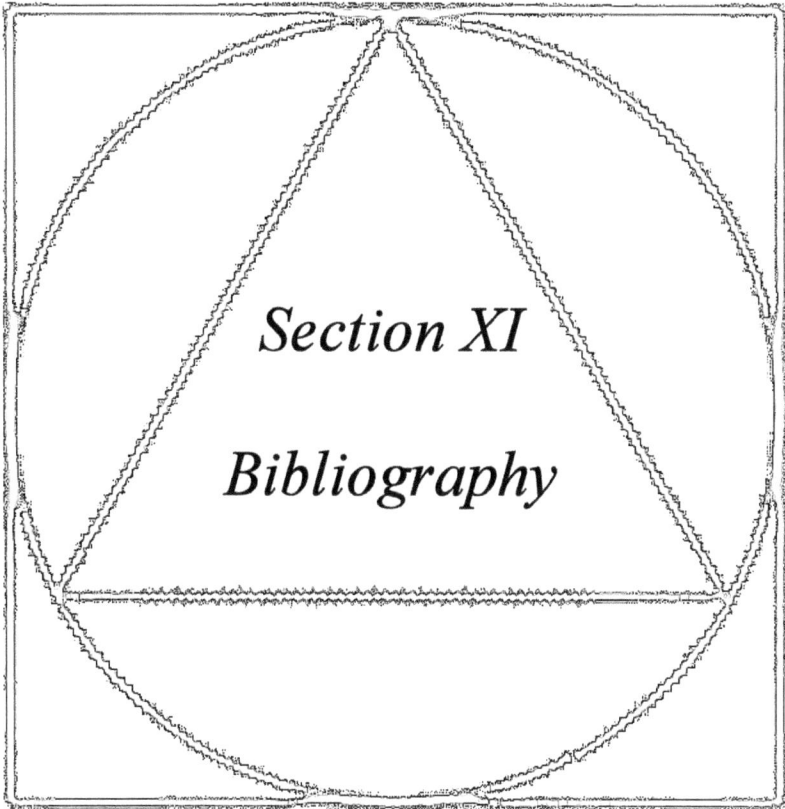

Section XI

Bibliography

Selected Bibliography

Books

Abe, Ryuichi. *The Weaving of Mantra: Kukai and the Construction of Esoteric Buddhist Discourse.* The Columbia University Press; paperback, 1999.

Adams, Ronald J. *Street Survival: Tactics for Armed Encounters.* Calibre Press, Inc.; hardcover, 1983.

Allen, James. *As A Man Thinketh.* Fleming H. Revell Company, hardback, first printing, 1957.

Ashcraft, Mark H. *Cognition*, Fourth Edition. Upper Saddle River, New Jersey, Pearson-Prentice Hall; hardcover, 2006.

Attenborough, Richard. *The Words of Gandhi.* Newmarket Press, Inc.; Book Club hardcover edition, 1982.

Armstrong, Thomas. *Multiple Intelligences in the Classroom.* The Association for Supervision and Curriculum Development; paperback, 1994.

Bailey, F. G. *The Prevalence of Deceit.* Cornell University Press; paperback, 1991.

Barnes, Hazel E. *Humanistic Existentialism: The Literature of Possibility.* Bison Books (University of Nebraska Press); paperback, 1962.

Cassirer, Earnst. *The Myth of the State.* Doubleday & Company, Inc., paperback, 1955.

Collum, Christina Vera. *Manifold Unity: The Ancient World's Perception of the Divine Pattern of Harmony and Compassion.* Charles E. Tuttle Company, Inc.; hardback, 1992.

Bibliography

Craig, William. *The Fall of Japan.* The Dial Press, New York, NY; hardback, first edition, 1967.

De Becker, Gavin. *The Gift of Fear.* Dell Publishing; paperback edition, 1998.

De Monthoux, Pierre Guillet. *Action and Existence: Anarchism for Business Administration.* John Wiley & Sons; hardback, 1983.

Del Rey, Lester. *Rockets Through Space.* Premier Books, a division of Fawcett World Library; paperback, 1960.

Doi, Takeo. *The Anatomy of Self: The Individual versus Society.* This book concerns the Japanese individual and his or her integration into Japanese society. Kodansha International, Tokyo, Japan; paperback, 1988, fifth printing (1994).

Ellwood, Jr., Robert. *Religious and Spiritual Groups in Modern America.* Prentice-Hal, Inc.; paperback, 1973.

Eliade, Mircea. *Cosmos and History: The Myth of the Eternal Return.* Harper & Row, paperback, 1959.

Eliade, Mircea. *Myth and Reality.* HarperCollins, paperback, 1968.

Eliade, Mircea. *The Sacred and Profane: The Nature of Religion.* Houghton Mifflin Harcourt, paperback, 1968.

Funikoshi, Gichin. *Karatedo: My Way of Life.* Kodansha International, Tokyo, Japan; paperback, first printing, 1981.

Gies, Joseph & Frances. *Life in a Medieval Castle.* New York, New York, HarperCollins; a Perennial book edition, 2002.

Hall, Calvin S. & Nordy, Vernon J. *A Primer of Jungian Psychology.* The New American Library, Inc.; a Mentor paperback book, 1973.

Hakeda, Yoshito S. *Kūkai and His Major Works.* The Columbia University Press; paperback, 1972.

Bibliography

Harner, Michael. *The Way of the Shaman: A Guide to Power and Healing.* Bantam Books, Inc.; paperback, 1982.

Hayakawa, S. I. *Language in Action.* Harcourt, Brace & Company, Inc.; hardcover, first edition, 1941.

Herbert, Jean. *Shinto: At the Fountainhead of Japan.* Allen & Unwin; hardcover, first edition, 1967.

Holiday, Linda. *Journey to the Heart of Aikido.* Blue Snake Books, an imprint of North Atlantic Books, Inc.; paperback, first edition, 2014.

Jung, Carl. *Modern Man in Search of a Soul.* Kegan Paul, Trench, Trubner & Co; hardback edition, first printing, 1941.

Jung, Carl. *Psychology and the East.* C. B. Jung Collected Works volume XX from the Bollingen Series, number XX. Princeton University; Bollingen Paperback Edition, 1978, fifth printing, 1990.

Jung, Carl. *The Undiscovered Self.* The New American Library, Inc.; a Mentor paperback book,1958.

Kaku, Michio. *The Future of Mind: The Scientific Quest to Understand, Enhance, and Empower the Mind.* Doubleday, a division of Random House; hardcover, first edition, 2014.

Kano, Jigoro. *Kodokan Judo.* Kodansha International; hardcover, first edition, 1986.

Kubose, Gyomay. *Zen Koans.* Henry Regnery Company; hardcover, first edition, 1973.

Knutsen, Roald. *Tengu: The Shamanic and Esoteric Origins of the Japanese Martial Arts.* Global Oriental, Ltd.; hardcover, first edition, 2011.

Lazear, David. *Seven Ways of Teaching: The Artistry of Teaching with Multiple Intelligences.* IRI/Skylight Publishing; paperback, 1991.

Bibliography

Maguire, Jack. *Essential Buddhism: A Complete Guide to Beliefs and Practices.* Simon & Schuster Publishers (Pocket Books); paperback, 2001.

Mannix, Daniel P. *The Way of the Gladiator.* iBooks, Inc.; paperback, 2001.

McKinnon, Richard. *Selected Plays of Kyōgen.* Uniprint, Inc. Printed in Japan by Komiyama Printing Company, Tokyo; oversized paperback, first edition, 1968.

Miller, Rory. *Facing Violence.* YMAA Publications; paperback, first edition, 2011.

Mimura, Janis. *Planning for Empire: Reform Bureaucrats and the Japanese Wartime State.* Cornell University Press; hardcover, first edition, 2011.

Ming, Shi, with Siao Weijia, translated by Thomas Cleary. *Mind over Matter: Higher Martial Arts.* Frog, Ltd.; paperback, 1995.

Mitchell, David. *The Young Martial Artist.* The Overlook Press; oversize paperback edition, 1992.

Mizuno, Kogen. *Basic Buddhist Concepts.* Kosei Publishing Company; paperback, English language first edition, 1987.

Morton, W. Scott. *Japan: Its History and Culture.* McGraw-Hill, Inc.; second paperback edition, 1994.

Murray, Henry A., editior. *Myth and Mythmaking.* George Braziller, Inc.; first edition, first printing, 1960.

Nelson, John K. *A Year in the Life of a Shinto Shrine.* University of Washington Press; paperback, 1996.

Nakamura, Hajime. *History of Japanese Thought.* Kegan Paul Limited; hardcover edition, 2002.

Noda, Yosiyuki. *Introduction to Japanese Law.* University of

Tokyo Press, Tokyo, Japan; hardcover, English edition, 1976.

Ono, Sokyo, in collaboration with William P. Woodard. *Shinto: The Kami Way.* The Charles E. Tuttle Company; hardcover, first edition, 1962, thirteenth printing, 1976.

Otto, Rudolf. *The Idea of the Holy: An Inquiry into the Non-rational Factor in the Idea of the Divine and Its Relation to the Rational.* Oxford University Press; hardcover, Oxford Bookshelf edition, 1936.

Phillipi, Donald L. *Norito: A Translation of the Ancient Japanese Ritual Prayers.* Princeton University Press; paperback, 1990.

Pranin, Stanley. *The Aiki News Encyclopedia of Aikido.* Published by Aiki News; oversized paperback, first edition, 1991.

Pyle, Michael. *The Study of Kanji.* The Hokuseido Press, Tokyo, Japan; hardcover, first edition, 1971.

Rodgers, David J. *Fighting to Win.* The Double & Company, Inc.; hardcover, first edition, 1984.

Saller, Sven and Koschmann, J. Victor. *Pan-Asianism in Modern Japanese History: Colonialsim, Regionalism and Borders.* Routledge, Oxon, England; paperback, first edition, 2007.

Sartre, Jean-Paul. *Existentialism and Human Emotions.* The Wisdom Library, a division of The Philosophical Library, Inc.; hardcover, 1957.

Sartre, Jean-Paul. *Literature & Existentialism.* The Citadel Press; paperback, 1966. Original title: *What is Literature?* First published by The Wisdom Library, a division of The Philosophical Library, Inc., 1949.

Sartre, Jean-Paul. *The Emotions -- Outline of a Theory.* Citadel Press edition; paperback, first printing, 1966. First published by The Wisdom Library, a division of The Philosophical Library, Inc., 1948.

Bibliography

Satchidanana, Sri Swami. *The Sutras of Patanjali.* Integral Yoga Publications; reprint edition, first printing, 1990.

Seward, Jack. *Hara-Kiri: Japanese Ritual Suicide.* Tokyo, Japan, Charles E. Tuttle Company, Inc.; paperback, 1973.

Shirer, William L. *Gandhi: A Memoir.* A Washington Square Press publication of Pocket Books, a Simon & Schuster division of Gulf & Western Corporation; paperback, 1982.

Shishida, Fumiaki and Nariyama, Tetsuro. *Aikidō Tradition and the Competitive Edge.* Shodokan Publishing, USA; paperback, first edition, 2001.

Shoho, Takuan, translated by William Scott Wilson. *The Unfettered Mind.* Kodansha International, Ltd.; first paperback edition, fourth printing, 1987.

Smith, Charles Page. *The Universal Curriculum.* Published by the William James Press, Santa Cruz, California; saddle-stitched paperback, 1975. [Author's comment: Though much of this small booklet was valid then as it is today, I'm uncomfortable with Smith's conclusion. It seems as if some of the radical ideas of the 1960s and 1970s unduly affected the reasoning of some learned and thoughtful academicians; his conclusion is influenced by those. For an improved alternative, let us consider Jaime Escalante's ideas about and efforts toward the education of all youth.]

Tanaka, Fumon. *Sword Techniques of Musashi and the Other Samurai Masters.* Kodansha USA; hardcover, English first edition, 2013.

Thompson, Maurice. *The Witchery of Archery;* published in 1878.

Tomiki, Kenji. *Judo and Aikidō.* Japan Travel Bureau, Japan; hardcover, sixth edition, 1963.

Tweed, Matt. *Essential Elements: Atoms, Quarks, and the Periodic Table.* Walker and Company; hardcover, first edition, 2003.

Ueshiba, Kisshomaru. *The Spirit of Aikidō.* Translated by Taitetsu

Bibliography

Unno. Kodansha International, Ltd.; paperback edition, first printing, 1987.

Ueshiba, Kisshomaru. 合気道 (Aikidō). Hozansha Publications, Ltd.; oversize paperback, 1985.

Ueshiba, Kisshomaru. *Aikido Ichiro* (My Life in Aikido). Published by Shuppan Geijutsusha, Tokyo, 1995.

Ueshiba, Morihei. *Budo: Teachings of the Founder of Aikido.* Kodansha International; first paperback edition, 1996.

Ueshiba, Morihei. *The Heart of Aikido: The Philosophy of Takemusu Aiki.* Edited by Hideo Takahashi. Compiled and translated by John Stevens. Kodansha International; hardcover first edition, 2010.

USA Wrestling: Coach's Guide to Excellence. The Cooper Publishing Group; oversize paperback edition, 1995.

Waley, Arthur. *The Nō Plays of Japan.* Alfred A. Knopf; hardcover, first edition, 1922.

Watts, Alan. *The Supreme Identity: An Essay on Oriental Metaphysic and the Christian Religion.* Random House, Inc.; Vintage Books edition, 1972.

Westbrook, A. and Ratti, O. *Aikido and the Dynamic Sphere.* The Charles E. Tuttle Company; hardcover first edition, 1970, twenty-seventh printing, 1985.

Westbrook, A. and Ratti, O. *Secrets of the Samurai.* The Charles E. Tuttle Company; paperback edition, 1991.

Weston, Mark. *Giants of Japan: The Lives of Japan's Greatest Men and Women.* Kodansha America; hardcover first edition, 1999.

Whiting, Robert. *The Samurai Way of Baseball: The Impact of Ichiro and the New Wave from Japan.* Warner Books, Time

Bibliography

Warner Book Group; trade paperback, first edition, 2005.

Yamamoto, Guji Yukitaka. *Kami no Michi.* Tsubaki America Publications; paperback, 1987.

Yoshida, Mitsuru. *Requiem for Battleship Yamato.* Translation and Introduction by Richard H. Minear. Naval Institute Press, Annapolis, Maryland; Bluejacket edition, paperback, 1999.

Yoshisaburo, Okakura. *The Spirit of Japan.* James Pott & Co., New York; first edition, 1905.

Yutang, Lin. *The Wisdom of Laotse.* Random House, Inc.; hardcover, first edition, 1976.

Articles

Abe, Ikuo; Kiyohara, Yasuharu; and Nakajima, Ken. *Sport and Physical Education under Fascistization in Japan.* June, 2000. Article was first published in *Bull, Health & Sport Sciences,* the University of Tsukuba, 13 (1990); subsequently reprinted with a few modifications in the *International Journal of the History of Sport,* 9:1 (April 1992). This version available at http://ejmas.com/jalt/jaltart _abe_0600.htm.

Agriculture in the Empire of Japan. http://en.wikipedia.org/wiki/ Agriculture_in_the_Empire_of_Japan; 2013.

An interview with Morihei Ueshiba O-Sensei and Kisshomaru Ueshiba, conducted by two unnamed newspapermen, appeared in the Japanese-language textbook entitled *Aikido* by Kisshomaru Ueshiba, Tokyo, Kowado, 1957, pages 198-219. It was translated from the Japanese by Stanley Pranin and Katsuaki Terasawa and presented in article form available from the Aiki News Journal.

Apophenia. http://en.wikipedia.org/wiki/Apophenia; 2013.

Boyd, James. *Faith, Race, and Strategy: Japanese-Mongolian Relations, 1873-1945.* A Thesis for Doctorate of Philosophy, Murdoch University, 2008.

Bibliography

Chiang Kai Shek. http://en.wikipedia.org/wiki/Chiang_Kai-shek; 2013.

Classifications of Religious Movments. https://en.wikipedia.org/wiki/Classifications_of_religious_movements; 2013.

Daito-ryu and Aikido. http://www.daito-ryu.org/en/daito-ryu-and-aikido.html.

Ellis, Henry. *Is Aikido a Martial Art.* Published online, 2001. http://EllisAikido.org.

Fukuka, Mahito. *A Cultural History of Tuberculosis in Modern Japan.* http://www.lang.nagoya-u.ac.jp/~mfukuda/english.html.

Fairchild, William P. *Shamanism in Japan.* Nanzan Institute for Religion and Culture, Nanzan University, Nogoya, Japan, 122 pages, 1962.

Gen'yōsha. http://en.wikipedia.org/wiki/Genyōsha; 2014.

Goldsbury, Peter. *Transmission, Inheritance, & Emulation* [of Aikido]. Article was published online at www.aikiweb.com, 2008 & 2009.

Goldsbury, Peter. *Touching the Absolute: Aikido vs. Religion and Philosophy*; published by the Aiki Journal Online, August 31, 2010.

Gojuon. https://en.wikipedia.org/wiki/Gojuon; 2011.

Gurovich, Dmitry. *Jiu-Jitsu and The Law.* Jiu-Jitsu Magazine, January 2013, Issue 11.

Hemp. http://en.wikipedia.org/wiki/Hemp; 2013.

Hierophany. http://en.wikipedia.org/wiki/Hierophany; 2013.

Homma, Gaku. *The Founder Morihei Ueshiba, a God? Reflections on the Anniversary of Japan's Surrender to the US Coalition*; 2005. http://www.nippon-kan.org/senseis_articles/05_uishiba-god/

05_ueshiba-god.html; 2013.

Hori, Ichirō. *Shamanism in Japan*. Japanese Journal of Religious Studies, December, 1975, 56 pages; 2103.

Industrial Hemp in Japan. http://www.japanhemp.org/en/ ya991003.htm; 2012.

Japanese Nationalism. http://en.wikipedia.org/wiki/Japanese_ nationalism; 2014

Kempeitai. http://en.wikipedia.org/wiki/Kempeitai; 2014.

Kōdōha (Imperial Way Faction). http://en.wikipedia.org/wiki/ Imperial_Way_Faction; 2014.

Kokutai. http://en.wikipedia.org/wiki/Kokutai; 2014

Kuomintang (Guomindang)*(KMT)*. http://en.wikipedia.org/wiki/ Kuomintang; 2013.

Kurihara, Akira. *The Emperor System as Japanese National Religion: The Emperor System Module in Everyday Consciousness*. Japanese Journal of Religious Studies, 1990, 17/2-3, 26 pages.

Li, Christopher. *Interview with Aikido Shihan Shigenobu Okumura*. Article published online at www.aikidosangenkai.org/ blog/interview-aikido-shihan-shigenobu-okumura-part-1/, May, 2013.

Lu Zhankui. http://en.wikipedia.org/wiki/Lu_Zhankui; 2013.

Manchuria. http://en.wikipedia.org/wiki/Manchuria; 2013.

Nakayama, Hakudō. http://en.wikipedia.org/wiki/Nakayama_ Hakudō; 2013.

Official Baseball Rules, 2011 version, as compiled by the Professional Baseball Playing Rules Committee.

Panpsychism. http://en.wikipedia.org/wiki/Panpsychism; 2013.

Pareidolia. http://en.wikipedia.org/wiki/Pareidolia; 2013.

Peace Preservation Laws. http://en.wikipedia.org/wiki/Peace_ Preservation_Law; 2013.

Pranin, Stanley. *What is the Origin of the Term "aikido"?* Article published online at the Aikido Journal Bulletin Board by the Aikido Journal, November, 1999.

Pranin, Stanley. *Escape to Mongolia.* Aiki News magazine, article #14, 1975.

Pranin, Stanley. *Sokaku Takeda and Daito Ryu Aikijujutsu.* Article published online by the Aikido Journal, article #104, 1995.

Pranin, Stanley. *Morihei meets Sokaku - The Untold Story.* Article published online by the Aikido Journal, November, 2011.

Pranin, Stanley. *Yoichiro* [Noriaki] *Inoue: Aikido's Forgotten Pioneer.* Article published online by the Aikido Journal, article #121, August, 2011.

Pranin, Stanley. *Morihei Ueshiba & Onisaburo Deguchi.* Published by Aiki News, magazine article #95, Spring/Summer, 1993.

Pranin, Stanley. *Interview with Morihiro Saito.* Article published online by the Aikido Journal, article #88, 1991.

Pranin, Stanley. *Morihei Ueshiba and the Ōmoto Religion.* Article published online by the Aikido Journal, February, 2005.

Pranin, Stanley. *Kobukan Dojo Era.* Article republished online by the Aikido Journal, July 27, 2012.

Pranin, Stanley. *The Elusive Chinese Connection.* Article published online by the Aikido Journal, September 18, 2012.

Pranin, Stanley. *Reminiscences Of Minoru Mochizuki (Part 1)* &

Bibliography

(Part 2). Article #71 & #72, *Aiki News* magazine, June, 1986 and September, 1986 respectively.

Pranin, Stanley. *Aikido in the Postwar Years - Part 1: 1946-1956*. Article published online by the Aikido Journal, December 18, 2010.

Pranin, Stanley. *Who is Koichi Tohei?* Article published online by the Aikido Journal, August 10, 2011.

Pranin, Stanley. *Kisshomaru Ueshiba's Stamp on Modern Aikido*. Article published online by the Aikido Journal, November 25, 2012.

Pranin, Stanley. *Kisshomaru Ueshiba and Morihei Ueshiba*. Article #96, Aiki News magazine, 1996.

Pranin, Stanley. *Interview with Minoru Hirai*. Article #100, Aiki News magazine, 1994.

Pranin, Stanley. *Interview with Shoji Nishio*. Article #91 and #92, Aiki News magazine, 1992.

Pranin, Stanley. *Interview with Kenji Tomiki Sensei*. Article #43, Aiki News magazine, 1981.

Pranin, Stanley. *Interview with Tetsuro Nariyama*. Article #121, Aiki Journal online, 2001.

Pranin, Stanley. *Interview with Shigenobu Okumura*. Article #203, Aiki News magazine, 1983.

Pranin, Stanley. *Interview with Aikido Doshu Kisshomaru Ueshiba*. Article #81, Aiki News magazine, 1989.

Pranin, Stanley. *Interview with Hiroaki Kogure Sensei*. Article #82 and #83, Aiki News magazine, 1989 and 1990 respectively.

Pranin, Stanley. *Behind the Scenes: The 1st Aikido Friendship Demonstration*. Published online at the Aikido Journal Blog site; July 1, 2012. http://blog.aikidojournal.com/2012/07/01/behind-the-scenes-the-1st-aikido-friendship-demonstration.

Bibliography

Pranin, Stanely. ***Morihei Ueshiba and Kenji Tomiki.*** Article published by the Wushu magazine (a Japanese publication) made available as article #70 at Aikido Journal's Internet site.

Pranin, Stanley. ***Morihei's Ueshiba Juku, Launchpad of a Martial Arts Career.*** Published online at the Aikido Journal Blog site; October 31, 2011. http://blog.aikidojournal.com/2011/10/31/morihei's-"ueshiba-juku"-launchpad-of-a-martial-arts-career-by-stanley-pranin.

Raja Yoga. http://en.wikipedia.org/wiki/Raja_Yoga; 2014.

Sakurakai. http://en.wikipedia.org/wiki/Sakurakai; 2014.

Satyagraha. http://en.wikipedia.org/wiki/Satyagraha; 2013.

Sease, Jason. ***Japanese Baseball: The Creation of a Philosophy.*** Asian Studies Thesis, Whitman College, 2010. http://www.whitman.edu/athletics/sport_texts/JasonSeaseAsianStudiesThesis.pdf.

Shamanism. http://en.wikipedia.org/wiki/Shamanism; 2013.

Sharov, Alexei A. & Gordon, Richard. ***Life Before Earth.*** Submitted as a pdf article on 28 Mar 2013 to Cornell University. Available at http://arxiv.org/abs/1304.3381v1.

Shishida, Fumiaki. ***Aikido.*** Article published online by the Aikido Journal, article #626, 1993.

Shishida, Fumiaki. ***Aikido and Injuries: Special Report.*** Published by the *Nihon Budo Gakkai Gakujutsushi* (Scientific Journal of Japanese Martial Arts Studies),Volume 21, No. 1, 1988.

Shishida, Fumiaki. ***The Process of Forming Aikido and Japanese Imperial Navy Admiral Isamu Takeshita: Through the analysis of Takeshita's diary from 1925 to 1931.*** A pdf document from: www.isdy.net/pdf/eng/2008_05.pdf.

Siddhaṃ Alphabet. https://en.wikipedia.org/wiki/Siddham_script.

Bibliography

Studies on Jigoro Kano: Significance of His Ideals of Physical Education and Judo. From: Bulletin of the Association for the Scientific Studies on Judo, Kodokan, Report 2 (1963) pp. 1-12. By M. Maekawa (Tokyo University of Education), Y. Hasegawa (Ministry of Education).

Sunadomari, Kanemoto. **Morihei Ueshiba Biography** article series of the book by the same title, 1969. Consists of seventeen articles which provide the first overview of the life of Morihei Ueshiba. Translated by Yoko Nonaka, edited by Stanley Pranin. Series of articles published by Aiki News, 1986 through 1991.

Taylor, James Standen. **Folk Religion in Tibetan Culture.** An essay in partial fulfillment of work toward a M.T.S. degree, Tyndale University College and Seminary, Toronto, Canada, 2000. From http://www.tibetanresearch.org/Shamanism.htm.

The First and Second Oomoto Incidents, a web article from the official Omoto-kyo site in Japan. http://www.oomoto.or.jp/English/enHist/jiken-en.html.

Theory of Mulitple Intelligences. http://en.wikipedia.org/wiki/Theory_of_multiple_intelligences; 2014.

Tohei, Koichi. **Tohei Resignation Letter,** May 15, 1974. Provided by the Aikido Journal online; 2012.

Tōseiha. http://en.wikipedia.org/wiki/Toseiha; 2014.

Tokubetsu Keisatsu-tai. http://en.wikipedia.org/wiki/Tokubetsukeibitai_(Navy); 2014.

Tokubetsu Kōtō Keisatsu. http://en.wikipedia.org/wiki/Tokubetsu_Kōtō_Keisatsu; 2014.

Tomiki, Kenji. **Greeting at the opening of Shodokan Aikido dojo.** March 28, 1976. http://homepage2.nifty.com/shodokan/en/aisatsu.html; 2013.

Tomiki, Kenji, translated by Robert W. Dzuibla & Fumiaki Shishida.

Bibliography

On Jujutsu and its Modernization, 1986. http://www.tomiki.org/
files/Article_Jujutsu_and_its_Modernization.pdf; 2014.

Tomiki Aikido: History. www.tomiki.org/tomikiaikido.html; 2014.

Tucker, Abigail. *The Science of Morality.* The *Smithsonian* magazine, January, 2013.

Ueshiba, Kisshomaru. *Founder of Aikido* article series, which consists of material translated from the Japanese language version of Kisshomaru Ueshiba's book *A Life in Aikido: The Biography of Founder Morihei Ueshiba*; forty-two articles. Edited by Stanley Pranin. Published by Aiki News, 1978 through 1986.

Ueshiba, Morihei. *Takemusu Aiki - Lectures of Morihei Ueshiba.* Article published online by the Aikido Journal, article #118, 1999.

Whiting, Robert. *The Japanese Way of Baseball and the National Character Debate.* *Japan Focus*, September 29, 2006. http://japanfocus.org/-Robert-Whiting/2235.

Web article concerning *Morihei Ueshiba's activities in the Shirataki* area, Hokkaido, Japan. http://www2.ocn.ne.jp/~aiki0325/
shiraaiki2.html; 2013.

Yamamoto, Yukitaka. *Kami no Michi* (The Way of the Kami): *The Life and Thought of a Shinto Priest.* Tsubaki Grand Shrine, Mie Prefecture, Japan, 1987. http://www.csuchico.edu/~gwilliams/tsa
/Kami_no_Michi_ToC.html; 2012.

Yasuaki Deguchi: The Omoto Religion and Aikido article series. Consists of fifteen articles in a series written by Yasuaki Deguchi, founder of Aizen-en, a branched-off religion of the Omoto-kyo religion. Edited by Stanley Pranin. Published by the Aiki News magazine/Aikido Journal online, 1993 through 1997.

Zhāng Zuòlín. http://en.wikipedia.org/wiki/Zhang_Zuolin; 2013.

Zhāng Xueliang. http://en.wikipedia.org/wiki/Zhang_Xueliang;
2013.

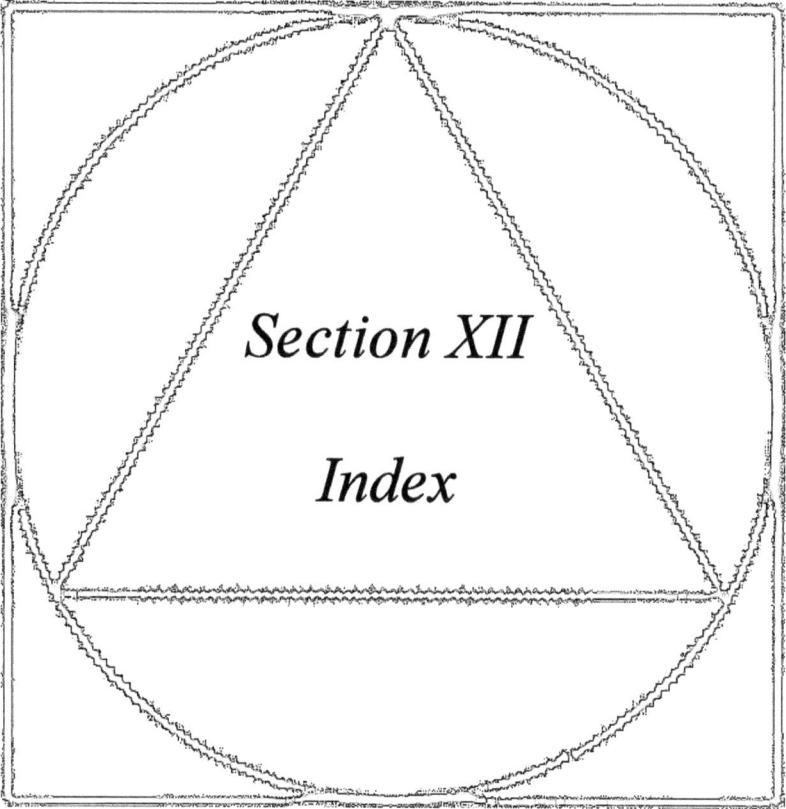

Section XII

Index

Index

Index

Index

I

L

M

Index

Z